THE J. PAUL GETTY MUSEUM JOURNAL
Volume II

The J. Paul Getty Museum
Malibu, California

Volume II
Jiří Frel, Editor

Published by the J. Paul Getty Museum, Malibu, California
© 1975 The J. Paul Getty Museum
All rights reserved
ISBN 0-89236-001-1

Produced in Chicago by Ares Publishers, Inc.

BERNARDO ASHMOLE OCTOGENARIO
DE MUSEO GETTIANO BENEMERENTI

PARS SECUNDA

Contents

Introduction

Bernard Ashmole, one of the greatest connoisseurs of ancient sculpture, after a fine career with the British Museum and at Oxford University, has spent the last five years helping us form the antiquities collection at the J. Paul Getty Museum. Thanks to him the quality of our collection has been maintained.

J. PAUL GETTY

The identity of the young girl portrayed on the grave stele of Myttion (Fig. 1), formerly among the Elgin marbles at Broomhall[1] and now the oldest of the large collection of fourth-century Attic funerary sculpture in the J. Paul Getty Museum in Malibu, has always presented something of a puzzle.[2]

The subject of the relief is common. A girl turns to her left, glancing at a bird which she holds in her outstretched left hand.[3] Her curly hair is short-cut and bound by a narrow, painted ribbon or band, evoking the image of Pollux' mask:

ἡ δὲ κούριμος παρϑένος ἀντὶ ὄγκου ἔχει τριχῶν
κατεψηγμένων διάκρισιν, καὶ βραχέα ἐν κύκλῳ
περικέκαρται, . . .

The slab itself is peculiar. It is disproportionately tall and narrow; the odd, trapezoidal pediment is free, without lateral pilasters. Carved architectural elements, including the moulding between relief and pediment, are absent. Above all, Myttion's coat, with its tubular sleeves and stiff fabric, knee-length and open over her chiton, is unique for an Attic grave stele. Few precise parallels have so far been cited for the coat in classical Greek art. The girl, therefore, has sometimes been hesitantly identified as a servant, a young barbarian, or both.

The monument, which was brought to Britain from Greece by Lord Elgin, was sculptured from a slab of fine-grained Pentelic marble (71 x 22.6 cm.). The rough-cut lower section was originally inserted into a base. The figure itself was carved at the very surface of the slab, and the surrounding area was cut back to produce a very shallow relief. Normal claw chisel marks appear on the sides, while the reverse is rough-picked. The fourth and little fingers of the right hand have been recut, the contours of the chin retouched. Traces of bright red from the original polychromy are retained on the right foot. The painted ornament of the pediment is very poorly preserved. The surface of the right side of the stele has been obliterated. Pale traces of the former paint can be distinguished with the aid of good light, however, on the left half of the pediment. The name of the deceased, Myttion, the *M* "almost certainly fourth-century", according to Sterling Dow,[5] is painted between two lightly incised lines. To the left, above, was depicted a roll of long cloth, laid parallel to the diagonal edge of the stone (Fig. 2). An identical roll was surely painted symmetrically on the right side, and, between the two, another appropriate ornament, such as a palmette. The bolt of fabric may represent the long *tainiai* which were tied around funeral monuments, or it may be a winding cloth.[6] Similar representations appear in relief on the pediments of several other grave stelai:[7]

1. Eupheros, Athens Kerameikos: *AM* 79 (1964) 48, 1; 49; 51, 1; *Propyläen Kunstgeschichte* (Berlin, 1967) Fig. 85; *Deltion* 24 (1969) pl. 126.
2. Kallisto, Athens N.M. 732: Conze 79 (36); *AM* 79 (1964) pl. 81, 2; *Deltion* 24 (1969) pl. 127b.
3. Pythodor[os], Athens N.M., from Boeotia: Conze 1455a (fig.), see also fig., p. 25.
4. Stele of a small boy (limestone), Athens N.M. 983, from Thebes: drawing of facade, Conze, p. 24; *Deltion* 24 (1969) pl. 127a.

I am very grateful to Burton Fredericksen and Jiří Frel, curators of the J. Paul Getty Museum, for permission to study and publish this stele, for photographs, and for their continued generosity and hospitality which has enabled me to use the museum facilities. I am particularly indebted to J. Frel for consenting to publish his revised list of the sculpture which he attributes to the Myttion Sculptor and to other artisans of the workshop with which the Myttion Sculptor was associated. To Ronald and Connie Stroud, and to D. A. Amyx, I owe thanks for assistance during the writing of the preliminary manuscript three years ago, and to Stella Grobel Miller and Sally Roberts for having offered useful comment.

ABBREVIATIONS

Blümel: C. Blümel, *Katalog der griechischen Skulpturen des 5. und 4. Jahrhunderts* (Berlin, 1928); Conze: A. Conze, *Die attischen Grabreliefs* (Berlin, 1893); Deubner, *Att. Feste:* L. Deubner, *Attische Feste* (Keller, Berlin, 1932); Helbig: K. Helbig, *Führer durch die öffentlichen Sammlungen klassischer Altertümer in Rom* (3rd rev. ed., 1912); Lullies-Hirmer: R. Lullies and M. Hirmer, *Greek Sculpture* (New York, 1957); Picard, *Manuel:* C. Picard, *Manuel d'archéologie grecque. La Sculpture* I-IV (Paris, 1935-54); Reinach, *RR:* S. Reinach, *Répertoire de reliefs grecs et romains* (Paris, 1909-1912); *SAA:* J. Frel, *Les sculpteurs attiques anonymes, 430-300* (Prague, 1969); Schefold, *Untersuch.:* K. Schefold, *Untersuchungen zu den Kertscher Vasen* (Berlin and Leipzig, 1934); van Hoorn: G. van Hoorn, *Choes and Anthesteria* (Leiden, 1951).

1) See A. H. Smith, "Lord Elgin and His Collection," *JHS* 36 (1916) 163ff.; I. Gennadios, Ὁ Λόρδος Ἔλγιν (Athens, 1930); W. St. Clair, *Lord Elgin and the Marbles* (London, 1962).

2) J. Paul Getty Museum I-72, purchased from Spink, London, November, 1952. Previous bibliography: A. Michaelis, *JHS* 5 (1884) 148f., No. 6; *CIA* II 4000; Conze 819, 156; *IG* II² 12220; G. Richter, *Sculpture and Sculptors of the Greeks* (3rd ed., New Haven, 1950) 91, fig. 258; C. C. Vermeule, *AJA* 59 (1955) 132; J. Paul Getty with E. Le Vane, *Collector's Choice* (London, 1955) 202, pl. before p. 193; *SSA* 77; M. del Chiaro, *Greek Art in Private Collections in California* (2nd ed., Santa Barbara, 1966) 17; G. Richter, *op. cit.* (4th ed., New Haven, 1970) 60, fig. 272.

3) E.g., Conze, nos. 821ff. For burials of children with birds: *AM* (1893) 175.

4) Pollux, *Onomastikon* 4, 140. For a possible representation of such a mask: L. Talcott, *Hesperia* (1939) 267-273, figs. 1 and 2.

5) Letter, October 26, 1968, to the J. Paul Getty Museum. Literally, "Myttion" should mean "little, damp girl." The spelling, of course, is Attic.

6) The interpretation is discussed fully by A. Kaloyeropoulou in her publication of a stele in Athens (second ephoria) on which such a piece of rolled fabric is held by a small servant: *Deltion* 24 (1969) 222ff., pll. 118-121.

7) I am indebted to J. Frel for these parallels.

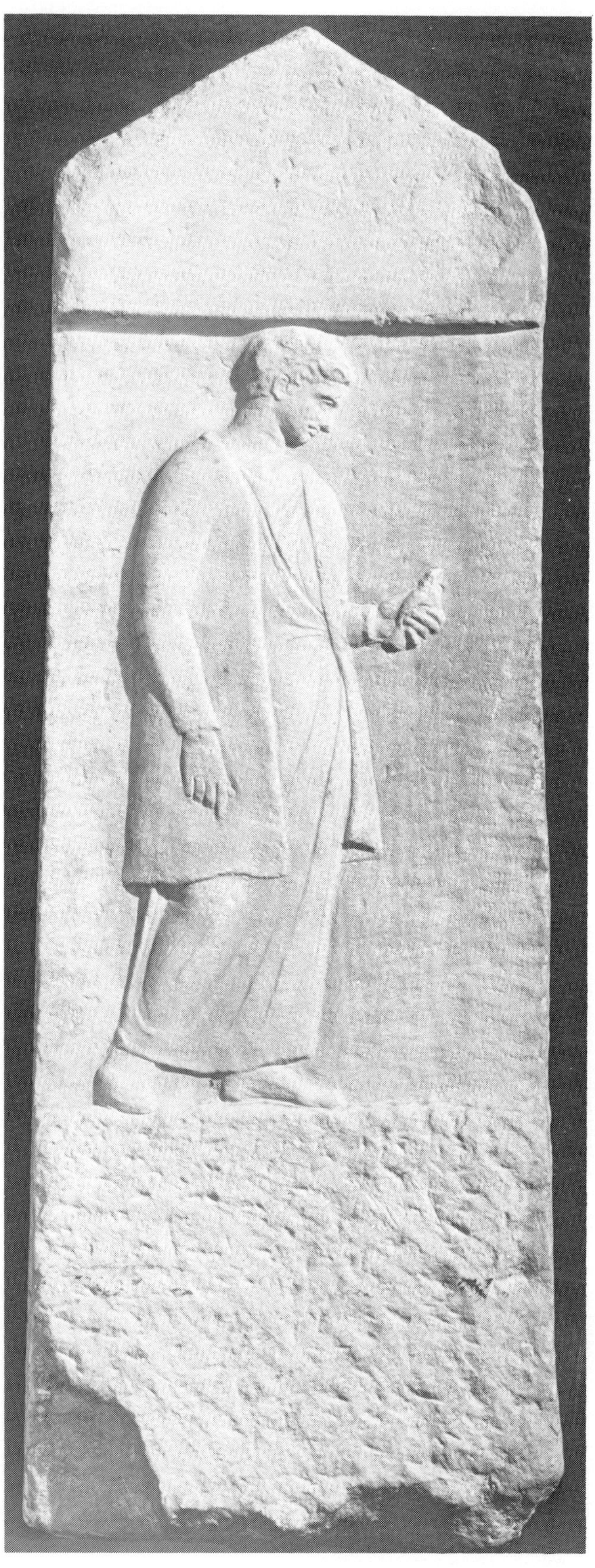

1   Stele of Myttion. J. Paul Getty Museum I-72,
     on loan from J. Paul Getty.

2   Detail of left side of pediment

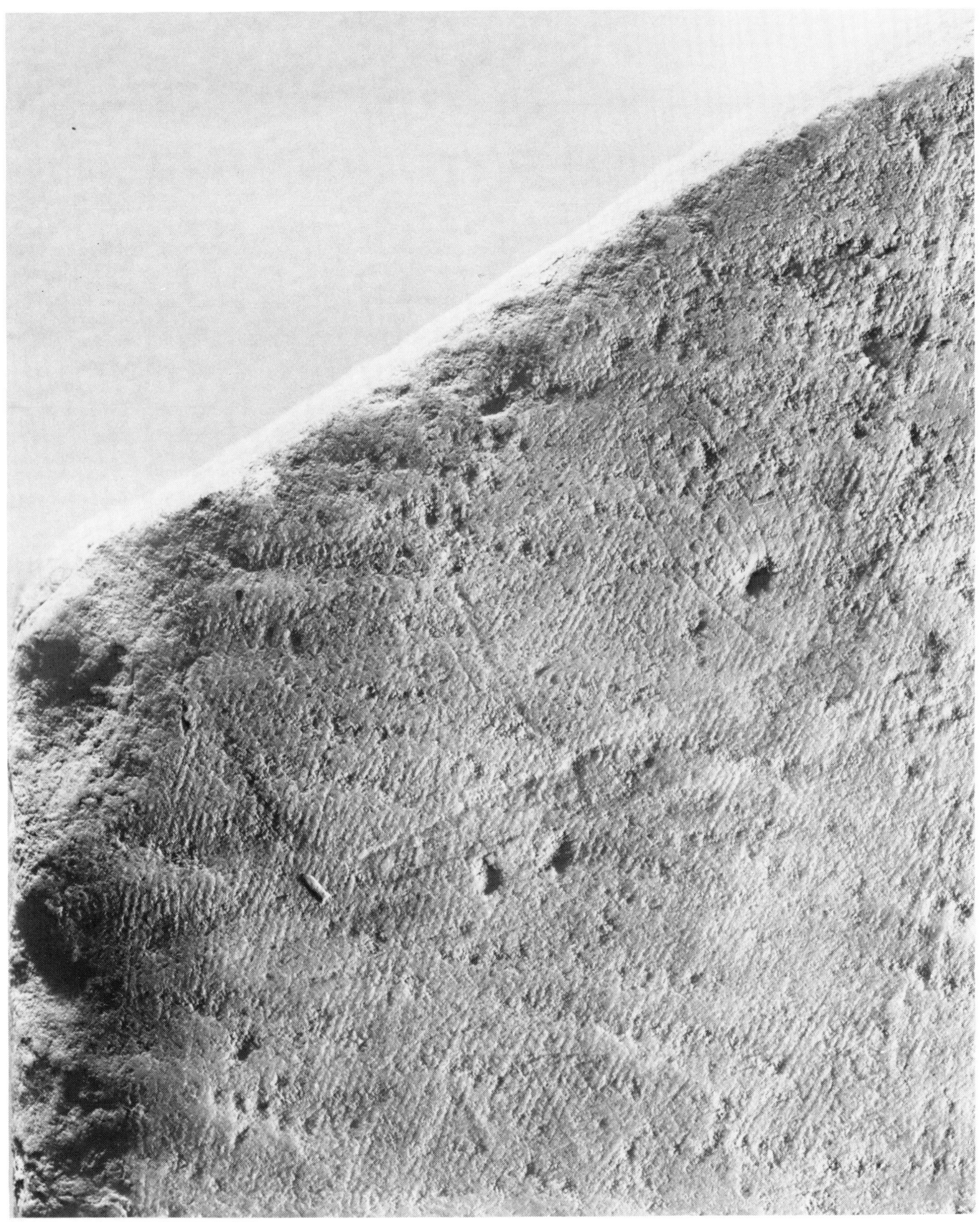

5. [Diphil]os Philionos (fragment), Brno, private collection: *Listy Filol.* 71 (1947) 2, pl. 4; *SAA* 356, 48.[8] (For this fragment the rolled fabric is roughly schematized.)

A painted, rolled *tainia* appears on a stele in Munich on which a loutrophoros is also painted: *JdI* 24 (1909) pl. 9; C. Picard, *Manuel* 4, 2 (Paris, 1963) 1440, 551.[9] Two rolled *tainiai* are symmetrically arranged at the foot of the loutrophoros; another is suspended near the neck of the vessel.

The workmanship of the stele is unpretentious. The pediment protrudes in a simple, angular step over the panel, marking the original thickness of the marble slab and the maximum height of the relief. The modelling of the figure is rather simplistic, suggesting that such details as hair and the figured fabric of clothing may have been painted. The attempt to render a foreshortened, frontal, right foot is clumsy, yet the treatment is nearly identical to that of the servant girl's foot on the more impressive stele of Hegeso.[10] A closer comparison of the two stelai indicates, in fact, that the sculptor of Myttion was following just such a model. The position of the legs and the drapery folds at the side of the skirt and across the right leg are in sketchy imitation of the sculpting of the same areas for the servant of Hegeso. It is such similarity to serving girls depicted on stelai, wearing, however, *sakkoi* and floor-length garments with which the tubular sleeves form one piece, which has sometimes relegated Myttion to the status of servant or slave.[10-bis]

Already in the last century W. Amelung had identified Myttion as an Attic child and her jacket as the *kandys,* a garment of Persian origin,[11] a judgment with which T. Linders has concurred in more recent times.[12] Amelung associated Myttion's *kandys* with the sleeved coats worn loose on the backs of figures on the Alexander sarcophagus and with that of the Medea in the so-called Peliades reliefs,[13] which H. Thompson has identified as copies of one of the sculptured slabs from the Altar of Pity in the Athenian Agora.[14] To the sculptured Medea should be added an Andromeda on an Attic kalyx crater in Berlin,[15] who likewise wears an upright tiara and a *kandys* draped over her shoulders with the sleeves dangling empty at her sides. So, too, probably, another Andromeda on an Attic white-ground kalyx crater in Agrigento,[16] and possibly still others found in Apulian red-figure, before the garment vanishes, becoming, perhaps, an anomalous cloak.[17]

The best parallel for Myttion and her coat has always been the Medea of the Attic volute crater which is the namepiece of the Talos Painter. [18] Although her upright tiara indicates her status as barbarian royalty, she wears a richly ornamented *kandys* as Myttion does, arms thrust into sleeves, the coat opened.

C. Greenewalt, Jr., has recently found what is probably the Persian *kandys* at a point of contact with Greco-Lydian art in Asia Minor in the late sixth century.[19] H. Thiersch, who also supported Amelung's identification of Myttion's coat as a *kandys,* traced other cult or court dress from the Near East to its appearance as theatrical costume in fifth-century Athens.[20] The earliest *kandys* to appear in fifth-century Attic vase-painting is probably that worn by a woman on a white-ground lekythos by the Sabouroff Painter in a scene for which the connotations are at once funereal, foreign, and theatrical.[21] The *kandys,* painted red and white in broad zigzag areas, is worn as a proper coat, with arms sleeved. The woman stands at the left of a grave stele which is mounted on a three-stepped base and tied with a tainia. To the right is a Persian male who wears the upright

---

8) By the Budapest Sculptor: *SAA, loc. cit.*

9) The old hypothesis, repeated by C. Picard, that the rolls depicted *volumina* with inscribed mystic texts, was refuted long ago by P. Wolters: *JdI* 24 (1909) 53ff.

10) Athens N.M. 3624: Conze 68, 30; Lullies-Hirmer 187; *Ant. Kunst* 7 (1964) pl. 4; Karouzou 77, 32.

10-bis) The Thracian slave of an early fourth-century stele in Athens, so identified by inscription, wears the floor-length sleeved dress; her wrap is a himation: S. Karouzou, Δημοσιεύματα Ἑταιρείας Μακεδονικῶν Σπουδῶν 15 (Saloniki, 1957) 311ff., pll. 6, 7, whence E. Simon, "Ein Anthesterien-Skyphos des Polygnotos," *Ant. Kunst* 6 (1963) p. 9, pl. 3,2.

11) *RE* III, 2207.

12) Notes in accession files, J. Paul Getty Museum, Malibu, California.

13) Rome, Lateran Mus.: Benndorf-Schöne 61ff., 92; Helbig II 1154; Wolters 1200; Alinari 29909. Berlin, Staat. Mus.: Blümel, *Kat.* 4 K 186, pl. 78, p. 46f; Reinach *RR* II 24.

14) H. Götze first associated the Peliades relief with the three others with which the original surely belonged: *RM* 53 (1938) 189ff., pl. 38, and *JdI* 63-64 (1948-49) 91, n. 2. H. Thompson assigned the four reliefs to the remodeling of the Altar of Pity in the Athenian Agora, possibly to a period just after the Sicilian catastrophe of 413 B.C.: *Hesperia* 21 (1952) 199ff., pll. 14-15, 17-18.

15) Attic kalyx crater, Berlin, Staat. Mus. 3237, by the Pronomos Painter, ca. 400 B.C., from Capua: *ARV²* 1690; K. Phillips, Jr., *AJA* 72 (1968) 7 and n. 51, pll. 6-7, 16-17; Webster and Trendall, *Illustrations of Greek Drama* (London, 1971) III. 3, 47.

16) Agrigento, Mus. Civ., by the Phiale Painter: *ARV²* 1017, 53; K. Phillips, Jr., *op. cit.,* 7, pll. 7, 15.

17) *Idem.,* pp. 1ff.; cf., especially pl. 6, 11, 12 and 14; pl. 7, 13; pl. 8, 19; and pl. 9, 22.

18) Attic volute crater, Ruvo 1501 (ex coll. Jatta): *ARV²* 1338, 1; H. Sichtermann, *Griechische Vasen in Unteritalien aus der Sammlung Jatta in Ruvo* (Tübingen, 1966), pll. 1, 24.

19) *Studies Present to George M. A. Hanfman* (Mainz, 1971) p. 28ff., esp. pp. 40-44 and nn. 24-27.

20) "Ependytes und Ephod," *Geisteswiss. Forschungen* 8 (Stuttgart, 1935) esp. pp. 36-37.

21) Tübingen E 67, by the Sabouroff Painter: *ARV²* 850, 270 (160). See A.S.F. Gow, *JHS* 48 (1928) 144ff.

tiara and a short, sleeveless jacket. S. Gow, writing in 1927, used the lekythos to support other evidence that *kandyes* and tiaras were worn by actors in Aischylos' *Persai,* first produced in 472 B.C., to render Persians and Persian royalty patently recognizable to Athenian audiences.[22] Certainly there is solid evidence for the use of the *kandys* and of the tiara, the latter upright to represent royalty, collapsed as a "Phrygian cap" for commoners, to represent non-Greeks in Attic art before 400 B.C.[23] For this reason, and because other sleeved garments are worn by actors, flautists, and other stage-folk in painted scenes of the later fifth and early fourth centuries, Myttion has also been suspected of having connections with the theater. A very explicit description of the *kandys,* drawn from a Hellenistic source, in Pollux 7.58, and the many references to the garment, beginning with Xenophon, leave no doubt as to the appearance of the sleeved coat for which the Greeks used the word, *kandys.*[24]

What had not been noted until recently,[25] however, is that the *kandys* is worn very frequently by children, real Attic youngsters, one assumes, on the class three oinochoai, the choes which have been associated with the Anthesteria and which have been found in burials, each surely with its matching skyphos, as E. Simon has pointed out.[26] A number of boys wear the jacket just as Myttion does, open, arms thrust into the sleeves. In no case is it worn by a toddler or a crawling infant, or by the post-adolescent males who appear in other scenes, although how accurately the painters have intended to depict ages has been disputed.[27] S. Karouzou has suggested that the small fellow seated on a *skimpous* between two other little boys (on Athens N.M. 17752), one of whom manifestly wears a comic phallic costume, is acting a child's parody of Orestes.[28] His patterned jacket, particularly the leaf-pattern on the sleeve, may be compared to the more carefully painted coat worn by the Medea of the Talos Painter (*supra.* n. 18). He holds his garlanded pitcher in his extended right hand, and his

loose curls are bound by a fillet in relief, once gilded, as are the heads of the other two children. The possibility that girls may have worn the same garment, but fastened closed, is supported by two other oinochoai, both also in Athens. A little girl[29] who carries a cake and runs with her Meliteian puppy toward a boy at the left, wears a garment for which the sleeve pattern is very like that of the boy (*supra*) seated on the *skimpous.* Other details evoke Medea's *kandys,* although in an even more cursory fashion than those of the boy's coat. L. Deubner noted that the *kandys* of another boy on an oinochoe of the same shape is laced crosswise from top to bottom.[30]

Studies in the last half-century which have concentrated on the Anthesteria pitchers leave little doubt that the scenes depicting these youngsters of mid-childhood reflect their participation in the ritual and fun of the three-day feast which occurred in the very early Spring, even if they also contain quasi-fantastical elements.[31] So far, however, little attention has been paid to what may be the distinct roles of the children who are portrayed wearing *kandyes.* H.R.W. Smith believed that they may very well have been intended to be dressed in "Sunday best".[32] Both he and Karouzou noted funereal allusions which are elements in some of the scenes and appropriate to the feast. In contrast, there are also mimicry of adult ceremonies, dramatic parody, drinking and carousing, races and games. In each scene in which the *kandys* appears, only one child wears the garment. He usually occupies an important position in the composition. Our boy in the laced jacket (*supra,* n. 30) stands almost as if posed for a snapshot, his wreathed *chous* held out to the left, but more attentive to his wheeled toy, right.[33] He wears a crown of white blossoms, which recalled for Deubner the tradition with which the very name of the Anthesteria was associated.[34] The jacketed child who drinks from a kantharos proffered by a nude youth while, behind him, another child chases a goat away from the pitcher of wine, has been identified as "young Dionysos" with satyrs.[35] A child, probably a boy

22) *Idem.*
23) Webster and Trendall, *op. cit., supra,* n. 15: pp. 56-57, III 2.21, 1.22. Compare the unusually fine fragment of an Apulian RF crater, ca. 400 (N.Y. M.M.A., 20. 195) showing Priam in upright tiara doing *proskynesis* before Achilles, to a silver relief cup in Copenhagen, depicting the same subject in a very similar scene (1st C., B.C., but thought to be a copy of Attic work of the late fifth century). In neither, however, can the *kandys* be identified.
24) For references to the *kandys* in literature: *RE* III, 2207, and C. Greenewalt, Jr., *op. cit., supra,* n. 19.
25) B. Kingsley, *AJA* 77 (1973) p. 217.
26) Collected by G. van Hoorn, *Choes and Anthesteria,* (Leiden, 1951). For the related skyphoi: E. Simon, *op. cit., supra,* n. 10-bis. S. Roberts has identified related sets of pyxides and lebetes gamikoi and stressed the importance of pairs for reading the iconography: in a forthcoming

publication, and *AJA* 76 (1972) p. 217; H.R.W. Smith noted complementary scenes in matched Apulian craters: *BABesch* 45 (1970) 68ff.
27) H.R.W. Smith, *CV San Francisco,* 1, p. 48.
28) Athens N.M. 17752, by the Jena Painter: *ARV* 880; S. Karouzou *AJA* 50 (1946) pp. 132ff, figs. 10, 10a,b,c,; van Hoorn, *op. cit.,* No. 117, fig. 148.
29) Athens, Agora Mus. P. 7685: van Hoorn, No. 184, fig. 552.
30) Athens N.M. 1226: *ARV²* 1601, 1; L. Deubner, *JdI* 42 (1927) 190, fig. 23; Beazley, *Hesperia* 24 (1955) p. 308, n. 7, fig. 61; S. Karouzou, *op. cit., supra,* n. 28: "...by a hand close to that of the Phiale Painter ...and by the same hand as Athens N.M. 17753, (from an Attic grave)."
31) Deubner, *Att. Feste,* p. 241.
32) Smith, *loc. cit., supra,* n. 27.
33) Karouzou, *op. cit., supra* n. 28, p. 121 and n. 14.
34) Deubner, *JdI* 42 (1927) pp. 190ff.
35) *Ibid.,* p. 98, pl. 9, 1; *Brit. Mus. Quarterly* 4 (1929) p. 7, no. 49, pl. 45a,b.

because no long undergarment shows below the coat, teases with a bunch of grapes the same Maltese puppy which is very nearly omnipresent on all the *choes*.[36] Boys who wear *kandyes* await jug-racers[37] or race (or dance?) themselves.[38] A child bearing an unidentifiable object approaches a seated, torchbearing woman who has been identified as the wife of the priest of Dionysos, or a priestess in her own right.[39]

Pre-adolescent girls are relatively rare in the Anthesteria scenes, but where they can be clearly recognized, they wear sleeved garments. A little girl sits on a *skimpous* facing a child who rides a rooster and extending a pitcher to him.[40] If her dress may be conjectured by a comparison with the girl of Agora P 7685 (*supra*, n. 29), she may wear a *kandys* closed over an ankle-length chiton.[41] If the garments are correctly identified, these little girls should not be servants, for they engage in activities identical to those of several of the boys.[42]

Many older girls, or young women, who appear on the *choes*, usually in the company of nude youths, also wear sleeved garments, banded down the front and about the knee-length hem. The Eastern *kandys* was often depicted with such broad bands from neck to hem.[43] Although, in most instances, insufficient detail is preserved to identify the garments they wear with any certainty, van Hoorn was able to recognize a sleeved, knee-length open coat worn by a young woman at an altar on a Kerch-style *chous* from Spina.[44] The young women, all similar, appear in two types of scenes: standing at altars[45] and running (or dancing?) with youths, carrying *choes*, torches (?), loaves (?), tympana, phialai, or flat trays of foodstuffs.[46] These are surely komasts, human or

36) Harvard, Fogg Mus. 2408: *CV* III, Ia, pl. 20, 16; van Hoorn no. 438, fig. 324.

37) Munich Ant. Kleinkunst 2466: *CV* pl. 90, 7-8, Deubner, *Att. Feste,* p. 242, n. 8; van Hoorn no. 710, fig. 194.

38) Deubner, *Att. Feste,* pl. 28, 4; van Hoorn, fig. 330 a,b.

39) Louvre CS 2527: *Att. Feste,* p. 99, pl. 9,2; van Hoorn, no. 842, fig. 87.

40) Istanbul Mus. 2493: van Hoorn, no. 560, fig. 348.

41) *Cf.* Kerch-style chous, Leningrad, Hermitage 14444 (1904); K. Schefold, *Untersuch.,* p. 36, 317; van Hoorn, no. 600, fig. 351 (or 531?). Also van Hoorn, no. 595, fig. 530.

42) Athens N.M. 1561, for example, should be a boy carrying a cake, for he lacks the long skirt: see Deubner, *Att. Feste,* p. 240, pl. 28, 5.

43) C. Greenewalt, Jr., *op. cit.,* p. 40, pl. 16b.

44) Van Hoorn, no. 870, fig. 69; London, Sotheby, *Cat.,* December 13, 1928.

45) Altar scenes: e.g. van Hoorn, no. 167, fig. 68 (fragmentary of c. 420 B.C.; no. 351, fig. 54-55, for which compare a youth at altar: Deubner, *Att. Feste,* pl. 13, 1 and 2, and van Hoorn, *RA* 25 (1927) 104ff.; van Hoorn, no. 829, fig. 32.

46) Komasts: e.g., British Museum E 554: *ARV*² 1504, 2; van Hoorn no. 651, figs 168a,b. Leningrad, Hermitage 1490 (1905), Kerch-style: Schefold, *Untersuch.* pp. 36 and 140, 319; van Hoorn, no. 601, fig. 107.

daimonic. A variant of the altar scene shows elements appropriate to an initiation.[47] Over the head of a seated youth, two of our young women dangle a garland and the Dionysiac bunch of grapes, in which might be recognized Smith's "dismemberment telete."[48] Each girl likewise holds a water laver of a type used in purificatory washing, similar to the Apulian dipper in Amsterdam, published by G. Schneider-Herrmann.[49]

The childish Anthesteria scenes begin to appear in Attica just after the mid-fifth century and continue into the fourth.[50] Many, therefore, are approximately contemporary with the stele of Myttion. So, too, may have been the six real Attic women who are recorded as having dedicated their *kandyes* to Artemis Brauronia in the inscribed inventories of just after 350 B.C., which were repeated ca. 343/2.[51] At least one of the dedicants, Aphide, who presented a ϑῶραξ, can be placed.[52] Her husband, Kallistratos, was a trierarch for Athens for either 371/70 or 370/69 B.C.,[53] hence a man of considerable wealth. At least four of the women who gave their *kandyes* to Artemis Brauronia are denoted as married.[54] The wording of the inventories, with the women's names in the nominative, seems to indicate that the clothing was dedicated by living women, rather than for them, after death. In view of the probable ages of the children who wear the *kandyes* on the *choes,* a very good possibility would be that the garments were among the childish articles dedicated to Artemis just before the final day of the Gamelion which, as M. Bieber has shown, was closely linked to the ensuing Anthesteria.[55]

The *kandys* appears to have been an expensive garment. That dedicated by Diophante, the Acharnian wife of Hieronymos, was described as 'ϱάκ', probably a very worn article, in the earliest entry preserved for this garment; either long wear or exposure to the elements might have produced its poor condition. It was decorated with πασμάτια ...χ[ϱ]υσᾶ.[56] The *kandys* of Teisikrateia was

---

47) *ARV²* 1504, 1; van Hoorn, no. 343, figs. 45a,b.
48) Smith, *op. cit., supra,* n. 26.
49) *BABesch* 36 (1961) 64ff; for its use, see Smith, *op. cit., supra,* n. 26.
50) S. Karouzou, *op. cit., supra,* n. 28.
51) *IG* II² 1524B, 180-181 (=1523, 8-9); 1524B, 202-205 (=1523, 26-29); 1524B, 216-220; *IG* II² 1514, 19 (=1515, 11). See T. Linders, *Studies in the Treasure Records of Artemis Brauronia Found in Athens* (Stockholm, 1972).
52) *IG* II² 1524B, 195-96.
53) R. Sealey, *Historia* 5 (1956) p. 179ff., whence *IG* II² 1609; *Fr.Gr. Hist.* II B 115 F. 97.
54) Of 1524B: Diophante (11. 180-81); the woman of 202-4 who may not be Lysimache; Phile of 204-205; Hediste, 219-20; from *IG* II² 1514, 19, probably Tesikrateia.
55) M. Bieber, *Hesperia* sup. 8 (1949) p. 33.
56) *IG* II² 1524B, 180-181.

ποικίλος,[57] that of Olympias, made of ἀμόργι, possibly linen from Amorgos, and decorated περιποίκιλ'.[58] Hediste's was also ποικίλ', of λινοῦ[ν], and βατραχειοῦν, which should indicate a green color.[59] Although no clear clues as to the form of the garments are given, especially as to whether or not they are sleeved, in two instances τὸ ἄγαλμα ἔχει.[60] The decorations would not be inconsistent with the elaborate ornament of the jacket worn by the painted Medea (*supra*, n. 18). The inventories suggest, furthermore, that by the mid-fourth century the *kandys* was regarded as normal wear for Greek women or girls, despite its iconographical use to depict the non-Greek. Elsewhere in the list a dedication is specified as foreign,[61] and foreign garments are noted as such among similar accounts of votive clothing from other sites.[62]

Although the stele of Myttion has commonly been dated to the end of the fifth century,[63] the epigraphy indicates a time soon after 400 B.C.[64] The closest stylistic parallels are also found among reliefs which were formerly regarded as late fifth-century works, but which have been definitely assigned to the first quarter of the fourth century in more recent studies.[65] J. Frel has attributed several of these to the same workshop which produced the Myttion stele, four of which are probably by the same hand. By his generous permission, his attributions, recently revised, are published in an addenda to this study,[66] since they are significant both to the identification of the sculptured figure and for the dating of the stele.

Frel has attributed the stele of Myttion to a workshop of sculptors whose surviving output is largely votive in nature and directly connected to several Attic cults. Particularly important to our attempt to identify Myttion is his recognition of a quality of "observed reality" in the other reliefs belonging to the group.[67] While the figure of our little girl would not, of course, be a portrait, it should reflect in an idealized way her age and status. Furthermore, given the sculptor's interest in representing specific details of real cult practices, it seems probable that the child's coat, which we now recognize as a *kandys,* denotes some aspect of Myttion's actual activity while she lived. The *choes* of the Anthesteria likewise belong to the trend, strong by the fifth century, toward representing generalized real-life situations, mingled with mythical elements.

The Brauronian inventories further confirm that the coat was familiar as an Athenian garment by the early fourth century, and the vases suggest that this may already have been so by the 440's B.C. Since the Anthesteria was celebrated early in the spring, when weather is often still chilly in Athens, Smith's suggestion that the coats were simply cold-weather finery for children has merit. The scenes, however, lend a strong flavor of ritual to support the connections with cult already hinted at by the stele itself. The relatively small numbers of *kandyes* among the Brauronian garments, the unique position of Myttion's coat among grave stelai, and the apparent special role of each jacketed child who appears on a *chous* combine to indicate that the wearing of the garment was in some way restricted, perhaps to children who performed special functions, or who possessed special status and wealth. It was a garment suitable for barbarian royalty; Diophante's gold sequins may be compared to the himation which Demosthenes sent to a gold-smithy to be decorated for his wear as a *choregos,* later in the fourth century.[68]

The contexts, therefore, within which we find the *kandys* would make it appropriate for wear at one or more of various rites, such as a person's enrollment as a citizen, initiation, or at other feasts thereafter, so long as it still fit. The children could, as Karouzou and others have shown, have been parodying adult theatrical costume or other ritual roles, such as the so-called sacred marriage of the archon-basileus to a worthy Athenian woman.[69] What is certain, however, is that both Myttion and her counterparts who romp through Dionysos' oldest Attic feast are Athenian children, for they lack the headgear with which contemporary art consistently signified its foreigners. Our little girl, therefore, surely belonged to some distinguished Athenian family who thus commemorated their daughter, although she did not live long enough to present her own elegant *kandys* to Artemis Brauronia.

Bonnie Kingsley
University of California, Santa Cruz

---

57) *IG* II² 1514, 19.
58) *IG* II² 1524B, 216-218.
59) *IG* II² 1524B, 219-220.
60) The Kandys of Moschos' daughter, 1524B, 202-4; and that of Phile, wife (?) of Democharidos, 204-205.
61) *IG* II² 1514, 49 (=1516, 26; 1517, 155-6).
62) T. Linders, *op. cit.,* n. 51, *supra.*
63) E.g., by H. Möbius, for IG 12221.
64) *Supra,* p. 7, n. 5.
65) J. Frel, "The Telemachos Workshop," *infra.* p. 16.
66) First studied in *SAA*.
67) Frel, *infra,* p. 16.
68) Demosthenes 21.6.
69) As Ariadne, perhaps, according to E. Simon, *op. cit., supra,* n. 10-bis.

The Telemachos Workshop

I.   The Myttion Sculptor

1.   Votive relief, woman spinning, Brauron 760, 761, 761b: *BCH* 86 (1962) 675, 7; *ÖaJh* 45 (1965) fig. 203, 89; *Ergon* 4 (1961) 24, 23.
2.   Stele, Myttion, the J. Paul Getty Museum, Malibu I-72: *Handbook* 25, pl. 14; *Conze* 819, 156.
3.   Votive relief to Asklepios, Athens 1341: *Svoronos,* pl. 34; joined by O. Walter to Epigraphical Museum 8745: *AM* 66 (1941) pl. 61. An important fragment from the Acropolis was added by L. Beschi, who published a new study of the entire monument: *Annuario* 47 (1969) 9, 1.
4.   Record relief (fragment), Athena, Kingston Lacy: *AJA* 60 (1956) pl. 104, 3.
5.   Votive relief of Telemachos, (A) Athens 2477 and (B) Acropolis 1530: joined by O. Walter 316; (C) London, British Museum: *Burlington Fine Arts Club* (1904) 39F 108ad; (D) Athens 2491: *Svoronos* 162; together with part of the inscription of Telemachos: *Annuario* 45-46 (1967-68) 402-403, figs. 9-11. All the fragments were re-assembled and restudied by L. Beschi in *Annuario* 45-46 (1967-8), especially 411, fig. 22.

II.   Comparable with the Myttion Sculptor

6.   Woman with mirror, Kerameikos, Athens: *BCH* 86 (1962) pl. 22; *Deltion* 17 (1961-62) Chron. pl. 18a.

III.   The Sculptor of the Replica

7.   Votive relief, (A) Athens 1358: *Svoronos* 26; *Ephemeris* (1908) 112, 3; *Annuario* 47 (1969) 16, 4; (B) Acropolis 2966; Walter 223 (no ill.); *Annuario* 47 (1969) 17, 5, joined by L. Beschi, *Annuario* 47 (1969) 18, 6.
8.   Votive relief to Artemis, Brauron BE 77: one fragment, *BCH* 86 (1962) 674, 6; *Ergon* for 1961, 25, 24; completed, *BCH* 87 (1963) 711, 18; *Ergon* for 1962, 35, 44; *Deltion* 22 (1967) pl. 105 (bottom).
9.   Replica (fragmentary) of votive relief of Telemachos: (A) Padua, Museo Civico: *Annuario* 45-46 (1967-68) 34; (B) Athens 2490: *Svoronos* 162; *Annuario* 45-46 (1967-68) 401, 6-8 (cf. L. Beschi, *Annuario* 45-46, 381ff.)

IV.   The AB Sculptor (Acropolis-Brauron)

10. Votive relief to Asklepios, Athens 2441: *Svoronos* 156; *Annuario* 47 (1969) 36, 16.
11. Relief, decree, Artemis and votaries, Brauron 1058: *BCH* 86 (1962) 675, 8.

Compare also

12. Votive relief, banquet, Berlin K 95: Blümel 78, 102.

The main characteristics of the entire Telemachos Workshop is its lack of monumentality. The group of sculptors, while they were not miniaturists, made no pretenses to grandeur in either subject or execution. They are obviously delighted with matter which is *genre* in theme and by the rustic appearance of individual figures. The quality is especially strong in the work of the Sculptor of the Replica. Both the dedicant in his votive relief, No. 7, and the driver in the ex-voto to Asklepios by the Myttion Sculptor, No. 3, could be good Acharnians as conceived by Aristophanes. A similar spirit is expressed in the topographic description which accompanies the detailed chronicle of the Telemachos inscription, No. 5, and, even more, in the narrative flavor of the Artemis decree, No. 11. This fondness for a folkloric quality, apparent in both the Sculptor of the Replica and the AB Sculptor, is tempered by a more sober, classicizing touch in the leading master. The woman with mirror, No. 6, may also be his work, although it is superior to his standard production. The Myttion Sculptor shows a predilection for a very flat relief, surely enhanced by a rich polychromy. The faces of his figures wear somewhat serious expressions, which are reduced to accidental grimaces at the hand of his immediate imitator and became mere comic faces with the AB Sculptor.

The workshop received orders from such respectable clients as the sanctuary at Brauron and Telemachos, the latter when he wished to issue a "claim" and to advertise his merits for having established Asklepios in Athens. Several grave stelai of the beginning of the fourth century, which have usually been dated to the late fifth, reflect a similar traditionalist trend in sculpture. They likewise present a direct vision of simple reality in which picaresque detail prevails over artistic merit.

Jiří Frel

Some time during the fourth century B.C. a statue of Herakles was set up in the gymnasium of Sikyon.[1] Although Sikyon was famous for the bronze sculptures produced by its native artists (notably Polyclitus and Lysippos), the Herakles was of stone; the reason for this was undoubtedly the personal preference of the sculptor employed, Skopas of Paros.[2] A bronze coin struck at Sikyon in the early third century A.D. by Geta almost certainly reproduces this statue.[3] The coin's usefulness as a guide to the statue's appearance is sometimes disparaged, as its poor state of preservation not only precludes stylistic analysis but makes recognition of some of the basic features quite difficult. So much seems sure: the left leg is the *Standbein,* the left forearm is outstretched and covered with drapery or the lion's skin, the right arm is lowered, and the head is turned sharply to the proper left. The head, very large in proportion to the body (as is common on figures reproduced on coins) is probably beardless and wreathed.[4]

The employment of even superior and well-preserved coins as aids in reconstructing the appearance of lost statues is generally, and correctly, very cautious. The value of the Sikyonian coin, moreover, has seemed further lessened by the apparent abundance of sculptural evidence related to Skopas' Herakles. Almost a century ago, B. Graef made a famous and influential study of a group of wreathed and unbearded heads of Herakles, most in the form of herms.[5] At that time the best known example was the British Museum head from Genzano,[6] which has given its name to the entire class. A few years previously, the Genzano head had been assigned to Praxiteles,[7] but Graef, noting a basic resemblance to several sculptured heads (among them a Herakles wearing the lion's skin) from the pediments of the Temple of Athena Alea at Tegea, declared for Skopas; Skopas designed the temple ca. 340 B.C., and it is generally agreed that the sculptures were the product of his workshop, if not of his own hand.[8]

For most attributions made to Skopas and most ideas of his style, these heads—which are cursory in their workmanship and severely weathered—have been the main criterion. Their appearance is striking: especially noteworthy are the massive structure with great depth from front to back, the square face tapering suddenly to a rather small chin, the large, round eyes which turn upward and are overhung by heavy flesh at the outer corners, and the lifted upper lip which gives the mouth a "breathing" expression.[9] The overall effect is one of great emotional intensity or "pathos".

The Genzano-type Herakles heads form a rather unruly class linked together by the fact that almost all wear a wreath—most frequently of white poplar, sometimes of ivy, vine, olive, or oak leaves—as well as by a basic resemblance to the presumably Skopadic heads from Tegea. The Herakles heads, however, tend to be fleshier, and their chins longer. Partly in consequence of these differences, the fire and energy of the Tegea heads (and of some others attributed to Skopas) has become a dreamy melancholy.[10] This softening of the pathos expected of Skopas could be explained as the work of copyists—but it should also be noted that the original of this Herakles seems to predate Skopas' activity at Tegea by several decades, and that in any case so versatile an artist as Skopas (who made a nude Aphrodite reputed more beautiful than Praxiteles' statue for Cnidus) can not always have worked in exactly the same style as at Tegea.[11]

---

1) Pausanias 2.10.1.

2) On Skopas see especially K. A. Neugebauer, *Studien über Skopas* (Leipzig 1913), C. Picard, *Manuel d'Archéologie Grecque: La Sculpture* III 2 (Paris 1948) 633-780 and IV 1 (Paris 1954) 1-236, and P. E. Arias, *Skopas* (Rome 1952). The only recorded bronze by Skopas is his Aphrodite *Pandemos* at Elis (Pausanias 6.25.1), while the testimonia for many Skopadic works specify stone as the material.

3) See P. Gardner and F. Imhoof-Blumer, "Numismatic Commentary on Pausanias," *JHS* 6 (1885) 79, pl. 53, no. 11, B. Graef, "Herakles des Skopas und Verwandtes," *RömMitt* 4 (1889) 212-214, G. Cultrera, "Una Statua di Ercole," *Memorie dei Lincei* 14 (1910) 186-187, Picard (*supra,* n. 2) III 2, p. 708, fig. 307, Arias (*supra,* n. 2) 108, no. 36, pl. I.5, S. Howard, *The Lansdowne Herakles (J. Paul Getty Museum Publication* No. 1, Los Angeles 1966) 3, fig. 3, A. Linfert, *Von Polyklet zu Lysipp* (Giessen 1966) iv, 33. It seems impossible that the coin could reproduce the Lysippian statue of Herakles in the agora of Sikyon, as Cultrera suggests, as that work was undoubtedly the original of the "weary" Herakles type best known from the Farnese statue in Naples.

4) See Graef, *loc. cit. (supra,* n. 3).

5) Graef (*supra,* n. 3) 189ff. Subsequent lists of replicas have been compiled, notably by A. Preyss, text to *Br.-Br. Denkmäler* 691-692, Arias (*supra,* n. 2) 104-108, Howard (*supra,* n. 3) 30-31, and Linfert (*supra,* n. 3) 71-75.

6) See Arias (*supra,* n. 3) 104, no. 4, pl. II.6-7.

7) See P. Wolters, "Praxitelische Köpfe," *JdI* 1 (1886) 54-56; more recently, B. Ashmole, "Notes on the sculpture of the Palazzo dei Conservatori," *JHS* 42 (1922) 242-244.

8) For the Tegea temple see especially J. Berchmans, C. Dugas, and M. Clemmensen, *Le Sanctuaire d'Aléa Athéna à Tégée au IVe siècle* (Paris 1924), E. Pfuhl, "Bemerkungen zur Kunst des vierten Jahrhunderts," *JdI* 43 (1928) 27-39, Arias (*supra,* n. 2) 78-81, 115-122, Picard (*supra,* n. 2) IV, 1, pp. 15-193. Berchmans *et al.* set the date ca. 360-330 B.C.; I follow Pfuhl, Arias, and Picard in dating the temple and its sculpture after 350. For Skopas' connection with the pedimental sculptures see recently Linfert (*supra,* n. 3) 38-39, and for a new reconstruction of the West pediment A. Delivorrias, "Σκοπαδικα I: Télèphe et la bataille du Caïque au fronton Ouest du temple d'Aléa Athéna à Tégée," *BCH* 97 (1973) 111-135.

9) For detailed description of the Tegea heads cf. Berchmans *et al.. (supra,* n. 8) 87-92, 124-125, nos. 7, 8, 17, 18, 106, E.A. Gardner, *Six Greek Sculptors* (London 1926) 184-186, F. P. Johnson, *Lysippos* (Durham 1927) 51-53 (who is reminded of the "blind will of Schopenhauer"), and Picard (*supra,* n. 2) IV 1, pp. 187-190.

10) For this reason Ashmole, *loc. cit. (supra,* n. 7) suggested that at

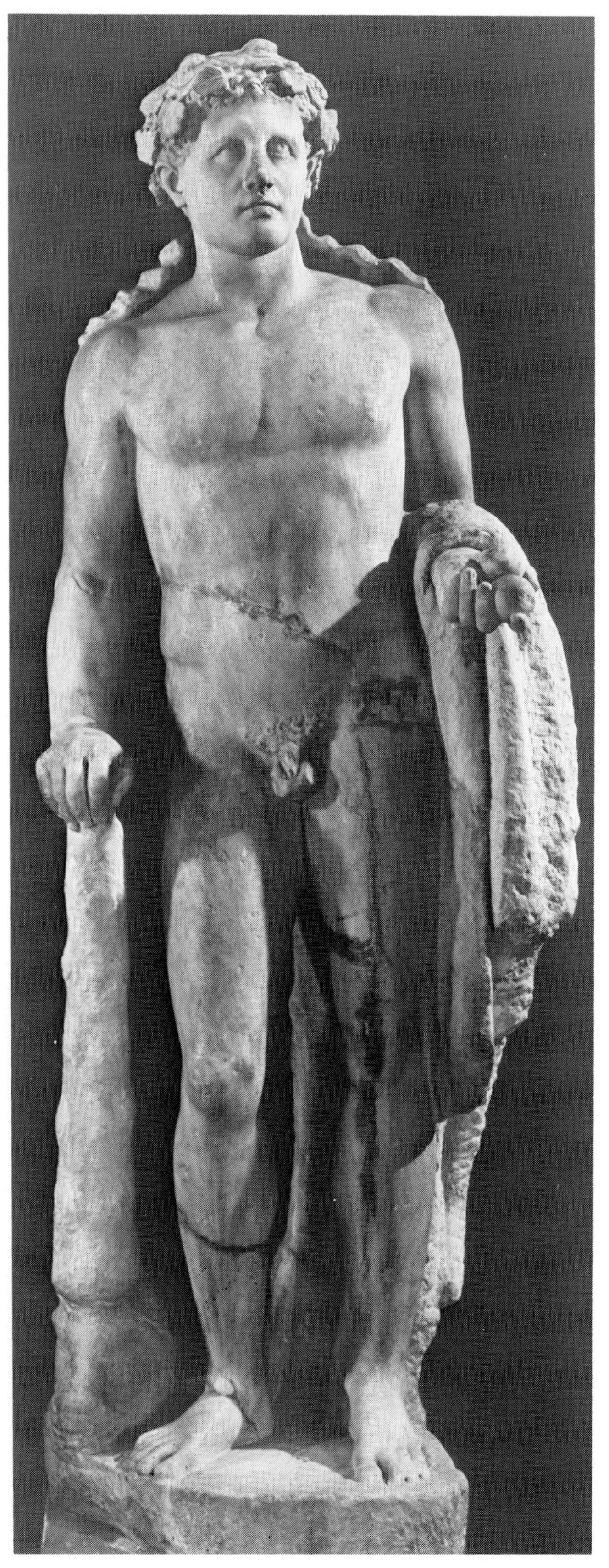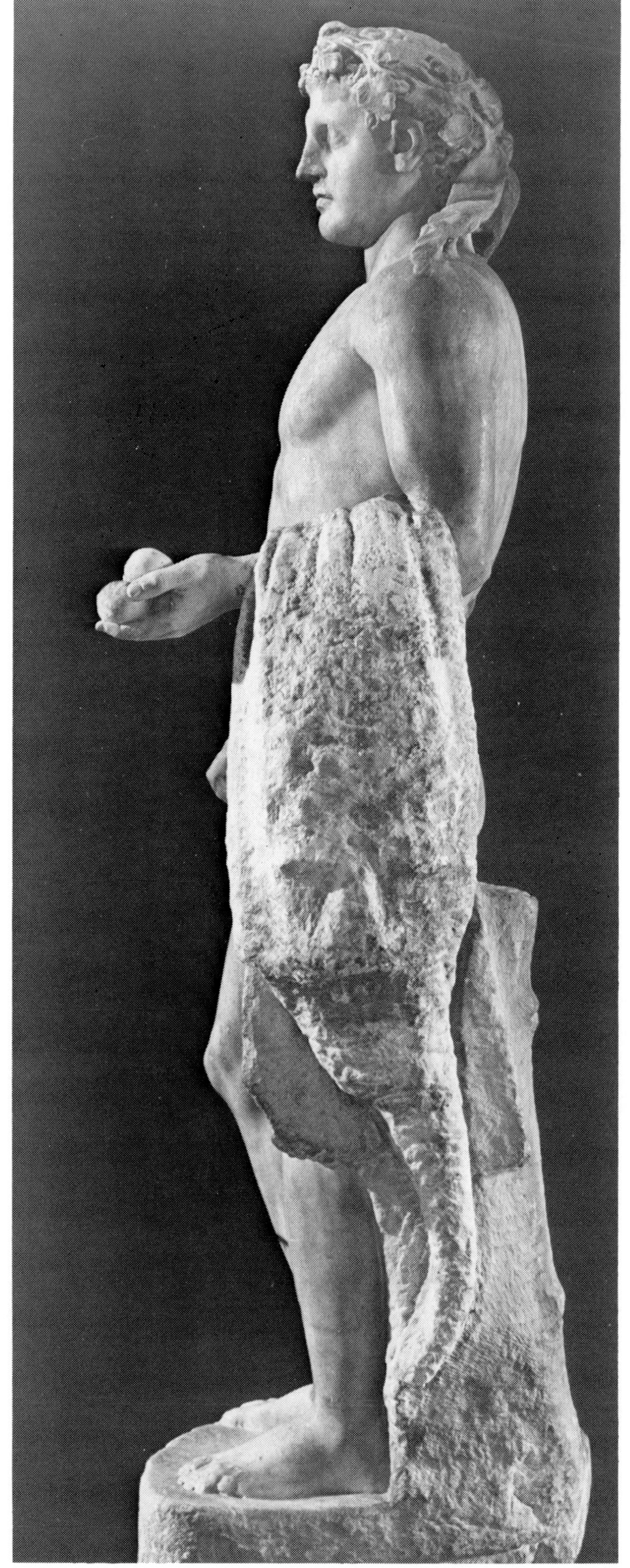

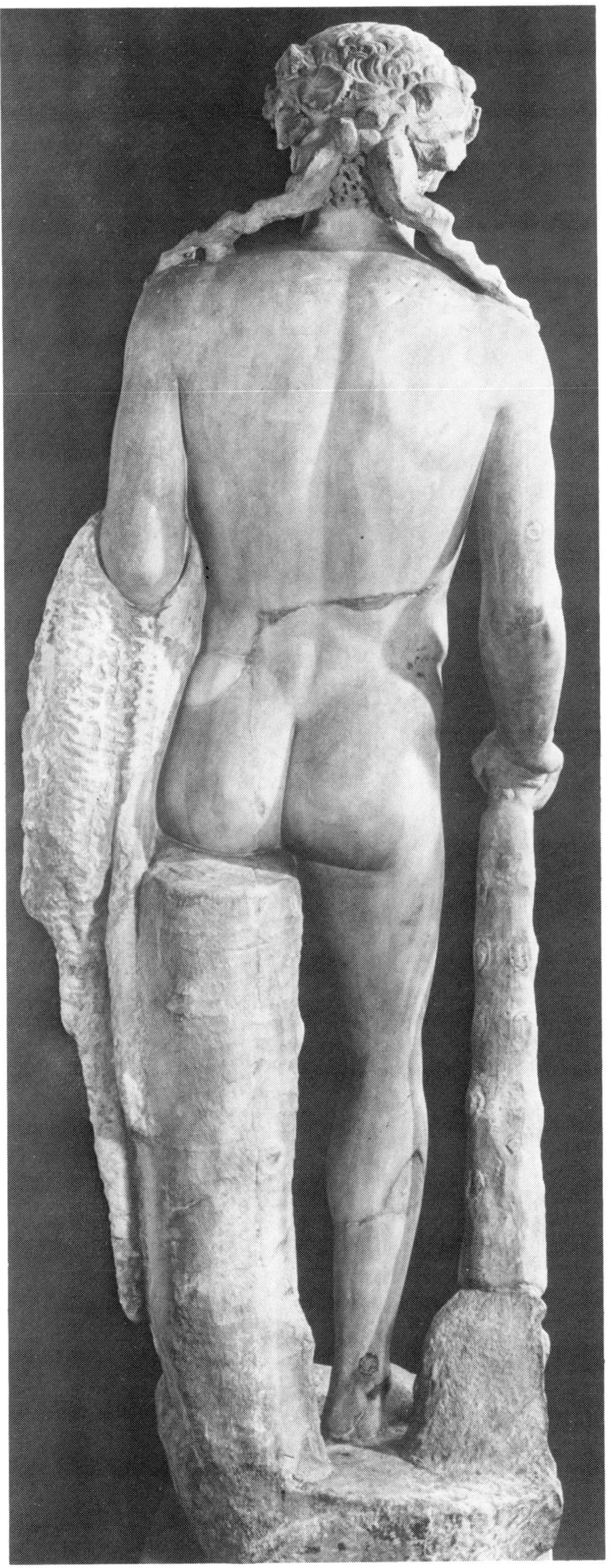

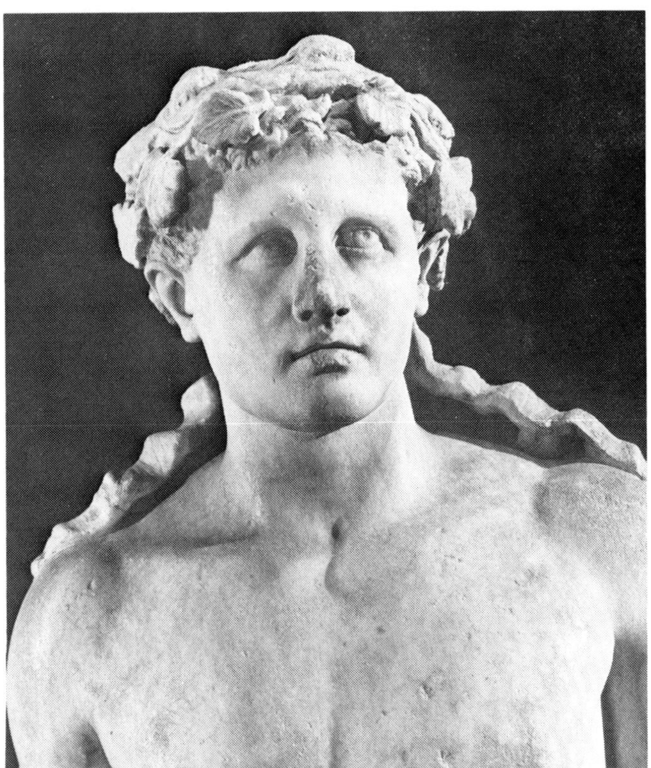

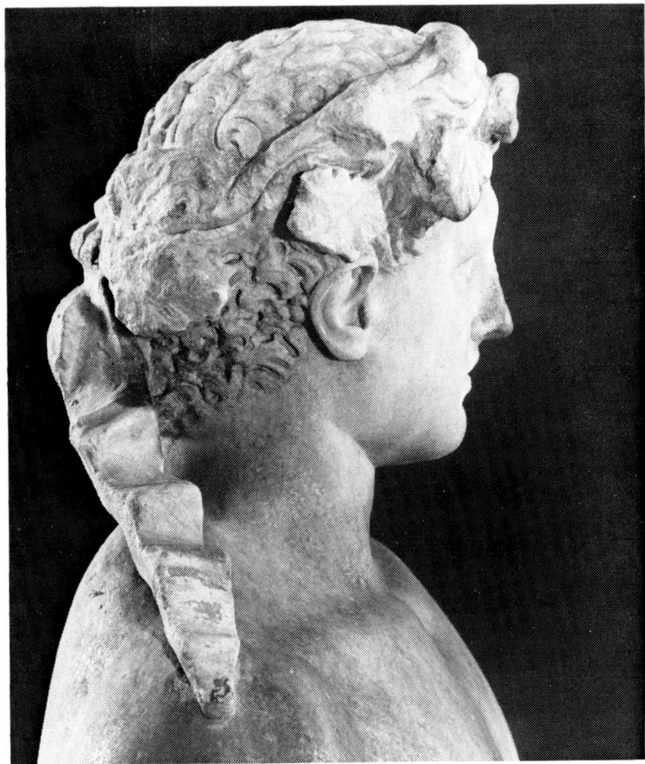

1-5   Hope Herakles, on loan in the J. Paul Getty Museum
from Los Angeles County Museum of Art,
William Randolph Hearst collection

Clearly an identification of the Skopadic Herakles for Sikyon on the basis of head types alone is an uneasy one, yet no definite body-type has been unanimously accepted as belonging to the Genzano heads. (The Lansdowne Herakles will be discussed below.) Graeco-Roman art produced many youthful Herakles figures which seem hybrids of earlier statues, and a type of head frequently disembodied to serve as a herm would be an almost inevitable ingredient in this mixing process. If, however, we return to the rather neglected coin from Sikyon, a single statue (also generally neglected) comes into the picture. This is the Hope Herakles, now in the J. Paul Getty Museum, on loan from the Los Angeles County Museum of Art (Figs. 1-5).[12] This life-size statue matches the coin in every detail which can be checked; in addition, we see that the outstretched left hand holds the golden apples, the lowered right hand rests easily on a heavy club which is supported by a small bull's head.[13] The head (Fig. 4) of the Herakles clearly belongs to the Genzano class[13a] and is at the same time closer than most of these to the heads from Tegea: the chin is compact, the fleshiness over the corners of the eyes and the square bony structure of the face are pronounced, the ears are placed quite far forward (Fig. 5), and the expression is somewhat more vigorous and less lugubrious than that characterizing the Genzano class. Like most of the other examples, the Hope head wears a wreath fastened with a broad fillet whose ends hang over the shoulders, a feature which has been called "ganz ungriechisch".[14] A wreath with similar hanging fastenings, however, is worn by a marble head of Herakles now dated ca. 300

B.C.[15] While it was a common practice of Roman copyists to add such wreaths to statues,[16] its presence on the Sikyonian statue may be corroborated by the coin; the "long hair" noticed by one scholar could be the hanging fastenings.[17]

Because the Hope statue has been very little known, opposition to its claims to represent the Skopadic Herakles[18] has hardly been voiced. Riis contents himself with pointing out that the basic type seems to go back to Attic art of the late fifth century.[19] Howard considers it "probably an Antonine pastiche", which incorporates a "body, which is too early in style, duplicating the stiff, unmastered contrapposto of mid-fifth century standing figures."[20] The stance of the Hope Herakles (Figs. 1, 3)— which is unfortunately a replica of poor quality—is in fact the most interesting feature of the statue. The supporting leg, outstretched hand, and turn of the head place an overwhelming emphasis on the left side; the right side seems to hang from the figure's axis (every anatomical detail is placed lower than on the left), and only the club prevents an appearance of toppling sideways.[21]

This unusual stance, with its ambiguous use of a support (the club) is in my opinion further evidence of an attribution to Skopas. The original of the Hope Herakles appears to have been made in the 360's.[22] Around the same time or slightly earlier, and probably close to the beginning of his career, Skopas gave his "Palatine" Apollo a similarly *einseitig* stance: again, the left arm is flexed, the left leg supports the body's weight, and the head is turned left; the entire right side is relaxed.[23]

<hr>

least one of the herms represented Dionysos rather than Herakles.

11) Moreover, Skopas may have had close followers or imitators, e.g., see *infra*, 5, n. 25. For the Aphrodite see Pliny, *NH* 36.26.

12) J. Paul Getty Museum L73.AA.3. S. Reinach, *Répertoire de la statuaire grecque et romaine* V, 81, no. 6, *idem*, "Un Héraclès du IVe siècle," *RA* 6 (1917) 460-461, O. Brendel, text to *E.-A.* 4168, A.H. Smith, *An Ancient Greek Statue of Herakles from the Arundel and Hope Collections* (London 1928), Howard (*supra*, n. 3) 35, Linfert (*supra*, n. 3), 33-39. Preyss (*supra*, n. 5) no. 35 listed the Hope Herakles as a terminal bust joined to an unrelated statue; contra, see Smith and Linfert, n. 20. I can detect no sign of breakage at the neck. The lion's skin has been extensively and crudely recut. The left hand and the apples appear to be antique but also recut; the club is restored.

13) This last attribute was mistakenly identified as a boar's head by Reinach in *RA* (*supra*, n. 12) 460; cf. Smith (*supra*, n. 12) 3.

13a) One of the closer parallels is a head in Venice; see *E.-A.* 2618, Linfert (*supra*, n. 3) 73, k.

14) By Brendel, *loc. cit.* (*supra*, n. 12).

15) See E. T. Wakely and B. S. Ridgway, "A head of Herakles in the Philadelphia University Museum," *AJA* 69 (1965) 156-160.

16) *Ibid.* 159, n. 24.

17) See Graef (*supra*, n. 3) 213.

18) Reinach, Smith, and Linfert (see *supra*, n. 12) accept the Hope statue as a replica of the Skopadic statue at Sikyon.

19) P. J. Riis, "The pedigree of some Herakles figures from Tarsus,"

ActaA 23 (1952) 154. The analysis below will attempt to show that the Hope statue displays an individuality and originality which distinguish it from superficially similar works such as those cited by Riis or the much-restored Madrid torso (Linfert [*supra*, n. 3] 72, A, c).

20) *Loc. cit.* (*supra*, n. 12). Howard 3, 35, associates the use of tree-trunks as supports with marble copies after bronze originals; applied to the Hope Herakles, this line of argument would seem to discredit Howard's pastiche theory to some extent as well as an attribution to Skopas. For supporting tree-trunks in later classical stone sculpture, however, see recently S. Adam, *The Technique of Greek Sculpture* (Oxford 1966) 100-101 and T. Dohrn, "Die Marmor-Standbilder des Daochos-Weihgeschenks in Delphi," *Antike Plastik* 8 (Berlin 1968) 46. It has been suggested from time to time that the frequency with which Roman copyists reproduced bronzes in marble affected their handling of such details as hair even when bronze originals were not involved; I think it is also likely that copyists always inclined toward caution and conservatism in supporting stone figures, to reduce the dangers of breakage (Roman statuary was a commercial proposition, and the results were not necessarily intended to bear close inspection). There are thus two ways of accounting for the presence of a tree-trunk in a copy after a marble original.

21) See the excellent analysis by Linfert (*supra*, n. 3) 34-35.

22) Its possible influence on other fourth-century Herakles figures is traced by Linfert (*supra*, n. 3) 35-39.

23) On the Palatine Apollo see especially G. E. Rizzo, "La Base di

Bulle, without considering this latter statue, has already suggested that a partiality to statues with a "closed" and "open" side was a central characteristic of Skopas' art, one that culminated in his image of *Pothos*.[24] We may also compare the Meleager type (as represented by the Fogg replica), which seems Skopadic—although I would attribute it to a close follower rather than to Skopas himself.[25] In both the *Pothos* and the Meleager the sideward motion is more pronounced than in the Hope Herakles, and the support more essential, yet the support remains somewhat ambiguous, each statue assuming a pose which seems impossible to sustain for more than a moment. Architectural sculpture made by Skopas or under his supervision seems to show a comparable interest in strong sideward motion.[26]

For Skopas, then, the Hope Herakles probably belongs to an early stage of a development whose beginning is marked by the one-sided but firmly-standing Palatine Apollo. The origins of this feature of Skopas' style, while apparently more sophisticated than "stiff, unmastered contrapposto", are not easy to find. Where Skopas received his training as a sculptor has in fact been a vexed question. His Ionian birth and blood are factors to be kept in mind but difficult to assess. Early studies of Skopas pointed to the Peloponnese and the school of Polyclitus, but it has been more recently and plausibly argued that Skopas began his career in Athens and was essentially an Attic sculptor.[27] Linfert believes that, though Skopas' workshop was in any case Peloponnesian, Skopas did not belong to the Polyclitan school but rather influenced it.[28] Both Linfert and Arnold have shown that Polyclitus' followers themselves often departed from the chiastically-balanced contrapposto of such works as the *Doryphoros;*[29] yet Linfert's judgment that the Hope Herakles is "'von Natur' unkanonisch, unpolykletisch"[30] seems brilliantly right.

For any discussion of Skopas' artistic origins and in particular of his connections with the Polyclitan school, the Lansdowne Herakles—one of the most common attributions to Skopas—is of great importance (Figs. 6-10).[31] The Herakles, discovered in Hadrian's villa near Tivoli and now in the J. Paul Getty Museum in Malibu (Acc. no. 70.AA.109), was one of the most admired of antique statues long before studies of Skopas' career commenced. The association of the statue with Skopas was preceded by the discovery of the pedimental fragments at Tegea and by Graef's study of the Genzano type; the Lansdowne Herakles has been sometimes grouped with the Genzano heads as a reproduction— even the only full-length one—of Skopas' statue at Sikyon,[32] sometimes thought to go back to a different original also made by Skopas.[33]

Augusto," *BullComm* 60 (1932) 51-66, G. Becatti, "Una nuova copia dell'Apollo Palatino," *BullComm* 64 (1936) 19-25, and Picard (*supra,* n. 2) III 2, p. 639ff. Originally the statue probably stood in Attica, as the Palatine temple was called "Aedem Apollonis Ramnusii" (*Notitia Reg. X*). The three true replicas are headless or faceless, and the original must be dated by drapery style. On this evidence, the Apollo should belong to the 370's; the drapery lacks the decorative flamboyance of the very early fourth-century rich style but is lighter and more abstract than that of the *Eirene* by Kephisodotos. The Athena on an Athenian record relief of 375-4 (*Br.-Br. Denkmäler* 533 r., H. K. Süsserott, *Griechische Plastik des vierten Jahrhunderts vor Christus* [Frankfurt 1938] pl. 3.2) and early fourth-century terracottas from Tiryns (Pfuhl [*supra,* n. 8] fig. 1) provide parallels.

24) H. Bulle, "Skopas und die Persönlichkeitsfrage in der griechische Kunst," *JOAI* 37 (1948), esp. 11-14. On the *Pothos* see recently E. Simon, "Neuerwerbungen des Martin von Wagner-Museums, Würzburg," *AA* 1968, 148-150.

25) See my article, "Meleager: New replicas, old problems," *Opuscula Romana* 9 (1973) and to my references add G. Kopcke, "Die Hündin Baracco. Beobachtungen und Vorschläge," *RömMitt* 76 (1969) 133. In doubting the attribution to Skopas himself I may have given too much weight to the argument that the original was bronze; see *supra,* n. 20. For the stance cf. also H. Sichtermann, "Das Motiv des Meleager," *RömMitt* 69 (1962) 43-51 and "Nachtrag," *RömMitt* 70 (1963) 174-177.

26) For the fragmentary figures from Tegea see Berchmans *et al.* (*supra,* n. 8) 134-136, E. Lapalus, *Le Fronton Sculpté en Grèce* (Paris 1947) esp. 208-211, Picard (*supra,* n. 2) IV 1, pp. 190-191; a recently discovered torso is published by G. Daux, "Chronique de fouilles 1967," *BCH* 92 (1968) 810, fig. 4. For the "Skopadic" reliefs from the Mausoleum at Halicarnassus see recently B. Ashmole, *Architect and Sculptor in Classical Greece* (London 1972) 178-187. H. Bulle, text to *Br.-Br. Denkmäler* 649 and *op. cit.* (*supra,* n. 24) 18-19 argued that the "Alba Jüngling" in Copenhagen is a fourth-century pedimental statue and associated it with Skopas, calling it "ein zu Boden gestossener Pothos." Cf. Delivorrias (*supra,* n. 8) 119-121.

27) See Picard (*supra,* n. 2) III 2, pp. 637-639, Arias (*supra,* n. 2) 97, G. Becatti, *La Scultura Greca* (Rome 1961) 34, G. Donnay, "Art et politique dans l'Athènes classique," *GBA* 104, no. 59 (1962) 16.

28) Linfert (*supra,* n. 3) 29-39.

29) *Ibid.* 34, 47, D. Arnold, *Die Polykletnachfolge* (*JdI Erg.-H* 25, Berlin 1969) 62, 117, 138, 176-177, 222. Both writers find *einseitig* compositions especially characteristic of Naukydes.

30) Linfert (*supra,* n. 3) 34.

31) See now Howard (*supra,* n. 3): full bibliography, excellent illustrations, detailed history of the piece since its discovery; also, C. Vermeule and N. Neuerberg, *Catalogue of the Ancient Art in the J. Paul Getty Museum* (1973), pp. 6-8, pl. 9. Another recent reference (from J. Frel): F. Hiller, *Formgeschichtliche Untersuchungen zur griechischen Statuen des Spät 4. Jahrhunderts* (Mainz 1971) 17, 19, Fig. 12.

32) E.g., by Lippold, *Kopien und Umbildungen griechischer Statuen* (Munich 1923) 159, A. della Seta, *Il Nudo nell'Arte* (Milan 1930) 285, B. Schweitzer, "Herakleskopf der Ny Carlsberg Glyptotek. Kopienkritisches zu Skopas," *JOAI* 39 (1952) 107, Howard (*supra,* n. 3); more tentatively, Brendel (*supra,* n. 12) and Arias (*supra,* n. 2) 104, no. 1. This theory seems to jettison the Sikyonian coin as evidence, as Linfert (*supra,* n. 3) iv protests, although Howard 3-4 accepts it as "meager corroborative evidence."

33) See Preyss (*supra,* n. 5), Reinach in *RA* (*supra,* n. 12) 461, E. Curtius, *Die klassische Kunst Griechenlands* (Potsdam 1938) 382.

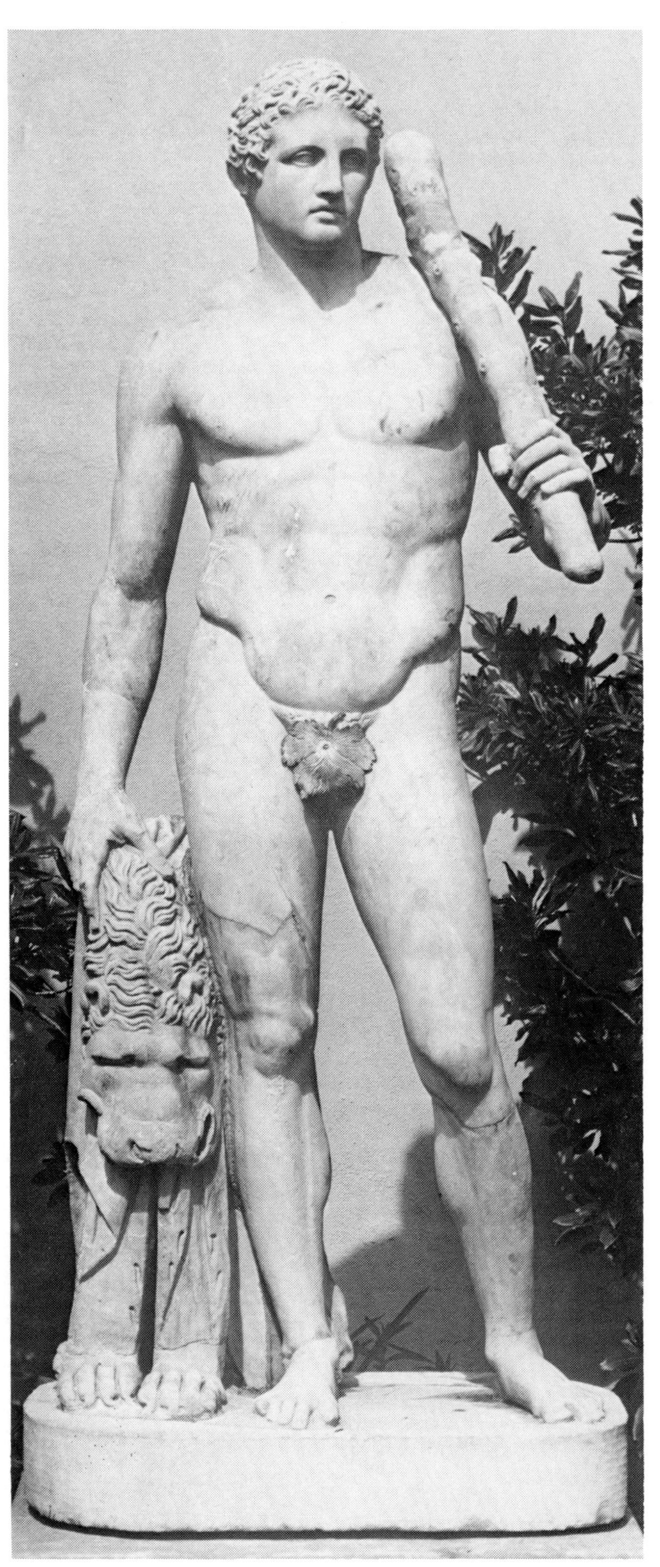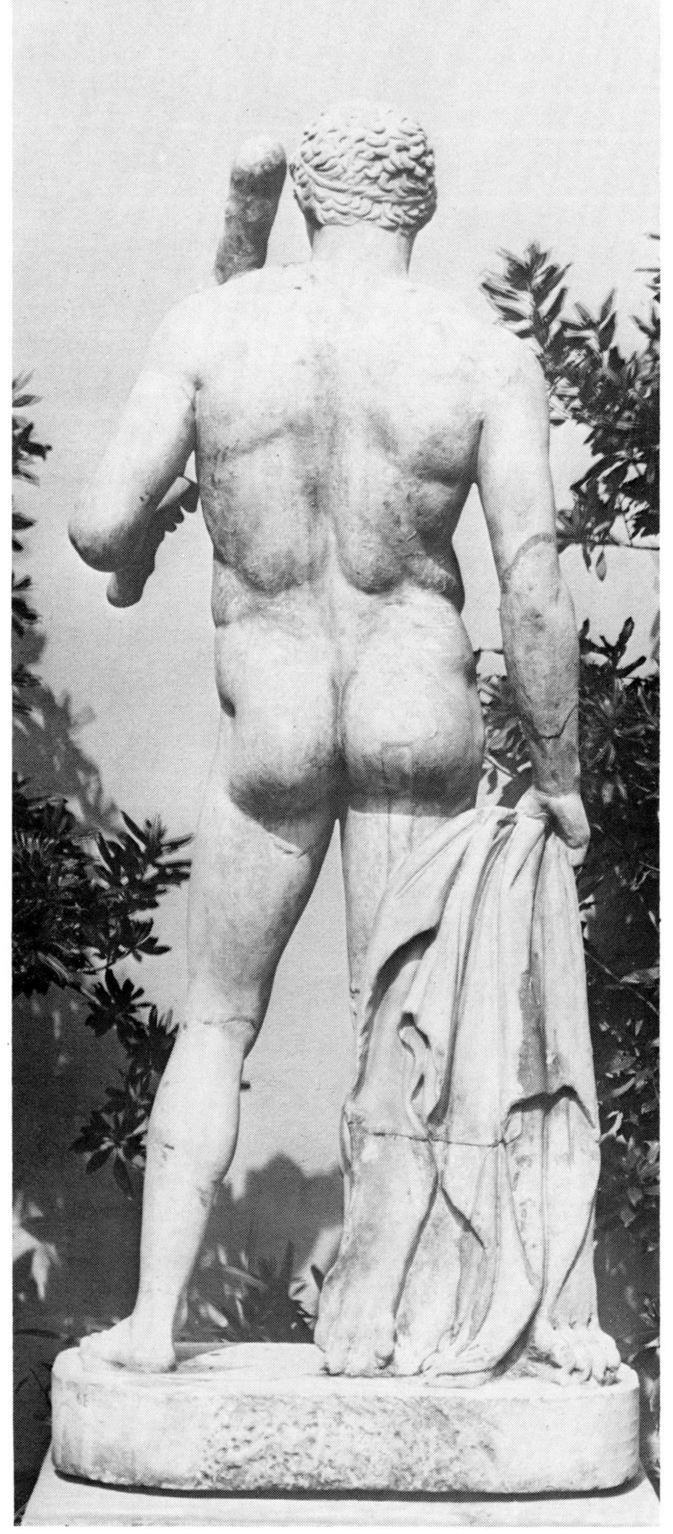

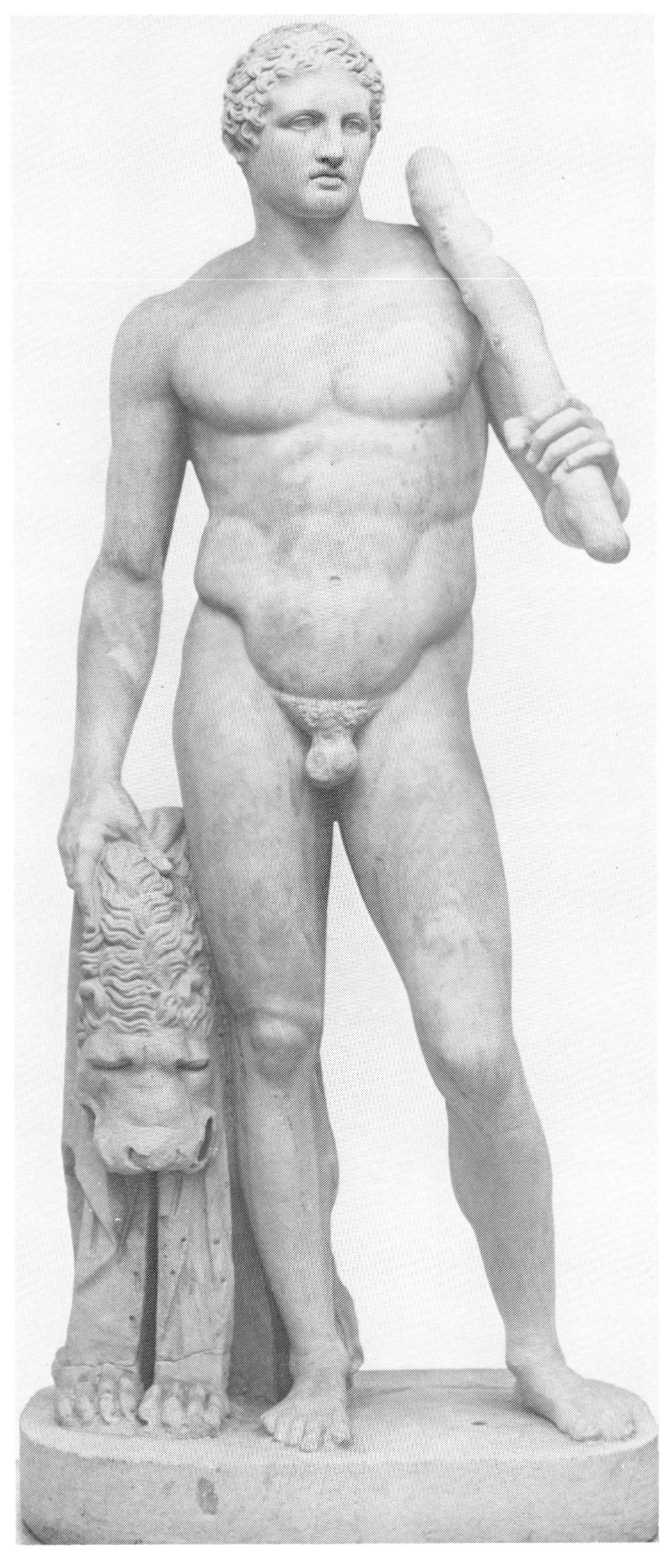

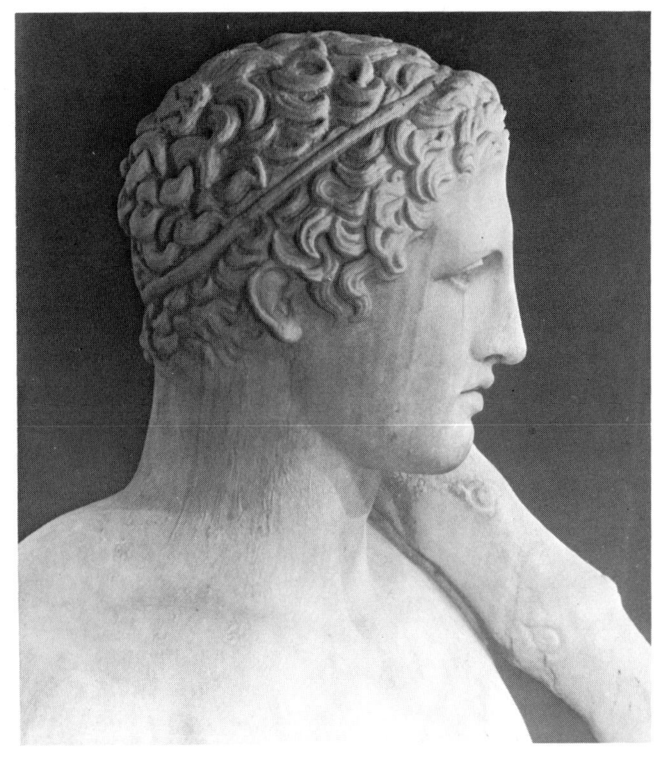

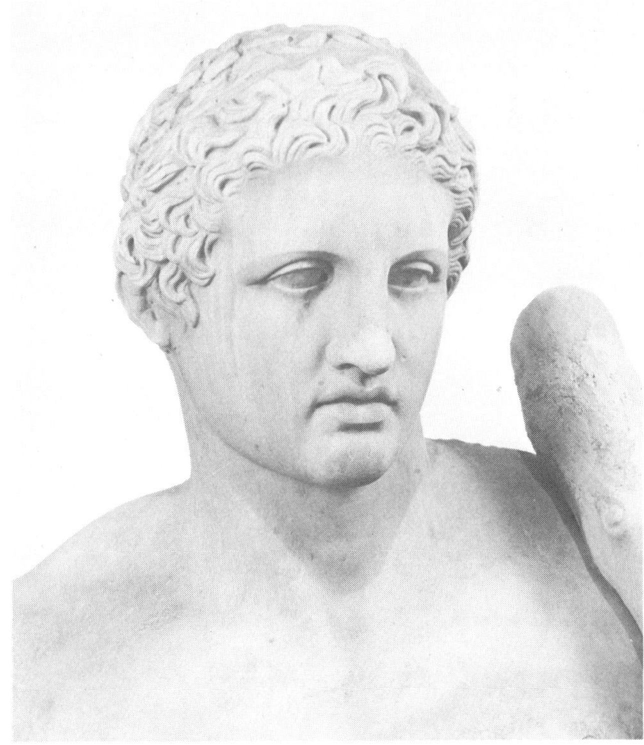

6-7   Pg. 22: L.H. Lansdowne Herakles, J. Paul Getty Museum
70.AA.109 (previous display)

8-10   Lansdowne Herakles, present display

The original of the Lansdowne Herakles is generally dated ca. 360, which would place it toward the beginning of Skopas' career; if accepted as his work the statue should provide some clues as to his training. There is an unmistakable similarity to Polyclitus' *Doryphoros* (Fig. 11), and several scholars accept the Herakles as a product of the Polyclitan school.[34] Alscher, however, considers the style Ionian,[35] while others believe the statue blends Peloponnesian and Attic stylistic features.[36] Arnold's opinion stands somewhat apart: Skopas made the statue, not as a Polyclitan follower—although he was deeply influenced by both Polyclitus and his school—but as an independent artist who returned to the *Doryphoros* for his inspiration with a wholly new understanding of that work.[37] A close relation with the *Doryphoros* is established by the chiastic balance of Herakles' stance, and more particularly by the position of the left arm. The proportions, moreover, seem those used by Polyclitus,[38] as do many anatomical details such as the long, graceful curve of the pectoral muscles.[39] It is difficult to see anything here which is definitely Attic.[40] Yet the way to an attribution to the school of Polyclitus is not clear. The head is unlike any created by the master himself and cannot really be paralleled among the works attributed to his successors. Perhaps equally important, the treatment of anatomical details lacks the careful articulation and the emphasis on the contraction and relaxation of individual muscles which was developed by Polyclitus and his school.[41]

As already mentioned, various scholars from Furtwängler on have found the style of the Lansdowne Herakles a mixture of Attic and Peloponnesian, conservative and innovative traits and have accepted as a solution the attribution to a young sculptor of great originality who had come under strong fifth-century, including Polyclitan influences: Skopas. Yet the original basis for this attribution—the style of the head—has been challenged. Comparing the Tegea heads, we find that the Lansdowne Herakles has a higher forehead and fuller chin,[42] the brow is slightly indented at the bridge of the nose, the ears are placed further back,[43] the fold of flesh over the outer corners of the eyes is attenuated and almost lacking, as is the overall expression of emotional intensity (Figs. 9-10). The Genzano heads share many of these same differences from the Tegea fragments but tend to be closer to them than is the Lansdowne head.[44] The Lansdowne Herakles, moreover, has a different handling of the locks of hair over the forehead and wears a simple fillet rather than a wreath.[45]

An especially interesting approach to the problems

34) E.g., K. A. Neugebauer, text to *Br.-Br. Denkmäler* 717-718, p. 6, and Linfert (*supra,* n. 3) 36. Neither attributes the original to Skopas; Linfert suggests Antiphanes of Argos.

35) L. Alscher, *Griechische Plastik* III (Berlin 1956) 172-173. Yet he believes that the Ionian sculptor cannot be Skopas (see *infra,* 9, n. 42).

36) See A. Furtwängler, *Masterpieces of Greek Sculpture* (Chicago 1964, reprint of 1895 edition) 297-299. Della Seta (*supra,* n. 32) 285, 288-289 stresses the Attic element, Howard (*supra,* n. 3) 6-7 the Polyclitan.

37) Arnold (*supra,* n. 29) 230. The view of Schweitzer (*supra,* no. 32) 107 is similar, although more generalized: Skopas had close ties with the Argive-Sikyonian school of sculptors but, rather than conforming, carried on a "dialogue" with Polyclitus.

38) For a variety of opinions about the pose cf. della Seta (*supra,* n. 32) 285, 288, Süsserott (*supra,* n. 23) 147-148, J. Charbonneaux, *La Sculpture Grecque Classique* 2 (Paris 1945) 88, Bulle (*supra,* n. 24) 13-14, Schweitzer (*supra,* n. 32) 108, Alscher (*supra,* n. 35) 172, G. Kaschnitz von Weinberg, *Ausgewählte Schriften* III (Berlin 1965) 308-309 (reference from E. K. Gazda), Howard (*supra,* n. 3) 6-7, 10-11, Linfert (*supra,* n. 3) 35-36. There is general agreement that the statue—placed in the context of early fourth-century sculpture—shows a new feeling for spatiality.

39) Neugebauer (*supra,* n. 34) 7, n. 1, specifies the bulge of muscle over the knee and the form of the pubes.

40) The position of the free leg, with the foot firmly planted to one side, has often been considered an Attic innovation. Arnold (*supra,* n. 29) 36-39 has shown that this stance, whether it came from Attic influence or Argive tradition, had already been taken up by Polyclitus' followers.

41) See especially Arnold (*supra,* n. 29) 230, n. 780, also Alscher (*supra,* n. 35) 172; contra, Linfert (*supra,* n. 3) 36. For the most detailed description of the anatomy see della Seta (*supra,* n. 32) 289.

42) See Alscher (*supra,* n. 35) 173.

43) The ears are placed unusually far forward on the Tegea heads, also on a female head from Attica which is closely related stylistically; see P. Croissant and C. Rolley, "Deux têtes féminines d'époque classique," *BCH* 89 (1965) 324-325, 329, figs. 7-8, pls. VI-VII. The ears are also placed well forward on the Hope head, although not on most of the Genzano heads. This placing of the ear is one of the few probable Skopadic features that definitely appear in the work of Polyclitus and his school.

44) Linfert (*supra,* n. 3), after enumerating the salient characteristics of the Genzano type (72), lists only five heads as true replicas (73, a-e); cf. *supra,* n. 13a. As defined by Linfert the Genzano type seems close to the Tegea style except in the limited depth of the rear portion of the head, a feature determined largely by the positioning of the ears; cf. *supra,* n. 43.

45) Linfert (*supra,* n. 3) 74 believes that none of the heads without wreaths can be regarded as copies of the Herakles by Skopas and remarks that he knows no replicas of the Lansdowne head (75, n. 21). The Jandolo head (*E.-A.* 2001-2002) is sometimes regarded as such, e.g., by B. Schweitzer, *Platon und die bildende Kunst der Griechen* (Tübingen 1953) 76, figs. 27-28, and Howard (*supra,* n. 3) 11, fig. 16, but the only real similarity is in the treatment of the hair. The hair over the forehead, especially, differs from that of the Genzano heads and seems related to that of the Meleager type; Neugebauer (*supra,* n. 34) 6 notes a similarity in the faces as well. A head in Copenhagen (*E.-A.* 1373-1374 and 4577-4578) associated with the Lansdowne head by Schweitzer (*supra,* n. 32) 101ff, figs. 41-42, is regarded, probably rightly, by Linfert 75, n. 21, as closer to the Meleager. Very similar to the Copenhagen head is one in Magdeburg, see E. Bielefeld, "Ein Skopasisches Meisterwerk," *JdI* 74 (1959) 158-163; the association with Naukydes made by Linfert 18, 20 seems unlikely.

presented by the Herakles statue is the one followed by Schweitzer. Accepting the work as a replica of the Skopadic statue, he deals with what he feels to be divergences from Skopadic style by emphasizing the copyist's own artistic personality.[46] The Polyclitan features of the statue, he suggests, have been exaggerated to the point of banality by the copyist's inclination to *Polykletesieren*.[47] The classicizing alterations perhaps do not end here but rather lead away from the careful Polyclitan handling of surface. Schweitzer observes that the surfaces of the body and, especially, head are reduced to large *Relieffläche* which sometimes make abrupt transitions or leave blank areas.[48] This "stereometric" structure, he believes, is due not so much to the style of the original as to a distinctly Roman classicism related to the "cubism" of early Italic sculpture.[49] A relief-like approach to the frontal view is responsible for the non-Skopadic widening of the upper forehead, which can be paralleled in many Julio-Claudian portraits.[50] Also consistent with an early imperial classicizing manner are such linear features as the sharp brows and the angular bridge of the nose.[51] As an example of a contrasting late-Hellenistic classicism Schweitzer cites a head in Copenhagen which he believes to be related to the original of the Landsdowne Herakles, although not a replica.[52]

After this review of the Hope and Lansdowne statues, perhaps some direct comparison will clarify the place of each work in the context of sculptural development in antiquity. Both reflect the late classical ideal of Herakles, which stands between the active and mature battler of earlier art and the stoical benefactor of mankind which, under Lysippian influence, dominated Hellenistic portrayals: miraculously young and beautiful, the hero approaches his apotheosis (often, like the Hope Herakles, holding the golden apples).[53] Yet the Hope Herakles, by its upturned gaze and restless stance, still shows the tension of an extraordinary career; the lackluster work of the copyist does not conceal the subtly controlled and highly original pathos of the prototype.[54] By comparison, the Lansdowne Herakles appears more poised and introspective (the surface of the eyes, in contrast to those of the Hope statue and apparently contrary to Skopadic practice, turns downward). Charbonneaux's characterization of this hero as "the ideal guardian of Plato's Republic" is strikingly apt.[55]

These admittedly subjective considerations, in conjunction with more objective criteria mentioned above, seem to point to the Hope statue as the more plausible replica of Skopas' statue at Sikyon. Tentative iconographical arguments can be added. There is some evidence that Skopas was intrigued by unusual local cults; at Sikyon Herakles was worshipped as a god as well as hero.[56] While Skopas may have been familiar with a similar dual cult on his native island of Paros,[57] there is also a connection with Crete: the practice of worshipping Herakles as a god is said to have been introduced to Sikyon by a stranger named "Phaistos".[58] The bull's head on which the Hope statue rests the club could, by representing the Cretan Steer, possibly allude to this. The popular wreath may also refer to the double cult, as the leaves of the white poplar, "aptior Herculae populus alba comae",[59] are bi-colored. But perhaps the poplar simply emphasizes the mortal Herakles' completion of his labors and triumph over death.[60]

The interest of the Lansdowne figure, which possesses only the most generalized of Herakles' attributes (club

---

46) Schweitzer (*supra*, n. 32) 108ff. Contrast the view of Neugebauer (*supra*, n. 34) 6, that what resemblance the Lansdowne Herakles has to the Genzano (probably Skopadic) type is due to mixing by copyists of the imperial period.

47) Schweitzer (*supra*, n. 32) 108.

48) *Ibid.* 108-109.

49) Bulle (*supra*, n. 24) 14 regarded this handling of surface and structure as a feature of Skopas' early style, while Schweitzer (*supra*, n. 32) 111 believes that the style of Skopas' original must have provided an excuse (*Ansatzmöglichkeit*) for the copyist's approach. The sculptural fragments from Skopas' temple at Tegea do show a simplified treatment of surface, but of a different sort; see Berchmans (*supra*, n. 8) 109-111. For detailed analysis of the role played by Italian "cubism" in the formulation of a Roman classicizing style in the early empire see the writings of G. Kaschnitz von Weinberg, e.g., "Der italische Charakter des offiziellen Porträts," *Römische Bildnisse*. Ausgewählte Schriften II (Berlin 1965) 89ff.

50) Schweitzer (*supra*, n. 32) 110. To some extent the Hope head shares this feature, as does the Genzano head and some others of the class.

51) *Ibid.* 111.

52) See *supra*, n. 45.

53) See K. A. McDowell, "Herakles and the Apples of the Hesperides: a New Type," *JHS* 25 (1925) 157-162, F. Brommer, "Herakles und die Hesperides auf Vasenbildern," *JdI* 57 (1942) 105ff, Howard (*supra*, n. 3) 11-14.

54) The spiritual quality of the Hope Herakles is very well conveyed by Linfert's assessment (*supra*, n. 3) 35: "Ganz krass formuliert ist das Ziel nicht 'eine Figure, die Herakles darstellt; sondern: 'ein Herakles, der—um darstellbar zu sein— (beinahe leider) eine Figure sein muss.'"

55) *Loc cit.* (*supra*, n. 38). Schweitzer (*supra*, n. 45) 75-76 finds "platonische Stimmung" here.

56) Pausanias 2.10.1.

57) See C. Picard, "Un rituel archaïque du culte de l'Héracles Thasien," *BCH* 37 (1923) 241-274.

58) Pausanias, *loc. cit.* (*supra*, n. 56).

59) Ovid, *Her.* 9.64.

60) For Servius, *ad Ecl.* 7.61 the dual coloration of the white poplar symbolized the twofold nature of Herakles' labors, on earth and below. While Homer, *Il.* 13.389 and 15.482 calls the white poplar *Acheroida*, most evidence for the tree's association with Herakles' conquest of the underworld is relatively late; see C. Bötticher, *Baumkultus der Hellenen* (Berlin 1856) 141.

and lion's skin—the simple fillet and cauliflowered ears are details which can simply denote an athlete) is, I think, of a different order. Schweitzer has shown that the work exhibits some characteristic features of Roman sculptural style. These features, moreover, are especially prominent in copies made during the reign of Hadrian,[61] in whose villa the statue was found. Had the Lansdowne Herakles been preserved only as a torso, Polyclitan in design but lacking Polyclitan anatomical articulation, it might possibly have been taken for a Hadrianic copy of the *Doryphoros*[62]—and yet the head cannot be Polyclitan. When we remember, however, that Hadrianic sculptors produced more than copies (notably the Antinous type), a new explanation suggests itself: the Lansdowne Herakles is—on the highest level—a pastiche, a new creation of imperial Roman sculpture.[63] A combination of fifth- and fourth-century styles in sculpture from Hadrian's Villa has been noted previously,[64] and the possible production of hybrid statues during the imperial age by combining the torsos of the *Doryphoros* or other Polyclitan figures with heads which are not necessarily Polyclitan has recently been suggested on good grounds.[65] As for the head, the connection with the Skopadic Herakles may be as casual as Neugebauer suggests,[66] or it might be regarded as a very free copy.[67] According to J.M.C.Toynbee, "Only once in the history of Roman sculpture did this copying of classical Greek statues result in a certain creativeness—in the idealized statuary types of the emperor Hadrian's favorite, the Bithynian youth Antinous."[68] I conclude that this statement is effectively challenged by another Hadrianic masterpiece, the Lansdowne Herakles.

Steven Lattimore
University of California, Los Angeles

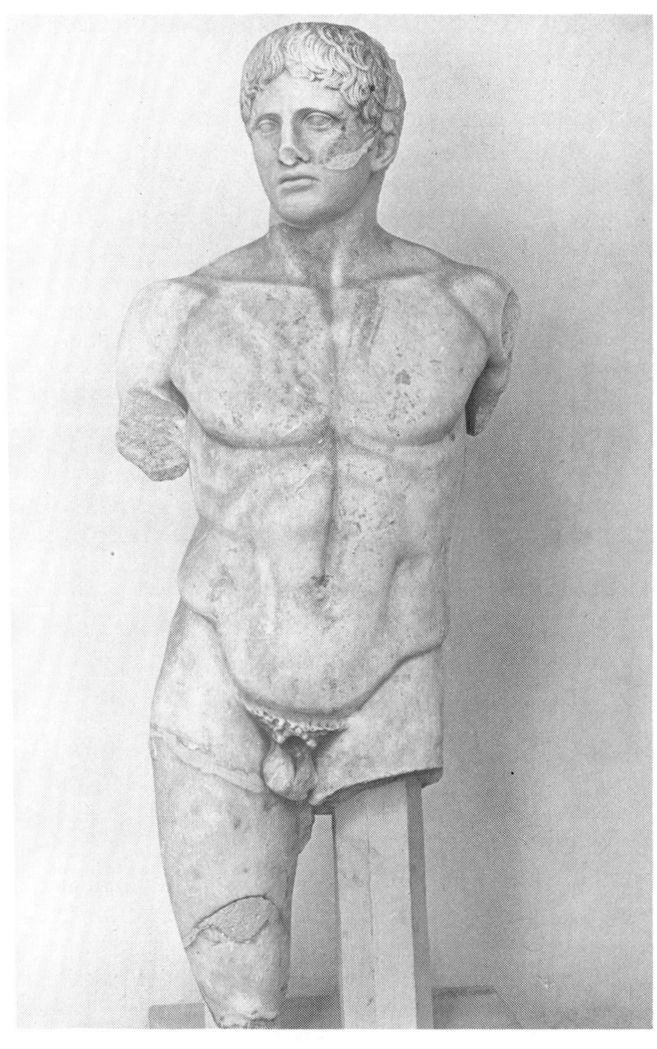

11   Copy of Polyclitus' Doryphoros, from Leptis. Photo courtesy of German Archaeological Institute 61.1767

61) See H. Lauter, *Zur Chronologie römischer Kopien nach Originalen des V. Jahr.* (Berlin 1970) 28, 34, 94, 125.

62) On the copy from Leptis Magna see *ibid.* 97 and T. Lorenz, *Polyklet* (Wiesbaden 1972) 78, pl. XXVII, 2 (the latter considers this copy Antonine rather than Hadrianic) and cf. Alscher (*supra,* n. 35) 172 and Arnold (*supra,* n. 29) n. 780.

63) It is not clear to me what Picard (*supra,* n. 2) III 2, P. 713 means by "composite". On the qeustion of "Roman originals in Greek style" see now B. S. Ridgway, "A Story of Five Amazons," *AJA* 78 (1974) 1-17, especially the last paragraph.

64) E.g., by P. E. Arias, *La Scultura Romana* (Messina 1943) 129, F. Preisshofen and P. Zanker, "Reflex einer eklektischen Kunstanschauung beim Auctor ad Herennium", *Dialoghi di Archeologia* 4-5 (1970-1971) 116-117 (reference from J. Frel).

65) See D. K. Hill, "Polykleitos: Diadoumenos, Doryphoros, and Hermes" *AJA* 74 (1970) 24.

66) *Loc. cit.* (*supra,* n. 46).

67) A colossal copy of the head of the Myronic Herakles, found at Hadrian's Villa (Furtwängler [*supra,* n. 36] 178-180, fig. 75, G. Traversari, *Aspetti Formali della Scultura Neoclassica a Roma dal I al III sec. d.C.* [Rome 1968] 52, figs. 32-32a) has a strong stylistic resemblance to the head of the Lansdowne statue. It is a somewhat eclectic work (hair and beard are archaized), and it would be of great interest to know how the body—which should have a one-sided stance like the Hope Herakles—was handled (Polyclitized?). For an interesting recent discussion of Hadrianic classicism see J. Fink, "Der grosse Jäger," *RömMitt* 76 (1969), esp. 251: "Diese Zeit versucht, klassische Kunst zu machen."

68) *The Art of the Romans* (New York 1965) 43-44. A good appraisal of the Antinous in its context is that of H. Sichtermann in *Propyläen Kunstgeschichte* 2 (Berlin 1967) 245 (reference from J. Frel).

A White Lekythos in the Getty Museum

In a collection of antiquities consisting mainly of sculpture and frescoes, no Greek vase could be more appropriate than an Attic white lekythos of the fifth century. White lekythoi were produced almost exclusively in the region of Athens, whose period of greatest artistic achievement spanned the seventh to fourth centuries B.C. As their iconography suggests and written evidence confirms, these vases held offerings for the dead; in this funerary purpose they resemble much of the great sculpture produced in Athens during the fifth and fourth centuries. Moreover, the sureness of the potting and their often considerable size render the finer lekythoi graceful but also imposing in a sense that may be called statuesque. Finally, the technique of decoration was the Greek vase-painter's closest equivalent to what we consider "painting". The artist was constrained neither by the inarticulable silhouette and laborious incision of black-figure, nor by the rigid contours and black background of red-figure; he had a neutral white surface on which to draw freely and apply color, chiefly for drapery. During the fifth century B.C., their *floruit,* white lekythoi were decorated by many important Athenian artists. The latter, while working in their own personal styles, often borrowed from one another and herein lies the special interest of the Malibu lekythos. It joins a small group of works that document a close connection between aspects of the Sabouroff Painter's work and that of his younger contemporary, the Bosanquet Painter.

The Malibu lekythos[1] (Fig. 1) survives today as a large fragment, broken irregularly at the lower part of the scene with everything below missing. What remains is complete, but repaired; a sizeable piece that includes the legs of the male figure has been rejoined. It is particularly unfortunate to have neither the complete body nor the foot of the vase, but from the preserved height of 38.1 cm. one can estimate the original height as about 45 cm. As is common in lekythoi of the early classical and classical periods, the inside and outside of the mouth, the neck, and the inside and outside of the handle are black; the topside of the mouth is reserved. A bone-white slip, with crackle and stains, covers the decorated portions of the vase: the shoulder and most of the body.

The ornament on the shoulder (Fig. 2) is organized around a pendant palmette placed opposite the handle. It is flanked by two horizontal palmettes and its framing tendril ends in two lotus buds. The drawing here, as on the body, is done with lustrous glaze rather than with the matte preparation which became prevalent after c. 440 B.C. Preliminary sketch lines are readily visible,

particularly beneath the tendrils. Each of the three palmettes consists of four glaze fronds and a larger central frond outlined with glaze and filled in with red. The same color was used in the palmette hearts and for an additional pair of fronds, now barely visible, just above the volutes. The lotuses have three fronds growing out of a bag-shaped calyx. An important, functional, feature of the shoulder is the vent-hole which appears inside the base of the handle; the first vent-hole, which can only be seen from within the vase, was wrongly placed and covered up by the handle.

The body of the Malibu lekythos is bordered on top by a continuous, or running, rightward maeander which extends the width of the scene, while the framing lines continue around the entire circumference. The representation, showing a man and a woman at a tomb, occupies the front of the vase without being aligned with either the shoulder decoration or the handle. In the centre of the picture stands the tomb: a base of three steps that decrease in width and height, surmounted by a rectangular shaft that ends in a cyma. The monument is drawn rather casually, with the result that it is asymmetrical, has imprecise edges, and generally gives the impression of a cardboard prop cut down to fit a given space. Rapid sketch lines for the steps suggest that they were originally intended to be wider. Offerings of two kinds have been brought to the deceased. On the shaft hangs a pair of long red fillets ending in thin matte black threads; the woman is in the process of adding a third. Upon the topmost step stand four vases, all of shapes which we know were used for holding oil; they are rendered here, however, with unusually mannered proportions. The first and fourth vases are lekythoi, the second an oinochoe shape 1, the third a plemochoe. The glaze is greenish-brown with the brushmarks evident. At the left edge of the steps hangs another red fillet, now mostly obliterated.

The figure to the left of the stele, with a chlamys and a spear, is a hunter or possibly a warrior (Fig. 3). The glaze contours and anatomical markings range from a golden to a dark brown, and the drawing is competent, except in such passages as the right hand, the right knee, and the back of the left leg. Preliminary sketch lines, readily visible in the left foot and lower leg, also appear under the right leg, right arm, and chest. In passages where the artist "painted" rather than drew with glaze his hand seems more supple. The hair and beard are rendered with a variegated yellowish-brown while strokes and curls of dark glaze indicate the crown of the head and thicker masses of hair. The spear has a heavy point

I should like to thank D. von Bothmer for reading over the text as well as B. Philippaki and K. Vierneisel for help with photographs.

1) J. Paul Getty Museum 73.AE.41. D. shoulder 14.46 cm.; D. mouth 8.69 cm.; H. of picture zone (ground line to first horizontal above scene) 18.18 cm.

or butt at its lower end, and a shaft whose color is as irregular as its shape; as in the representation of the tomb, there is no insistence on plausibility. Finally, the short cloak or chlamys, draped over the man's left shoulder and arm, is drawn in a combination of glaze and added matte paint. The former, diluted to a golden tone, defines the garment's major, rather stiffly falling folds. The same red as the fillets' was applied on top, with black lines added for borders and secondary folds. The artist's use of glaze as well as color here is noteworthy, for the later tendency was to use color alone for drapery.

On the other side of the tomb, but certainly on this side of the hereafter, stands the woman with a fillet (Fig. 4). While the Malibu lekythos was drying, another vase must have been pushed against this figure. There is a dent on her head and part of her hair has misfired; moreover, a yellowish double line at the top of her left arm and a single line near her left elbow are ghosts of the other vase's decoration. What remains of the woman today is only the glaze outline: of her head and limbs as well as of her chiton, with its full sleeves and large overfold at the waist. The garment was originally painted red, which has disappeared but for a very few traces. Although the figure has thereby lost in substance, the preliminary sketch of the body beneath the chiton has been gained; from the middle of the torso to the legs, lightly drawn lines define the form beneath the rather shapeless dress. Despite the streaky hair and the awkward position of her left shoulder, this figure is probably the most successful part of the picture.

Below the slipped portion of the lekythos, only a bit of the reserved groundline and of the black-glazed wall remains. While relatively little of the figurework is missing, the real loss is not to have such a large vase complete. In its present state, however, it does allow one to look into the cylinder (Fig. 5). The latter contains, intact, a false bottom which reduced the oil offering from the capacity of the vase to that of an elongated receptacle about 9.5 cm. long.

The Malibu vase is typical of Attic white lekythoi in shape, technique, and iconography. Stylistically, its connection is with the oeuvres of two artists: the Sabouroff Painter,[2] an early classic painter principally of cups and lekythoi, and the Bosanquet Painter,[3] a classic painter known only from lekythoi. Among the lekythoi of both

artists, the favorite motif is a man and a woman at the tomb, rather than the prothesis, "mistress and maid" either in an indoor setting or at the tomb, or again, Charon with his bark coming for the deceased. The tomb itself often consists of a rather insubstantial-looking shaft rising above a three-stepped base, and characteristic of both artists are the oil containers of various shapes placed on the steps. Further connections exist in the drawing style and in details like the frequent use of a rightward maeander above the scene, and the location of the vent hole on the shoulder within the handle. The similarities that can be found between selected vases of the Sabouroff and Bosanquet Painters do not, however, imply identity; the personalities are distinct, and Donna C. Kurtz first recognized that the Malibu lekythos belongs within the oeuvre of the Sabouroff Painter and it is her forthcoming monograph on Athenian white lekythoi which will do justice to its context. Our interest here is restricted to the Malibu vase and the convergence of two painters which it documents.

The feature which points the vase to its proper stylistic setting is the shoulder ornament. Far from being peculiar to a specific hand, the combination of a pendant palmette with a pair of lotuses and a pair of horizontal palmettes is typical of early classic red-figure lekythoi. It is a formula, which the Sabouroff Painter uses on a red-figure lekythos like Stockholm G 1701[4] and on a small number of white-ground examples[5] of which Berlin inv. 3262 (Fig. 6) is the least inadequately published. E. Buschor included this group with other lekythoi showing offering vases on the tomb, and he placed the whole series early in the oeuvre of his "Thanatosmeister".[6] J.D. Beazley reattributed most of the pieces, but the three in Athens and Berlin remain together, near the beginning of his list of Sabouroff white lekythoi. Although the forms have become rather dry and attenuated, the palmette-lotus ornament drawn in glaze is one of the major indications that the Malibu and related lekythoi are relatively early works. In any event, their connection is with the early classic tradition rather than with the new formula evolved by the Achilles Painter, and adapted by his contemporaries and successors. This formula, which appears on the majority of Sabouroff Painter lekythoi, places the palmettes among elaborated tendrils and substitutes volutes for the lotuses. Compared with the entire oeuvre of the Sabouroff Painter, that of the Bosanquet Painter is small,[7] yet none of his lekythoi has

2) J. D. Beazley, *Attic Red-figure Vase-painters* 2nd edition (Oxford, 1963), 837 ff (hereafter *ARV²*).
3) *ARV²* 1226 ff.
4) *ARV²* 844,145; cf. also the palmette beneath the handle of Honolulu 2892 (*ARV²* 844,153).
5) Athens 12747 (*ARV²* 845,166); Athens 12739 (*ARV²* 845,167);

Berlin inv. 3262 (*ARV²* 845,168).
6) E. Buschor, "Attische Lekythen der Parthenonzeit," *Münchener Jahrbuch der bildenden Kunst* N.F. 2 (1925), 180.
7) The Sabouroff Painter is credited by Beazley with almost three hundred vases of a dozen shapes; the Bosanquet Painter's oeuvre comprises about a dozen lekythoi, all but one white.

the palmette-lotus ornament. In his treatment of the shoulder, he calls to mind the late black-figure tradition, favoring three rather full palmettes with the central one upright; moreover, he draws them in matte paint, not glaze. While its importance might seem secondary, the shoulder ornament is the first and clearest of several criteria which allow one to place the Malibu vase.

A second detail is the ornamental border above the figural representation. The Getty lekythos has a continuous rightward maeander that is somewhat unevenly executed; as a result, several of the vertical strokes touch the framing lines above and below. The same border, drawn with the same quirks, recurs on the lekythoi Berlin inv. 3262 and Athens 12747. Comparing the border used by the Bosanquet Painter (Fig. 7), one consistently finds a stopt meander, consisting of self-contained units whose beginning and end touch the framing horizontals. The distinction here is even finer than with the shoulder ornaments, but the evidence provided by these very straightforward features attunes the eye for the main scene.

As mentioned above, the tomb scenes of the Sabouroff and Bosanquet Painters correspond in many respects so that our task is, again, mainly one of distinction. There are three points which allow one to attach the Malibu lekythos to the Sabouroff Painter's oeuvre. First, the shaft of the tomb monument, with a narrow cyma at the top, recurs in virtually identical form on the Sabouroff Painter's lekythos Athens 12747 (Fig. 8). The latter also shows a similar treatment of the stepped base and of the oil vessels on the upper step; lekythoi occupy the left- and rightmost positions and are placed so that they cover the outer edges of the shaft. The Bosanquet Painter either ends the stele somewhat below the maeander zone or he allows a crowning member to project into the ornament. Moreover, he carefully disposes the offerings inside or outside the contours of the shaft.

The second feature which links the Malibu vase to the Sabouroff Painter is the treatment of the figures. The man and woman stand to the left and right of the tomb, as is the case with Athens 12747 and the small group of related pieces; in the majority of Sabouroff and Bosanquet Painter tomb scenes, the woman stands at the left, the man at the right. Athens 12747 also provides an excellent parallel for the head of the hunter; one finds the same wedge of face set within a curly mass of hair and beard. Further correspondences exist in the awkward hands with their large palms and tentacle-like fingers. The women can be compared as well, particularly in the rendering of their hair-styles and right arms. Relatives of the Malibu pair also appear on other Sabouroff Painter lekythoi. For example, the man occurs in a

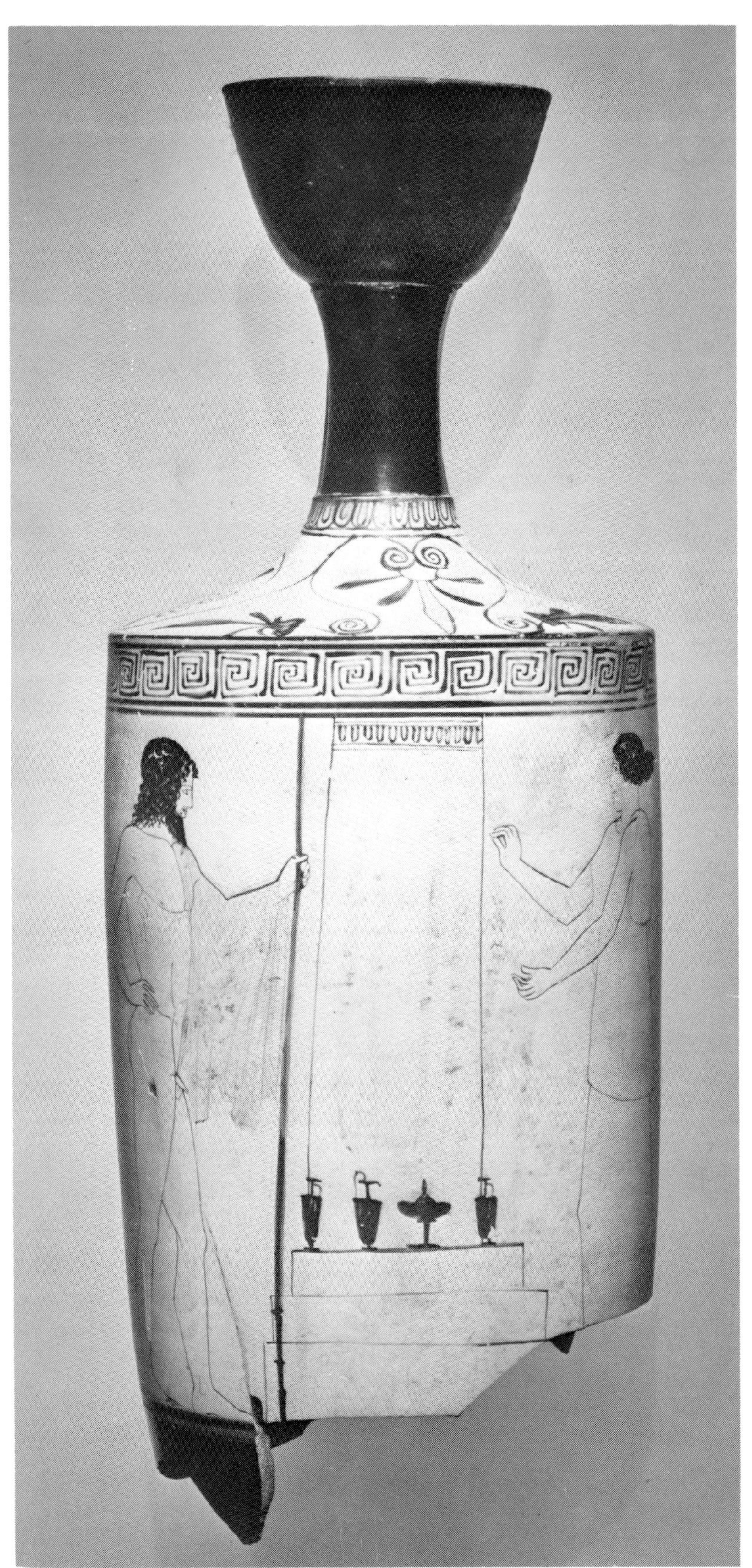

1   J. Paul Getty Museum 73.AE.41
(photo: Metropolitan Museum of Art)

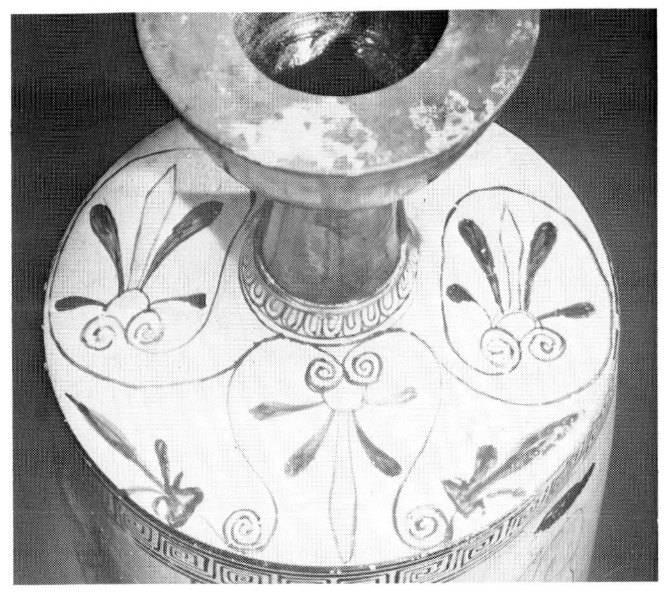

2   73.AE.41, detail of shoulder
     (photo: Metropolitan Museum of Art)

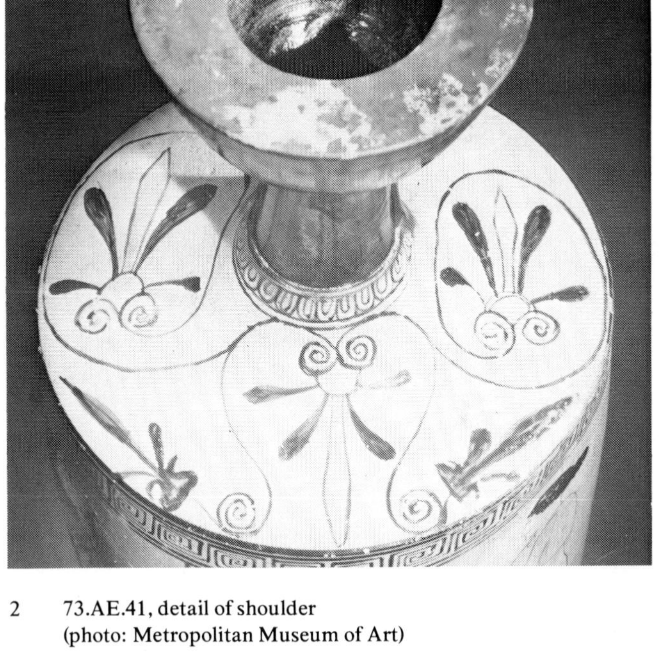

5   73.AE.41, interior of vase, with oil
     container (photo: Metropolitan Museum of Art)

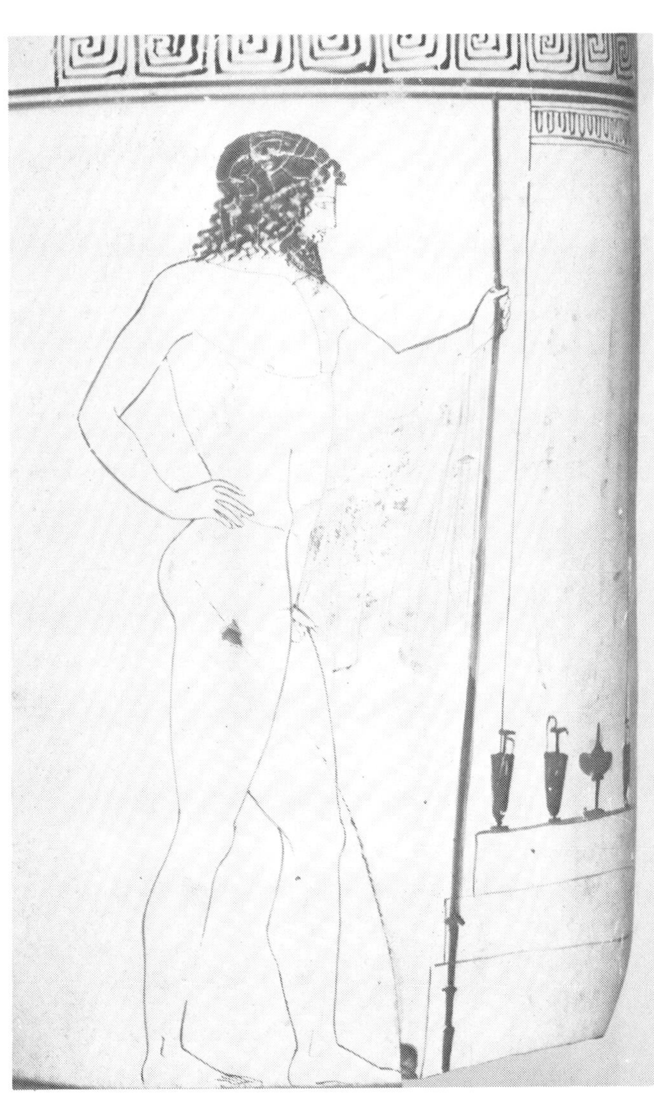

3   73.AE.41, detail of man
     (photo: Metropolitan Museum of Art)

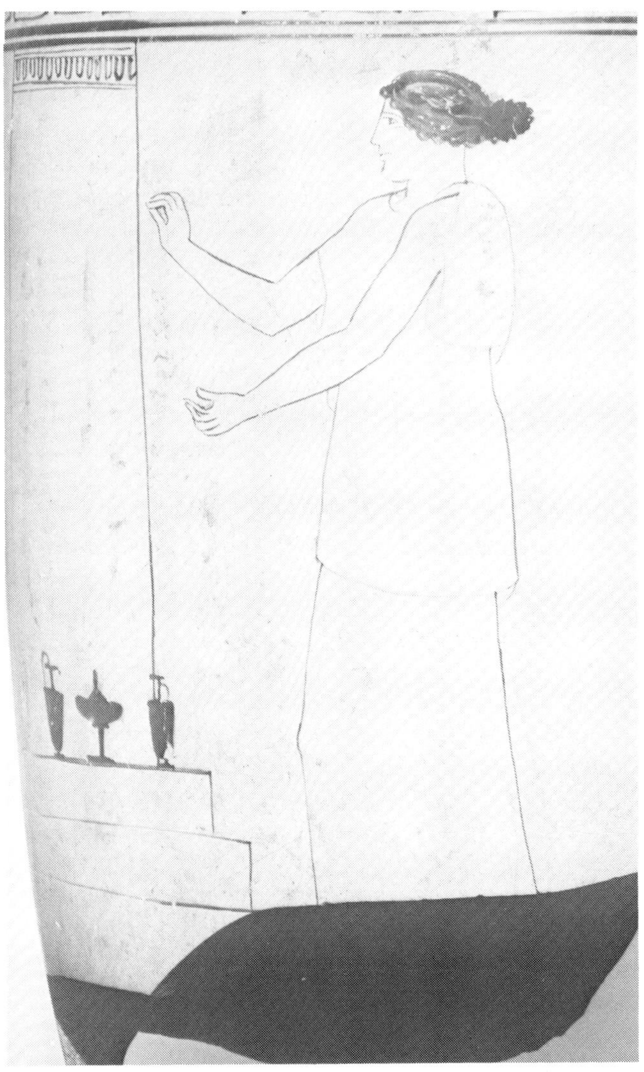

4   73.AE.41, detail of woman
     (photo: Metropolitan Museum of Art)

younger version on Oxford 1966.922,[8] and in the form of Charon and Hermes on Berlin 2455.[9] The woman has counterparts on the Mitchell vase once at San Simeon,[10] on one of the von Schoen vases now in Munich,[11] and on Villa Giulia 15729.[12] These comparisons point up not only similarities in detail but also the generalized, undynamic, occasionally rubbery quality of the Sabouroff Painter's people. Those of the Bosanquet Painter, especially the men, appear athletic and capable of coordinated, energetic movement, a feature which may be ascribed to the Achilles Painter's influence. The Bosanquet Painter has left us several representations of a spear-holding youth by a tomb; the articulation of the musculature, the differentiated stance of the legs, the tensed fingers differ markedly from what one finds in the Malibu warrior. The women present less of a contrast except in the small eyes and downturned lips of the faces and in the drapery which is elaborated into unlikely folds (Fig. 9).

The Bosanquet Painter's interest in articulating a form and, to a certain extent, in drawing for its own sake reveals a basically different hand from that of the Sabouroff Painter and furnishes a third criterion for distinguishing the two artists. Though entirely competent, in his white lekythoi the Sabouroff Painter gives the impression of being somewhat stiff-wristed. With the figures as with the maeander border, he proceeds from one point to the next, without too much regard for transitions; only rarely does he swing a line smoothly, as in the contour of the Malibu warrior's back and buttocks. The Bosanquet Painter seems more nervous, slightly finicky. It may, in addition, be a sensitivity to texture that leads him to differentiate the man's hair, the woman's, the branches, and the wreaths on New York 23.160.38,[13] for example. In size and variety, his oeuvre cannot compare with that of the Sabouroff Painter; nonetheless, he has a freshness which his older contemporary lacks.

In the process of attributing the Malibu lekythos, the resemblance of the Bosanquet Painter's style to aspects of the Sabouroff Painter's will have diminished somewhat. It does, however, exist, and an effort should be made to account for it. The essence of the matter obviously lies in the influence exerted by one artist on the other, but the first question is: at what distance? One of the most interesting lines of inquiry is to be found in the potting of the lekythoi, with particular attention to the shape of the false bottom and to the position of the vent-hole. While he is not the first to study them, D. von Bothmer has established that, on the one hand, these two features are variable and that, on the other hand, they tend to remain constant in the work of a given painter.[14] Careful attention to the potting of a vase, to details like the false bottom and vent hole, to the distribution of the decoration, and character of the ornament can indicate not only which vases a painter decorated for a certain potter but also how many different hands this potter employed. Thus, while it is not a decisive criterion, the cylindrical oil container corroborates other evidence for attributing the Malibu lekythos to the Sabouroff Painter.

On the other hand, the small amount of information currently available provides no firm ground for postulating that the Sabouroff and Bosanquet Painters worked for a time in the same shop. In favor of such a hypothesis one can cite the vent-hole placed within the handle and thoroughgoing stylistic connections ranging from the composition of the scene to the execution of the offering vessels. The negative considerations begin with small variations in shape, at the neck for instance, and are reinforced by the entirely different shoulder ornament and maeander pattern. X-rays taken to determine the shape of the oil containers in two restored Bosanquet Painter lekythoi in New York produced disappointing results. They show that the upper end is cylindrical but that everything below shoulder level is broken off and missing. While promising, this approach requires much more evidence to be truly useful. As for the question at hand, one may tentatively conclude that the Bosanquet Painter lekythoi and the group to which the Malibu vase belongs come from different workshops; their similarity may therefore be due to extensive borrowing of one artist from the other.

The Sabouroff-Bosanquet connection also has a temporal aspect, which entails the question of who influenced whom. As we have seen above, the Malibu vase belongs with a small group that occurs early in the Sabouroff Painter's production of white lekythoi. The latter do not, however, stand at the beginning of his career. One imagines the Sabouroff Painter to have started during the decade before 450 B.C. with red-figure work on cups and pots, and to have taken up white lekythoi shortly before 450, stimulated perhaps by the Achilles Painter.[15] The Malibu vase would seem to belong here, before the shape becomes elongated,

8) *ARV²* 845,165.
9) *ARV²* 846, 196.
10) *ARV²* 850,267; J. D. Beazley, *Paralipomena* (Oxford, 1971), 424.
11) *ARV²* 845,179.
12) *ARV²* 849,246.

13) *ARV²* 1227,5.
14) J. V. Noble, *The Techniques of Painted Attic Pottery* (New York, 1965), 24-25.
15) The extent and form of the Achilles Painter's influence is a factor that complicates the already unclear Sabouroff-Bosanquet Painter

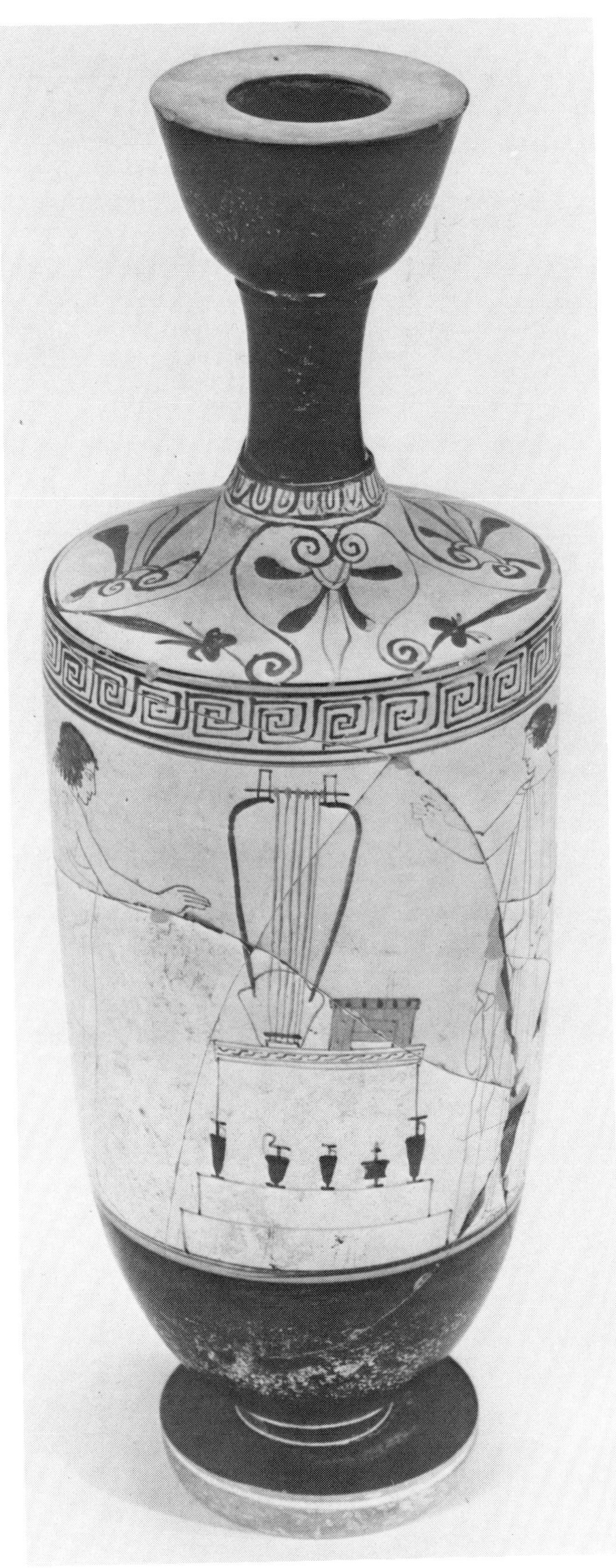

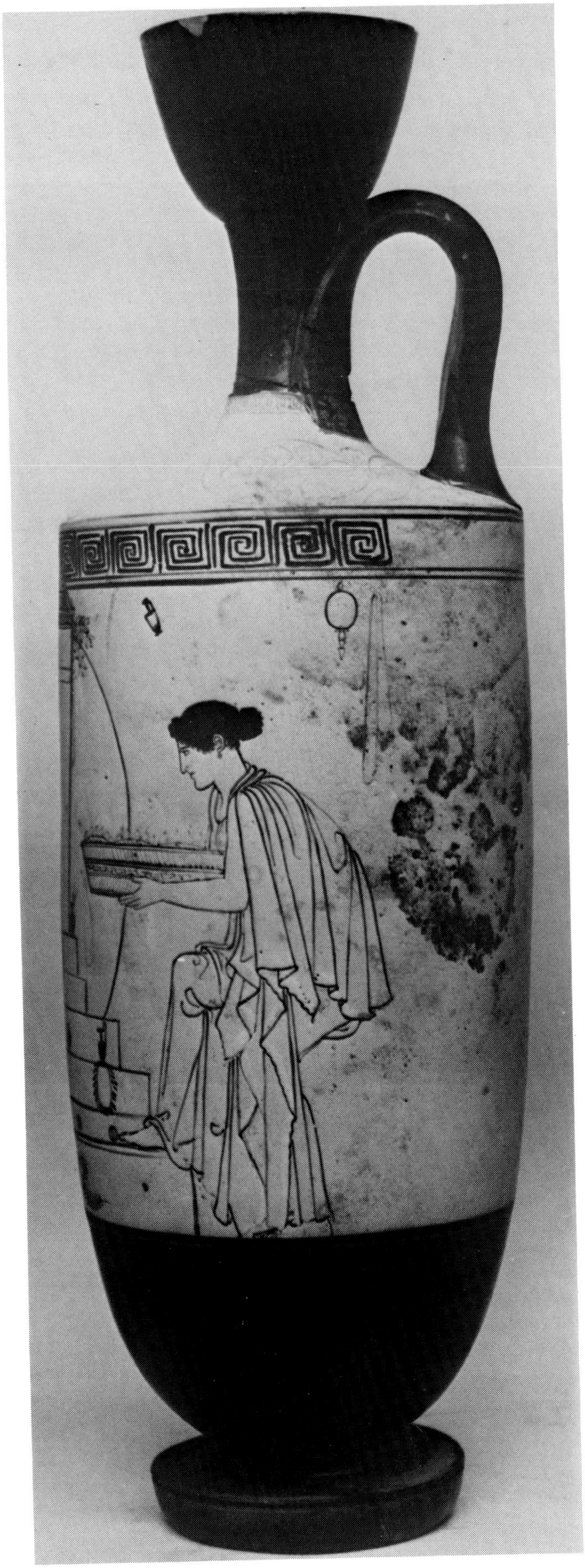

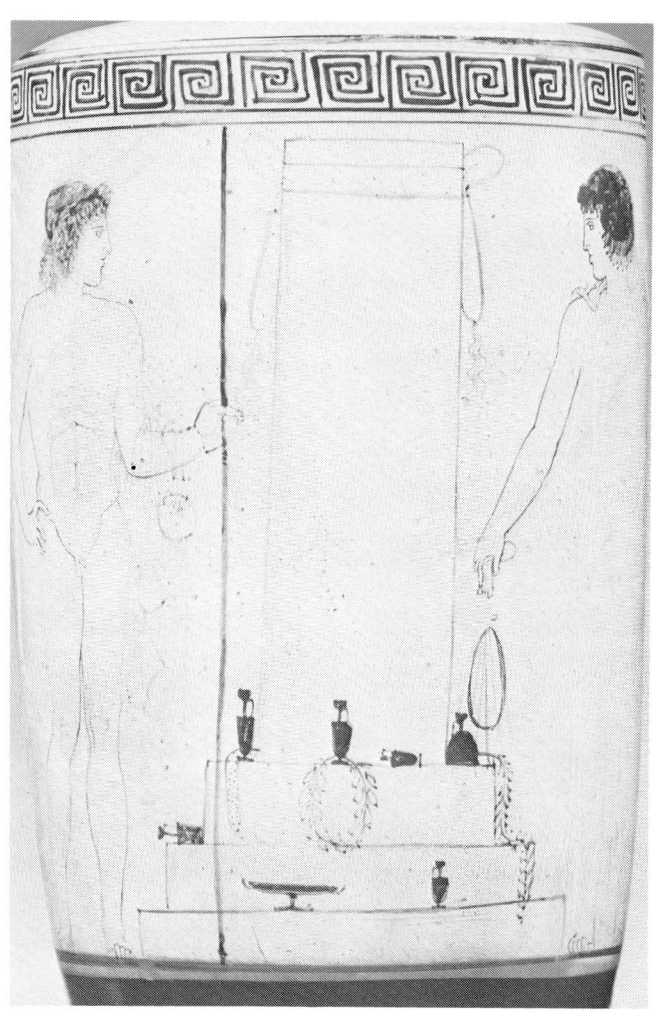

7   New York 23.160.38 (photo: Metropolitan
Museum of Art, Rogers Fund)

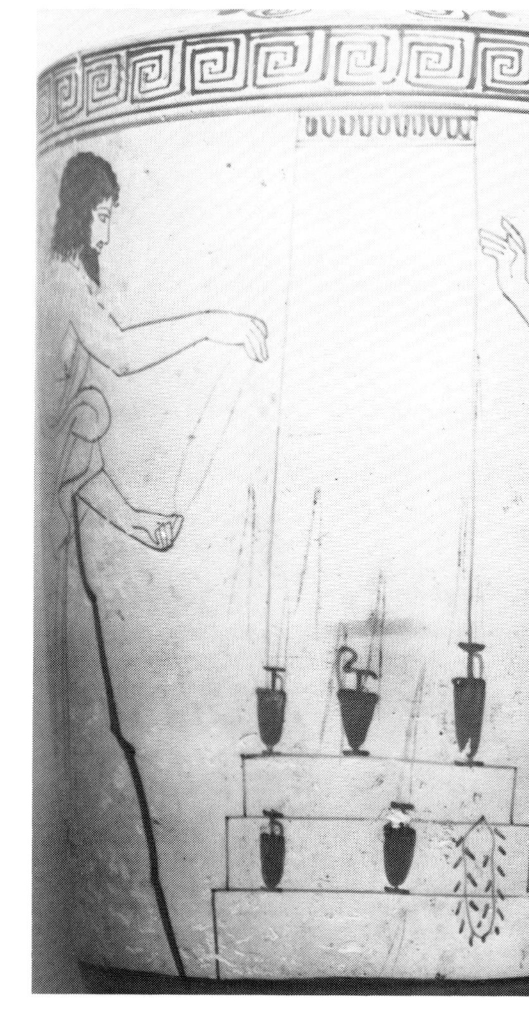

8   Athens, N.M. 12747 (photo:
Athens, National Museum)

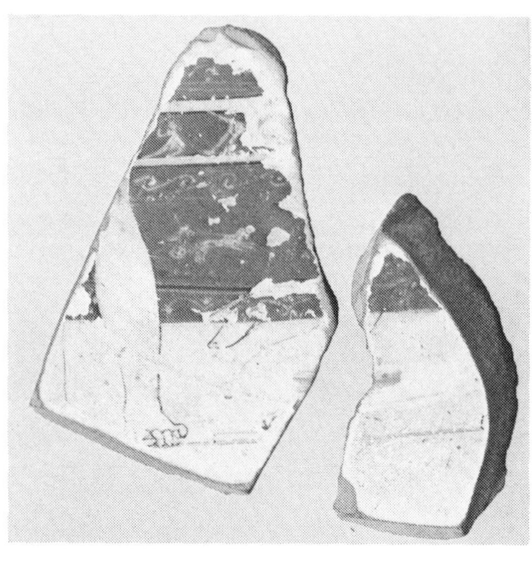

10a   Other fragment of interior
of Berlin F4059

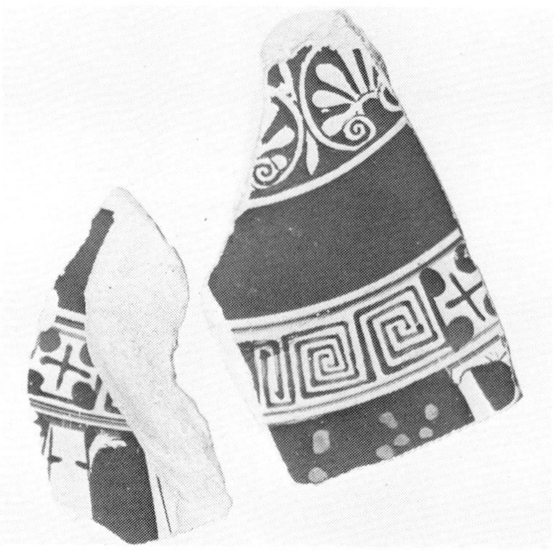

11a   Fragment of exterior

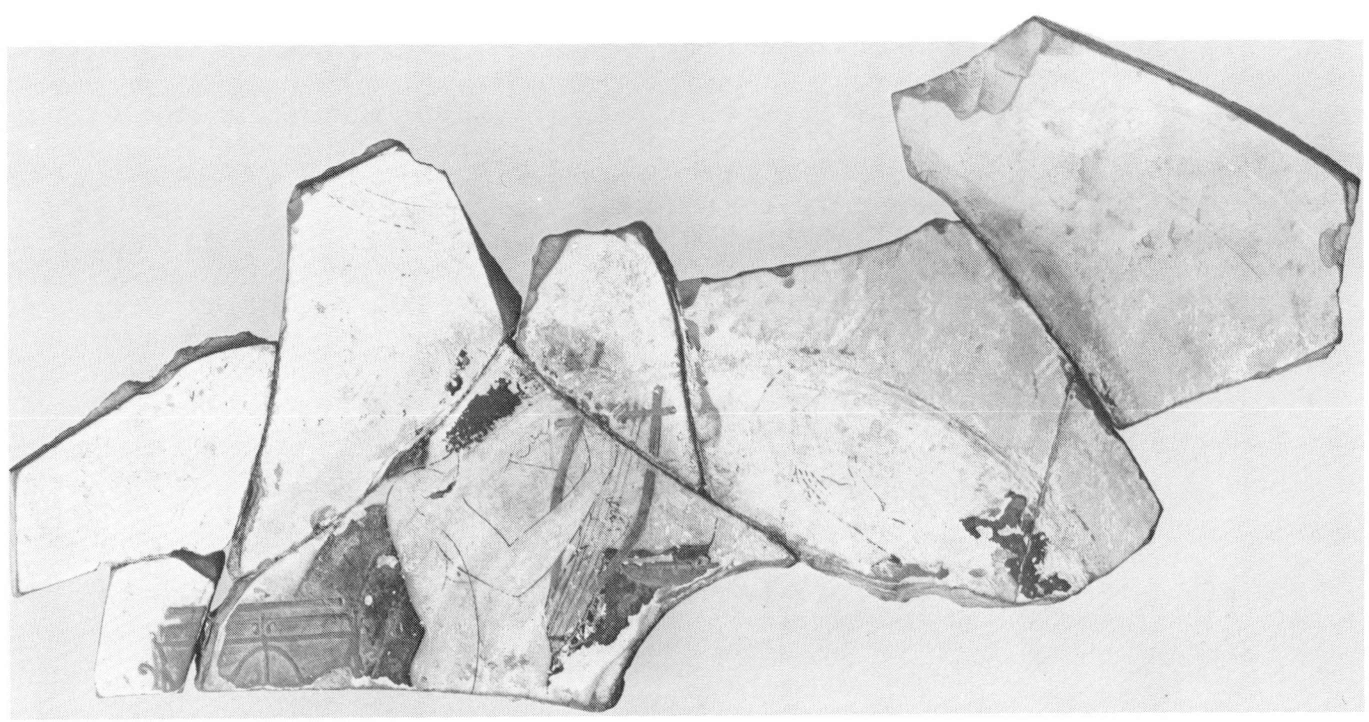

10 Berlin F 4059, interior of cup (photo:
Staatliche Museen, Antikenabteilung)

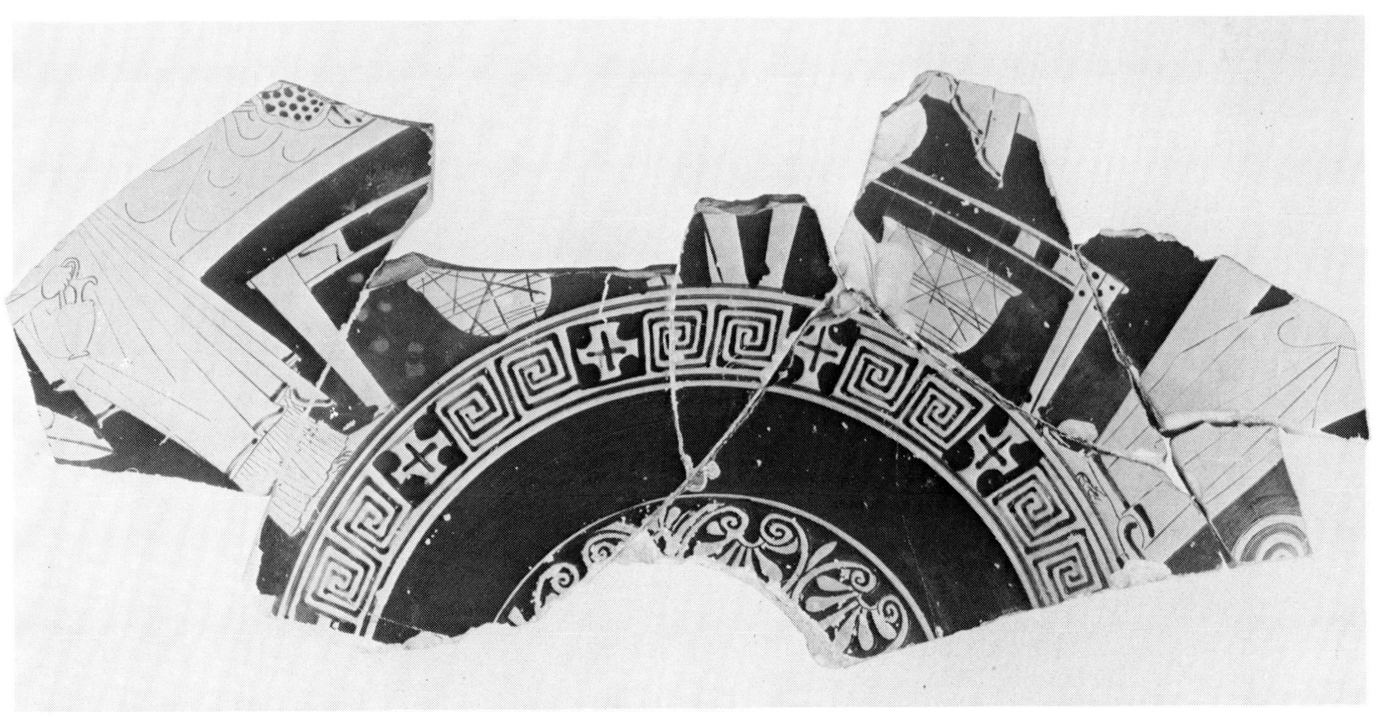

11 Berlin F 4059, exterior of cup (photo:
Staatliche Museen, Antikenabteilung)

glaze lines give way to matte, and the drawing deteriorates. Moreover, this and the related pieces in Athens and Berlin seem to antedate those of the Bosanquet Painter. The shoulder pattern, with its lotus and circumscribed palmettes, provides the first indication; it associates the "Malibu group" with the Sabouroff Painter's red-figure lekythoi and distinguishes them from his more numerous funerary lekythoi with the Achilles Painter's type of shoulder. The second indication appears in the different rendering given by the Sabouroff and Bosanquet Painters to the subject of a man and woman at a tomb. The Malibu vase, like its counterparts, has an outdoor setting with vases and other "props" limited to the grave stele. The offering vases painted in opaque glaze add not only a decorative but also a realistic element to the rather plain scenes. The Bosanquet Painter, on the other hand, occasionally suspends a vase or other object on an imaginary wall by the tomb; such details produce an impossible combination of interior and exterior space, intensifying the effect of his restless hand and rather fussy style. Though the Bosanquet Painter may have drawn on works of the Achilles Painter for features like the suspended utensils or the build of his youths, he integrates them into what seem to be elaborations of the Sabouroff Painter's early representations.

Our discussion of the Malibu lekythos has led us to compare those aspects of the Bosanquet and Sabouroff Painters which are most similar; an extensive juxtaposition of the two is of little use given the differences between their attributed oeuvres in size and scope. Since the Sabouroff painter worked on cups as well as lekythoi, however, we may conclude with a well-known white-ground cup that reminded Beazley of the Bosanquet Painter.[16] Berlin F 4059 (Figs. 10-11) was found on the Akropolis and, except for one fragment,[17] it is now in West Berlin.[18] Though badly preserved, its original diameter was about 40 cm. and it was decorated with symposia on both the white-ground interior and red-figure exterior. The strongest connection between this work and the lekythoi we have considered lies in the lyre-playing youth; the treatment of his chest, leg, and toes, for instance, can be compared with similar features on lekythoi in Athens[19] and Basel[20] by the Bosanquet Painter. The latter cannot, however, match the soulful features, fine fingers, and wire-like contours that suggest an

exceptionally able hand. Moreover, the polychrome couch cover and the mixing bowl in relief on the interior, the band of palmettes around the stem on the exterior point to an artist or artists versed in the tradition of Attic display pieces; the work is a perfect example of the large and elaborate cups often dedicated in sanctuaries and executed in a combination of techniques. The identity of the obviously ambitious painter—and potter —eludes us, although he would seem to belong in the chronological and stylistic orbit of the Pistoxenos Painter. He may well have been a contemporary of the Sabouroff and Bosanquet Painters, but otherwise, the Berlin cup represents an entirely different facet of activity in the Athenian Kerameikos of the mid-fifth century B.C.

Joan R. Mertens
The Metropolitan Museum of Art

---

connection. F. Felten has published the most recent analysis of this question (*Thanatos- und Kleophonmaler* [München, 1971], see especially 23 ff. and 32 ff.); one would certainly agree with his emphasis on the Philadelphia loutrophoros and his relative chronology of the early Bosanquet lekythoi.

16) J. D. Beazley, Review of H. Philippart, *Les Coupes à Fond Blanc* in *Gnomon* 13,6 (1937), 292.

17) Athens, National Museum C 27.

18) For a recent publication with previous bibliography, see A. Greifenhagen, *C.V.A. Berlin* 3 (Munich, 1962), 10-11 and pl. 107.

19) *ARV²* 1227,2.

20) *ARV²* 1227,3.

The so-called Cottenham relief (Figs. 1 and 2), said to have been found by a farm laborer in 1911 near Cambridge, England, was first published in 1917 in a brief article by A.B. Cook,[1] and since that time has been mentioned by various scholars.[2] The relief remained at Cottenham until 1953 when it entered the collection of Mr. J. Paul Getty.

About one-fourth of this small marble relief, which depicts a youth with a horse, is preserved. The youth's head, his outstretched right arm and part of his torso remain; of the horse, only its head, neck and shoulder are preserved. At the top of the relief there is a moulding 4.4 cm. high. The background in front of the horse bears traces of the claw chisel, perhaps the result of reworking, and some of the carved surface is worn, notably part of the moulding, the area around the horse's eye and below its ear, the eye, temple and ear of the youth, and also his right hand and wrist. Pick marks and scratches are visible in places. Between the head of the youth and the mane of the horse, the surface of the stone has flaked, suggesting that the marble may be Pentelic. The back of the relief is roughly picked (Fig. 3), its top and left side are more smoothly worked (Figs. 4 and 5), though traces of the claw chisel remain. The surface of the right side and its small drilled hole are not ancient, but are the result of later reworking. The broken surface bears traces of cement. The preserved dimensions of the relief are: height 27.9 cm; length, 30.5 cm; the maximum thickness, 5.0 cm. Its original height must have been about 45 or 50 cm,[3] and the length perhaps about 50 or 55 cm. These dimensions would allow ample room for the missing parts of both the horse and the youth.

The torso of the youth is frontal, his head in profile to the spectator's left. The young man's hair, cropped short in the late archaic fashion, has a stippled surface, instead of separate locks which are more common, and the superior carving of his nose, mouth and chin indicates that his eye and ear, though no longer well preserved, must have been carved with equal care (Fig. 6). The youth leans slightly to the viewer's right, restraining the horse which he holds firmly by reins, now missing, but once attached in bronze as the three small holes, two at the youth's hand and one at the corner of the animal's mouth, indicate (Fig. 7). The horse has raised its head very high so that its muzzle points upward; it has opened its jaws to relieve the pressure caused by the metal bit.[4] Its lips are flexed slightly revealing its tongue and some of its teeth. The boney structure of the horse's head is carefully worked, the flaring nostril and alert ear are those of a high-strung, spirited beast. What remains of the eye suggests that it was small in proportion to the size of the head. The horse's neck is smooth and rather short, the sloping shoulder barely articulated, and the short upright mane is parted just below the poll to permit the cheekstraps of the bridle to pass over the top of the head.[5] The absence of a hole here suggests that the headstall of the bridle, unlike the reins, was painted.

I wish to thank Dr. Jiří Frel, Curator of Antiquities at the J. Paul Getty Museum, for inviting me to publish this relief and for his generous cooperation in all phases of the research. I am grateful to Professors Peter H. von Blanckenhagen and J. K. Anderson, and to Dr. Dietrich von Bothmer who read the manuscript and offered many suggestions for its improvement. As always, Dr. von Bothmer generously permitted me to draw on his large collection of photographs for much of the comparative material. I also wish to thank Dr. Christoph Clairmont for calling my attention to bibliographical references which I did not know.

1) A. B. Cook, "A Pre-Persic Relief from Cottenham," *JHS* 37 (1917), pp. 116ff.

2) Beazley, *The Lewes House Collection of Ancient Gems* (Oxford, 1920) (hereafter, Beazley, *Lewes House*), p. 15; Picard, *La sculpture antiques des origines à Phidias*, I (Paris, 1923), p. 355; Casson, *JHS* 45 (1925), pp. 177f; Langlotz, *Frühgriechische Bildhauerschulen* (Nuremburg, 1927), pp. 127, no. 18 and p. 130; Buschor, *AM* 54 (1929), p. 151; Jacobsthal, *Die melische Reliefs* (Berlin, 1931), pp. 93 and 134; Picard, *Manuel d'archéologie grecque, La sculpture*, II, I (Paris, 1939) (hereafter, Picard, *Manuel*), p. 20; Markman, *The Horse in Greek Art* (Baltimore, 1943), p. 118; *Time Magazine*, March 11, 1946, p. 51; Chittenden and Seltman, *Greek Art* (London, 1947), no. 45, pl. 10; Lippold, *Die griechische Plastik* (*Handbuch der Archäologie* 5,1 [Munich, 1950]), (hereafter, Lippold, *Handbuch*), p. 84, note 15, pl. 27,3; C. Vermeule, *AJA* 63 (1959), p. 143; Karouzos, *Aristodikos* (Stuttgart, 1960), p. 57; Cooper, *Great Private Collections* (New York, 1963), p. 183; Schlorb, *Untersuchungen zur Bildhauergeneration nach Phidias*

(Waldsassen, 1964), p. 67, note 21; Getty, *The Joys of Collecting* (New York, 1965), pp. 19, 47-48, 50-51; Fuchs, *Die Skulptur der Griechen* (Munich, 1969), pp. 504f, fig. 586.

3) This estimated height is based on a calculation of the height of the youth and the horse, and does not take into account that there may have been a base moulding.

4) For bits in antiquity, cf. J. K. Anderson, *Ancient Greek Horsemanship* (Berkeley, 1961), chs. 3-5; P. Vigneron, *Le cheval dans l'antiquité gréco-romaine* (Nancy, 1968), ch. 2; more recently, M. A. Littauer, "Bits and Pieces," *Antiquity* 43 (1969), pp. 289ff.

5) The parting of the mane to allow the cheekstrap of the bridle to pass over the head is a detail of horse trappings that in Greek art seems to be introduced in Attic vase painting by Psiax (*ABV* 292ff; *ARV²* 6ff and 1617; *Paralipomena* 127f and 321) and is used by his followers, the Priam Painter (*ABV* 330ff and 694; *Paralipomena* 146f) and the Rycroft Painter (*ABV* 335ff and 694; *Paralipomena* 148f). This feature is, however, very rare in sculpture. On equestrian statues or statues of horses, there is usually a hole drilled at the poll and another at the mouth to permit attachment of a cheekstrap made of bronze. We may cite as examples the two late sixth century statues of horses from the Acropolis, Acr. 697 (H. Schrader, *Die archaischen Marmorbildwerke der Akropolis* [Frankfurt-am-Main, 1939] [hereafter, Schrader], no. 320, pls. 147-150; P. Charbonneaux, *Archaic Greek Art* [New York, 1971], fig. 93) and Acr. 700 (Schrader, no. 314, pls. 140-141, 149-150), a rider slightly earlier than these, Acr. 4119 (Schrader, no. 317, pl. 143), and also the horseman in oriental dress, Acr. 606 (Schrader, no. 313, pls. 138-139; Charbonneaux, *Archaic Greek Art*, fig. 292). On reliefs,

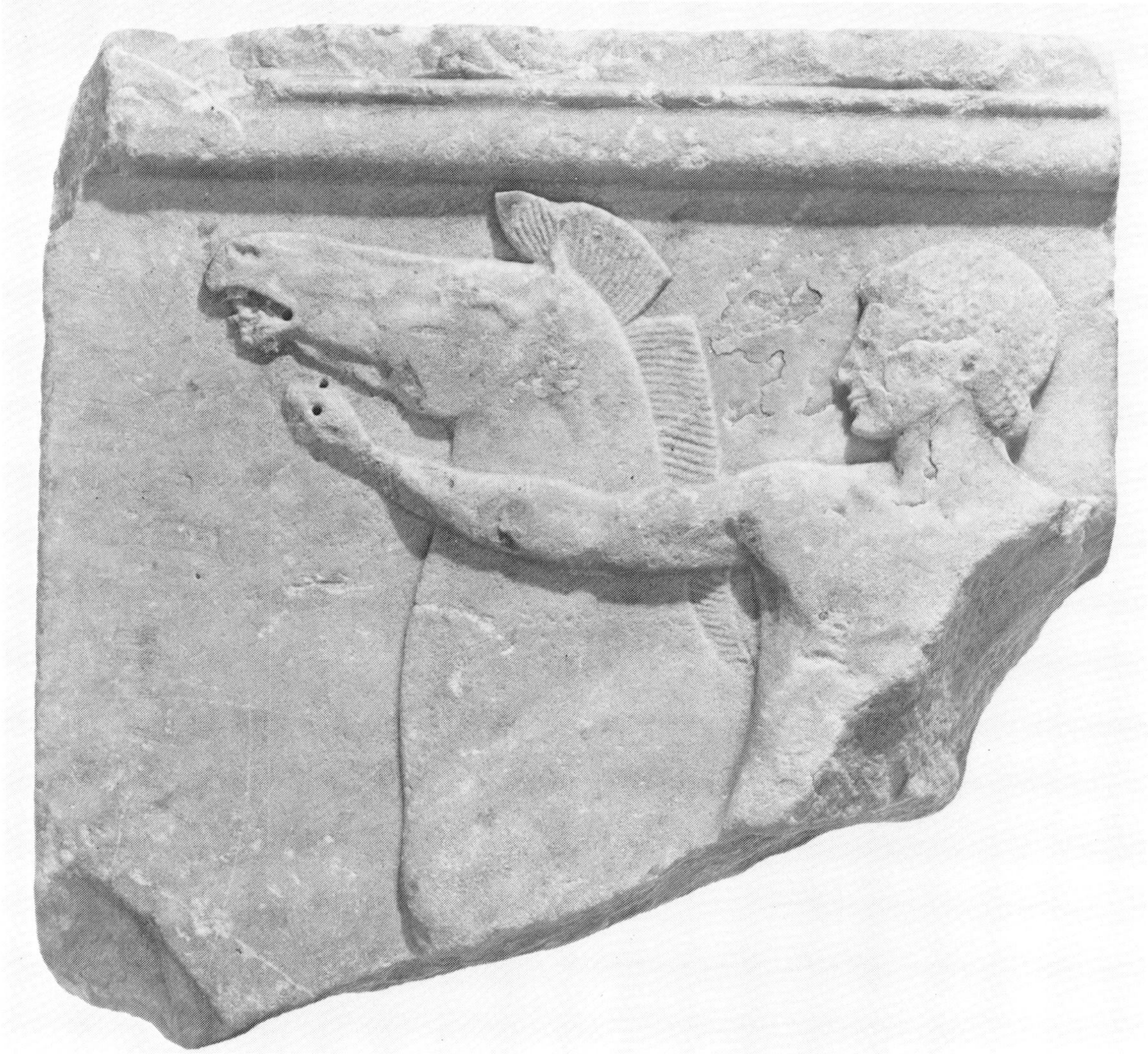

1 Cottenham Relief, J. Paul Getty Museum I-75

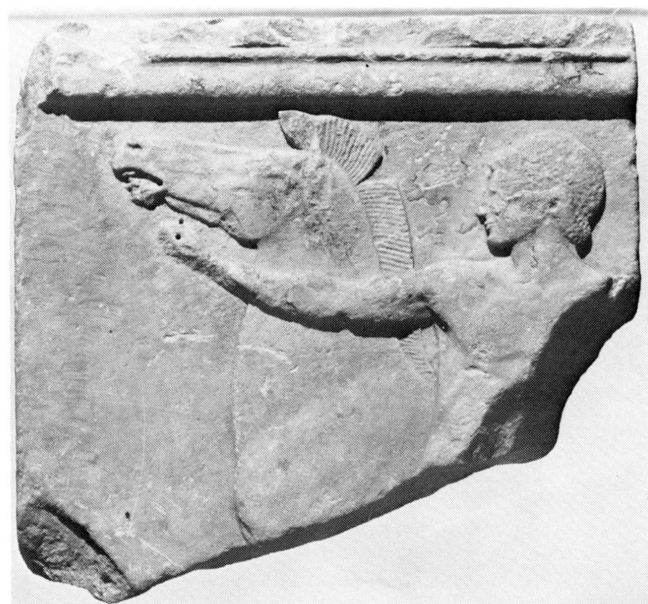

2 Cottenham Relief, photographed in sunlight before last cleaning;
two little chips of marble—later additions—were afterwards removed from the cheek above the mouth

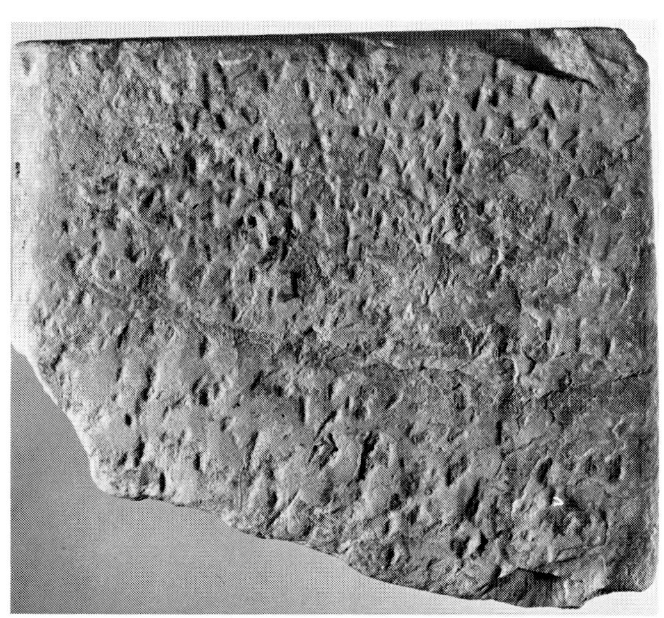

3 Cottenham Relief, back

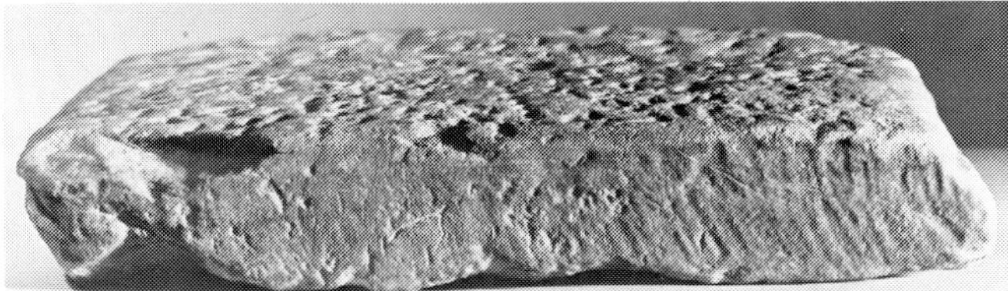

4   Cottenham Relief, top

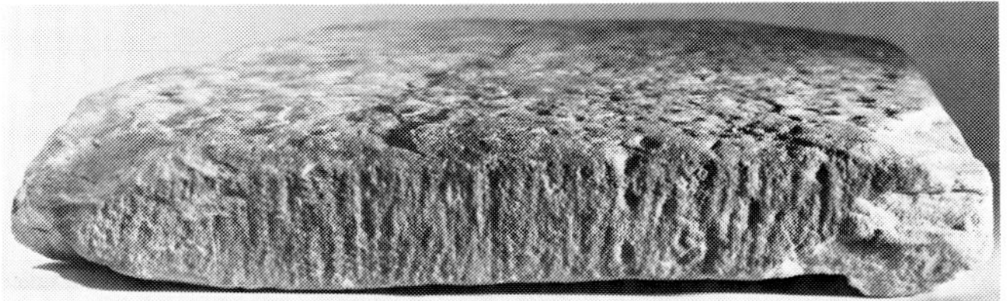

5   Cottenham Relief, left side

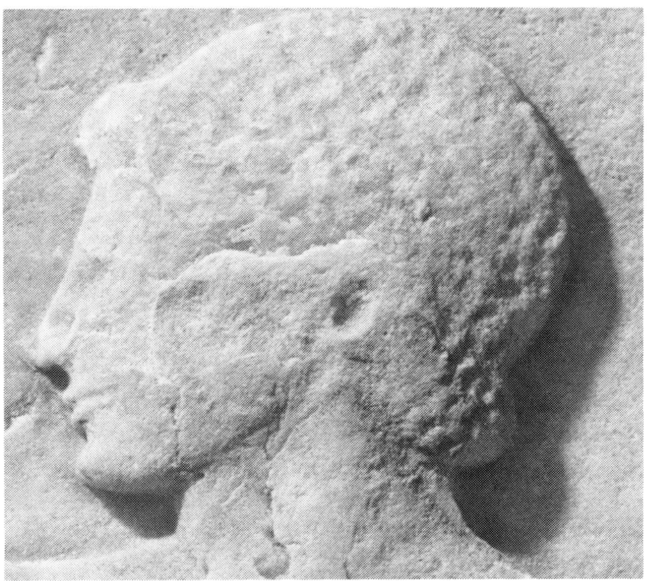

6   Cottenham Relief, head of youth

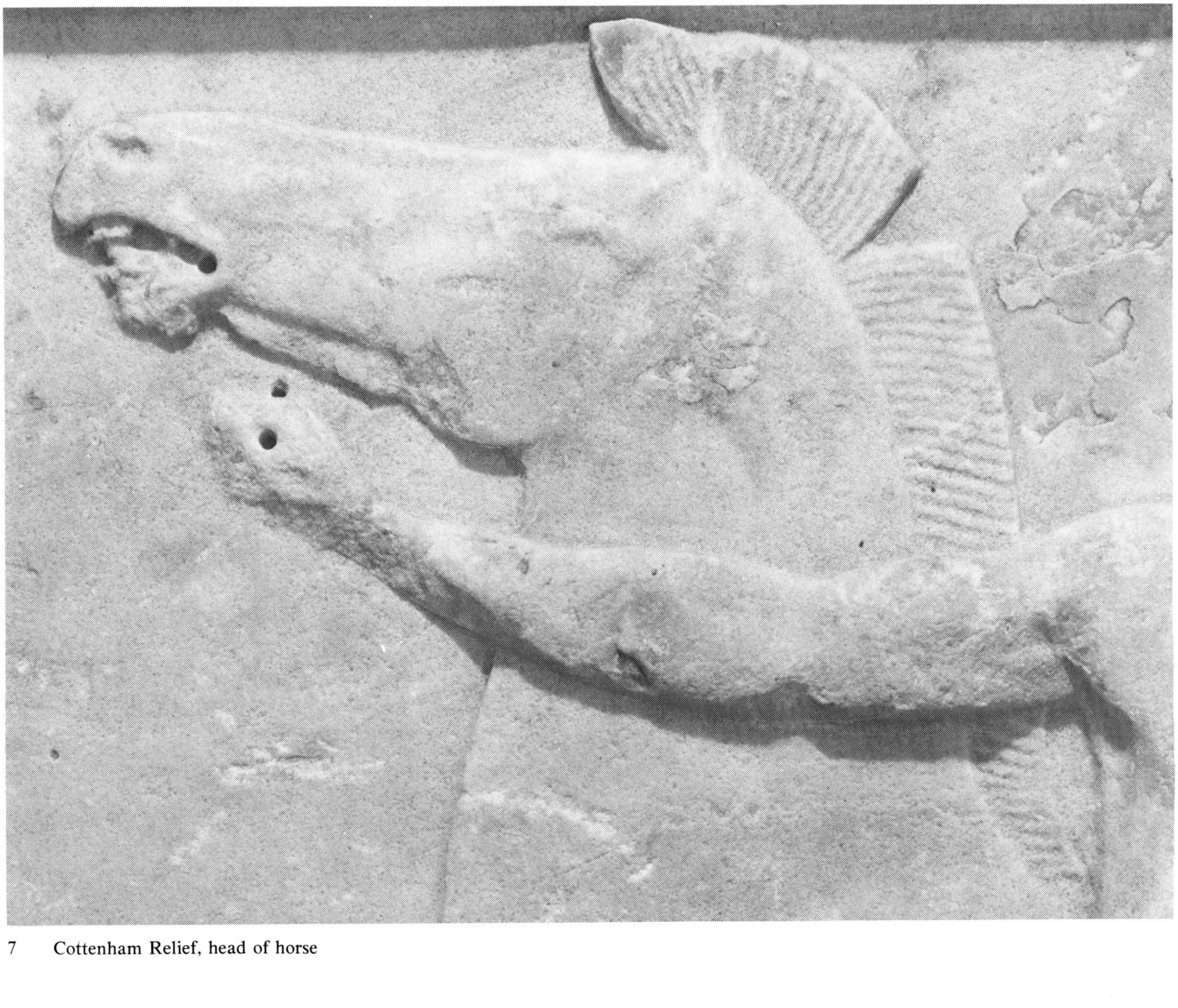

7   Cottenham Relief, head of horse

The horse and youth on the Cottenham relief compare best with some of those carved or painted in the late sixth and early fifth centuries, and a date of about 500 for this relief seems an appropriate one.[6] The youth recalls athletes carved on the sides of the bases that supported marble statues used as grave monuments, especially some of the athletes on the ball-player base in Athens, National Museum NM 3476 and on one from the Kerameikos, inv. P 1002, both from the Themisto-klean Wall (Figs. 8 and 9).[7] The combination of profile head with frontal torso is the same, even though the poses of the athletes are more active and their muscula-ture more sharply articulated than are the pose and anatomy of the Cottenham youth whose less vigorous activity permits a quieter stance. A contemporary example of the stippled surface of the youth's hair is preserved in the statue of Aristodikos (Fig. 10),[8] yet the Cottenham youth's head is broader than that of Aristodikos and has a very high cranium. In these two features it compares favorably with the kouros, Ptoon 20,[9] and with Athena on a votive relief from the Acro-polis.[10]

The horse resembles one carved on the right side of the athlete base already mentioned that was found about a decade ago, Kerameikos inv. P 1002 (Fig. 11).[11] On this side of the base there are two riders to right. Of the two horses it is the left one that is closest to the one on the Cottenham relief, for its head, although badly preserved, points upward. Elsewhere in archaic sculpture this un-usual position may be seen twice on the Siphnian Treasury, once on the West frieze where it is used for the right hand trace horse of Aphrodite's chariot and once on the South frieze for the left hand pole horse of a chariot team,[12] and it also occurs on a fragmentary relief from Thasos in the collection of Dr. Papageorgiou, which depicts a horse and rider to left.[13] I do not know other examples in archaic sculpture of horses with their muzzles pointed upward, but this rare position of the head appears on a few horses painted on late archaic vases, mainly by black-figured artists,[14] and on the Epimenes gem in Boston which shows a youth restraining a rearing horse (Fig. 18).[15]

Other comparisons for the style of the Cottenham horse are to be found among horses painted on late archaic vases. The general proportions of the head and neck of the Cottenham horse match those of the horse painted in each tondo of two cups by Epiktetos that are now in London. One, in red-figure, shows a warrior with

there is considerable variation in how bridle parts are indicated. Cf., for example: Acr. 3702 (Schrader, no. 419, pl. 173) where a hole at the corner of the mouth suggests a bronze attachment, but as there is no hole at the poll, probably the cheekstraps were painted and the reins were in bronze as on our relief; a stele fragment in Chios (Berger, *Das Baseler Arzt-Relief* [Basel, 1970], p. 39, fig. 38) where the straps were probably painted; an Attic stele found in Rome, now in the Barracco Museum (Fuchs in Helbig, *Führer*⁴ vol.2, no. 1857) which has the bridle parts carved in relief; the small fragmentary stele found recently in the Dipylon excavations (*AA* 84 [1969], p. 34, fig. 6), which preserves the poll, part of a flame-like mane, and a hole for a bronze cheekstrap; an Attic statue base with a war chariot departing for battle, Athens, NM 3477 (*BSA* 57 [1962], p. 127, no. 2; *AJA* 67 [1963], p. 338, note 28, no. 9, pl. 77, 52) where all of the harness parts were painted. An exception to these is Acr. 1340 (Schrader, no. 476, pl. 200): here the mane is parted slightly and there are two holes for bronze attachments, one at the part, the other at the corner of the mouth. The strands of the forelock are carved, the mane is solid and its hairs were very likely indicated by paint. The ear was carved separately, the eye inlaid.

6) A date of about 500 has been proposed by several scholars, but the matter has not been fully discussed. Cf. Karouzos, *Aristodikos,* p. 57; Jacobsthal, *Melische Reliefs,* p. 134; Langlotz, *Frühgriechische Bild-hauerschulen,* p. 130; Lippold, *Handbuch,* p. 84; Getty, *Joys of Collect-ing,* p. 47; and Fuchs, *Skulptur der Griechen,* p. 504. Cook's date of ca. 485 seems too low (*JHS* 37 [1917], p. 122).

7) Athens, NM 3476 (*AM* 78 [1963], Beil. 65,3 and 66,2; *AM* 84 (1969), pl. 27; Charbonneaux, *Archaic Greek Art,* fig. 302); Kerameikos inv. P 1002 (*AM* 78 [1963], Beil. 64,2 and 66,1; *AM* 84 [1969], pl. 3,1).

8) Karouzos, *Aristodikos,* esp. pl. 10; Richter, *Kouroi*² no. 165. For a similar treatment of the hair, cf., also, Acr. 306 (Schrader, no. 326, fig. 275), the child on the grave stele from Anavysos, NM 4472 (Richter, *The Archaic Gravestones of Attica* [London, 1961] [hereafter, Richter, *Gravestones*], no. 59; *AM* 84 [1969], pl. 3,2), and a youth on an early

fifth century relief in the Metropolitan Museum, 12. 59 (Richter, *Cata-logue of Greek Sculpture in the Metropolitan Museum of Art* [Cam-bridge, Mass., 1954], no. 22, with a brief discussion of this hair style).

9) Richter, *Kouroi*², no. 155; J. Ducat, *Les kouroi du Ptoion. Le sanc-tuaire d'Apollon Ptoieus à l'époque archaïque* (Paris, 1971), no. 202.

10) Acr. 121 (Schrader, no. 425, fig. 350).

11) *AM* 78 (1963), Beil. 65,1.

12) For the west frieze, cf., de la Coste-Messelière, *Delphes* (Paris, 1957), pl. 67; Charbonneaux, *Archaic Greek Art,* fig. 206; for the south frieze, *Delphes,* pl. 72; Charbonneaux, fig. 207.

13) *BCH* 97 (1973), pp. 151ff and fig. 6 on p. 152; dated ca. 520.

14) Here are the most important examples: Attic black-figure: the *Rycroft Painter,* Syracuse 21956 (*ABV* 336,22), Munich 1720 (*ABV* 337, 24), Hamburg 1917.476 (*ABV* 337,25), Boston 03.880, a fragmentary hydria that shows a harnessing scene, attributed by the author; the *Leagros Group,* London B 326 (*ABV* 362,28; *JdI* 85 (1970), p. 77, fig. 44) Capesthorne Hall (*ABV* 365,64; *Paralipomena,* 162,64); Vatican 416 (*ABV* 365,65; *Paralipomena* 162,65); the *Diosphos Painter,* Boston 99.528, here, fig. 20 (Haspels, *ABL* pp. 111 and 235, 69; *Paralipomena* 248,69), Hamburg 1927.143 (*ABL* 239,142; Bothmer, *Amazons in Greek Art* [Oxford, 1957], p. 106, no. 182); four unattributed examples: an amphora type A, Petit Palais 304 (*CVA* pl. 7,1 and 3, 5-6); a hydria, Würzburg 310 (*ABV* 666); a lekythos, Palermo, Coll. Mormino 27 (*CVA,* pl. 12, 9-10); and an olpe, Rhodes 12331 (*CVA* pl. 14,4); *Attic red-figure: Manner of the Epeleios Painter,* Montauban 2, the horse painted in the tondo (*ARV*² 129,22; *AJA* 73 [1969], pl. 31, fig. 10); *Onesimos,* Bryn Mawr P 246, here fig. 14 (*ARV*² 324, 72; *CVA* pl. 8,3) and Orvieto, Faina 65 (*ARV*² 329,132).

15) The most recent bibliography is: Richter, *Engraved Gems of the Greeks and the Etruscans* (London, 1968), no. 116; Boardman, *Archaic Greek Gems* (London, 1968), no. 246; Boardman, *Greek Gems and Finger Rings* (London, 1970), pl. 355.

a horse to left (Fig. 12).[16] Unfortunately, much of this tondo is missing, but parts of the horse that remain depict an animal with the same long head, small eye, and short neck as the horse on the Cottenham relief. The other tondo is painted in black-figure on a bi-lingual cup signed by Epiktetos as painter and by Hischylos as potter (Fig. 13).[17] Here a horseman rides to right and, as before, the proportions and details of the horse's head and neck are similar to those of the Cottenham horse. However, the muzzle of neither painted horse points upward nor do its teeth show.[18] For the combination of these rare features, it is necessary to turn to a painter of the next generation: Onesimos. A fragmentary cup by him in Bryn Mawr preserves the head of a horse that resembles the Cottenham horse more than do those by Epiktetos (Fig. 14),[19] for not only is the head of this painted horse raised so high that its muzzle points upward, but also it has the same small nostril, open mouth with teeth showing, and parted mane as the sculpted horse has. For these latter three details, the horses of a chariot team painted on the exterior of a cup in London by the same artist also offer important comparison (Fig. 15).[20] Furthermore, these chariot horses by Onesimos have short necks, a characteristic of the Cottenham horse already mentioned, and one common among horses painted and carved in the late archaic period. Thus similarities between the Cottenham relief and late archaic sculpture and painting indicate that its sculptor was a contemporary of vase painters such as Epiktetos and Onesimos and of the anonymous sculptors of such works as the statue bases, Aristodikos, and the kouros, Ptoon 20.

Although the Cottenham relief has appeared many times, there has been only one attempt to reconstruct the missing parts of its composition. In the initial pub-lication of the piece, Cook proposed a reconstruction based on a relief in London of the Roman period which depicts a youth who restrains a rearing horse (Fig. 16).[21] Standing behind the two is a dog. A.H. Smith suggested that this relief imitates one carved about 500 B.C.,[22] and Cook concurred, adding that perhaps the Cottenham relief was even the model.[23] Thus the viewer is asked to imagine that our horse is rearing, forelegs in mid-air, hind legs well under the body, being controlled by a youth. The youth's legs are in profile one behind the other as he braces himself against the strong action of the beast. Such a reconstruction is perfectly plausible, but this restoration of the horse presents certain icono-graphic difficulties.

In archaic relief sculpture representations of rearing horses are few. The two examples known to me are not animals controlled by a groom or a dismounted rider, but are the trace horses of frontal chariot teams. One is carved in the panel of a small limestone metope recently found at Selinus, the other is a small terracotta plaque from Metatauros, now in the Metropolitan Museum (Fig. 17).[24] The Selinus relief probably dates in the sec-ond quarter of the sixth century. Here, the yoked pole horses appear in the standard way, chests in front view and heads turned, but the more mobile trace horses, which are not yoked to the chariot pole, but are attached to the vehicle only by trace lines, have become excited and have reared very high so that their heads are at the same level as those of the figures standing in the chariot. The New York relief (Fig. 17), though later in date, is similar, but that the head of the preserved trace horse faces outward, not inward. In archaic vase painting, the examples of rearing horses that appear in combat scenes are too numerous to list here. But unmounted or unhar-nessed rearing horses are rare indeed.[25] Other species

<hr>

16) London E 35 (*ARV²* 74,38).

17) London E 3 (*ARV²* 70,3; *Wissenschaftliche Zeitschrift der Univ. Rostock* 16 [1967], pl. 52,1).

18) For a very general overview of representations of painted horses with teeth depicted, cf., Cook, *JHS* 37 (1917), pp. 120ff.

19) Bryn Mawr P 246 (*ARV²* 324, 72; *CVA* pl. 8,3).

20) London E 44 (*ARV²* 318,2).

21) A.H. Smith, *A Catalogue of Sculpture in the British Museum*, vol. 3 (London, 1904), pp. 266ff, no. 2206; Cook, *JHS* 37 (1917), p. 123, fig. 10; W. Fuchs, *Die Vorbilder der neuattischen Reliefs* (Berlin, 1959), p. 135, note 69 and p. 182, note 56.

22) Above, note 21.

23) Cook, *JHS* 37 (1917), pp. 124ff.

24) From Selinus, now Palermo (*AJA* 75 [1971], p. 81, pl. 17, fig. 24, whence part. Richter, *The Sculpture and Sculptors of the Greeks* [New Haven, 1970], p. 47, fig. 166; *Arch. Class.* 21 [1969], 162ff, pls. 43-46). New York 22.139.54 (Lippold, *Handbuch*, p. 93).

25) I know only the following examples, all of them in black-figure: *Attic: Exekias*, Boston 89.273 (*ABV* 144,4; *Paralipomena* 59,4; *CVA* pl. 5, 29-32); *Manner of Exekias*, Zurich Market (*ABV* 147,3; *Para-lipomena* 61,3); two vases with the same scene by the *Amasis Painter*, Leningrad inv. 161 (*ABV* 151,15; *Paralipomena* 63,15) and New York 62.11.1 (*Paralipomena* 66; *Madrider Mitt.* 12 [1971], pl. 28 b); *Psiax*, Leningrad (*ABV* 294,22; *Paralipomena* 128,22); three by the *Swing Painter* with similar compositions, Richmond 62.1.2 (*Paralipomena* 133,6 ter), London, Blundell (*ABV* 305,23), and Würzburg 256 attrib-uted by the author (Langlotz, *Griechische Vasen in Würzburg* [Munich, 1932], pl. 83; three unattributed examples, a cup, Acr. 1551 a-b (Graef, *Die antiken Vasen von der Akropolis zu Athen* [Berlin, 1915-44], pl. 81), and two neck-amphorae, Louvre F 223 (*CVA* pl. 57,3; I. Scheibler, *Die symmetrische Bildform in der frühgriechischen Flächenkunst* [Kallmunz, 1960], pl. 51) and Port Sunlight (unpublished) on which two horses rear over a fallen archer.

Non-Attic examples: Laconian: London B 2 (Stibbe, *Lakonische Vasenmaler des Sechsten Jahrhundert v. Chr.* (Amsterdam, 1972), p. 274, no. 96); *Corinthian:* Toronto 161 (*BSA* 44 [1949], p. 204, no. 25), Bonn inv. 2055 (*BSA* 44 [1949], p. 228, no. 1); *Caeretan:* Amsterdam 1346 (Hemelrijk, *De Caeretaanse hydriae* [Rotterdam, 1956], no. 19), Dunedin E53.61 (Hemelrijk, no. 15).

Two possible exceptions where the forelegs are raised only slightly

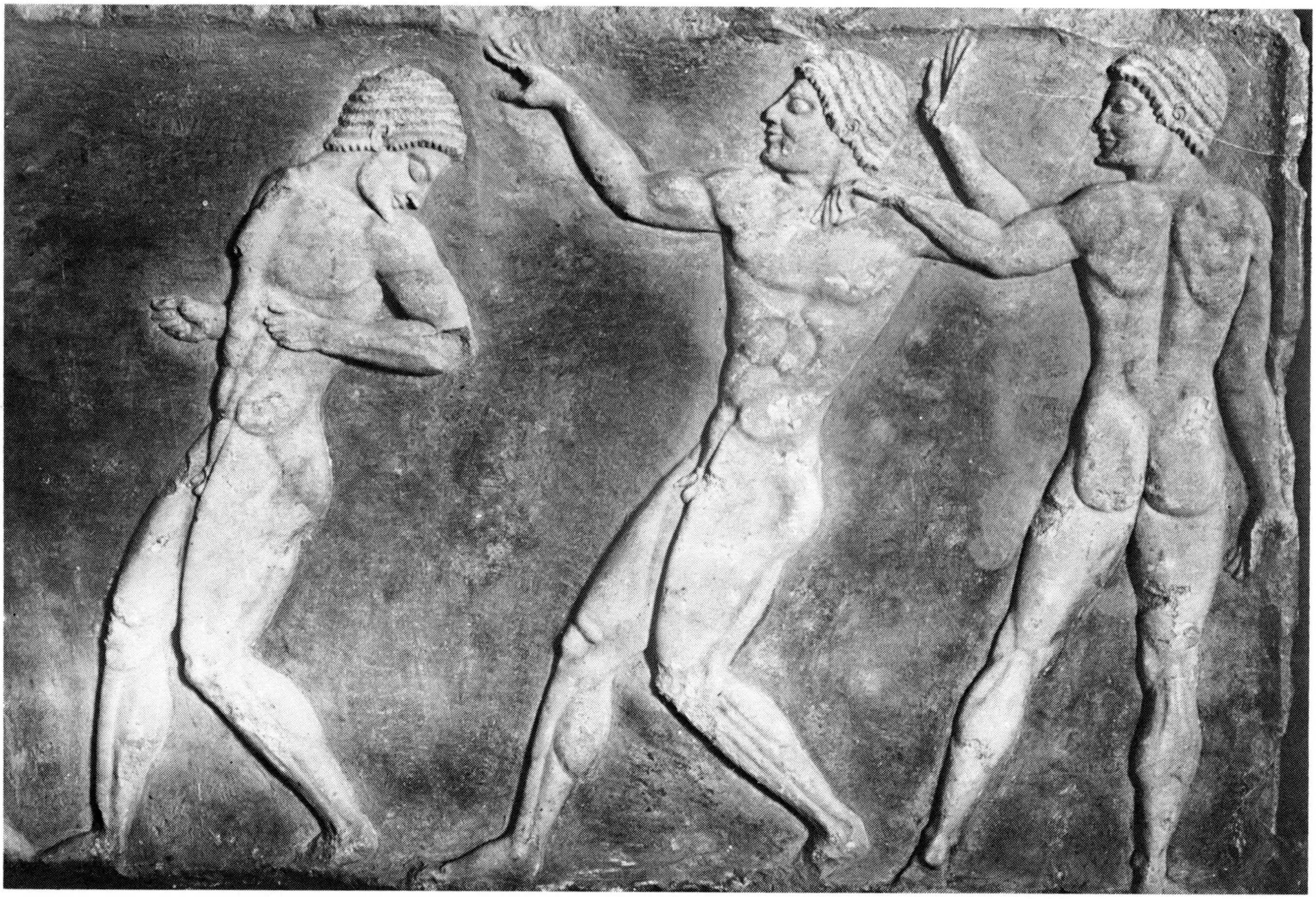

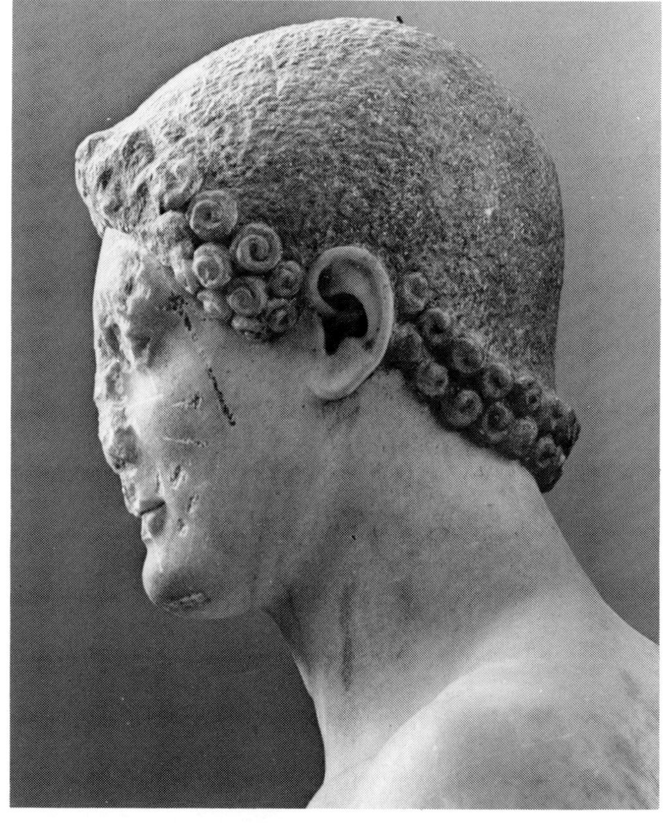

8   Statue base, Athens NM 3476 (Photo: DAI Athens)

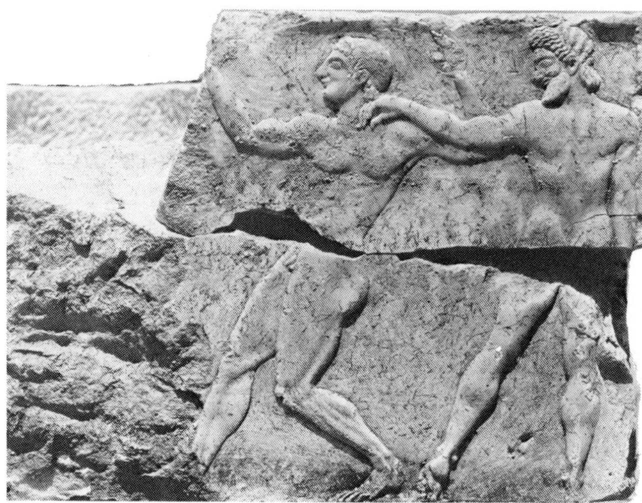

9   Statue base, Kerameikos inv. P 1002 (Photo: DAI Athens)

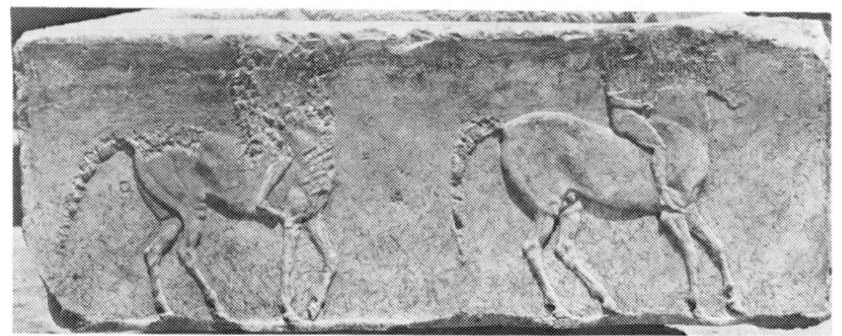

11   Statue base, Kerameikos inv. P 1002 (Photo: DAI Athens)

10   Aristodikos, Athens NM 3938 (Photo: DAI Athens)

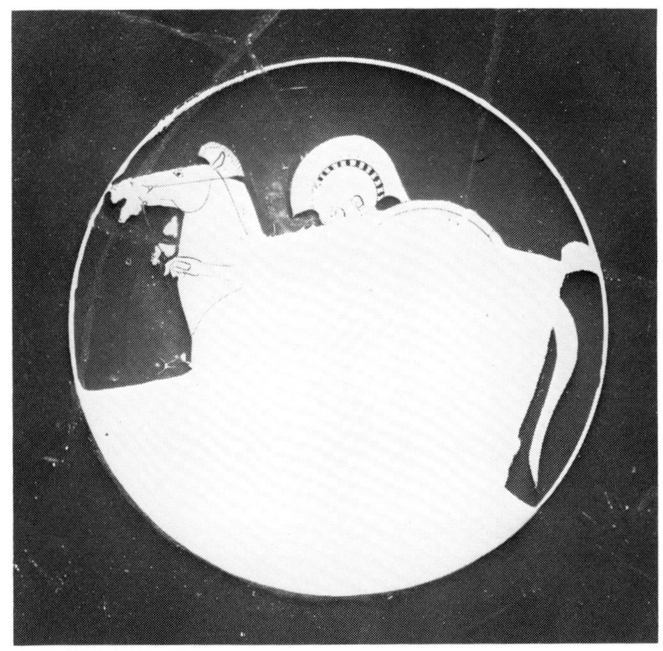

12 Epiktetos, London E 35 (Courtesy The Trustees of the British Museum)

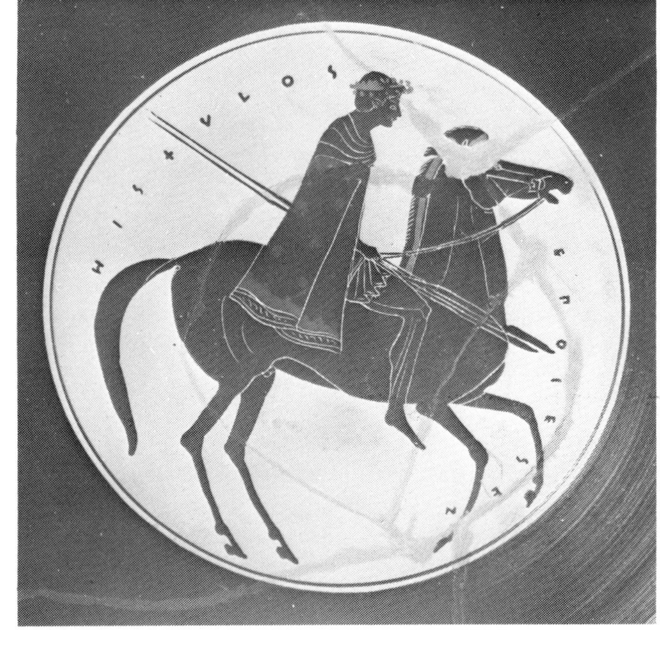

13 Epiktetos, London E 3 (Courtesy The Trustees of the British Museum)

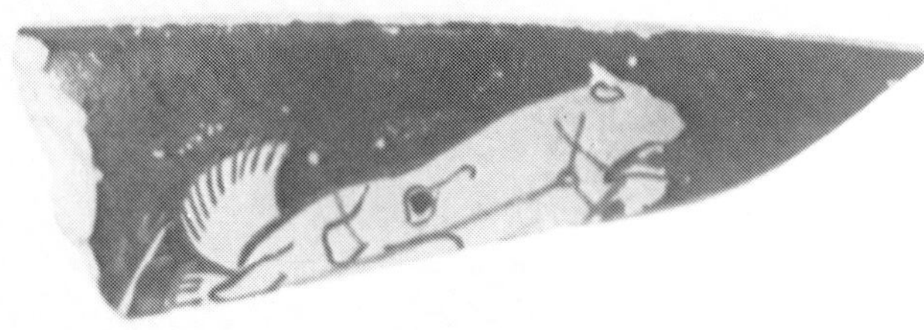

14 Onesimos, Bryn Mawr P 246 (Ella Riegel Memorial Museum)

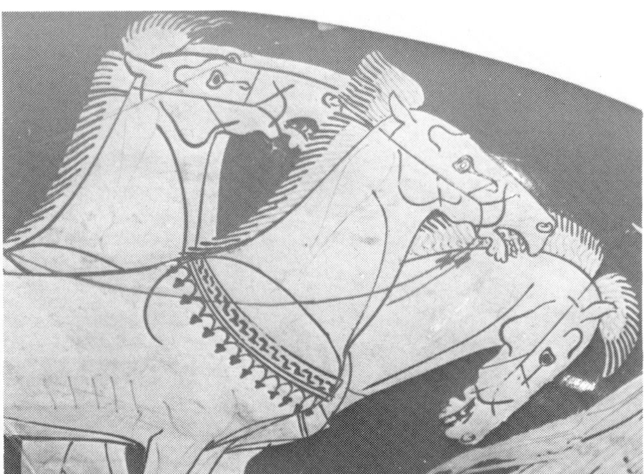

15 Onesimos, London E 44 (Courtesy The Trustees of the British Museum)

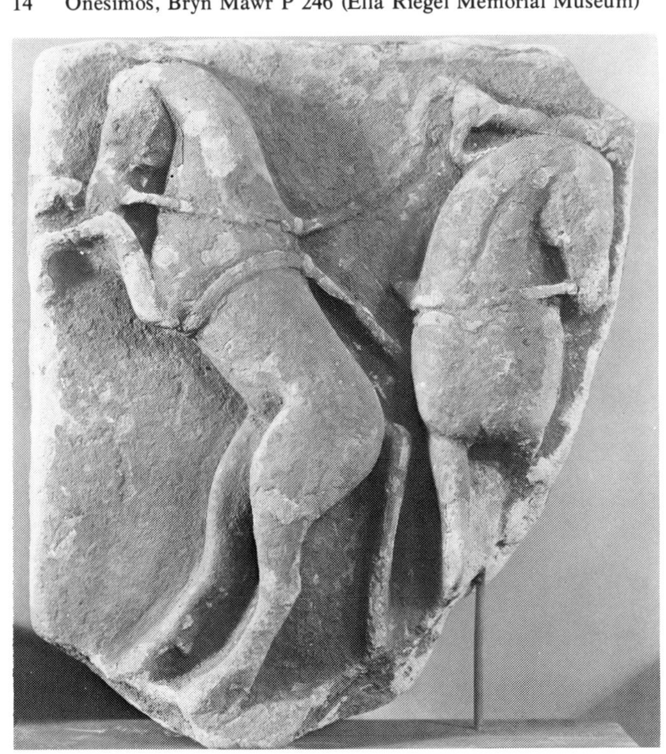

17 New York 22.139.54 (Rogers Fund, 1922)

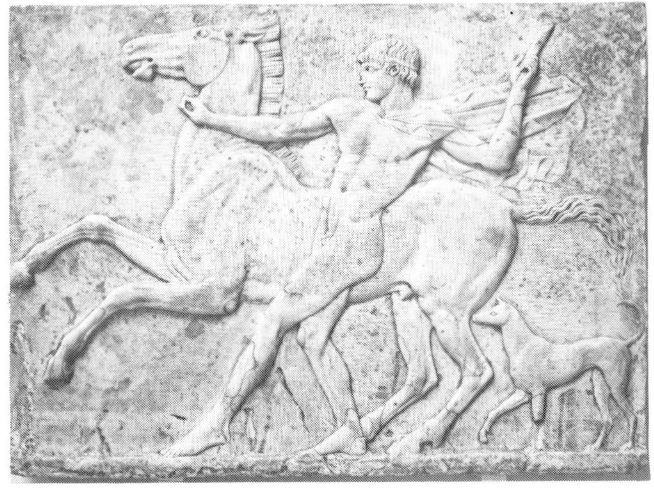

16 London 2206 (Courtesy The Trustees of the British Museum)

such as gems (Fig. 18) confirm that account.[26] Thus the contemporary visual evidence hardly presents a strong case for reconstructing the Cottenham horse as a rearing one. Furthermore, in the archaic period, a horse with its forelegs raised does not always denote one that rears, but often one that gallops, and horses moving at such a speed may be either mounts or chariot horses.[27] Also, at least some parts of the forelegs of a rearing or even of a galloping horse, especially as represented in Greek sculpture, are raised at least as high as the body, and the neck of a rearing horse is usually bent backward slightly.[28] Therefore, if the horse on the Cottenham relief were a rearing one, part of its forelegs should be preserved near the lower edge of the relief just above the break, and its neck should be bent backward slightly, instead of being almost vertical.

Other features of the London relief also suggest that this composition should not be used as a source for reconstructing the original appearance of the Cottenham relief.[29] Smith thought that the London relief imitates one carved about 500 B.C.,[30] yet it actually depends on later prototypes. This composition of a youth wearing a billowing chlamys and restraining a rearing horse recalls the similar composition on Slab 8 of the West Frieze of the Parthenon.[31] Here, however, the human figure

stands on the far side of the horse and the horse is the center of attention. It is a spirited, high-strung animal, overexcited by the noise and commotion of the preparations for the procession going on around it. The position of its limbs, forelegs raised one higher than the other, hind legs placed well under the body, is a sculptural convention of the classical and later periods that expresses excitement or rapid motion.[32] The heads of the two horses are also similar, although that of the London horse has less detail. Noteworthy too is the ear of each horse which is laid back against the top of the head, instead of pricked forward alertly as is customary in the archaic period.[33] Also, the unevenness of the short mane of the London horse finds better parallels in the classical period than it does in the archaic.[34] The legs of the youth on the London relief are placed in approximately the same position, though right and left reversed, as those of the Parthenon cavalryman, and if the Parthenon slab is indeed the prototype for the composition on the London relief,[35] this explains the awkward carving of the right hip of the London youth, for the hips and thighs of the Parthenon cavalryman are obscured by his horse.

The squarish proportions of the youth's head and the style of his hair, loose locks which radiate from a central point and are held by a narrow fillet, fit, however, neither

---

appear in early red-figure: *Epiktetos,* London 1929.11.11.1 (*ARV²* 74,35) and the *Euergides Painter,* London Market (*Cat. Sotheby, June 18, 1962,* no. 123) attributed by Bothmer, which on Side A depicts a youth putting on his greaves watched by a youth leaning on a stick, the two flanked by warriors holding horses. The position of the horses on these two cups is awkward.

26) Here are three certain examples: New York 74.51.4173 (Richter, *Engraved Gems of the Greeks and the Etruscans,* no. 98; Boardman, *Archaic Greek Gems,* no. 135); Boston 27.677, the gem by Epimenes, here, fig. 18 (Richter, no. 116; Boardman, no. 246; also Boardman, *Greek Gems and Finger Rings,* pl. 355); fr. Olympia (Furtwängler, *Die antiken Gemmen* [Leipzig and Berlin, 1900], pl. 8, 59; *JHS* 37 [1917], p. 125, fig. 12). Three others may be mentioned: London 88.10-15.4 (Richter, no. 132); London 88.10.15.2 (Richter, no. 133; Boardman, *Archaic Greek Gems,* no. 137); Boston 27.670 (Richter, no. 135; Boardman, no. 268 where the accession number given is 27.674). These latter three show the forelegs bent, but owing to the restriction of the oval format, the gem cutter was unable to show the animal as truly rearing. Nevertheless, his intention is clear.

27) These are just a very few examples of galloping horses: the chariots from the East frieze of the Siphnian Treasury (de la Coste-Messeliere, *Delphes,* pls. 78-79; Group E, Berlin 1716 (*ABV* 137,62); Manner of Exekias, Tarquinia 623 (*ABV* 147,2); the Amasis Painter, Munich inv. 8763 (*Paralipomena* 65).

28) Cf., for example, the monuments mentioned in notes 24-27.

29) Fuchs, *Skulptur der Griechen,* p. 504 states that the London relief is unsuitable for restoration of the motive of the Cottenham relief, but he does not give reasons.

30) Above, note 21.

31) G. Rodenwaldt, *Die Akropolis* (Berlin, 1930), pl. 33; M. Collignon, *Le Parthénon* (Paris, 1912), pl. 82, top.

32) Although this convention appears in vase painting as early as the

second quarter of the sixth century, for example, on the namepiece of the Painter of Acropolis 606 (*ABV* 81,1; *Paralipomena* 30,1; Charbonneaux, *Archaic Greek Art,* fig. 70), it is rarely used by sculptors until the high classical period. Other than the galloping horses on the Siphnian Treasury (above, note 27), the Amazons from the Athenian Treasury (*Fouilles de Delphes* IV, 4 pls. 87-88, and the two rearing trace horses mentioned in note 24, the only other pre-Parthenon example in stone relief sculpture of this Convention known to me is the metope from the Temple of Zeus at Olympia where Herakles restrains one of the mares of Diomedes (Ashmole, *Olympia, The Sculptures of the Temple of Zeus* [London, 1967], pl. 179).

It is only on the Parthenon frieze that for the first time this composition is used repeatedly, both for rearing and for galloping horses, and surely this frieze provided the model for many of the later examples of this motive.

33) Compare, for example, the horse on the London relief with the statues of archaic horses from the Acropolis, Acr. 697 and 700 (Schrader, nos. 320 and 314), Acr. 606 (Schrader, no. 313), and the relief fragment, Acr. 1340, where the position of the hole for insertion of the ear makes clear that it was vertical, not laid back (Schrader, no. 476); also the statue base, Athens, NM 3477 (above, note 5). Unless horses of the archaic period are galloping, their ears are not laid back as flatly against the tops of their heads as some of those on the Parthenon. Compare, for example, the ears of galloping horses on the neck-amphora attributed to Group E, Berlin 1716 (*ABV* 137,62), or one in the tondo of a cup by Onesimos, Orvieto, Faina 65 (*ARV²* 329,132).

34) Compare some examples in the previous note with such classical examples as the Parthenon frieze, the Dexileos stele (Lullies, *Greek Sculpture* [New York, 1957], pl. 191), or the Villa Albani relief (von Steuben in Helbig, *Führer⁴* vol. 4, no. 3241).

35) Smith, *Catalogue of the Sculpture in the British Museum,* 3, p. 267, mentions that Overbeck thought that the London relief might date

the archaic nor the classical periods, but originate in the Early Classical era. Two general comparisons that immediately come to mind are the "Omphalos Apollo" and the Artemision bronze.[36] Neither of these gods wears a fillet, for the long hair of each is braided and wound round the head, but the forelocks are combed forward and neatly arranged. On the London youth, a fillet replaces the braids and the arrangement of the locks is looser and livelier,[37] but an Early Classical source for this hair style seems apparent. Thus the iconographic and stylistic features of the London relief indicate that it depends on models carved later than the Cottenham relief and that its composition is unsuitable for reconstructing that of the Cottenham relief. Therefore a different route must be taken in order to reconstruct its original appearance.

The horse presents a suitable starting point. Since a rearing horse may be ruled out, we may examine representations of late archaic horses which are walking, mounted or led, and which show some indication that they are being restrained. Similarities between the Cottenham horse and those on the base from the Kerameikos, which on one side shows two mounts walking slowly to right (Fig. 11), have been mentioned above. Of these two horses, it is the one on the left which exhibits more evidence of being restrained for it has raised its head very high, its hind legs are well under its body, and one foreleg supports the forehand while the other is raised slightly. The fragmentary horse and rider stele from Thasos,[38] which preserves the foreparts of the mount, presents another important comparison, for the muzzle of this horse also points upward and its forelegs are in the same position as those of the Kerameikos horse. A fragmentary painted stele, Athens NM 31, shows a mount similar to these two.[39] A fragmentary double-sided relief from the Acropolis depicts on one side a mounted horse walking slowly to right.[40] Here the right foreleg supports the forehand, the left is raised slightly; most of the hindquarters are missing, but the small portion of the left hind leg that is preserved indi-

cates that it was supportive. On late archaic red-figured vases, there are numerous representations of youths with horses, both mounted and on foot, and many of these compositions contribute evidence for reconstructing the Cottenham horse. A few of the most important ones may be mentioned here. In the tondo of a cup in Leningrad signed by the potter Kachrylion (Fig. 19),[41] a youth to left leads a horse which he holds firmly by reins held in both hands, and on the outside of a cup in Naples attributed to the Manner of the Epeleios Painter,[42] youths lead horses, two to right, one to left. On the exterior of a fragmentary cup in the Louvre attributed to the Proto-Panaitian Group, a man in Thracian costume leads two horses,[43] and on a fragmentary cup by the Thalia Painter in the collection of Dr. Herbert Cahn, Basel, a rare subject, the Dokimasia, is represented.[44] Here, cavalrymen bring their horses to the Council for the annual inspection. The tondo of a fragmentary cup in the collection of Dr. Dietrich von Bothmer, attributed by him to the Ambrosios Painter, shows a helmeted warrior armed with a round shield leading a horse to left. The warrior holds the reins close to the bit. The left foreleg of the horse is raised, the right is supportive. The hindquarters of the horse, the youth's left arm and part of his shield are missing. An early fifth century white-ground lekythos in Boston attributed to the Diosphos Painter depicts a warrior leading his horse to right (Fig. 20).[45] On this vase, the artist has drawn the warrior in black with his helmet crest in outline, the horse in outline with a black mane. Although this composition is a reversal of the one on the relief, it is nevertheless of particular importance, for the neck of the painted horse is almost vertical and its muzzle points upward, similar to these parts of the Cottenham horse. Two more examples of walking horses central to our reconstruction are by Onesimos. One is the youthful rider to right painted in the tondo of a cup in the Louvre signed by Euphronios as potter and by Onesimos as painter (Fig. 21).[46] The other, on the outside of a cup in Munich (Fig. 22),[47] shows a mounted youth leading a

from the time of Phidias.

36) For the "Omphalos Apollo", cf., most recently, B. Ridgway, *The Severe Style in Greek Sculpture* (Princeton, 1970), figs. 94-95; for the Artemision bronze, cf. Ridgway, fig. 99. The Apollo Choiseul-Gouffier in London belongs with the "Omphalos Apollo" and has the same hair style (Ridgway, fig. 96). For others, cf. H. von Steuben and P. Zanker, "Wagenlenker and Omphalosapollo," *AA* 81 (1963), pp. 68ff.

37) On this feature, cf., Ridgway, *Severe Style*, p. 112.

38) Above, note 13.

39) Richter, *Gravestones*, no. 71, figs. 163-164.

40) Acr. 3702 (Schrader, no. 419, pl. 173).

41) Leningrad inv. NB 6484 (*ARV²* 108,25). Bothmer attributes this cup to the Thalia Painter. For the work of this artist, cf *ARV²* 112ff and *Paralipomena* 332.

42) Naples 2616 (*ARV²* 149,21; *AJA* 73 [1969], pl. 30, 7-9).

43) Louvre G 26, G 26 bis (*ARV²* 317, 13; *Paralipomena* 332; *RA*, 1973, p. 16, fig. 11). These fragments are now in New York on permanent loan to the Metropolitan Museum (L. 1970.48). Bothmer has seen that they join a fragment given by him to the Metropolitan Museum (69.44.1). This cup is now almost complete.

44) Basel, Cahn 133 (*ARV²* 1626 and 1708; *Paralipomena* 332; *RA* 1973, pp. 6-7, figs. 3-6).

45) Boston 99.528 (Haspels, *ABL* pp. 111 and 235, 69; *Paralipomena* 248,69).

46) Louvre G 105 (*ARV²* 324, 60; *Wissenschaftliche Zeitschrift der Univ. Rostock* 16 (1967), pl. 52,2). Cf. also, the horses represented on the outside of this cup (*RA*, 1973, p. 17, figs. 12-13).

47) Munich 2639 (*ARV²* 324,61).

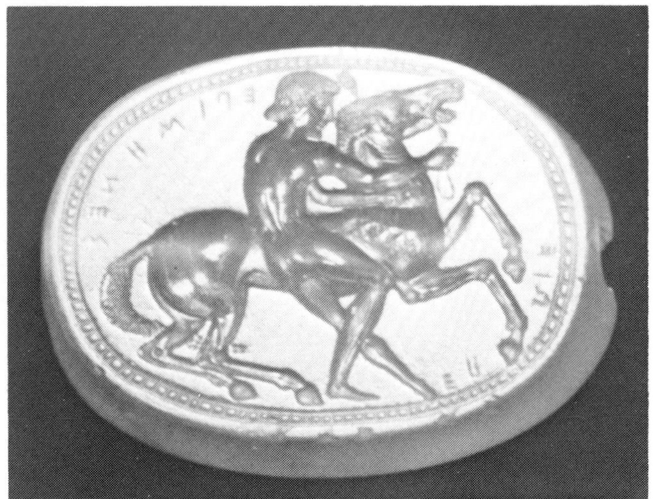

18

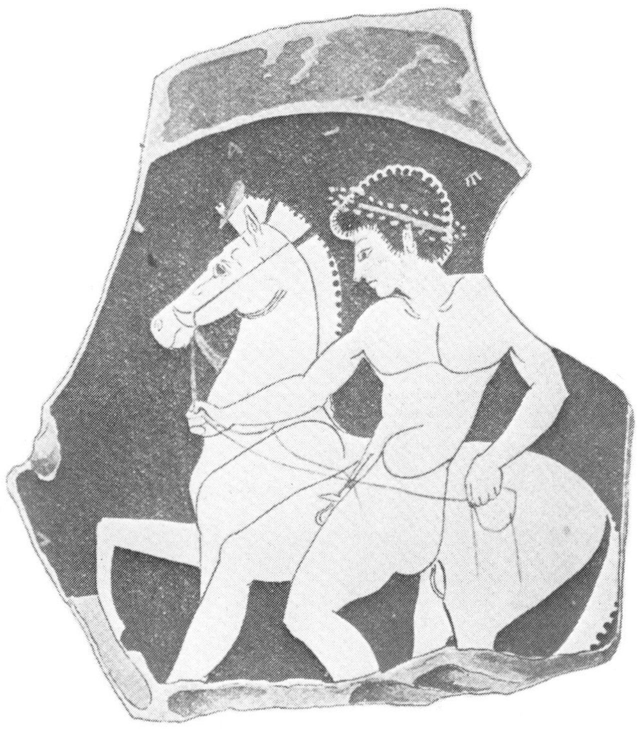

19

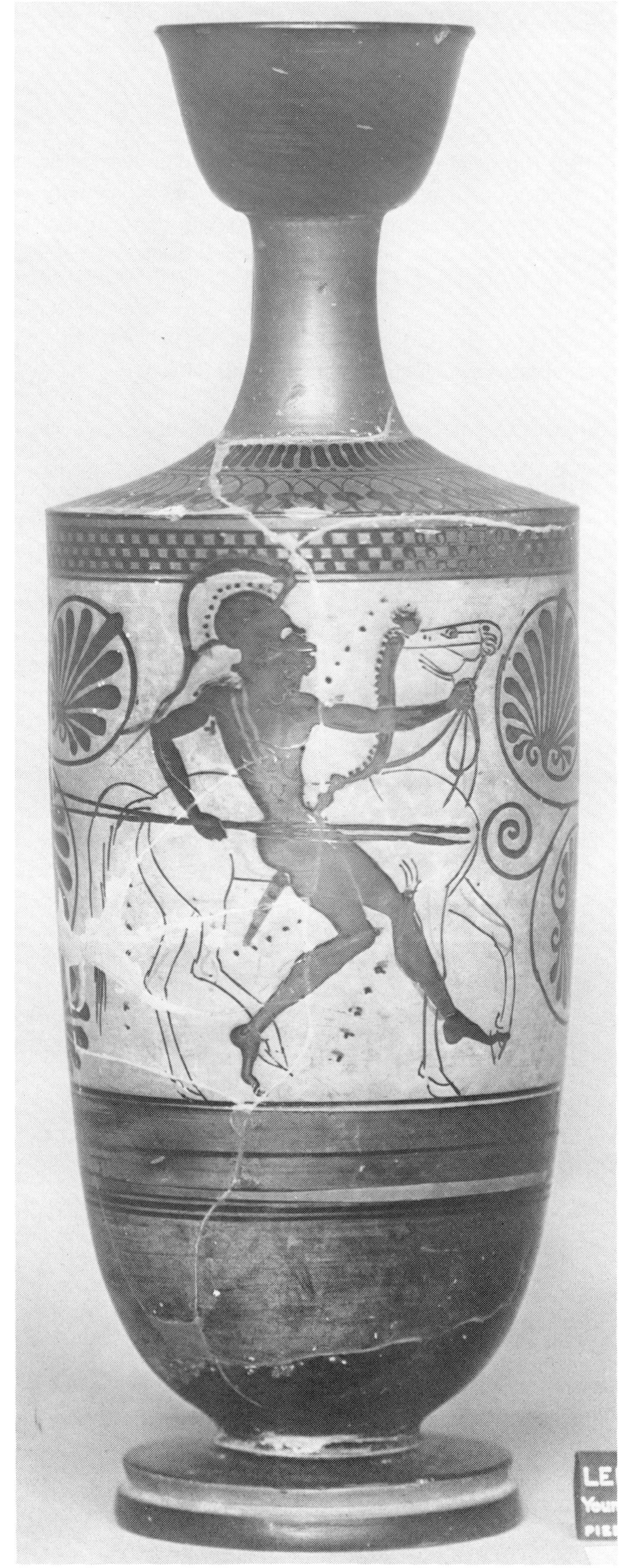

20

18   Epimenes gem, Boston 27.677 (Courtesy, Museum of Fine Arts, Boston, Francis Bartlett Donation)

19   Kachrylion, Leningrad inv. NB 6484 (after *Izvestiya Rossiiskoi Akademii Istorii Materialnoi Kultura*)

20   Diosphos Painter, Boston 99.528 (Courtesy Museum of Fine Arts, Boston, H. L. Pierce Fund)

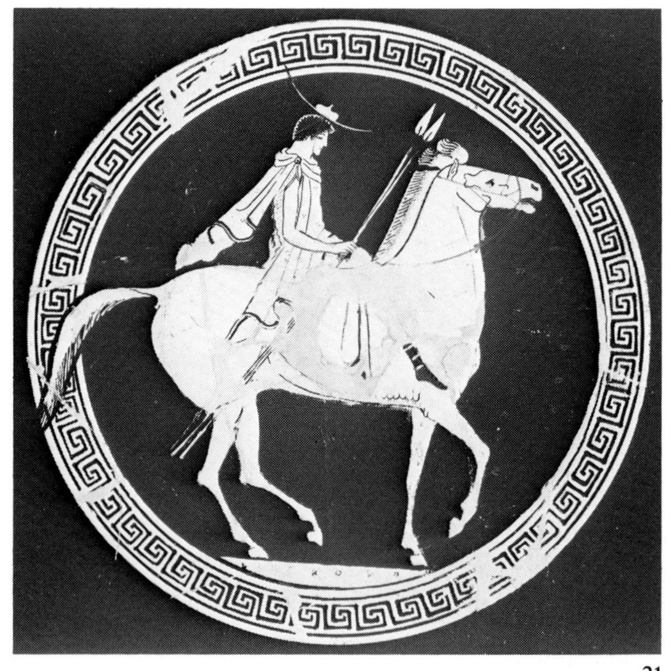

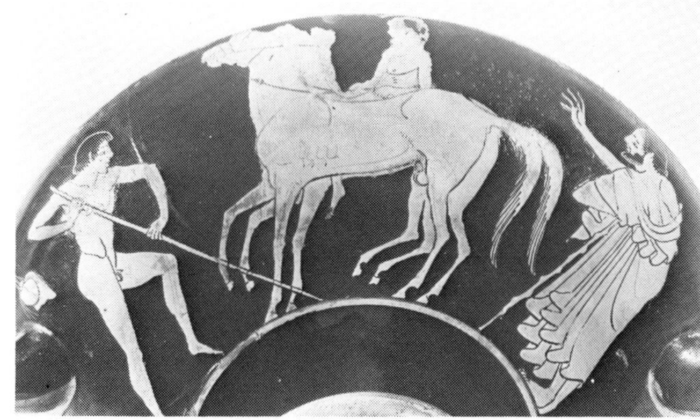

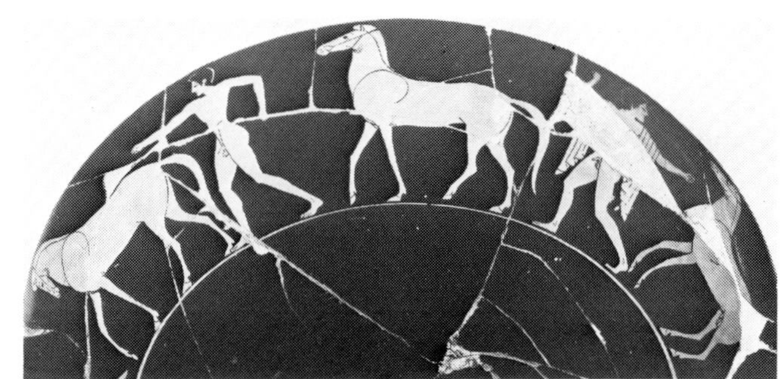

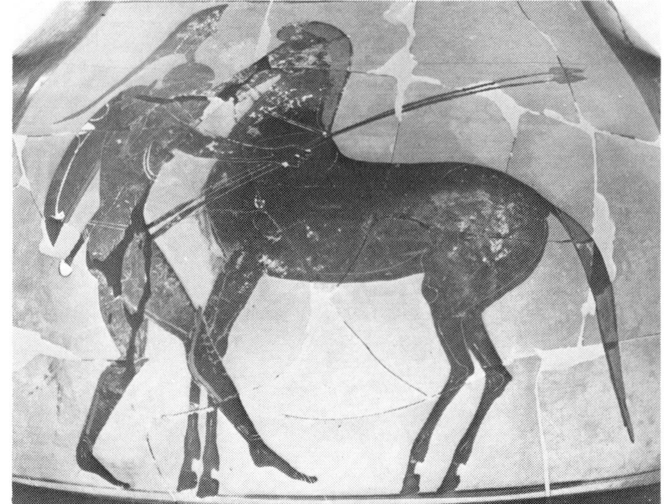

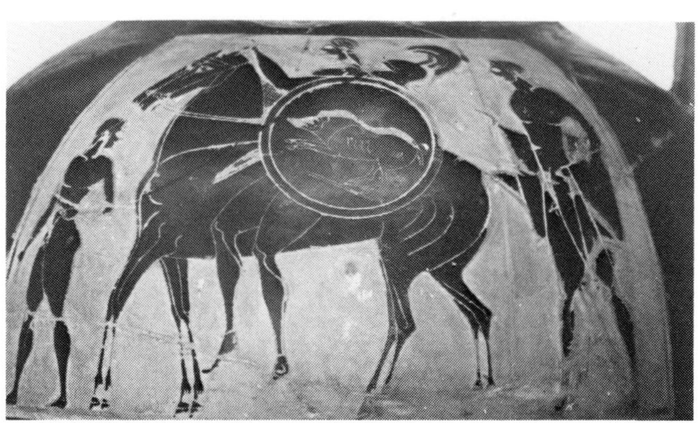

21   Onesimos, Louvre G 105 (Photo: Chuzeville)

22   Onesimos, Munich 2639

23   Euergides Painter, Louvre G 15 (Photo: Chuzeville)

24   Hypobibazon Class, Kerameikos inv. 158 (Photo: DAI Athens)

25   Amasis Painter, London B 151 (Courtesy The Trustees
      of the British Museum)

void horse to left. None of these late archaic sculpted and painted horses walks calmly or is led quietly, such as a contemporary example by the Euergides Painter (Fig. 23),[48] for each exhibits tension in the contours of its body and neck and in the position of its head, which indicates resistance to control.[49] Each has one foreleg raised; the one by the Diosphos Painter and the two by Onesimos have one hind leg off the ground as well. Also the heads of these latter two horses are raised very high and they have opened their mouths, two notable features of the horse on the Cottenham relief, paralleled elsewhere in the work of Onesimos.[50]

This brief review of late archaic representations of walking horses which, mounted or led, show some resistance to control, suggests a more plausible reconstruction of the missing limbs and body of the Cottenham horse: one foreleg supported the forehand, the other was raised slightly; the hindquarters were placed well under the body with one or both legs supporting them. Such a composition is compatible with contemporary representations in both sculpture and vase painting.

Reconstruction of the youth presents fewer problems. It is clear from what remains that his torso is in front view and his right arm is outstretched holding the reins. His left arm may also have been held out and raised somewhat in order to complement the right one and to fill an otherwise void space above the horse's hindquarters. The legs of the youth were very likely in profile like those of some of the athletes on the two bases in Athens (Figs. 8 and 9),[51] and the youths on two of the cups mentioned above, one in Leningrad (Fig. 19), the other in Naples.[52] The suggestion of Fuchs that the youth on the relief is about to mount seems to me untenable,[53] for, in order to swing himself up onto the animal's back, the youth would have to face his horse, as we know from Xenophon and from the namepiece of the Hypobibazon Class which shows a warrior about to mount (Fig. 24).[54] Nor does it seem likely that the youth is dismounting for, as comparison with representations on vases (Fig. 25) and gems reveals,[55] the eye level of the youth would be higher than that of his mount and his hand would not hold the reins so close to the animal's mouth. Furthermore, a dismounting rider presents an awkward appearance, perhaps not suitable for stone sculpture, though it is known from a late archaic terracotta relief shield from Corinth,[56] and from Etruscan statuettes.[57] Rather than these alternatives, it is more likely that the Cottenham relief simply depicts a youth who restrains a horse that has become slightly excited and tries to move forward (Ill. 1).

A few words need to be said about the original provenance of the relief. External information is lost forever; all remarks must be based on internal evidence. Previously, Attic as well as Ionian origins have been suggested. Picard, in 1923, was the first to opt for Ionian,[58] and his opinion was accepted by Langlotz who, in *Frühgriechische Bildhauerschulen,* included the Cottenham relief in his chapter on Naxian sculpture, comparing the head of the youth with those on the South frieze of the Siphnian Treasury.[59] Buschor, [60] and Jacobsthal,[61] also supported the opinion of these two scholars that the Cottenham relief is Ionian. In 1939 Picard repeated

---

48) Louvre G15 (*ARV*² 91,51). Horses led by a groom or a rider are a frequent subject on late archaic vases. Here are a few more examples of quiet horses: *the Euergides Painter,* Louvre G 61 (*ARV*² 91,45), Louvre G 21 (*ARV*² 92,68); *Manner of the Epileios Painter,* Naples 2616, the middle horse of side B (*ARV*² 149,21; *AJA* 73 [1969], pl. 30, fig. 9), Lerici (*ARV*² 1628, 22 bis); *Myson,* Boston, Alpers and Shulman (*ARV*² 1638, 23 bis), Greenwich, Bareiss 342 (*Paralipomena* 349, 29 ter). For the method of leading a horse considered proper in antiquity, cf., Xenophon, *On Horsemanship* VI, 4-6; also M.A. Littauer, *Iraq* 33 (1971), pp. 29ff.

49) An exception may be the middle horse on the cup in Naples mentioned above in notes 42 and 48 (*ARV*² 149,21).

50) Above, notes 17 and 20.

51) Above, note 7.

52) Kachrylion, Leningrad inv. NB 6484 (*ARV*² 108,25); Manner of the Epileios Painter, Naples 2616 (*ARV*² 149,21; *AJA* 73 [1969], pl. 30, figs. 8-9).

53) Fuchs, *Skulptur der Griechen,* p. 504.

54) Xenophon, *On Horsemanship,* VII, 1-4; Kerameikos inv. 48 (*ABV* 339,2). A warrior mounting a horse also appears on a small neck amphora in Oxford attributed to the Diosphos Painter (Oxford 317: Haspels, *ABL* p. 238, 129; Bothmer, *Amazons,* p. 91, no. 7). I have not seen this vase. For late red-figure examples, cf., Brunn, "Ὑποβιβάζεσϑαι," *AZ* 38 (1880), p. 18f.

55) Compare the following examples: *Attic black-figure: the Amasis Painter,* London B 191, here, fig. 25 (*ABV* 152,24; *Paralipomena* 63, 24); *Related to Lydos,* New York 25.78.4 (*ABV* 119,9); *Leagros Group,* Palermo 1170 (*ABV* 378,255; Bothmer, *Amazons,* p. 102, no. 139); two unattributed examples, Vatican 369 (Albizzati, *Vasi antichi dipinti del Vaticano* [Rome, 1925-39], pp. 153-154, figs. 93-94) and New York 06.1021.85 (to be published in the forthcoming *CVA* fascicule); *two gems:* London 1907.10-1.21 (Richter, *Engraved Gems of the Greeks and the Etruscans,* no. 134, with bibliography; Boardman, *Archaic Greek Gems,* no. 200) and Leningrad (Boardman, no. 201). For dismounting riders, cf., also Haspels, *ABL,* p. 52, note 2 and Boardman, *Archaic Greek Gems,* pp. 81 and 86, notes 8-9 with bibliography.

56) Corinth KN 1. Cf. Haspels, *ABL,* p. 52, note 2; *AJA* 35 (1931), pl. 2; Bothmer, *Amazons,* p. 122; *Gestalt und Geschichte (Festschrift Schefold),* pl. 7,2.

57) Cf., two in London B 32 and B 30 (*Festschrift Schefold,* pl. 8, 1-2). The mounted Amazons that once adorned the Athenian Treasury (*FdD* IV, 4, pls. 34-35 and 87-91) may, at eye level, appear to dismount, but in their original position on the building more likely appeared to the spectator below to be Amazons sitting sideways on their mounts.

58) Picard, *La sculpture antique des origines à Phidias,* p. 235.

59) Langlotz, *Frühgriechische Bildhauerschulen,* p. 130.

60) Buschor, *AM* 54 (1929), p. 151.

61) Jacobsthal, *Melische Reliefs,* p. 134.

his opinion,[62] and two decades later Karouzos not only agreed, but compared the relief with the gem in Boston signed by Epimenes (Fig. 18).[63] Recently, Fuchs has suggested that the piece comes from Thasos.[64] In the initial publication of the Cottenham relief, however, Cook assumed that its provenance was Attic and its marble either Pentelic or Hymettan,[65] and Beazley took the piece to be Attic as did Lippold and Vermeule.[66] These various views, however, have never been discussed at length. The style of the relief and the marble, indeed if it is Pentelic, argue more strongly for an Attic origin than they do for an Ionian or a Thasian one. Comparison of the Cottenham relief with the South frieze of the Siphnian Treasury, or even with the western one, reveals more differences than similarities. On these two friezes, both men and gods are sturdy, with heavy limbs and stocky bodies, the horses short-coupled with thick necks and short heads, whereas both the youth and the horse on the Cottenham relief have the slender, refined, elegant proportions typical of late archaic figures by Attic sculptors and painters. The Epimenes gem also offers few criteria on which to base an argument for an Ionian origin, for, as Beazley has seen,[67] Epimenes was an Ionian artist strongly influenced by the innovations in rendering of human anatomy made by sculptors and by vase painters of the Pioneer Group during the latter part of the sixth century. The lively rendering of the youth on this gem recalls some of the athletes on the two bases in Athens (Figs. 8 and 9) and also contemporary painted figures such as the athletes and their attendants on the Berlin krater by Euphronios,[68] while the three-quarter view of his back is one preferred by Onesimos for some of the figures painted on many of his finest cups.[69] As pointed out by Beazley,[70] the fiery spirit of the horse by Epimenes, the decorative treatment of its mane and tail, and the details of the harness parts are unquestionably Ionian and may best be compared with horses on Clazomenian vases and sarcophagi. The style of the Epimenes gem, then, is a spirited blend of Attic and Ionian elements. Beyond the most general similarities, it has little in common with our relief. The Cottenham relief compares best with purely Attic monuments of the late sixth and early fifth centuries, in particular the Athenian statue bases with horsemen and athletes, and horses on cups by Onesimos.

The purpose for which the Cottenham relief was carved requires some discussion. Although several possibilities come to mind, only one or two may appear feasible. Cook, who thought that the original shape of the relief was trapezoidal, suggested that it was the predella of a grave stele,[71] and such a use has been accepted by Vermeule.[72] Several features of the relief, other than its rectangular format, eliminate such an interpretation. First of all, predellae of grave stelai are not separate panels, but are carved in one piece with the shaft.[73] Also, the thickness of the moulding suggests that it should terminate the relief rather than separate the shaft of a stele from the panel below, especially when compared with mouldings on Attic stelai which are usually a simple fillet.[74] Furthermore, since the top surface of the Cottenham relief is ancient, unlike that of the right side which was reworked at a later time, there is no way that the relief could have continued upward to form the shaft of a stele.

Decoration of a statue base, such as those found in Athens,[75] may also be excluded, for not only is the Cottenham relief too short, but in the archaic period, such reliefs are carved from the same block of stone that supported the statue. They are not separately-worked panels attached to the base by dowels and clamps. Nor does the Cottenham relief seem to be part of an architectural frieze, for there are no clamp cuttings for attachment to frieze backers and the subject matter is unsuitable for a continuous frieze. The rectangular shape of

62) Picard, *Manuel*, II, 1, p. 20.

63) Karouzos, *Aristodikos*, p. 57. For the gem, cf. note 15 above.

64) Fuchs, *Skulptur der Griechen*, p. 504.

65) Cook, *JHS* 37 (1917), p. 116.

66) Beazley, *Lewes House Gems*, p. 15; Lippold, *Handbuch*, p. 84; Vermeule, *AJA* 63 (1959), p. 143.

67) Beazley, *Lewes House Gems*, pp. 21ff.

68) Berlin 2180 (*ARV²* 13,1; *Paralipomena* 321,1; Charbonneaux, *Archaic Greek Art*, figs. 370-371).

69) Some examples: Louvre G 104, side B, Theseus and the bull (*ARV²* 318,1; *Paralipomena* 358,1); Boston 01.8020, tondo (*ARV²* 321,22; *Paralipomena* 359,22; Charbonneaux, *Archaic Greek Art*, fig. 392); Louvre G 287, tondo (*ARV²* 321,24); Munich 2637, sides A and B (*ARV²* 322,28; *Paralipomena* 359,28).

70) Beazley, *Lewes House Gems*, pp. 22ff.

71) Cook, *JHS* 37 (1917), p. 117.

72) C. Vermeule, *AJA* 63 (1959), p. 143.

73) Cf., for example, New York 36.11.13 (Richter, *Gravestones*, no. 45, fig. 126); Rome, Barracco Museum (above, note 5).

74) Besides the two sculpted examples in note 73 above, add New York 11.185 (Richter, *Gravestones*, no. 37, fig. 96; Berger, *Baseler Arzt-Relief*, fig. 122), the stele of Aristion, Athens NM 29 (Richter, no. 67, fig. 156; Berger, fig. 121), Athens, NM 34 (Richter, no. 65, fig. 162) which have unsculpted predellae that once may have contained painted decoration. A non-Attic stele may also be added here: Istanbul, from Syme (Berger, fig. 58). Compare these narrow fillets with the top mouldings of each of the following reliefs: Aigina, grave stele from Aigina (Berger, fig. 23); Loryma, a base that once supported the shaft of a grave stele (Berger, figs. 35-36); Athens, NM, stele by Alxenor, from Orchomenos (Berger, fig. 46). An exception may be the fragmentary relief found at Chios (Berger, fig. 38), which depicts a rider to left. It is uncertain whether this is a grave relief or a votive relief (Berger, pp. 39 and 170, note 74, with bibliography).

75) Above, note 7; also, Acr. 2993 and 203 (Schrader, no. 420, fig. 347)

our relief in its original state may suggest that it once served as a metope for a small building, yet the moulding seems too intricate for this purpose and the subject matter unsuitable.[76]

There is one more category in relief sculpture: votive reliefs.[77] Although Greek votive dedications form a large and impressive group of monuments from the classical period on, there is very little information about archaic votive monuments. Many, such as the well-known plaques from Pitsa,[78] were probably made of wood or of clay with painted decoration and only a fraction of the original number survives.[79] Furthermore, not many archaic stone votive reliefs are known, and these vary considerably in format as well as in subject,[80] thus indicating that this species of relief was hardly a prescribed one. The shape may be broad or narrow, the edges framed or unframed (though more often the latter), the subject human or divine. Occasionally, these reliefs bear inscriptions, the most famous example being the "Potter Relief" from the Acropolis which has a fragmentary inscription that once gave the name of the dedicator and that of the sculptor whom he commissioned to carve it.[81] Sometimes a figure may be identified by an attribute, such as Athena on several reliefs from the Acropolis, in particular the Sacrifice relief and the gigantomachy relief,[82] or Herakles on a slightly later relief from Athens which depicts the hero about to hurl the boar.[83] Most of the votive reliefs that have come down to us, however, are more enigmatic than these, bearing neither an inscription nor a figure identified by an attribute. A few examples, all from the Acropolis, may be mentioned: the so-called Charites relief which may represent Hermes and the Graces;[84] the fragmentary relief which depicts the lower right leg and foot, as well as some drapery, of a woman, perhaps Athena, who strides to right;[85] the fragmentary double-sided relief which

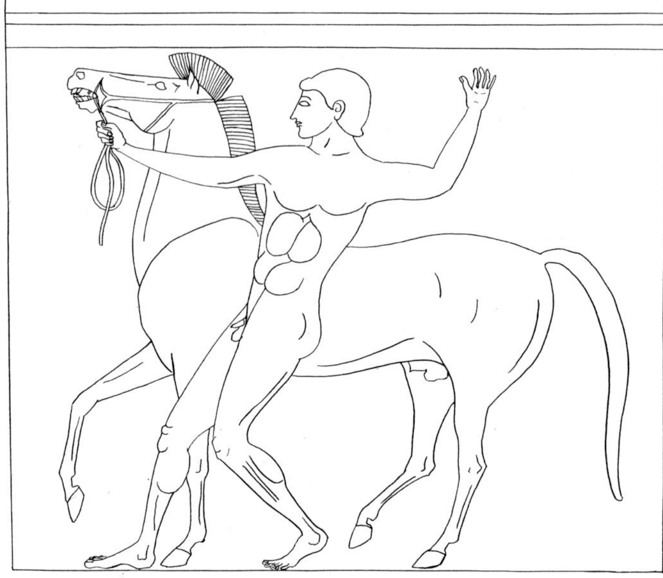

Illus. 1   Proposed reconstruction of the Cottenham Relief

shows a horseman to right on one side and a seated sphinx on the other.[86]

Thus it is among these enigmatic and varied monuments that the Cottenham relief seems most at home, for it is unlikely that the name of its dedicator and the event for which it was commissioned will ever be known. Possibly, however, the representation on the relief offers a clue and, if so, then perhaps it is not going too far to suggest that the dedicator of the Cottenham relief was a victor in a horse race.

Mary Moore
Hunter College of the
City University of New York

and Athens NM 3477 (above, note 33).

76) For metopes, cf., Kähler, *Das griechische Metopenbild* (Munich, 1949), especially pp. 28ff for a detailed discussion of the development of pictorial metopes. For simple top mouldings of metopes and the frequent lack of frames, cf., for example, those from the temple at Assos (Kähler, pl. 37), or those of the Athenian Treasury (Kähler, pls. 42-49; de la Coste-Messeliere, *Delphes*, pls. 123-137).

77) The most recent discussion of archaic votive reliefs is Berger, *Baseler Arzt-Relief,* especially, pp. 104ff. Cf., also, Hausmann, *Griechische Weihreliefs* (Berlin, 1960), pp. 10ff; Fuchs, *Skulptur der Griechen,* p. 501ff.

78) For the Pitsa pinakes, cf., Berger, *Baseler Arzt-Relief,* pp. 104f, fig. 127 and p. 184, note 262, with bibliography; also B. Philippaki, *Vases of the National Archaeological Museum of Athens* (Athens, 1973), p. 70, fig. 29.

79) For archaic votive plaques, cf., Boardman, "Painted Votive Plaques and an early Inscription from Aegina," *BSA* 49 (1954), pp. 183ff, especially pp. 186ff.

80) Above, note 77.

81) Acr. 1332 (Schrader, no. 422, pl. 176; Raubitschek, *Dedications from the Athenian Acropolis* (Cambridge, Mass., 1949), p. 75, no. 70; Beazley, *Potter and Painter in Ancient Athens (Proc. Brit. Acad.* 30 [1946], p. 22; most recently, Deyhle, *AM* 84 (1969), pp. 14f, pls. 23,2; 28; and 30,1).

82) Acr. 581 (Berger, *Baseler Arzt-Relief,* p. 108, fig. 129, pp. 109 and 184, note 270, with bibliography; Harrison, *Archaic and Archaistic Sculpture. The Athenian Agora* XI [Princeton, 1965], p. 25; Charbonneaux, *Archaic Greek Art,* fig. 263) and Acr. 120 (Schrader, no. 423, pl. 174). Cf. also, the following: Acr. 121, Athena striding to left (Schrader, no 425, fig. 350); Acr. inv. 290, 290a and 3532, Athena mounting her chariot (Schrader, no. 426, figs. 351-352).

83) Athens NM (Berger, *Baseler Arzt-Relief,* p. 104, fig. 125 and pp. 107 and 184, note 266, with bibliography).

84) Acr. 702 (Schrader, no. 430, pls. 178-179; Hausmann, *Griechische Weihreliefs,* p. 11, fig. 1).

85) Acr. inv. 191 (Schrader, no. 427, fig. 353).

86) Acr. 3702 (above, note 40).

Mosaic of A Lion Attacking a Horse

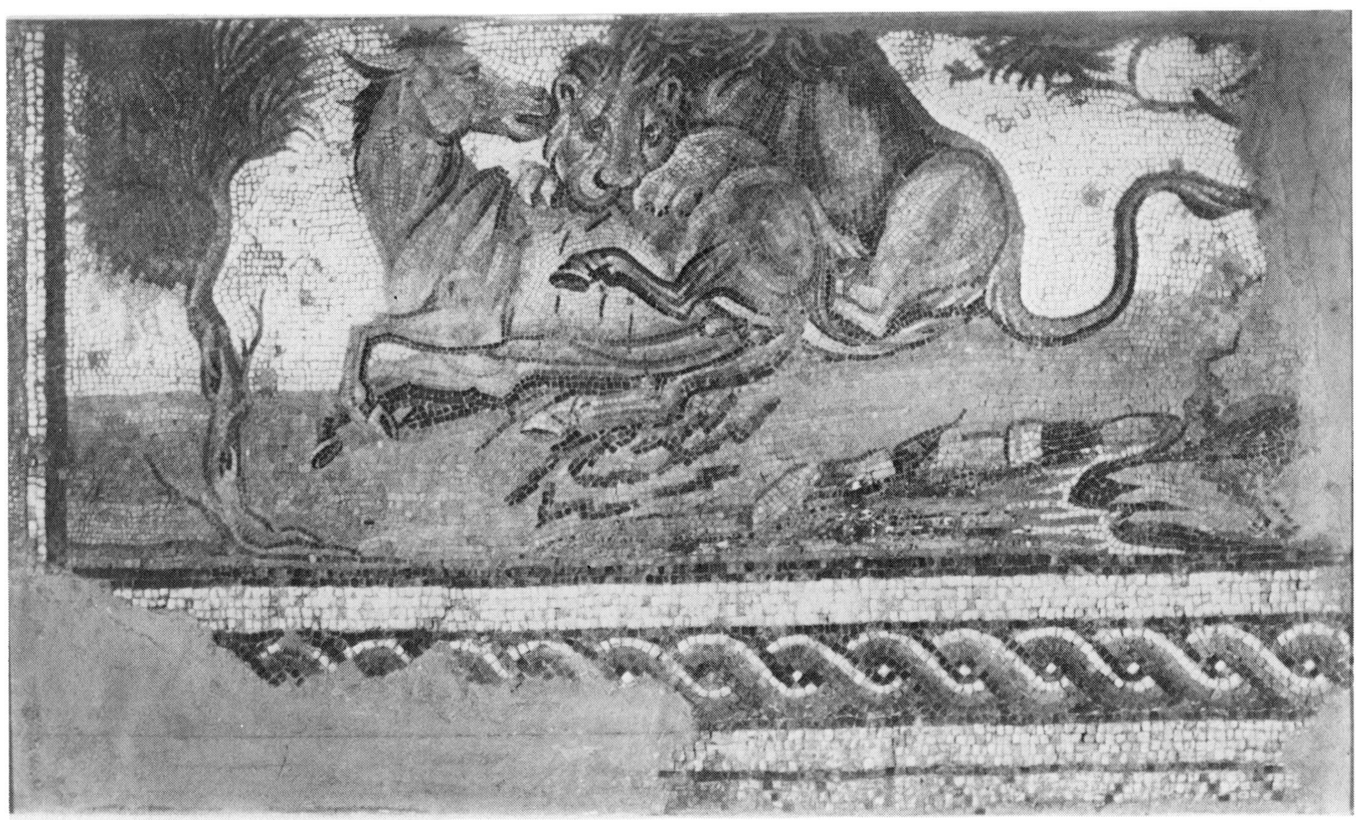

Date: c. 2nd Cent. A.D.

Dim.:   57¾" x 33¾"

This fragmentary floor mosaic shows a lion attacking a horse (J. Paul Getty Museum 73.AH.75: Fig. 1); the lion is biting the stallion on his back and blood flows on the ground. The outdoor setting is a stretch of ground with a pool, or edge of a stream, in the foreground between two trees; the background is a neutral white suggesting the sky. The naturalistic treatment is essentially pictorial as are many mosaics of the period throughout the Roman Empire, but we have no way of knowing whether it might closely follow a painted model or not. The quality of the execution is relatively good, but some parts appear to have been restored in ancient times. Only parts of the border survive on two adjoining sides, though apparently little of the composition is lacking. A black line of two rows of tesserae borders the scene; this is followed by a white band, two rows wide on the left side and four rows below. The left side then has three rows of yellow tesserae forming a band while below there can be seen a typical single polychrome guilloche. This in turn is followed by a band of white similar to that above and a single line in black above a sort of open work design. This, along with the relatively small size of the piece suggests that the mosaic may only be part of a rather larger floor containing several scenes. Although the theme of a stronger animal attacking a weaker one has a long history in Mediterranean art, this scene of a lion attacking a horse may be unique; at any rate it is certainly uncommon.

The mosaic is said to have been found at Oued Kharroub near Sousse (the Roman Hadrumetum) on the east coast of Tunisia.[1]

Norman Neuerburg
California State College, Dominguez Hills

1) *Le Bien Public,* Dijon, 19 April 1961.

Two Attic Funerary Stelai in the J. Paul Getty Museum

Among the collection of Attic funerary monuments in the J. Paul Getty Museum (Malibu, California), the two inscribed stelai published here attracted my especial interest during a visit in January, 1975.

The two stelai are very important, but for two different reasons. The first is a fine specimen of an Attic funerary tombstone. It preserves, in relief, the heads of two standing figures, and may be attributed to one of the great unknown masters who worked in Attica during the first quarter of the 4th century B.C. Its inscriptions are important for Attic prosopography. Thanks to these we learn of two more uses of a very rare Attic name; thus the stemmata of two ancient related Athenian families may be more closely connected. As for the second stele, a glance at the illustration tells immediately that its relief is the work of a mediocre ancient 'artist', who, according to his ability, worked standard subjects in relief for the market of 'ready-made' funerary monuments. This stele, however, is of great interest; it has a fake inscription, which was executed by a forger of our own times, using a dated epigraphic alphabet copied from an encyclopaedia or other reference work. Since this is the first fake Attic funerary inscription I have been able to identify in twenty-five years of work on Greek inscriptions, I can say with conviction that this is a very important documentation of the first known 'opus' of a forger who must have produced similar inscriptions for genuine antiquities in the past, and who may be planning to produce more in the future.

1. *THE STELE OF OPSIADES AND POLYSTRA[TE].*

ca. the first quarter of the fourth century B.C. *Height:* 0.37 m; *width:* 0.47 m; *depth:* 0.055 m; Pentelic marble. The total width was 73 cm at the epistyle. *Provenance:* purchased by the Museum in 1973 (73.AA.116). The back was sliced thinner to make it easier to transport.

The stele, of which only the upper part is preserved, takes the form of a shrine with Ionic pilasters, a pediment with one chipped acroterion, and epistyle. The stele's width is short by about one-third of the total. The first part of the inscription appears on the horizontal geison of the pediment, the second part is engraved on the epistyle at the extreme right of its preserved width.

Two heads belonging to the figures in the relief have been preserved in the niche. There is an impressive profile of a male bearded head, with strong features, of which only the nose is chipped. Next to it is a head of a young girl. The nose is chipped on this second head, also the lower lip and part of the chin.

The inscription engraved on the horizontal geison of the pediment has lost the first letter and part of the second; this is due to a fracture. (Height of letters: 0.012 m to 0.015 m). The *vacat* before the fracture verifies the actual size of the inscription:

.ΨΙΑΔΗΣΟΨΙΑΔΟΥΕΞΟΙΟΥ

['Ο]ψιάδης 'Οψιάδου ἐξ Οἴου.

The inscription engraved on the epistyle is obviously the name of the person for whom the stele was made. From the many parallel reliefs on Attic stelai we understand that this person was seated, facing left, and extending a hand to the standing Opsiades as a last farewell. I think it is safe to assume that this person was the wife of Opsiades (almost invariably ladies and old men were represented seated in Attic funerary reliefs). We may thus restore the missing part of the inscription (height of letters: 0.013 to 0.020 m).

ΠΟΛΥΣΤΡΑ

Πολυστρά[τη' Οψιάδου

ἐξ Οἴου γυνή]

The young lady standing between Opsiades and Polystrate must be their daughter, or another relative. Even though she is not identified by inscription, I am inclined to think that this young lady is 'Ιερόκλεια, the daughter of Opsiades and Polystrate, whom we know from another Attic grave monument (*IG* II² 7711) as being buried with her husband.[1] Her husband was Τηλέμαχος, son of Spoudocrates of Phlya (*ca.* 365 B.C.), residing in the area of Piraeus.

IG II² 7711.

Τηλέμαχος | Σπουδοκράτος | Φλυεύς.

"Ω τὸν ἀειμνήστου σ' ἀρετᾶς παρὰ πᾶσι πολίταις
5 κλεινὸν ἔπαινον ἔχοντ' ἄνδρα ποθεινοτατον
παισὶ φίλει τε γυναικί· τάφο δ' ἐπί δεξιά, μῆτερ,
κεῖμαι σῆς φιλίας οὐκ ἀπολειπόμενος.

'Ιερόκλεια | 'Οψιάδου | ἐξ Οἴου.

Telemachos/son of Spoudocrates/of Phlya. *Alas, for you, most praised among the citizens for your unforgettable virtue; man most beloved of your sons and loving wife— Just to the right of your grave, mother, my body lies to be not far from your love.*
Hierokleia/daughter of Opsiades/of Oion.

1)

'Οψιάδης (I) ἐξ Οἴου
JPGM 73.AA.116-IG I² 950
col. 1, line 34 - IG I² 579.

∞ 'Οψιάδης (II) 'Οψιάδου (I) ἐξ Οἴου
Πολυστρά[τη]　　JPGM 73.AA.116-
JPGM 73.AA.116　　IG II² 7711,
line 8.

'Ιερόκλεια 'Οψιάδου (II) ἐξ Οἴου
IG II² 7711, line 8.

Τηλέμαχος (I) Φλυεύς
IG II² 7708

Σπουδοκράτης Τηλεμάχου (I) Φλυεύς ∞
IG II² 7708, IG II² 7695　　Μελίτη
IG II² 7711, line 1.　IG II² 7695

∞ Τηλέμαχος (II) Σπουδοκράτους Φλυεύς
IG II² 7711, line 1.

-X and X-- Τηλεμάχου (II) Φλυεῖς.
IG II² 7711, line 6.

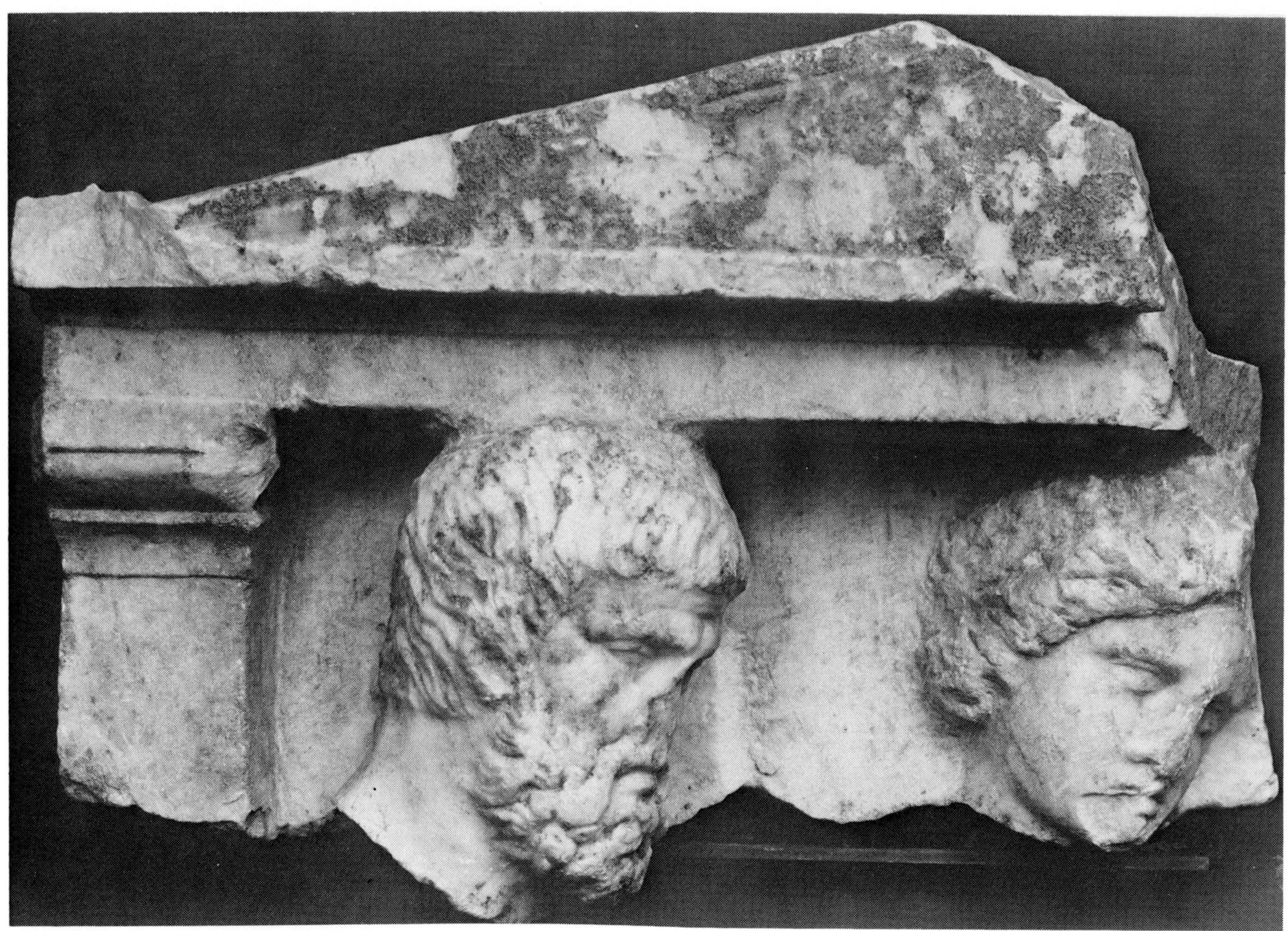

1 The stele of Opsiades and Polystrate

J. Kirchner has observed that the name of Hierokleia has been inscribed on Telemachos' funerary monument sometime after it was made. This helps us to understand that after the death of her husband Telemachos, Hierokleia stayed with her sons and her father-in-law Spoudocrates, who had already lost his wife Melite, before his son died (*IG* II² 7695). We cannot firmly say that the old man Spoudocrates survived after the death of his daughter-in-law, but we may suspect that he did because Hierokleia was buried with her husband in their family plot instead of returning to the house of Opsiades, her father, to die, as Attic law would have required. If our assumptions are correct, the death of Spoudocrates after all the other members of his family (*IG* II² 7708) ends the use of the family plot, since no grave monuments of the sons of Telemachos and Hierokleia are known.

The extreme rarity of the name of Opsiades which we know only from the epigraphical references to this Opsiades and his father in post-Eukleidean Attic inscriptions (JPGM 73. AA.116 and *IG* II² 7711), helps us to gather the prosopographical data. The stele for Opsiades' wife Polystrate can be dated between 400-375 B.C., and the funeral inscription for his daughter Hierokleia *ca.* 365 B.C.; this means that Opsiades Jr. must have been born in the last decades of the fifth century B.C. His father must have lived and died in the fifth century B.C. So it is easy to identify Opsiades Sr. as the one recorded as being among the dead in a sea-battle of the Peloponnesian war (*ca.* 412/1 B.C.? *IG* I², 950, col. I, 34), the same battle in which the famous comic poet Eupolis was killed (*IG* I² 950, col. I, 52).

Another Attic inscription (*IG* I² 579) in which an Opsiades is recorded as dedicating an offering to Athena is also easily connected with Opsiades Sr. This last document completes the prosopographical data currently available.

2. *ATTIC STELE OF A YOUNG BOY WITH MODERN INSCRIPTION. ca.* Middle of the fourth century B.C. *Height:* .62 m; *width:* .294 m (at widest

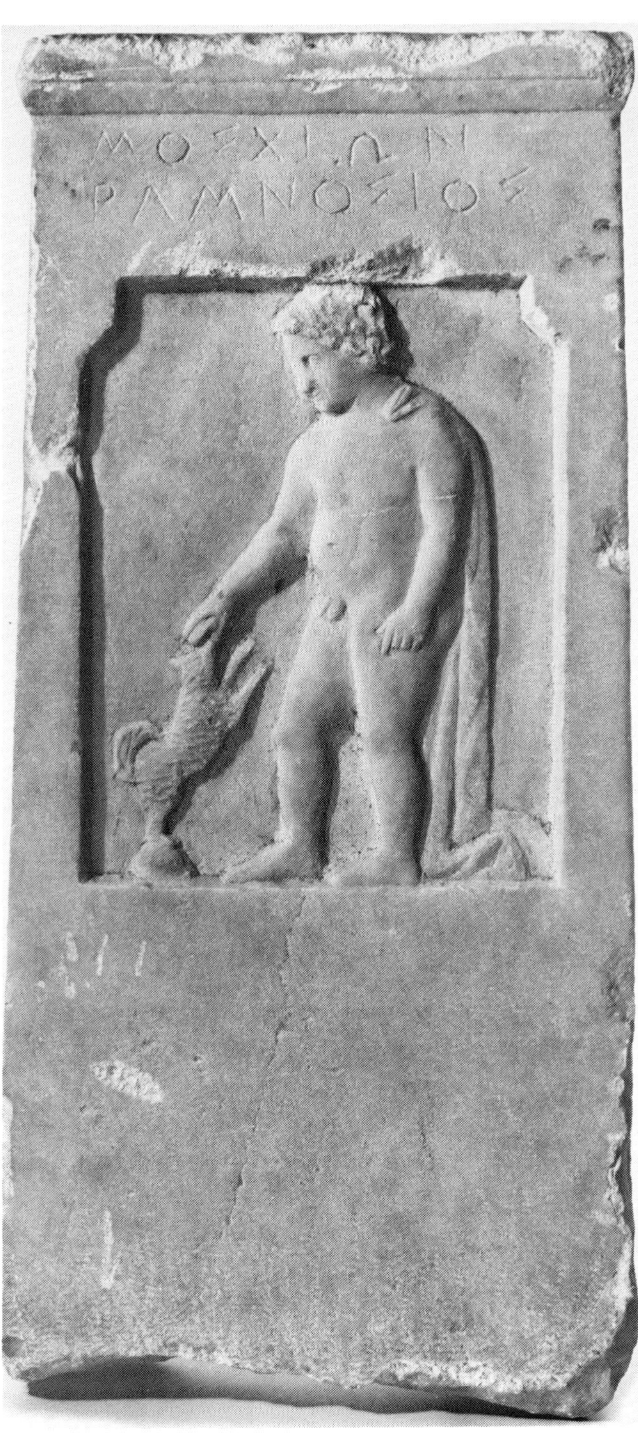

2   The stele of the alleged 'Moschion'

part); *depth:* .069 m (at widest part); Pentelic marble. *Provenance:* Purchased by the museum in 1973 (73.AA.117).

The stele belongs to the group of 'necessity artworks' produced by minor sculpture workshops in Attica in order to comply with the demand for low cost, ready made, standard subject grave stelai.

The relief depicts a young, rather plump boy, who stands nude and is petting the head of a small dog (species is obscure), which stands in front of the boy on its hind legs. The way that both the boy and the dog have been depicted by the sculptor leaves little doubt that he was an apprentice in his first years, or a simple marble-cutter attempting to transform himself into an artist. Many similar stelai have been found to date in Attica, and the fact that a great number of them are not inscribed indicates that they were probably re-used several times. The inscription with the name of the deceased was added to those stelai with paint, which undoubtedly lasted as long as was necessary for each use.

The inscription was obviously added by a twentieth century hand, its sole purpose being to give the piece greater interest for a prospective antique buyer. The forger did not do a 'rush job'. He possibly visited a museum, looked at similar stelai and their descriptions, concluded that his stele was dated 'roughly' at the fourth century B.C., and then consulted an encyclopaedia or other reference work in order to copy the form of letters from another grave stele typical of ones in the fourth century B.C. Thus far, our forger appears to have been rather clever. But he was overconfident in his ingeniousness in thinking that he knew enough to fool the 'American' or 'European' for whom this inscription was prepared.

Our forger selected an ancient name and a demotic (possibly agreeing with the area in which the stele was found), pencilled the planned inscription on the marble, and then engraved it with a chisel following his outline.

An archaeologist without special training in Attic epigraphy might be easily fooled by this forgery as there is nothing wrong with any part of the stele; only the inscription. The epigraphist, however, if he knows his inscriptions, and if he has learned to read them from stones rather than from photographs and squeezes, can see immediately that the cutting of the letters does not agree with their form or the date indicated by the relief figures and other cut surfaces of the stele. The manufacturer of this stele did not have the knowledge or talent to make a good relief, but he knew well how to cut straight lines and surfaces on stone with a sure hand. If the inscription were authentic the strokes of the letters would display the same sureness of hand and not the unsure, miserable cutting that the forger's hand produced:

ΜΟΣΧΙΩΝ   Μοσχίων
ΡΑΜΝΟΣΙΟΣ   Ραμνο(ύ)σιος.

The form of the letters imitated by the forger certainly belongs to the earliest quarter of the fourth century B.C. But the stele and its relief can by no means be dated before the middle of the fourth century B.C.; this interval of time is sufficient to prove a limited knowledge on the part of the forger. The same limited knowledge is shown by the poor layout of the inscription using a monumental alphabet. Certainly no ancient engraver using this form of letters would fail to equalize the empty spaces before the first letter and after the last in laying out the name of *MOSCHION*. If the demotic *Rhamnousios* had to be added below the name, it would have followed the same centering as adopted in the line above. This type of mistake is quite inconceivable for any craftsman of the period, even a bad one.

But the forger outdoes himself, and makes a very grotesque blunder; the Attic name is formed by the name, the patronym, and the demotic; the name and the demotic alone appear here. Why is this? It must have been that the forger was unaware of the necessity, in this particular stele's case, of using the patronym. A young boy's stele had to be provided by the family; mother, father, or other close relative. None of those persons would have omitted the patronym for the inscription, particularly if it were a young boy born of Athenian citizens, which is the main reason for the addition of the demotic.

Al. N. Oikonomides
Loyola University, Chicago

The handsome red-figure lekythos[1] shown in Figure 1 belongs to the J. Paul Getty Museum, Malibu, and was for a time generously loaned to the Ashmolean Museum, Oxford, where I was able to examine it. I am most grateful to Dr. Frel for inviting me to contribute a note on it to this volume in honour of a scholar to whom both institutions (and I myself) owe so much.

The history of the lekythos at Athens has been traced by Miss Haspels[2] from its beginnings early in the sixth century down far into the fifty. Though the subject of her magisterial study is the black-figure lekythos, she has important things to say also on early red-figure examples. There are several such from the sixth century, and one in the most primitive red-figure style and technique has appeared since she wrote,[3] but it is only in the early fifth, in the generation after the Pioneers, that the shape takes a regular place in the production of red-figure workshops, and it is to this phase that our vase clearly belongs. The first red-figure painter to decorate lekythoi in quantity is the Berlin Painter, and his name has been suggested as the painter of the Malibu pot. An alternative attribution to the Eucharides Painter, proposed by Dr. D.C. Kurtz, appears to me certainly correct; but I think, and hope to show, that the relation to the greater artist's work is closer than simply contemporaneity and a common decorative scheme. I have thought it worth going into some detail in the following pages for two reasons: first, the problem of acceptable attribution has become acute since Beazley's death; and secondly, the relation between different artists and workshops is a subject on which more work needs to be done, work for which Beazley's lists lay the foundation.

The vase[4] is all black except for the upper surface of the mouth (the mouth interior is blacked), a band of tongues at the top of the shoulder (below the vestigial ridge which sets off the neck), the single figure and the band of egg-pattern on which he stands, and the edge and underside of the foot. Underneath is a simple graffito, a large M, to which I shall return.

The picture (Fig. 2) shows a youth, fair-haired and whiskered, standing to left, right foot slightly advanced, wearing only a himation, wrapped over the left shoulder and round the elbow, the end hanging over the forearm. In his left hand he holds a lyre (shell towards us) and plectrum, high against his body, while his bare right arm is advanced, the hand resting on top of a vertical knotted stick. He is very like youths and men whom the Berlin Painter delights to draw, especially as single reverse-figures on his panathenaics or small neck-amphorae.[5] To certain specific points which also recall the painter I shall return, but the detailed renderings are not in the main his, nor it seems to me is the character of the drawing in a more general sense.

To take detail first: the deep chest, with a wide very shallow triangle at the bottom of the black central line, the top of which is joined by straight black lines for the collar-bones, is a hall-mark of the Eucharides Painter's work. The Berlin Painter's chest, though constructed from similar basic elements, is significantly different, particularly in the form of the triangle at the base and in the drawing of the collar-bones and their relation to the central line. The brown lines on breast and arm are much the same in both painters; the two on the upper arm vary a good deal in the Eucharides Painter's work, but often approximate, sometimes even more closely than they do here, to the addorsed arcs regular in the Berlin Painter's.[6] For the youth's right hand one may compare the goddess's raised one (right drawn there for left as happens curiously often) on the Eucharides Painter's London neck-amphora with the death of Tityos; for his left, closed with protruding thumb, a warrior's on a stamnos by the same painter in Würzburg.[7] The outlining of the whole face (and virtually the whole figure) with relief-contour would be very unusual in the Berlin Painter's work, but is the rule with the Eucharides Painter; and the forms of the features, especially the narrowness of eye and chin, seem to me his.[8] The drawing of the ear is exceedingly summary, but in its broad proportion it resembles those of the Eucharides Painter, and it is almost exactly paralleled on the only lekythos ascribed by Beazley to this painter (apart from an unpublished fragment), that in the Ashmolean with Triptole-

---

1) J. Paul Getty Museum 73.AE.23. Details in n.4.

2) C.H.E.Haspels, *Attic Black-figured Lekythoi,* Paris, 1936.

3) Oxford 1949.751; *ARV²* 9, bottom no.1, with refs.

4) H. 0.34. No groove at top of foot; the slight 'stalk' at junction of foot and body not clearly defined as a fillet. Made up from fragments but complete. Some lines broken by cracks or scratches, but virtually nothing missing and no restoration. Glaze discoloured (thin and greenish) in area from mouth to base between handle and back of figure. Relief-contour: lower border of tongue-pattern on shoulder (the upper is formed by the very slight ridge setting off the neck); upper, lower and left-hand border of pattern-band below figure; whole of figure (including stick and lyre) except hair, lower lip and lower himation-weight. Thinned glaze: hair, whisker, lines on neck, chest and right arm, rim of lyre-shell. Re: wreath, plectrum and string.

5) See below, n.10.

6) Eucharides Painter's style: Beazley in *BSA* 18 (1911/12) 217-33 with figs. 1-5 and pls. 10-15. Berlin Painter's style: Beazley in *JHS* 31 (1911) 276-95 with figs. 1-9 and pls. 8-17. Further references to both in following notes.

7) Hand on British Museum neck-amphora (E 278): *BSA* l.c. pl. 14; *ARV²* 226 no. 2 with other references; on Würzburg stamnos (516): *BSA* l.c. pl. 15 above; *ARV²* 229 no. 36 with other references. Two left or two right hands: see *JHS* 74 (1954) 229f.

8) Relief-contour, especially for faces, differing practice of Eucharides Painter and Berlin Painter: Beazley in *BSA* l.c. 230, *JHS* l.c. 288 bottom.

mus standing by his winged car,[9] one of the painter's most attractive works (of which there will be more to say). For figures clothed and posed like this one, the Berlin Painter has a very distinctive treatment of the folds across the legs, noted by Beazley in 'Citharoedus' where he illustrates a large number of them.[10] The long, sweeping folds from the back do not reach the front contour of the advanced leg, and they alternate with shorter folds coming in from that edge. This rendering gives a plasticity and life to the garment which should check any tendency one may have to think of the painter as only a master of calligraphic contour and line. It is something found, so far as I know, in no other painter's work; our vase shows the common practice—the long folds brought right across. The Eucharides Painter has not many figures of quite this kind, but good parallels are given by a bearded man pouring a libation at an altar on the interior of a cup in the Fondazione Lerici at Rome, and by the youth on the front of Staehler's pelike.[11] The simple lyre is not very common in the Eucharides Painter's work, and when he draws it, it is generally shown from the other side. The shell is seen on a cup in Frankfurt, but an arm crosses it and the indication of markings is summary in the extreme. The careful but schematic rendering on the lekythos is very different from the Berlin Painter's on the panathenaic in Naples.[12]

To explain what I mean about the character of the drawing, I cannot do better than quote Beazley on two other painters: "The two boys…are from different cups…How admirable the drawing in both! only, the Brygan boy is made like us out of flesh and air: the other is a most captivating marionette."[13] I believe, however, that the Eucharides Painter had been looking at the Berlin Painter's work and wished to emulate it. I have said that this is a favourite type of figure with the Berlin Painter, rare in the other's *oeuvre;* and this figure, and the other two by the Eucharides Painter I have quoted share with those of the Berlin Painter the drawing of the front contour of the rear leg as though seen through the garment. To show this line, and not the back contour of either leg, is not uncommon in the Berlin Painter's work as a means of articulating clothed figures of either sex in various forms of dress,[14] but I cannot find it used in any other figure by the Eucharides Painter. Then, the boy on the lekythos is fair—that is, his hair is rendered in thinned glaze. I know only one other example in the Eucharides Painter's work: Triptolemus on the lekythos in Oxford.[15] The Berlin Painter loves a golden head: the Louvre Ganymede, the boy Achilles brought to Cheiron on a stamnos in the same collection, the baby Herakles strangling the snakes on another, the Boulogne Eros, Dionysus on a neck-amphora and a music-making silen on a panathenaic, both in Munich, Apollo on the Vatican hydria and the London volute-krater, Thetis there, the New York citharode,[16] a boy pouring a libation at an altar on a charming little oenochoe.[17] Other artists show the same usage, but none this strong predilection. Among those who sometimes use it is the Harrow Painter. Of a pair of charming oenochoai with boys, one blond, for which he later accepted, surely rightly, an attribution to this painter, Beazley first wrote: "The drawing is extremely close to the Berlin Painter himself, and has much of his χάρις. These are not mere imitations of the Berlin Painter's style, but careful copies of two vases by the Berlin Painter himself."[18] It is my impression that the Harrow Painter often looked directly to the Berlin Painter's work for models, as the Troilos Painter did to that of the Kleophrades Painter. The Eucharides Painter is a better and more independent artist than these, but it seems to me that when he came

9) 315; *ARV²* 227 no. 47 with references; *CV* 1 pl. 33, 1.
10) *JHS* 42 (1922), remarks on pp. 75ff, with figs. 2, 4-8, and pls. 2 right, 3 right, the corresponding figure in fig. 3 is repainted (pp. 75f.).
11) Lerici cup: *Paral.* 348 no. 88. Pelike in Münster: K.P. Staehler *Eine unbekannte Pelike des Eucharidesmalers,* Köln etc., 1967. Staehler's attribution of the pelike is surely right, but I cannot agree with his vigorous dismantling of the majority of the painter's *oeuvre* put together by Beazley; see *Gnomon* 41 (1969) 318f. A similar figure, partly concealed, on a stamnos in the Louvre: *ARV²* 228 no. 32; *Miscellanea Libertini* (Florence, 1958) pl. 2 right.
12) Eucharides Painter's Frankfort cup: *Paral.* 348 no. 89. Berlin Painter's Naples panathenaic: Beazley *Berliner Maler* pls. 10 and 12,4; *ARV²* 198 no. 18 with other references. For the black lines on the lyre-arms see Ashmole in *Bull.MFA* 66 (1968) 154.
13) *Attic Red-figured Vases in American Museums* 93. The other picture is by the Foundry Painter.
14) E.g. Gorgon on Panathenaic in Munich, *Berliner Maler* pl. 9,1, *ARV²* 197 no. 11 with other references; Athena on panathenaic in Vatican, *Berliner Maler* pl. 11, *ARV²* 197 no. 5 with other references; Nike on panathenaic in Philadelphia, *Mus.J.* 23 (1932) 28 fig. 6, *ARV²* 198 no. 15; Athena, Apollo, Thetis and Eos on volute-krater in British

Museum, *Berliner Maler* pls. 29-31. *ARV²* 206 no. 132 with other references; Athena on stamnos in Munich, *CV* pl. 228,1, *ARV²* 207 no. 137 with other references; maenads on stamnos in Oxford, *JHS* 31 (1911) pl. 17, *CV* pl. 25, 1-2, *ARV²* 208 no. 144 with other references; Europa on hydria in Oxford, *Berliner Maler* pl. 23,2, *CV* pl. 61,4, *ARV²* 210 no. 157; Polyxena on hydria in Leningrad, *Berliner Maler* pl. 24,1, *ARV²* 210 no. 174 with other references.
15) Above, n.9.
16) *ARV²* 196ff., nos. 124, 140, 160, 48, 21bis (p. 1700), 9, 166, 132, 3 with references and cf. *Berliner Maler* pls. 6, 16, 21, 21, 25f., 29ff. In all these, and in the jug in next note, fairness is indicated by thinned glaze; a different method on the Berlin amphora (*Berliner Maler* pls. 1-3 and 22,2; *ARV²* 196 no. 1 with other references).
17) *ARV²* 1635 no. 185bis; *Aukt. xxii Basel* pls. 49 and 56, 164. Another possible blonde: see *Paral.* 343 no. 172.
18) *ARV²* 1635f.; cf. ibid. 1705 bottom, where they are added to the Harrow Painter's list as nos. 78bis and ter. The boy on the Harrow Painter's name-vase (*ARV²* 276 no. 76 with references) is fair; and so is a Nereid on the hydria Louvre G 178, *CV* pl. 54.2, 5 and 7, *ARV²* 218 top no. 3, where it is classed as an imitation of the Berlin Painter, with the gloss "Some details recall the Harrow Painter".

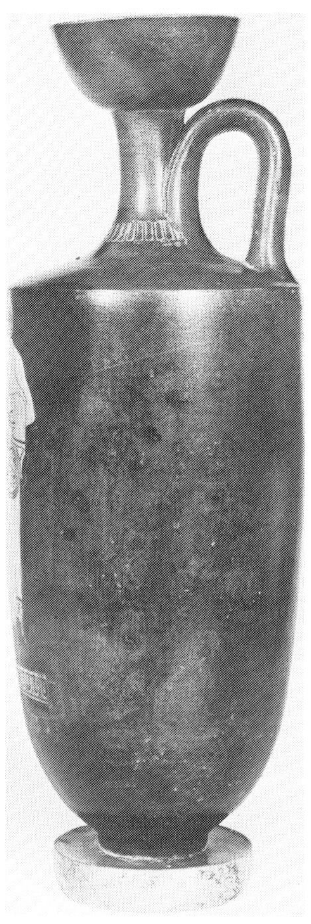

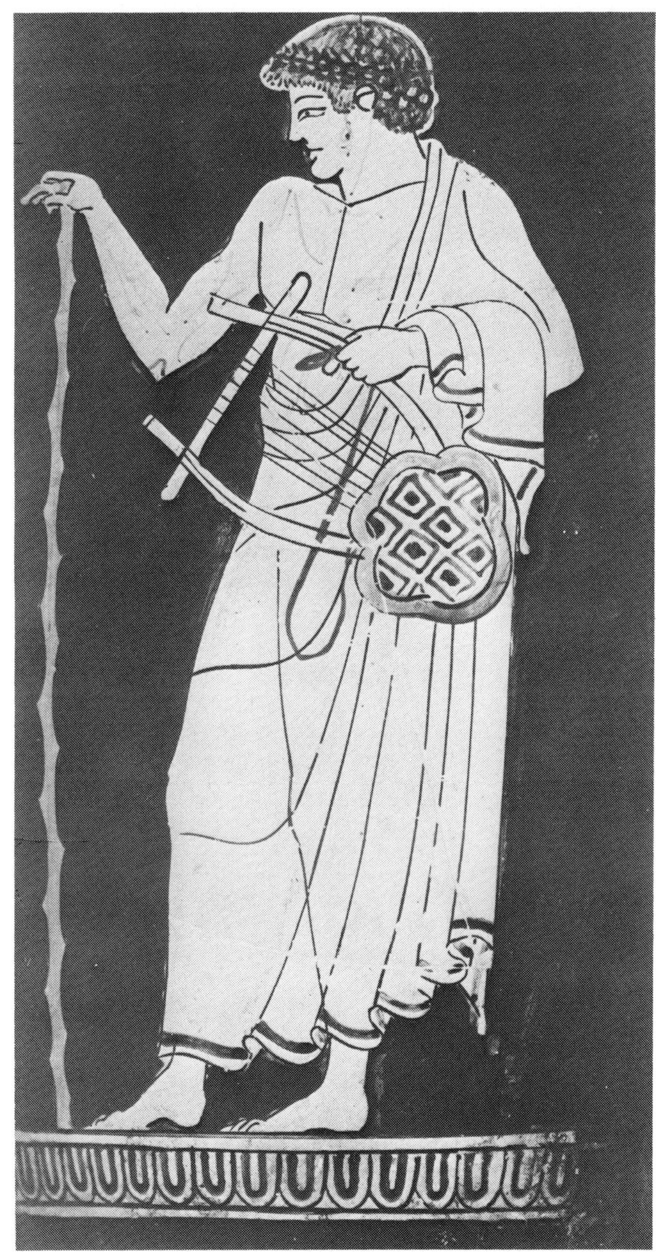

to paint a lekythos, he deliberately and directly took something from the greater artist who was popularizing the shape as a vehicle for red-figure.

The absence of a groove at the top of the foot is perhaps an early sign; at least a good many early vases are without it, while later it becomes invariable in careful work. A clearly defined fillet between foot and body is regular in careful vases, even early ones. The Eucharides Painter's Triptolemus vase has it, and in our vase it is perhaps carelessly slurred rather than deliberately omitted. Of the Oxford lekythos Beazley writes that it has "tongues on the shoulder instead of the commoner egg-pattern."[19] So has the Malibu vase, and the incidence of this usage is possibly of interest. On a rough spot-check I find that among lekythoi ascribed to the Berlin Painter in his early period, three have tongues and seven egg-pattern; on two this area is lost, and three more I have not seen. In his later period egg-pattern is regular and I have not found any tongues among those I have been able to check. Of nine lekythoi ascribed to his close imitator the Tithonos Painter, I have seen tongues on three and egg-pattern on two; and I have noticed one example each of tongues in the work of his pupils the Providence Painter and Hermonax. Tongues occur in this position on a number of other lekythoi, all

1   (above left) Red-figure lekythos, J. Paul Getty Museum 73.AE.23

2   (above) Detail of same

those I have noted rather early. They include the only vase of this shape ascribed to the Kleophrades Painter (and this has another feature, to be discussed in a moment, that relates it to the Malibu piece), and all those I have checked by the cup-painter Douris; the Brygos Painter, on the other hand, regularly uses egg-pattern.[20] I have an impression of the Berlin Painter initiating experiments in the design of a red-figure lekythos, including the pattern most appropriate to the shoulder-top, other painters imitating him, and the egg-pattern finally winning acceptance in his own work and others as the norm for this position. Of a particular design of stopped maeander, Beazley writes: "This principle of pattern is almost confined to the Berlin Painter, his followers, and to painters who are not his followers, but for the nonce, in certain kinds of vase, are working in his tradition."[21] The last phrase seems to me applicable to many painters of red-figure lekythoi in this period.

Egg-pattern does indeed occur, both on the Oxford and on the Malibu lekythos, but in different positions, both exceptional: above the picture of Triptolemus, below that of the boy with the lyre. This pattern is common throughout red-figure, but in the archaic period it is normal only (with certain exceptions to be noted in a moment) in 'architectural' positions: to decorate a moulding (as the lips of stamnoi or hydriai), or to mark a junction of parts sharply set off from each other (shoulder from neck, handle from body). On the Triptolemus vase, though the choice is unusual, the painter follows this rule; as often with the forms of maeander found in this position on lekythoi by the Berlin Painter and others, the pattern circles the vase, emphasizing the edge of the shoulder, and is not simply related to the figure as the short pattern-band below is. On the vase in Malibu the shoulder below the tongues is black and there is no pattern-band to mark the junction at the top of the body (another scheme common in the early lekythoi of the Berlin Painter and his circle); but the egg-pattern is chosen for the short band under the figure, which marks no junction. Such a usage is never to my knowledge found elsewhere in the Eucharides Painter's work or in the Berlin Painter's. The Kleophrades Painter is fond of a special, careful, squared form of egg-pattern, and this he does use in positions which are not 'architectural'. He in fact places it in this very position on the one lekythos ascribed to him, already noticed as having tongues on the shoulder.[22] He sets it similarly under the pictures of Theseus on his London stamnos,[23] but regularly employs it only in one position: enclosed by other pattern-bands under the framed pictures on the shoulders of kalpis-hydriai.

Similar forms of the pattern are used in the same position on earlier hydriai by several of the Pioneers, which form a single, coherent series with the Kleophrades Painter's.[24] This is the only case in which I know any form of egg-pattern to be regularly used outside the 'architectural' positions at this period. The Pan Painter, however, employs the ordinary form above, and sometimes below, the pictures on his little pelikai;[25] and in later red-figure it becomes common in such positions on many shapes, the 'architectural' limitation forgotten. The heavy, squared form is found twice in the Berlin Painter's work, both times at junctions,[26] but one could imagine him experimenting with it in this position on a lekythos. On the two lekythoi of the Eucharides Painter the form is the ordinary one, drawn carefully and rather large.

I mentioned a graffito, a large M, under the foot of the Malibu lekythos. Alan Johnston informs me that there is an analogous graffito under the foot of a black-figure hydria from Cumae in Naples ascribed to the Eucharides Painter;[27] and points out another, slightly more complex, on a red-figure lekythos in the Embiricos collection.[28] This has a foot without groove, fillet at the junction of the foot and body, black body with a form of maeander-band at the junction of the shoulder, and on the shoulder tongues and a sphinx. Of this vase Beazley wrote: "The pattern-band derives from the Berlin Painter, but he does not come in question for the drawing." I would not ascribe this piece with any confidence to the Eucharides Painter. There are no sphinxes among the works given to him, and the scale is smaller than that of most of his work. The profile, however, particularly the chin, is not unlike his, and I think it not impossible that he is the author. In any case it fits well into the general picture we have formed of artists in this period who, when they paint a red-figure lekythos, turn to the Berlin Painter.

Martin Robertson
Ashmolean Museum

---

19) *CV* Oxford L pl. 33,1.
20) Tongues: Berlin Painter, *ARV²* 211 nos. 188,196, *Paral.* 345 no. 194ter; Tithonos Painter, *ARV²* 309f. nos. 10, 12, 15; Providence Painter, *ARV²* 640 no. 67; Hermonax, *ARV²* 490 no. 119; Kleophrades Painter, *ARV* 189 no. 78, *Op.Ath.* 2 (1965) pl. 4, 13-14; Douris, *ARV²* 446f., nos. 267, 270, 272, 273; another, *ARV²* 1644 to p. 308.
21) *Berlin Painter* Melbourne, 1964, 7.
22) Above, n.20.
23) *ARV²* 187 no. 57 with references.
24) *ARV²* 34, note to nos. 13-13. A large number of the hydriai classed together there have this feature, including examples by Euphronios,

Euthymides, Hypsis, the Kleophrades Painter and others.
25) *ARV²* 555 nos. 88-93; cf. *Panmaler* pl. 23. One with the pattern below the picture: *ARV²* 1650 no. 93bis and *Paral.* 387; *Aukt. xxvi Basel* pl. 49, 137.
26) *ARV²* 205 no. 114bis, neck-pelike from Spina with lion and lioness, square egg-pattern at top of shoulder (the published replica, no. 114, has tongues in this position); no. 116, calyx-krater fr. from Corinth, *Hesp.* 35 pl. 136,f, square egg-pattern at top of *cul.*
27) Naples RC 192, *ABV* 397 no. 35, the ascription a little doubtful in tone.
28) Not in *ARV²* or *Paral.*; *Aukt. xxvi Basel* no. 134 (Beazley's letter quoted), pl. 47.

Zu Zwei Sarkophagplatten im J. Paul Getty Museum

Das J. Paul Getty Museum in Malibu konnte in letzter Zeit einen römischen Sarkophag sowie zwei Vorderseiten von Sarkophagen derselben Epoche erwerben. Alle drei Stücke sind von besonderem Interesse. Im folgenden sollen zunächst die beiden Platten vorgestellt werden, während das dritte Monument in einer eigenen Abhandlung untersucht werden soll[1].

Das erste hier zu behandelnde Denkmal, Inv. 72.AA.158 (Abb. 1)[2] stammt von einem stadtrömischen Guirlandensarkophag. In der Renaissance wurde der Kasten, von dem die Platte stammt—einem damals verbreiteten Brauch folgend—als Brunnen verwandt. Dabei wurden an mehreren Stellen Metallröhren durch die Sarkophagwand gelegt, was zu störenden Entstellungen führte. Dies gilt vor allem für die Zerstörung der Augen der Herme in der Mitte des Frieses[3]. Rechts von ihr war eine grosse runde Öffnung, durch die das Wasser rasch abfliessen konnte. Sie wurde mit einem Marmostück geschlossen, das jetzt wieder herausgenommen ist.

Die zwei Putten und die Herme tragen eine reiche Guirlande aus Lorbeerblättern, in deren Mitte jeweils eine Blüte angebracht ist. Über dem linken Blütenstern erscheint die frontale Maske eines Panthers. Die beiden in Ausfallstellung gegebenen Eroten an den Ecken der Platte halten die Enden der Guirlanden mit über ihre Schulter hinter den Kopf geführten Händen, wobei der linke Arm des linken Eros und der rechte des rechten durch die Guirlande verdeckt sind. Der Hermeros in der Mitte hat beide Arme angehoben und hält in der Linken das Ende einer um die Guirlande gelegten Binde. Mit seinen Schultern stützt er das Verbindungsstück der zwei Guirlanden. Weitere Tänien flattern von den anderen Manschetten der Guirlande herab. In den Schwüngen der Guirlanden sind je zwei antithetisch angeordnete dionysische Masken zu sehen, links zwei mit Weinlaub bekränzte Mänaden, rechts Pan und Silen. Bockshörner und Bocksohr kennzeichnen den bärtigen Gott, Pferdeohren den Satyr. Die Zusammenstellung von Masken des Pan und eines Silens findet sich auch auf anderen Sarkophagen[4]. Sarkophage mit guirlandentragenden Eroten setzen—nach einigen Vorläufern aus flavischer Zeit—in der Spätphase trajanischer Kunst ein[5], um dann recht beliebt zu werden. F. Matz hat die dabei vorkommenden Typen der Eroten in 7 Gruppen zu teilen versucht. Die Eroten unserer Platte gehören zu der 5. der von ihm geschiedenen Gruppen: Eros in Ausfallstellung[6].

Sehr häufig sind in den Schwüngen der Guirlanden der hier zu vergleichenden Sarkophage Masken angebracht, ein Motiv, das, wie so viele andere, aus dem Repertoire der Grabaltäre und Aschenurnen in die Bildwelt der Sarkophage übernommen wurde[7]. Dabei sind die Masken auf den stadtrömischen Sarkophagen in der Regel im Profil dargestellt, während sie auf östlichen—analog den dort besonders verbreiteten Medusenhäuptern—meistens in Vorderansicht erscheinen (Abb. 2)[8]. In dieser Form finden wir sie auf stadtrömischen Sarkophagen, vor allem unter den Clipei[9], aber auch auf Nebenseiten von Sarkophagen[10]. Ebenso ausgerichtet sind sowohl auf römischen als auf östlichen Sarkophagen auch die Bildnisbüsten in den Bögen der Guirlanden[11]. Der bekannte horror vacui auf stadtrömischen Sarkophagen führte dazu, dass die Masken, anders als im Osten, in den Guirlandenbögen häufig in

---

1) Vgl. vorläufig Recent acquisitions. Ancient Art. The J. Paul Getty Museum 1974, Nr. 13.

2) Sotheby 4.12.72,120 Taf. 19. Aus Slg. Lansdowne. A. Michaelis, Ancient marbles in Great Britain (1882) 362,80. H. 47,5,L. 196 cm. Aus Fragmenten zusammengesetztes Stück über den re. Masken mit Teil des Pan weggebrochen.

3) Weitere Stellen, an denen Röhren sassen: Penis der Eroten, Mund aller 4 Masken und des Eros rechts.

4) Michaelis a.O. und andere (z.B. H. Jucker, Das Bildnis im Blätterkelch 37 zu Taf. 7, Museo Torlonia) sprechen von 2 Satyrn.

5) J. Toynbee, The Hadrianic school (1934) 202 ff. mit älterer Lit. F. Matz, Ein römisches Meisterwerk (1958) 48 ff. G. Hanfmann, The season sarcophagus at Dumbarton Oaks II Nr. 290 ff. H. Wiegartz, Kleinasiatische Säulensarkophage (1965) 41.44. Ders., Festschr. Mansel I 373 für Vorläufer des 1. Jhs. M. Honroth, Stadtrömische Guirlanden (1971) passim. H. Gabelmann, Die Werkstattgruppen der oberitalischen Sarkophage (1971) 128 f. N. Himmelmann, Sarkophage in Antalya (1970) passim. Mansel-Akarca, Excavations and researches at Perge (1949) 49 ff.

6) a.O. 50.Die Typenscheidung von Matz berücksichtigt m.E. nicht alle Motive und ist nicht in allen Punkten klar. Dies liegt z.T. daran, dass die Motive nicht immer so streng sich scheiden sind wie Matz meinte und es bei Einteilungen dieser Art stets allerlei Übergangsformen gibt.

7) Toynbee a.O. Taf. 43 ff. Hanfmann a.O. Nr. 200 ff. Vgl. die Grabara Inst.Neg. 71.751, Mazara d. Valle, Dom (nach Gips).

8) Abb. 2 Ephesos, hier nach Inst.Neg. Rom 71.830 mit freundlicher Erlaubnis von R. Vetters: Bammer-Fleischer-Knibbe, Führer durch das Museum in Selçuk-Ephesos (1974) Taf. 27. Vgl. weiter u.a.: Lehmann, Hartleben-Olsen, Dionysiac sarcophagi in Baltimore (1942) Abb. 26, Boston, Gardner Museum. Auf dem Sarkophag ebenda Abb. 19 f., Baltimore, werden die Masken von Porträtbüsten bzw. Medusenköpfen gerahmt. Auf dem östlichen Sarkophag Festschrift W. Blavatski (1966) 25 Abb. 1 (von der Chersonnes) sind 2 Guirlandenbögen mit je 2 sich anschauenden Masken angebracht. Zur Zahl der Guirlandenbögen auf östlichen und westlichen Sarkophagen s. hier S. 64 und Anm. 34.

9) Z.B.: G. Pesce, Sarcofagi Romani di Sardegna (1957) Taf. 48 f., Cagliari. Für andere Möglichkeiten der Aufstellung von Masken unter Clipei s. hier Anm. 17. Der östliche Sarkophag Wiegartz a.O. Taf. 14,1, Smyrna, zeigt eine frontale Maske unter der mittleren Guirlande.

10) Z.B.: Robert, SR. III Nr. 425, New York. So auch auf Wannen: Inst.Neg. 65.1341 f., Badia di Cava.

11) Z.B.: Matz a.O. Taf. 8a, Clieveden. Toynbee a.O. Taf. 48,2, Neapel.Inst.Neg. 65.1339-43, Badia di Cava. Östlich etwa: Festschrift Mansel (1974) Abb. 23a, Rom, Casino Rospigliosi. Antalya (3 tragische Masken, 2 Niken u. 2 Eroten, frei im Raum stehend). H. Wiegartz, Kleinasiatische Säulensarkophage Taf. 9d, Afyon. Giuliano, RIA, 8,1959,194 Abb. 38, Smyrna. Vgl. auch den in Anm. 8 erwähnten Sarkophag in Baltimore. Die Eckfiguren sind im Osten meist Niken.

der Zweizahl erscheinen[12]. Sie können—wie bei dem Sarkophag Genf 19024—sowohl antithetisch (Abb. 3)[13] als in meist nur leichter Überschneidung und vorwiegend mit Blick nach der Sarkophagmitte angeordnet werden (Abb. 4.5)[14]. Sind die Masken antithetisch dargestellt, ist mitunter je eine von ihnen mehr oder minder stark nach vorn gerichtet[15]. Ungewöhnlich ist in diesem Punkt ein auch sonst eigenartiger Sarkophag in Warschau[16], auf dem die Masken sich am Hinterkopf überschneiden, also nach aussen blicken, wie wir dies sonst von Masken, die unter Clipei gesetzt sind, kennen (Abb. 6)[17]. Der möglicherweise in Ägypten entstandene Sarkophag gehört allerdings nicht eigentlich zu unserer Gruppe, da die Guirlanden nicht von Eroten gehalten werden. Schmücken drei Guirlanden die Sarkophagfront, was in stadtrömischen Werkstätten nicht übermässig häufig vorkommt, sind mitunter nur in die äusseren Bögen

Masken gesetzt, in das mittlere Feld dagegen ganze Figuren[18]. Gibt es somit für die Anordnung der Masken in den Bögen allerlei Variationen, gilt dies auch für das Mittelmotiv des Kastens selbst. Nicht immer erscheinen in der Mitte ein einfacher Eros. So sind etwa auf einem Sarkophag im Museum Torlonia und einem Fragment in Treviso die zwei Guirlandenbögen gewissermassen verselbstständigt, so dass jede Guirlande durch zwei Eroten getragen wird, zwischen die eine Porträtbüste uber Akanthoskelch gesetzt ist.[19]. Auf einem Kasten in S. Paolo in Rom tragen zwei Fackeln, die die aus einem Blütenkelch sich erhebende Büste rahmen, die Guirlanden (Abb. 7)[20]. In den Zwickeln der Guirlanden erscheint hier jeweils nur eine Maske. Auf einem Sarkophag im Louvre stützen die inneren Eroten nicht nur die Guirlanden, sondern zugleich einen Schild mit Büste[21]. Auf einer Platte der Villa Albani rahmen die

12) Als Beispiel für die Zweizahl im Osten vgl. den in Anm. 8 zitierten Sarkophag aus der Chersonnes. Natürlich kennt man auch im Westen die einzelne Maske im Profil, vgl. etwa G. Calza, La necropoli del Porto di Roma nell'isola sacra (1940) 192 Abb. 96 u. Vatikan 9879 mit ehemals 4 Schwüngen (ex Lateran). Vatikan 9255 (Gall.Lapid.). Vgl. auch hier Abb. 7.
13) Hier nach einer N. Dunant verdankten Aufnahme. Deonna, Genava 28,1950, 3.Ders., Musées suisses 5/6,1949,123 ff. Der Sarkophag diente bis 1949, wie unser Sarkophag in Malibu, als Brunnen.— Sichtermann, AA. 1970,226 Abb. 18, Vatikan. Sotheby 13,6.70.169. Poulsen, Ny Carlsberg Glyptotek, La sculpture, Ancient sculpture Nr. 788 a. C. Vermeule, The Dal Pozzo-Albani drawings I (1960) Nr. 94 Abb. 39. 124 Abb. 45. Inst.Neg. 8173, Frgt. der Villa Doria Pamfili. Dasselbe Schema bei Viktorien mit Guirlanden (z.B. in Rom, Villa Borghese, Garten, sowie 69.324, V. Doria Pamfili) und Satyrn (z.B. Inst.Neg. 73.1620, Villa Wolkonsky). Vereinzelt erscheinen die Masken nur in den äusseren zwei von insgesamt drei Schwüngen: Matz. SR. IV 1 Nr. 27, Neapel. (Frgt.). Fur diesen Typus im Osten s. Anm. 8 Ende.
14) Hanfmann a.O. I 20.232 f. II 170.394. S. Aurigemma. Le Terme di Diocleziano e il museo nazionale Romano[4] (1958) Nr. 404. Inst.Neg. 63.847-50, hiernach unsere Abb. 4. Abb. 5, Vatikan, nach Inst.Neg. 72.598: Amelung I Taf. 26,150. Hier überschneiden sich die Masken stark.—Alinari 29335, Pieve di S. Giuliano e Settimo. Auf dem Sarkophag Inst. Neg. 69.2771, S. Quattro Coronati, sehen alle 4 Masken nach rechts.
15) Z.B. Sichtermann a.O. 219 Abb. 8, Rom, S. Maria Antiqua. Vatikan 10060 u. 10064, Frgte. Helbig, Führer[4] Nr. 2131, Thermenmuseum. Charbonneaux, La sculpture grecque et romaine au musée du Louvre (1963) 220,451. Vgl. den in Anm. 12 genannten Sarkophag in Ostia. Dies Schema findet sich auch auf Sarkophagdeckeln: Forma Italiae I 4, Tellennae, 98 f. Abb. 220 ff., Casale di S.Giacinta (nur in einem von ehemals 4 Schwüngen 2 Masken).
16) Schauenburg, AA, 1975.
17) Abb. 6, Genua, Museum, hier nach Inst.Neg. 68.1416 (Dufour, Sarcophages romains à Genova Taf. 11.—Inst.Neg. 59.689, Rom, S. Paolo (Gegenstück dazu mit Elefanten über Panther an den Ecken vor kurzem im Kunsthandel). Pesce a.O. Taf. 44 f., Cagliari. Reinach, RR. III 210,3 und 211,2, Capitolinische Museen. Mustilli, Museo Mussolini Taf. 58,232 u. 233. Jones, Pal d. Conservatori Taf. 26 unten. V. Tusa, Sarcofaghi Romani in Sicilia (1957) Nr. 5, Agrigent. Michaelis a.O. (oben Anm. 1) 692,11, Wilton House. Inst.Neg. 59.15, Thermenmuseum 124709. Inst.Neg. 68.1416, Genua, Museum. Inst.Neg.61-109-112, Rom, Via Giulia 16. Inst.Neg. 68.1219, Rom, Via di Ripetta 246. Vatikan 5375, Frgte. Inst.Neg. 65, 163, Rom Palazzo Sacchetti. Inst.

Neg. 33. 956, ehemals Rom Pal. Merolli. Ostia 1154, Frgt. Mitunter werden 2 von 3 Masken unter einem Clipeus nach aussen gewandt, während die mittlere frontal gestellt ist: Scrinari, Bd'A. 55,1972, 65 ff. Abb. 1, Thermenmuseum. Die drei Masken des Sarkophags Pesce a.O. Nr. 29, Cagliari sind fast frontal ausgerichtet. Wieder andere Ordnung auf dem Sarkophag H. Jucker, Das Bildnis im Blätterkelch Taf. 10 S. 15, Pisa u. einem anderen in Camaiore Pieve (bei Lucca) Inst.Neg. 74.871, mit Niken, Jahreszeiten (nur 2 Masken). Zwei antithetische Masken um Gefäss auf dem Sarkophag Benevent 616, Inst. Neg. 68.406.
18) So auf dem Frgt. Matz, SR. IV 1 Nr. 27, Neapel.
19) Jucker a.O. Taf. 7,9. Ebenda Taf. 11,20, Saloniki, Das Frgt. in Treviso ist erwähnt in Städel-Jahrbuch 1,1967.50. An Akanthosbüsten auf Sarkophagen kommen zu den bisher bekannten u.a.: Ostia 10128, Frgt. BulAntBesch. 48,1973,124 ff. Abb. 1, Frgt. in Amsterdam. Inst. Neg. 73.1618, der Villa Wolkonsky. Saloniki 5697, Ehepaar. Frgt. im grossen Chiostro des Thermenmuseums (Kopf verloren). Erotensarkophag im Thermenmuseum (8 stehende Eroten, die meisten mit Speeren, Clipeus auf Akanthoskelch. Auf dem Deckel li. spielende Eroten, re. Eroten auf Hasenjagd.). S. hier Abb. 6. Vgl. auch die Ara in Antium, Villa Spignarelli, Inst. Neg. 69.1001.
20) Hier nach Inst.Neg. 70.2182. MD. 2437. Fehlt noch bei Jucker. Entsprechend diesem Sarkophag ist wohl das Frgt. v. Kaschnitz-Weinberg, Sculture del maggazino Vaticano Taf. 85,556 zu ergänzen.
21) Foto Marburg 180411. Auf einem Sarkophag in Ostia wird der mittlere Guirlandenbogen von einer Inschrifttafel weitgehend überdeckt: Honroth a.O. (oben Anm.5) Taf. 10,2 (in den Schwüngen Gorgoneia, keine Masken). Vgl. als weitere Variante: Inst.Neg. 64. 1650. Timgad, Clipeus in der mittleren Guirlande, li. u. re. je frontale Maske (lokal). Auf dem Sarkophag NSc. 1931,532 Abb. 16, Ostia, rahmen Guirlanden mit je einer Maske eine Ädikula (über den Pilastern weitere Masken). Inst.Neg. 65.1344, Badia di Cava, Tabula statt mittlerer Guirlande (ohne Eroten in der Mitte). Ebenso Inst.Neg. 54.847, Neapel. Kasten im grossen Kreuzgang des Thermenmuseums (nur auf letzterem Sarkophag je eine Maske, sonst keine Masken), Kranz statt Mittelbogen. Inst.Neg. 65.1350, Benevent, Amelung, Vatikankatalog II Taf. 113,217. Tusa a.O. Nr. 57, Palermo. Einen Clipeus u. keine Masken haben statt der Mittelbögen ein Sarkophag in Salerno, Inst.Neg. 64.1445, sowie ein weiterer in Terracina, Inst.Neg. 69.939. Clipeus u. je 2 antithetische Masken in den Schwüngen trägt der Sarkophag Charbonneaux a.O. 238,1536.—Die kanonische Form der Guirlandensarkophage ist vollends aufgelöst auf Sarkophagen wie Tusa a.O. Nr. 13, Catania.

Eroten mit den Guirlanden die Gruppe von Amor und Psyche[22]. Ein Sarkophag vor der amerikanischen Kirche in Rom zeigt in der Mitte einen Kandelaber anstatt der Eroten[23], während auf anderen an derselben Stelle ein Gefäss erscheint[24]. Wird somit bei einer Reihe von Sarkophagen der mittlere Eros verdoppelt, bei einer anderen durch eine Vase oder andere Geräte ersetzt, bietet ein Sarkophag im Thermenmuseum[25] eine andere Lösung: das Ende der beiden Guirlanden ist jeweils um einen Baum geschlungen, neben dem aussen je ein Korb steht. In den Lunetten befindet sich je eine Maske, an der sich ein Eros zu schaffen macht. Alle hier angeführten Sarkophage mit Ausnahme derjenigen in S.Paolo und im Thermenmuseum weisen in den Guirlandenbögen jeweils zwei Masken auf. Natürlich gibt es noch zahlreiche weitere Typen an Guirlandensarkophagen mit Eroten, doch sollen hier nur diejenigen erfasst werden, die in Verbindung mit Masken in den Bögen verwandt wurden.

Wir konnten aus dem kurzen Überblick über verwandte Sarkophage ersehen, dass der Ausgangspunkt für unsere Betrachtungen, die Sarkophagplatte in Malibu, in den wesentlichen Punkten keine von der üblichen Typologie abweichenden Züge aufweist. Eine kleine Besonderheit stellt allenfalls der Pantherkopf der linken Guirlande dar. Wir haben allerdings bisher ein Motiv des Sarkophags noch nicht berührt, das, soweit ich sehe, ohne Parallele ist, die Erosherme in der Mitte des Frieses. Hermen von Eroten sind an sich schon selten[26] und auf Sarkophagen meines Wissens erst zweimal nachgewiesen, auf einem attischen Sarkophag in Kyrene[27] wie einem verschollenen, wohl stadtrömischen Fragment[28].

Unsere Herme unterscheidet sich jedoch von den eben genannten Parallelen einmal darin, dass sie geflügelt ist, zum anderen dadurch, dass der Körper des Eros nicht unmittelbar in den Hermenschaft übergeht, sondern aus einem Akanthoskelch herauswächst[29]. Die Kombination des Eros mit einem Blütenkelch ist in den verschiedensten Denkmälerbereichen nachweisbar[30], auf Sarkophagen aber nicht allzu geläufig[31]. Bei einem guirlandentragenden Eros bot sie sich gewissermassen an.

Die chronologische Einordnung der Sarkophagplatte in Malibu ist nicht einfach. Das ausserordentliche reiche Material der Guirlandensarkophage ist bisher noch in keiner Form geordnet, nur weniges publiziert. Von den drei hier abgebildeten Sarkophagen ist das Exemplar im Thermenmuseum eindeutig das früheste, kaum viel später als 150 n.Chr. anzusetzen. Die zwei übrigen stehen sich in manchem recht nahe. Der Kasten in Genf ist aber nicht nur in der Auflösung der Haarpartien, sondern auch in der stärkeren Füllung des Grundes mit allerlei Getier sowie dem Korb zweifellos der jüngste in unserer Reihe. Bemerkenswert ist bei ihm auch, dass in der Mitte der Guirlanden jeweils eine Blüte mit Früchten herabhängt, was an die Trauben der norditalischen und östlichen Sarkophage erinnert[32]. Zusammenfassend wird man den Sarkophag im Getty-Museum in früh-, den Genfer Kasten in spätseverische Zeit datieren dürfen. Bei beiden sind die Guirlanden, verglichen vor allem mit den allerdings geringen Resten der Guirlanden des Sarkophags in Rom, bereits fühlbar verhärtet.

Die zweite Sarkophagplatte, mit der wir uns beschäftigen wollen, stammt ebenfalls von einem Guirlandensarkophag (Abb. 8)[33]. Es handelt sich bei ihr um ein präch-

22) Orlandi, ArchCl. 24,1972 Taf. 26,2. Honroth a.O. (oben Anm. 5) Taf. 10,1.

23) Honroth a.O. Taf. 12,1. Inst.Neg. 60.890.

24) Sichtermann a.O. 231. In den Bögen mitunter Masken (Sichtermann Abb. 26.34 sowie Inst.Neg. 69.446-48, Orvieto), manchmal andere Motive.

25) Honroth a.O. Taf. 112. Auch auf oberitalischen und östlichen Sarkophagen ist oft nur in der Sarkophagmitte ein Eros dargestellt, während die Enden an Bukranien, Ringen oder dgl. aufgehängt sind. Siehe z.B. Gabelmann a.O. 127 ff.

26) Keil, ÖJh. 23,1926,278 ff. zu Plinius, n.h. 36.33. Poulsen a.O. (oben Anm. 13) Nr. 182. R. Lullies, Die Typen der griechischen Herme (1931) 74.76 ff. Pietrogrande, AfrIt. 3,1930,129.

27) Pietrogrande a.O. 114 Abb. 9.

28) Matz-Duhn II 2736, damals DAI. Rom, Palästraszenen mit Eroten. Man könnte auch auf Jahreszeitenhermen verwiesen: Matz. SR. IV 1 Nr. 8 Taf. 10-12, Janina. Sie sind ungeflügelt wie die eben genannten Eroshermen. Matz a.O. IV 2 S. 94 f. möchte auch auf dem Sarkophag Nr. 78, Subiaco, zwei Jahreszeitenhermen erkennen. Es handelt sich aber wohl um Hermen Priaps, zumal beim Fehlen ausreichender Indizien die Zweizahl die Deutung von Matz nicht unterstützt. P. Kranz, der Bearbeiter der Jahreszeitensarkophage, teilt die hier vertretene Auffassung.—Nicht sicher ist auszumachen, ob die 4 Hermen dem verschollenen Sarkophag Vermeule a.O. (oben Anm. 13) Nr. 124 Abb. 45 solche von Putten waren.

29) Zu diesem Motiv zuletzt Schauenburg, Städel-Jahrbuch 1,1967,50 ff. mit Lit. Horn. BJBb. 172,1972,164 ff.

30) Vgl. etwa: Amelung, Vatikankatalog I Taf. 53,297, Gebälkfrgt. Amelung II Taf. 46,253 a u. Taf. 48,256 a, Grabaren. Grabrelief Vatikan 7507. Vatikan 9998, Relieffrgt. vom Hateriergrab. Lippold, Vatikankatalog III 2 Taf. 8,44.91.51.115,24 f., Kandelaber. Vjesnik 3,1971 Taf. 8,2, Relief in Leibnitz, Schloss Seggau. Jucker a.O. Abb. 64 u 67, Frgt. von Grabrelief im Grabmal der Caecilia Metella bzw. Friesrelief in Triest. Inst.Neg. 67.408 f., Ara in Rom, S.Passera. Inst.Neg. 75.256, Florenz, Dommuseum. Ergon 1971, 157 Abb. 193, Kapitell aus Messene. v.Rohden-Winnefeld, Architektonische römische Tonreliefs der Kaiserzeit 189 ff. Allgemein dazu Toynbee-Ward-Perkins, BSR. 18, 1950,1 ff. Schauenburg, JdI 78,1963,303 Anm. 41.

31) Vor einigen Jahren befand sich das li. Ende eines Wannensarkophags im Handel. Es zeigt einen guirlandentragenden Eros, der aus Akanthos herauswächst. Vgl. auch die Köpfe auf dem Guirlandensarkophag in Tartous, hier Anm. 48. P. Kranz verweist auch noch auf das Frgt. 121794 im Thermenmuseum, Knabe als Jahreszeitengenius: Inst.Neg. 72.3014 (Ns.eines dionysischen Sarkophags).

32) Rodenwaldt, AA. 1938,399 ff. Gabelmann a.O. 128.

33) Inv. 72. AA. 152. Sotheby 1.7.68,137. Michaelis (oben Anm. 2) 494,49, Lowther Castle. N. Himmelmann, Der Sarkophag von Megiste (1970) 19. Inst.Neg. Rom 70 1025-29. B. Cook, Journal of the J. Paul Getty Museum 1(1974) 34, Abb. 4. Zu kleinasiatischen Guirlandensarkophagen zuletzt Koch, AA. 1974,306 mit Anm. 61.

tiges kleinasiatisches Gegenstück zu dem soeben besprochenen stadtrömischen Denkmal. Die östlichen Sarkophage mit Eroten und Guirlanden zeigen meist drei Schwünge[34] wie wir sie auch hier sehen und im allgemeinen an den Ecken Niken, keine Eroten. Typisch für diese Klasse sind weiterhin die frontalen Masken, wobei nicht selten in der Mitte ein Medusenhaupt die Stelle der Theatermaske einnimmt[35]. Dabei ist auch bemerkenswert, dass im Osten die tragischen Masken, im Westen rein dionysische bevorzugt werden. Ebenso charakteristisch für kleinasiatische Herkunft der Platte ist die Ornamentik am Sockel: Spitzblattguirlande, Palmettenfries, Perlstab, Mäander. Einige weitere Motive des Reliefs sind nicht ganz so geläufig oder überhaupt bisher nicht nachgewiesen.

Die zwei Eroten stehen auf einem Seeochsen beziehungsweise einem Hippokamp (rechts). Die unteren Partien der beiden Ecken sind verloren, doch darf man in Analogie zu den Eroten und im Hinblick darauf, dass der Gewandsaum der Niken deren hohe Position erweist, annehmen, dass auch diese nicht frei im Raum schwebten, obwohl dies auf attischen und kleinasiatischen Sarkophagen durchaus geläufig ist[36]. Vermutlich standen die Siegesgöttinnen, wie viele Vergleichsbeispiele auf östlichen Sarkophagen nahelegen, auf Globen (Abb. 9)[37]. Die Guirlanden tragen in ihrer Mitte je einen grossen Blütenstern. Von den beiden äusseren Guirlanden hängen Früchte herab, an denen jeweils zwei Vögel (Perlhühner ?) picken. Die Früchte lassen wieder an die eben schon erwähnten östlichen Trauben denken[38]. Unter der mittleren Guirlande schliesslich ist ein breiter Blätterkranz angebracht, aus dem die Büste eines die Arme spreizenden Eros herausschaut. Von der

Verbindung des Eros mit Rankenwerk war bereits bei Besprechung der ersten Platte in Malibu die Rede. Im Sockelornament sowie in den Guirlanden mit den Trauben und den Masken ist die nächste Parallele zu unserem Sarkophagfragment ein Sarkophag aus Perge, auf den schon verwiesen wurde[39]. Vor allem das Ornament stimmt völlig mit dem unseren überein[40]. Sehr eng verwandt ist aber auch, wie N. Himmelmann bereits kurz hervorhob, auch ein Sarkophag in Konya[41]. Dort finden sich auch andere Übereinstimmungen, die für die Ikonographie und ihre Symbolik bedeutsam sind[42]. Der Sarkophag in Konya ist von Himmelmann-Wildschütz bereits exakt beschrieben worden, so dass ein erneutes Eingehen darauf hier nicht erforderlich ist. Einige Punkte werden später noch erörtert werden. Wichtig ist, dass auf beiden Langseiten der dritte Guirlandenbogen durch eine Gruppe von zwei beziehungsweise drei Figuren ersetzt ist[43]. Unter der auf einem Felsen sitzenden Frau sehen wir wieder einen Vogel, der an einer Traube pickt, also ein in reicherer Gestaltung auf der Platte in Malibu ebenfalls dargestelltes Motiv. In den Schwüngen finden wir in Konya auf A zwei Porträtbüsten, auf B zwei Medusenhäupter. Die Eck-Niken stehen auf Globen, wie wir dies für unser Relief ebenfalls annahmen. Auf dem Sarkophag aus Perge sind es Sphingen[44], über denen die Siegesgöttinnen erscheinen. Der verfügbare Raum reicht wohl kaum aus, um die weggebrochenen Ecken der Sarkophagplatte im Getty-Museum in dieser Form zu ergänzen.

Die Niken auf dem Globus haben ikonographisch und in ihrer Symbolik eine bis in den Hellenismus zurückreichende Geschichte[45]. Das den Römern durch die berühmte Victoriastatue in der Kurie bestens ver-

34) Natürlich gibt es auch im Westen Belege für 3 Guirlandenbögen, so z.B. JRS. 17,1927 Taf, 1 a-c, Pawlowsk.

35) Oben Anm. 8.

36) Vgl. etwa: Matz a.O. 50,4 b. Matz, 50,4 a ist eine stadtrömische Imitation (verschollen). Kasten in Antalyia (3 tragische Masken). Auch die Basen, auf denen Niken und Eroten stehen, können weit über dem Sockel der Sarkophage angebracht sein: Mendel Nr. 1158, Wiegartz a.O. 15. Mendel Nr. 1160, Wiegartz a.O. Taf. 14, Smyrna. Inst.Neg. 72. 500-506, Thermenmuseum. Ward-Perkins, Archaeology 11,1958,98 Abb. 1, Washington, Smithsonian Institute. Sarkophag aus Perge (3 Bögen, in 2 davon Gorgoneia, im mittleren Inschrifttafel). Matz 50,11, Antiochia, syrisch. Ebenda 51,6, New York. Himmelmann (oben Anm. 5) passim.

37) Z.B.: Brüssel, Syrisch. 1946 durch Brand beschädigt, Zuletzt bei Himmelmann a.O. 7 Abb. 5.6.24. J. Balty-F. Vandenabeele-W. van Rengen, Recherches dans la nécropole nord d'Apamée (1975). J. Balty bin ich für die Aufnahme u. Hinweise sehr dankbar. Lehmann-Hartleben-Olsen a.O. 48 ff. Mansel-Bean-Inan, Die Agora von Side (1956) Taf. 32,118 Nr. 4, Taf. 33.120 Nr. 6: die Globen schweben in der Luft. Bull.Mus. de Beyrouth 18,1965 Taf. 2 u. 4, zwei lokale Sarkophag. Auf dem Sarkophag Nr. 120 steht auch Eros auf Globen. Wiegartz a.O.51 f. (Konya), Himmelmann a.O. 19. Den von Parlasca RM. 77,1970,130 genannten Sarkophag in Izmir gedenke ich,

demnächst an anderem Ort zu behandeln. Bull.du Musée de Beyrouth 18,1965 Taf. 2 u. 4, Tyrus.—Zu Eckfiguren allgemein Pietrograde a.O. 126 ff. Bovio, Bul. Com. 52,1924,150 ff. Michon, Syria 2,1921,295 ff. Auf dem Sarkophag Morey, Sardes V Abb. 99 zu S. 56, Florenz, Pal. Riccardi rahmen Niken auf Globen die Grabtür. Die Siegesgöttin auf Himmelskugel kommt auch auf Grabaltären vor, so etwa auf dem Altar in Ravello. Inst.Neg. 68,477. Auch dies Motiv ist somit auf den Urnen bzw. Altären nachweisbar, bevor es von den Sarkophagwerkstätten übernommen wird (s.oben 61). Vgl. auch Turcan, Mél. 72,1960,158 ff. zu einer Ara im Thermenmuseum (Dioskuren ? auf Globen). Zu den pickenden Vögeln vgl. den in Anm. 50 genannten Sarkophag aus Kolossoi. Koch, Gnomon 45,1973,316.

38) Oben Anm. 32.

39) Wiegartz a.O. 37.178,17.

40) Zum Mäander dieser Form Wiegartz a.O. 35. Zur Traube hier S.

41) Wiegartz a.O. 51. Himmelmann-Wildschütz a.O. (oben Anm. 33) 19 f.

42) Das Ornament weicht leicht von dem unserer Platte ab.

43) Zu verwandten Schemata auf stadtrömischen Sarkophagen oben S. 61.

44) Hierzu Wiegartz a.O. 37. Mansel-Bean-Inan a.O. 71 f. Taf. 31. Zur sepulkralen Sphinx Schauenburg AA. 1975. Lehmann-Hartleben-Olsen a.O. Abb. 23-26, Boston, Gardner Museum.

45) T. Hölscher, Victoria Romana (1967) 1 ff.

traute und in vielen Denkmälergattungen verbreitete[46] Motiv hat in der Sepulkralkunst natürlich seine spezifische Bedeutung. Wie es neuerdings durch die Bronze aus Augst mit der allgemeinen Symbolik der Akanthosbüste verbunden wurde[47], so kennen wir andererseits auch Niken auf östlichen Sarkophagen, die auf Akanthoskelchen stehen[48].

Interessanter als die Niken sind aber die auf den Seetieren stehenden Eroten. Wir kannten bisher bereits mehrere kleinasiatische Sarkophage mit auf Delphinen stehenden Eroten[49]. Die Kombination mit Seeochsen ist in dieser Form dagegen meines Wissens singulär. Auf einem Sarkophag in Adana und dem erwähnten in Konya erheben sich die Eroten allerdings über Seepanthern, auf einem fragmentarisch erhaltenen aus Kolossoi stehen sie auf Seepferden[50].

Die Verbindung von Eros mit Meerwesen, insbesondere dem Delphin, reicht in der Bildkunst in spätarchaische Zeit zurück. Auf einer Schale in Palermo, die ins spätere 6. Jahrhundert gehört, ist erstmals das in der Folgezeit so beliebte Motiv des Eros, der auf dem Delphin reitet und meist musiziert, zur Darstellung gelangt[51]. Es findet sich, vor allem vom Hellenismus an und ganz besonders in der Kaiserzeit, in fast allen Denkmälergattungen. Wir kennen es sowohl in der Toreutik[52] als von Tonreliefs verschiedenster Art[53], aber auch aus der Glyptik[54] und von Münzen[55]. Auf Mosaiken lässt es sich ebenso nachweisen[56] wie auf Grabreliefs[57] und Sarkophagen der Rundplastik[58]. Ganz besonders sind aber rotfigurige und auch plastische Vasen zu nennen[59], da hier ungewöhnlich reizvolle Schöpfungen erhalten sind. Auch auf unteritalischen[60] Vasen und etruskischen Denkmälern[61] finden wir auf dem Delphin reitende Eroten. Das Motiv mag von da aus in die römische Kunst gelangt sein[62]. In vorrömischer Zeit war es, wenn man von den Vasen absieht, noch nicht allzu verbreitet. In einer anderen Kombination des Eros mit dem Delphin wird ein von Eros gelenktes Gespann von den gelehrigen Fischen gezogen, wobei die Lenker oft auf den Fischen stehen. Auch hierfür gibt es in der

46) Hölscher a.O. 1 ff. 180 ff. (Frühzeit) mit Lit. Jucker, Mus. Helv. 25, 1968,200 (für Dougga). Vgl. ausser den dort zu findenden Denkmälern an Bronzefiguren u.a.: R. Fleischer, Die römischen Bronzen aus Österreich (1967) Nr. 119.121.122. Guida Ruesch 832, Neapel. Neapel 5260, Anderson 25818, Inst.Neg. 66,1702, Tischfuss. Inst.Neg. 60.492, Neapel. Babelon-Blanchet, Cat. des bronzes ant. de la bibl. nat. Nr. 679 f. De Ridder, Les bronzes ant. du Louvre I Taf. 55,808 u. 810 (Nikekniet). Berlin, Friedrichs Nr. 1991-93. Inst.Neg. 32,940, Triest. Inst.Neg. 62.370, Chieti. Inst. Ph. 31.3413, Marseille, Zadocs-Jitta, Roman bronzes from the Netherlands II (1969) Nr. 62, Wychen. Arte e civiltà Romana nell' Italia settentrionale (1964) Taf. 168,349, Lausanne. Ebenda Taf. 114,229. Turin (Dreifuss). Ebenda Nr. 190, Statuette in Reggio Aem. Statuette in Bologna. H. Menzel, Die römischen Bronzen aus Deutschland, Speyer (1960) Nr. 14. Zwei Statuetten in Bonn, Rhein. Landesmuseum. Vermeule, CIJ. 60,1965, 293 Abb. 6, Boston. An Arbeiten aus Ton vgl.: S. Loeschke, Lampen aus Vindonissa (1919) 244 Anm. 133 und im Katalog Nr. 63 f. 389 mit Lit. Opusc.Athen 6,1965 Taf. 11,249, Lampe im Victoria und Albert Museum. Waldhauer, Die antiken Tonlampen der Ermitage (1914) Nr. 213. Lampe in Bologna (Victoria mit Kranz und Palme). Deneauve, Lampes de Carthage (1969) Nr. 299. Sparbüchse in Ostia. Vermeule, The Dal Pozzo-Albani Drawings II Nr. 8247 Abb. 17, verschollenes Relief. An Reliefs aus Marmor bzw. Stein: Corolla E. Swoboda (1966) 105 ff. mit Lit. (Diez), Giebel in Carnuntum. Titusbogen in Rom. Ostia 547, Pilasterfrgt. A. Frova, L'Arte di Roma e del mondo Romano (1961) 809 Abb. 693, Ascalona. Fundber, aus Schwaben 14, 1957 Taf. 54, Viergötterstein in Mühlacker Glyptik: Vollenweider, Schw.Münzbl. 13/14, 1964,76 f. Antike Gemmen in Deutschland, München 3 Nr. 190. Statue: R. Bartoccini, Le terme di Lepcis (1929) 153 ff.

47) Hölscher a.O. 37.47.138 f. mit Lit.

48) Z.B.: Inst.Neg. Rom 67.1838, Saloniki. Wiegartz a.O. 179,37, Ephesos. Annales Arch. de Syrie 7,1957 73 ff. Taf. 1 ff. Ward Perkins, BMus Beyrouth 22,1969,143, Ich habe G. Koch für Auskünfte zu danken. Er teilt mir mit, dass das Stück sich in Tartous befindet, Inv. T 290. Mit Akanthos sind mitunter auch die Basen unter den Eroten u. Niken verziert, so auf dem Sarkophag Mendel Nr. 1160, Istanbul. Vgl. auch die aus Akanthos herauswachsenden Jahreszeiten auf dem Sarkophag Wiegartz a.O. 178,16, Providence.

49) Mansel-Akarka a.O. (oben Anm. 5) Taf. 16,70. Frgt. in Istanbul.

Mansel-Bean-Inan a.O. 73 zu Nr. 5. Rodenwaldt, AA. 1938,397 ff. Abb. 6, verschollen. Lehmann-Hartleben-Olsen a.O. Abb. 16, Boston, Gardner Museum. Inst.Neg. 67.1838 Saloniki, St. Georg.

50) Syria 2,1921 Taf. 41,1. MMA. V 18,51 Taf. 10.

51) CVA. Palermo 1 Ic Taf. 3,4, Schale. Im folgenden werden jeweils nur wenige Beispiele herausgegriffen, da die Gesamtheit der Monumente den Rahmen dieser Untersuchung sprengen würde. Allgemein zum Motiv Rumpf, SR V 1,112.124.138 f. Brommer, AA. 1942,67. Ridgway, Archaeology 23,1970,86 ff.

52) AJA. 67, 1963 Taf. 95,6, Tischfuss aus Pompeji. Comstock-Vermeule, Greek, Etruscan and Roman Bronzes (1971) Nr. 361.367, Spiegel.

53) Berlin 30219.22. V. Rohden-Winnefeld, Architektonische römische Tonreliefs der Kaiserzeit 186. Tarsus I 324 zu 106 (Goldman). Hier auch Verweis auf Lampen u. Mosaiken. Weitere Lampen z.B. in Corinth IV T. II zu 606. Lampe im Vatikan. AA. 1911,202 f., Lampe aus Tanais.

54) Antike Gemmen in deutschen Sammlungen, Braunschweig, zu Nr. 64 (Scherf). Karneol in Belgrad.

55) Riggauer, ZfNum. 8,1881,74.87.98.

56) ILN.1961, 672 Abb. 14, Chichester. B. Cunliffle, Excavations at Fishbourne (1971) Taf. 50. Vgl. hier auch Anm. 53.

57) EA 3630, Villa Albani. Rumpf, SR V passim, z.B. Nr. 46 u. 269.

58) Ostia 4977: 2 Gruppen von Brunnen. Auktion Fischer, Luzern 1936 Taf. 11,2. Vgl. F. Muthmann. Statuenstützen (951)91 f.

59) Trumpf-Lyritzaki, Griech. Figurenvasen (1969) 130 mit Lit. in Anm. 179. Dazu u.a. Neapel, RC. 123, Lekythos. G. van Hoorn, Choes and Anthesteria Abb. 370 f., Oxford u. Kerameikosmuseum. Als Schildzeichen findet sich die Gruppe auf dem Krater Beazley, ARV² 227,11, Louvre, beim Parisurteil auf der Hydria ARV². 1187,32, Berlin. Vgl. die plastische Vase Maximova. Les vases plastiques (1927) Taf. 38, Villa Giulia.

60) Trendall, LCS. 375,114, Hydria in Neapel. Apulischer Krater ebenda H. 3252. Kantharos Brit.Mus. F 439. Vgl. die Reliefs in Pästum Zancani, RM.70,1963,27 f.

61) J. et L. Jehasse, La nécropole préromaine d'Aléria (1973) S. 264 f., rf. Stamnos. Mehrfach haben Eroten einen Delphin in der Hand, z.B. auf der Oinochoe Rom, Villa Giulia 19772, Beazley, EVP. 173.

62) Zur Übernahme grossgriechischer Motive in der römischen Kunst zuletzt Schauenburg, AA. 1972,513.

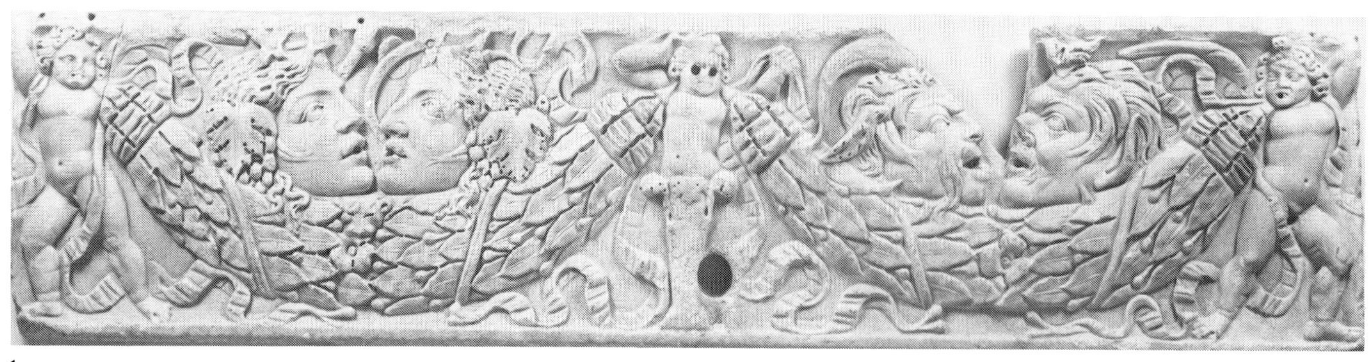

1

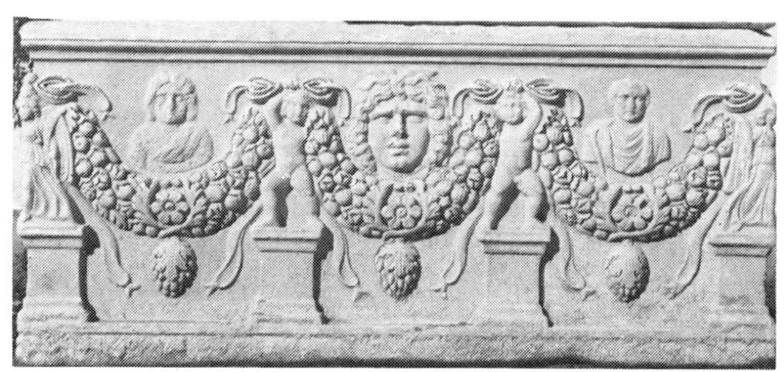

2

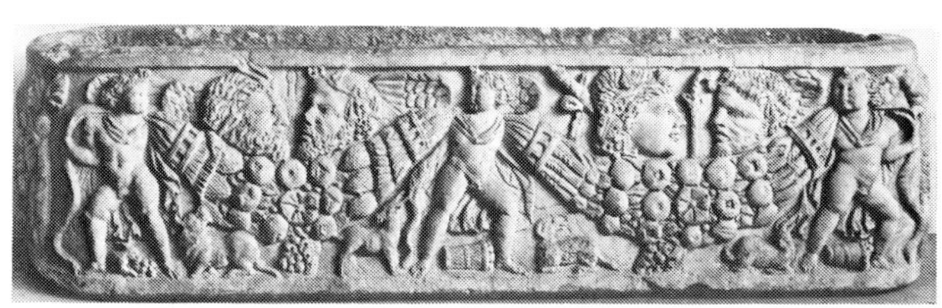

3

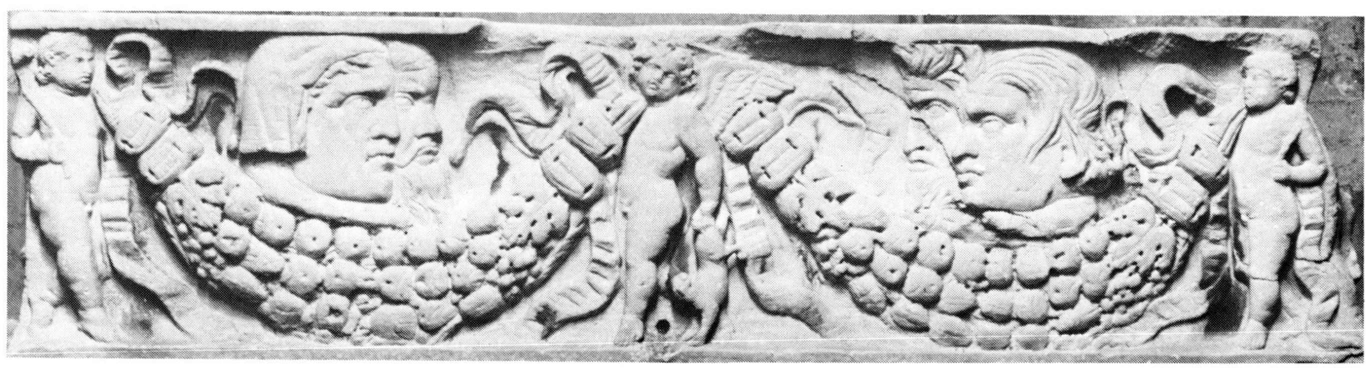

4

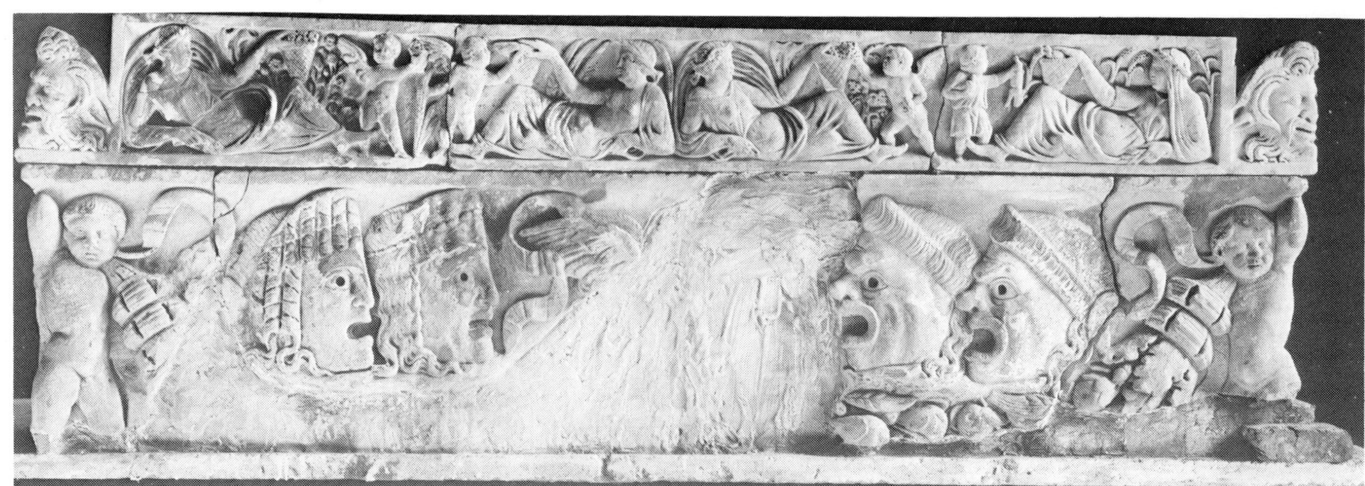

5

1   Sarkophagplatte in Malibu, J. Paul Getty Museum

2   Sarkophag in Ephesos

3   Sarkophag in Genf, Musée d'art et d'histoire

4   Sarkophag im Vatikan

5   Sarkophag in Rom, Thermenmuseum

6   Sarkophag in Genua, Museum (Detail)

7   Sarkophag in Rom, San Paolo

8   Sarkophagplatte in Malibu, J. Paul Getty Museum

9   Sarkophag in Brüssel

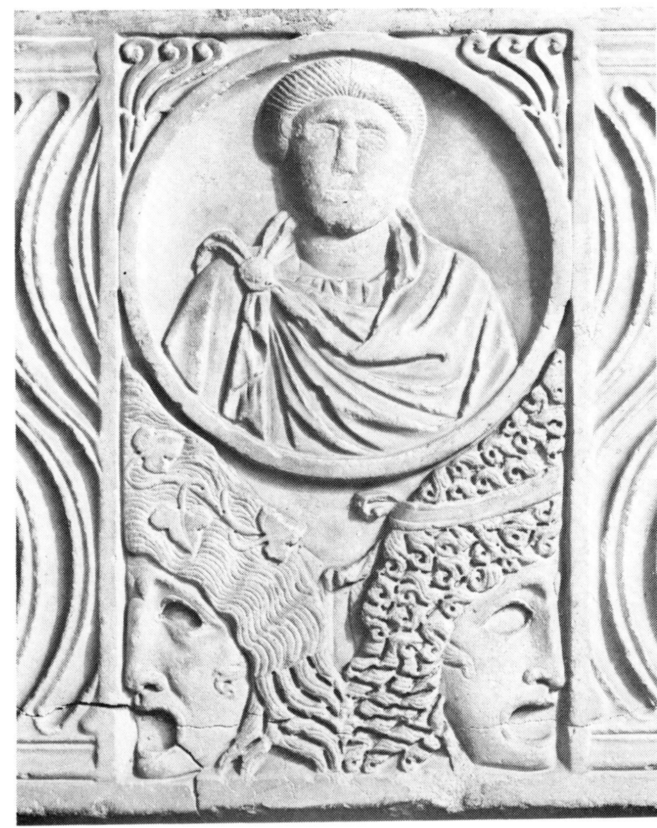

6

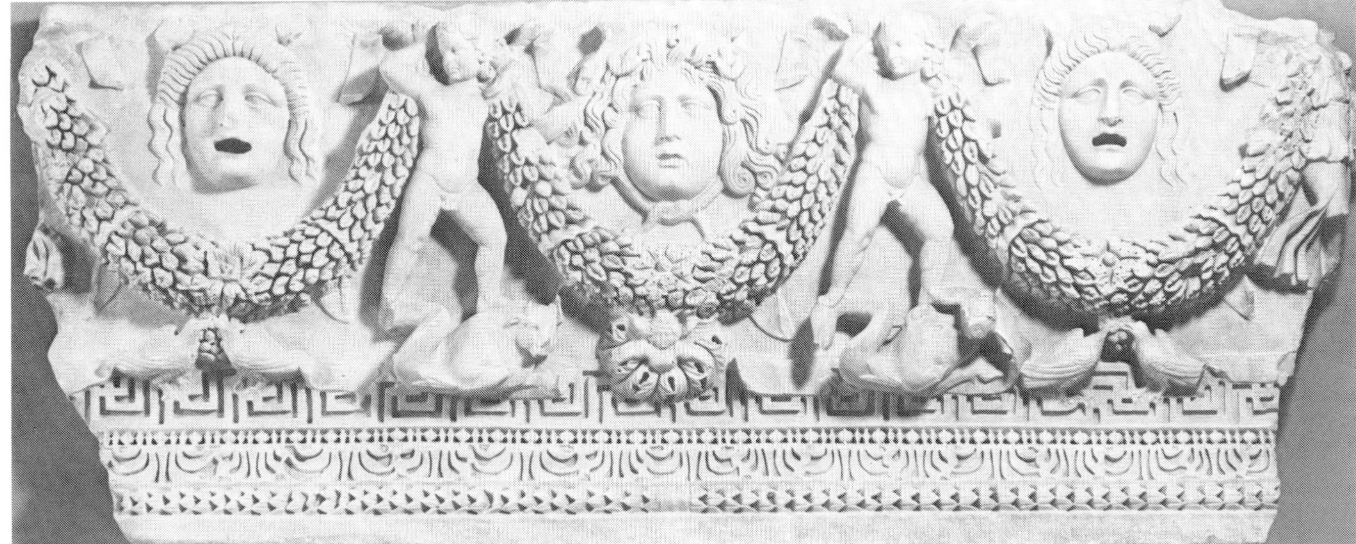

8

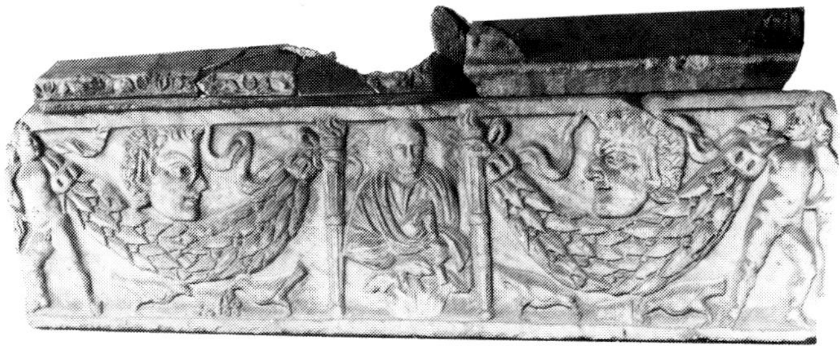

7

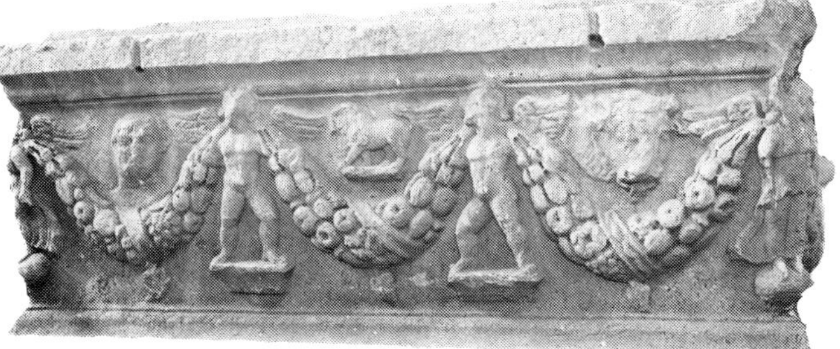

9

Nereide des Berliner apulischen Kraters F 3241 einen ikonographischen Vorläufer aus Unteritalien[63]. Später liebten vor allem die Gemmenschneider die von Delphinen gebildeten Gespanne[64]. Auf den Meeressarkophagen und kaiserzeitlichen Mosaiken erweitert sich dann die Verbindung Eros und Meer in ungewöhnlicher Weise. Auf letzteren sehen wir die Eroten vor allem beim Fischfang, oft vom Boot oder auch vom Delphin aus[65]. Das Motiv des Fischfangs der Eroten ist aber auch auf Sarkophagen nicht selten nachweisbar[66]. Das älteste Beispiel ist wieder eine apulische Vase, ein Krater, der sich in Berlin befindet und von E. Rohde demnächst publiziert werden wird[67]. Sowohl auf Sarkophagen als Mosaiken bedienen sich die Amoretten auch der Seepanther und anderer Mischwesen verwandter Art als Reittier, wie wir diese von den hier behandelten östlichen Sarkophagen kennen. Das Motiv der fischenden Eroten gehört ganz allgemein in den Bereich der Amoretten, die Tätigkeiten von Erwachsenen ausüben und somit nicht eigentlich in den Motivkreis unserer kleinasiatischen Sarkophage. Dasselbe gilt—wenn auch nur bedingt—für die "Nereidensarkophage" mit ihrem Seewesenthiasos. Wenn Eros relativ früh mit dem Delphin in Zusammenhang gebracht wurde, dann spielte dabei wohl die Meeresgeburt der Aphrodite eine Rolle. Wenn speziell der Delphin für den reitenden Eros ausgewählt wurde, so vermutlich wegen seiner Musikalität und auch deshalb, weil er der allgemein beliebteste und bekannteste grosse Fisch im alten Griechenland war. In der kaiserzeitlichen sepulkralen Bildwelt hat man ihn wohl dann auch als Hinweis auf die Reise der Toten

63) E. Gerhard, Apulische Vasenbilder Taf. 7. Mosaiken wie J. Salomonson, La mosaïque aux chevaux (1965) 22 Taf. 10,3, Louvre. Scavi di Ostia IV 340 ff. Taf. 124.161 (Becatti). Sarkophage: Rumpf, SR. V Nr. 29.
64) Gymn. 64,1957,225. Vgl. Sarkophage wie Rumpf, SR. V Nr. 273, Louvre, Mosaiken wie die aus Ostia (Anm. 63).
65) Z.B.: Tripolitania I Teil I (1960) Taf. 87 f. Salomonson a.O. Taf. 10,1, Karthago u. 37,1, Tunis. EAA. II. 798, Kos. NS.1951 308, Piazza Amerina. Fendri, Découvertes archéologiques dans la région de Sfax Taf. 14 ff. D. Levi, Antiochia I 162.177 ff. 198 ff. Scavi di Ostia IV Taf. 156.161, S. 340 ff. mit Lit. Auch rundplastisch nachweisbar: Gallia 23,1965,277, Musée du Puy.
66) Dazu im Sarkophagcorpus. Wichtig der Sarkophag in Karlsruhe, Thimme, Jb.d.staatl.Kunstslg. Baden-Württemberg 7, 1970, 128 f. M. Gütschow, Das Museum der Prätextatkatakombe (1938) 57 ff. B. Andreae, Studien zur römischen Grabkunst (1963) 131 ff. 154 ff. und in Helbig[4] zu 2121. Zu Eroten im Schiff auf Gemmen: Die antiken Gemmen in Deutschland, München 3, zu 2291 (Brandt). E. Diehl, Die antiken Gemmen d. kunsthist. Museums in Wien I (1973) zu 443. Eros mit kleinen Schiffchen auch auf Vasen: Lekythos K. Neugebauer, Führer durch das Antiquarium II, Vasen 121. Apulischer Glockenkrater Louvre K 132.—Vgl. jetzt den wichtigen Sarkophag J. Jacopi, L'antiquarium Forense 30 Abb. 35.
67) Schneider-Herrmann-Maler (Trendall); zu diesen Schauenburg, JdI. 87,1972,258 ff. Ein wenig jünger als der Krater wohl die attische Reliefkanne AM.79,1964,46 Taf. 37 d.

zu den Inseln der Seligen verstanden[68]. Die Meerwesensarkophage, die im Osten nicht hergestellt wurden, sind in ihrer allgemeinen Symbolik unter dem zuletzt besprochenen Aspekt auch für die hier behandelte Sarkophaggruppe von Interesse. Ausserdem sind jene auch in einem speziellen Punkt, der noch zu erörtern ist, vergleichbar, in dem Ersatz des Delphins durch Mischwesen aus Säugetier und Fisch. Denn zum Meerthiasos gehören auch zahlreiche Mischbildungen dieser Art. Innerhalb der kleinasiatischen Guirlandensarkophage stehen in diesem Punkt die Stücke in Malibu, Kolossoi und Adana für sich. Das Stehen, nicht Sitzen, auf einem Delphin, ist auf den Sarkophagen darin begründet, dass die Eroten die Funtion des Guirlandenträgers ausüben. Es ist aber ein Motiv, das uns auch sonst bekannt ist, vor allem durch Mosaiken, die Eroten beim Fischfang zeigen[69]. Wir sahen auch, dass auf einem apulischen Krater in Berlin eine Nereide auf einem Delphin steht. Wenn nun auf den vier genannten Sarkophagen der Delphin durch Seepferd, Seeochse oder Seepanther ersetzt wurde, wird dies wohl nicht ohne Sinn sein. Da es sich um grosse beziehungsweise gefährliche Tiere handelt, aus denen der Vorderteil der Mischwesen gebildet wurde, liegt der Gedanke nahe, dass man den Eroten, die die Seele zum Jenseits geleiteten, eine möglichst mächtige Unterstützung verleihen wollte. Der Pegasos ist überdies eines der bekanntesten Sinnbilder für die Reise ins Jenseits, allerdings nicht für die zu den Inseln der Seligen. Es ist dabei nicht zu übersehen, dass die Kombination Eroten-Seewesen als Symbol der Reise auf die Inseln der Seligen nicht zur Funktion der Eroten auf unseren Sarkophagen passt, auf denen sie ja Guirlandenträger sind. Andererseits wirkt das Stehen auf einem Delphin oder einem anderen Seewesen—schon aus statischen Gründen—nicht eben glücklich. All dies zeigt nur erneut die Vielschichtigkeit und mangelnde Logik in der Bildsprache römischer Sarkophage. Den Entwerfern der Bildprogramme kam es vor allem darauf an, möglichst viele Bereiche sepulkraler Vorstellungen anzusprechen.

Noch ein Wort zu den Nebenseiten des Sarkophags in Konya, der ja eine besonders enge Parallele zu dem Relief in Malibu ist und uns verdeutlicht, dass auch letzteres von einem wahren Prachtsarkophag stammt. Die linke Schmalseite zeigt eine offene Tür, in der die Verstorbene steht, gerahmt von einem Mann und einer Frau. Die beiden Frauen haben ideale Köpfe, also keine Porträts, der männliche Kopf ist verloren. Auf den Türflügeln erscheinen innen Medusenhäupter, darunter die aus der römischen Sepulkralkunst vertrauten Attisfiguren. Letzteres Motiv ist natürlich in Kleinasien, wo Attis beheimatet war, besonders gut verständlich. N. Himmelmann hat in seiner Publikation eines in Stil und Motiv als enge Parallele zu bezeichnenden Sarkophag der Villa Rospigliosi in Rom bereits darauf verwiesen[70], dass die Türen kleinasiatischer Sarkophage, die im Gegensatz zu den stadtrömischen Sarkophagen stets auf den Nebenseiten angebracht[71] sind, fast immer geschlossen dargestellt werden und dass vor ihnen meistens, ein Opfer dargebracht wird. Er hob auch hervor, dass die geöffnete Tür stadtrömischer Sarkophage, die die Mitte der Sarkophagfront einnimmt[72], Vorläufer auf römischen Grabaltären und Urnen hat. Das Motiv der zwei von ihm behandelten kleinasiatischen Sarkophage[73], die Verstorbene in der offenen Tür zeigen, ist ebenfalls nicht nur auf westlichen Sarkophagen[74], sondern auch auf den Urnen nachweisbar, wobei auf letzteren fast immer ein Ehepaar in der Tür erscheint[75].

N. Himmelmann hat bereits die Frage gestellt, ob bei den Türen kleinasiatischer Sarkophage eine Abhängigkeit von stadtrömischer Sepulkralkunst anzunehmen ist und dies für höchst unwahrscheinlich erklärt. Grundsätzlich wäre es nicht unmöglich, hier an Abhängigkeit in der einen oder anderen Richtung oder gar an Wechselbeziehungen zu denken, denn gerade bei Guirlandensarkophagen sind derartige Beziehungen längst erwiesen[76]. Andererseits liegt sowohl in Kleinasien als in Italien eine reiche Tradition älterer Denkmäler der Grabkunst vor, bei der die Tür eine Rolle spielt—für Rom bietet sich etwa die etruskische Sepulkralkunst als Quelle an—, so dass hier in beiden Gebieten durchaus mit eigener Entwicklung gerechnet werden darf. Auch die wenigen kleinasiatischen Belege mit Figuren in der Grabtür scheinen mir nicht gegen

68) F. Cumont, Recherches sur le symbolisme funéraire des Romains (1942) 83.157 f. mit Lit.
69) Oben Anm. 63.
70) Festschrift Mansel 49 ff. Zu kleinasiatischen Grabtüren auch Anadolu Arastirmalari 1965 II, In memoriam T. Bossert 104 (Boysal). Eichler, Jb. der Kunsthist. Slg. in Wien 13,1944,27 ff. Lambrechts, L'AntCl. 38,1969,43 f. (Gräber in Pessinus). Zur Symbolik der Tür auch Mansel, Bull.Inst.Bulg. 13,1939,162 (Thrakien). Ch. Picard, RA. 1958 I 102 f. Lehmann-Hartleben-Olsen a.O. 38 f. Boyance REA, 54, 1952,283. R. Turcan, Les sarcophages romains à représentations dionysiaques 617 f.
71) Auch auf Urnen finden wir die Tür manchmal auf den Nebenseiten: Pietrogrande BulCom. 63,1939. App. 17 ff. Taf. 1.

72) Auf dem christlichen Sarkophag H. Brandenburg, Repertorium der christlichantiken Sarkophage I Nr. 392, San Callisto, sind an beiden Enden der Vorderseite Türen angebracht.
73) Für einen möglichen dritten Beleg ebenda 50 Anm. 23. Der Sarkophag Mansel-Bean-Inan a.O. Taf. 32,118 f. zeigt Kerberos in der Tür.
74) Lawrence, AJA. 62,1958,274. Matz, Madrider Mitt. 9, 1969, 300 ff. mit vielen Abb.
75) Festschrift Mansel 51 Anm. 34. Ausnahme: Altmann, Die röm. Grabaltäre der Kaiserzeit (1905) 55 f. Nr. 11. G. Picardl L'art romain (1962) Taf. 36, Chantilly (Silen).
76) Mansel-Akarca a.O. 52 mit Verweis auf Rodenwaldt. Koch, AA. 1974,307 f.

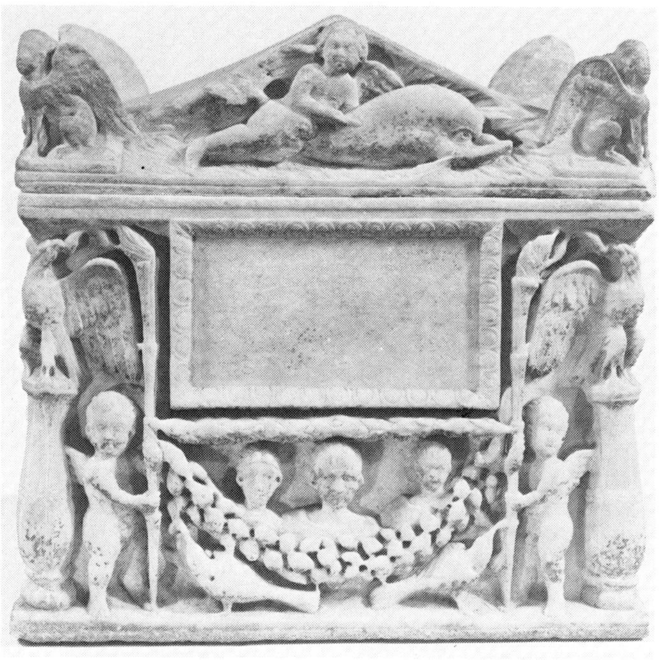

diese Auffassung zu sprechen, zumal die Figur—anders als in Rom—stets eine einzelne bleibt.

Interessant ist aber auch die rechte Nebenseite des Sarkophags in Konya. Von dem Eros auf dem Meerpanther war schon die Rede. Er trägt die zwei Guirlandenschwünge, in denen sich je ein mächtiger Adler erhebt. Zweifellos ist hier der Vogel der Apotheose gemeint, der in doppelter Gestalt die Hoffnung auf Unsterblichkeit versinnbildlichen soll[77].

Es zeigt sich, dass fast jede Einzelheit des Sarkophags in Konya—und auch der Platte in Malibu—Unsterblichkeitsgedanken zum Ausdruck bringt, die Eroten mit den Meerestieren ebenso wie die Trauben, die Adler, die Hadestür mit der Verstorbenen oder auch die dionysischen Masken. Für die Amazonomachie und die drei Figuren in der Mitte der Vorderseite des Sarkophags in Konya darf somit dasselbe angenommen werden, wenn auch letztere bisher nicht präziser interpretiert werden konnten. Auch hier also, wie so oft auf römischen Sarkophagen, eine sehr heterogene Unsterblichkeitserwartung.

Ein grosser Teil der hier besprochenen sepulkralen Motive, die Adler, die Verbindung Eros-Delphin, die von Eroten gehaltene Guirlande mit Porträtbüsten sowie Sphingen sind bereits auf einer augusteischen Urne in Cleveland nachweisbar (Abb. 10)[78]. Auch dies wieder ein Hinweis darauf, wieviele Elemente aus dem Figurenschmuck römischer Sarkophage von den Grab-

altären und den Aschenurnen übernommen wurden[79].

Die ungewöhnlich enge Verwandschaft des Sarkophags in Konya mit der Platte im Getty-Museum erlaubt es, letztere derselben pamphylischen Werkstatt zuzuweisen wie jenen. Vermutlich ist sie aber ein wenig jünger, um 170 n.Chr., gearbeitet worden.

Von G. Koch höre ich, dass er seit langerem daran zweifelt, dass die hier im Mittelpunkt stehenden Sarkophage alle in Pamphylien entstanden. Er teilt mir freundlicherwiese auch mit, dass in Kurze eine Arbeit von Asgari erscheint, in der der Nachweis erbracht wird, dass die Werkstatt erst in einem relativ späten Zeitpunkt aus Phrygien oder Lydien nach Pamphylien verlegt wurde.

Die Erwerbung der bei den hier besprochenen Sarkophagreliefs durch das Getty-Museum darf als besonderer Glücksfall auch für die Forschung angesehen werden. Selten hat man die Möglichkeit, zwei so wichtige Vertreter zweier grosser Zentren römischer Sarkophagkunst, der stadtrömischen und der kleinasiatischen, nebeneinander studieren zu können. Besonders deutlich werden dabei die Unterschiede, aber auch manche Gemeinsamkeiten. Besonders förderlich ist dabei natürlich, dass es sich um zwei Reliefs handelt, die in der grundsätzlichen Typologie, den von Eroten getragenen Guirlanden, übereinstimmen.

Konrad Schauenburg
Kiel

77) Zum sepulkralen Adler Schauenburg, JdI. 81,1966,299. Ders., AA. 1975. Vgl. jetzt Delt. 26, 1971 Taf. 149, attischer Sarkophag in Patras, Adler als Guirlandenträger. Inst.Neg. 62.851, Neapel (gleiches Motiv wie auf dem Sarkophag in Patras). Inst.Neg. 69.2519, Thermenmuseum (Adler im Giebel des Deckels). Vgl. auch die Stele in Adana: Gentse Bijdragen 18,1959/60,35 (2 Adler unter Knabenbüste). Für Oberitalien s. jetzt Gabelmann a.O. 123 zu Taf. 25, Sarkophag in

Modena. Interessant das Relief Vatikan 7562, Gall.lapid. 25: zwei fliegende Viktorien mit Guirlande, in deren Bogen ein Adler steht (verwandt das Motiv des Sarkophags AA. 1973,506 Abb. 8, Louvre). Dazu auch das Grabrelief Vatikan 7027. Gall.lapid. Inst.Neg. 74.247, Ara im Thermenmuseum: Eroten tragen Muschel mit Adler darin.
78) G. Chase, Greek and Roman sculpture in American coll. (1924) Abb. 229. Für die Aufnahme danke ich der Museumsleitung sehr.
79) Vgl. oben. S. 61 und 64, Anm. 37.

Die Büste von Eleusis und ihre Repliken

Die Büste in Athen, Nat.-Mus.181, der sogenannte Eubouleus aus Eleusis, füllte in den Jahrzehnten nach ihrer Auffindung im Jahre 1885[1] die Seiten der Fachliteratur wie kaum ein anderes Kunstwerk. Die Diskussion entbrannte vor allem um die Fragen, ob der Kopf den inschriftlich überlieferten Eubouleus des Praxiteles darstelle und ob es sich bie ihm um das Original oder eine römische Kopie handle. Die Büste schien sich jedoch in einer der Verschlossenheit ihres Ausdrucks adäquaten Weise dem ordnenden und klärenden Zugriff der Fachwelt zu entziehen. So wurde es in den letzten Jahrzehnten merklich stiller um sie, bis nach der Auffindung einer weiteren Büste des sogenannten Eubouleus auf der Athener Agora im Jahre 1959 E. Harrison die insgesamt 9 nach und nach bekanntgewordenen Exemplare dieses Typus als Alexander den Grossen erklärte[2]. "It is as if a hard white spotlight had been suddenly thrown onto an object which we have been accustomed to see only by candlelight", so charakterisiert sie den Unterschied zwischen der alten und neuen Betrachtungsweise[3].

Die Unterschiedlichkeit der vertretenen Meinungen— hier griechisches Original[4] oder zumindest Werkstattwiederholung aus der Zeit gegen 320 v.Chr.[5], dort römische Kopie[6], bis jetzt eleusinische Gottheit und nun plötzlich Alexander der Grosse[7]—scheint eine nochmalige Betrachtung des Werkes, von dem all die Unstimmigkeiten ausgingen, der Büste von Eleusis und ihren Repliken, zu rechtfertigen.

A) Büste Athen, Nat.-Mus.181 (Abb.1,4,11)[8]

Die Büste wurde im Jahre 1885 im Ploutonion von Eleusis zusammen mit anderen Weihegaben, unter denen sich auch ein Inschriftblock mit einer Weihinschrift fur Eubouleus befand, entdeckt[9]. Der Jünglingskopf zeigt eine auf den ersten Blick überraschende

Physiognomie: Unter einer verhältnismässig schmalen, stark gebuckelten Stirn verbreitert sich das Gesicht zu den Schläfen hin und führt in flachen Kurven zum runden Kinn. In diesem auffallenden Oval stehen die kleinen Augen seltsam hoch und nahe beieinander, die Wangen sind weich und langgezogen, der Mund sehr klein und voll. Eine Lockenzange, deren eines Ende über dem rechten Auge tiefer hängt, beschattet die Stirn, darüber ist ein fünfteiliger Lockenstern geschichtet. Unter einem Reifen fällt die Masse der Haare seitlich längs der Wangen dicht und ungeordnet herab und rückwärts tief in den Nacken. Am Hinterhaupt fliessen die Strähnen von einem Längsscheitel geteilt nach beiden Seiten. Der blühende Jünglingskopf ist auf einem starken Hals, bei dem der rechte Halsmuskel kräftig vortritt, zur linken Schulter gedreht. Die Büste ist mit einem Chiton bekleidet und an den Schultern von verschiedener Breite: Während von der linken Schulter ein grösseres Stück vorhanden ist, wurde die rechte ziemlich knapp am Ansatz abgeschnitten.

In seiner malerisch-pastosen Bearbeitung hebt sich das Haar wirkungsvoll von der zart schimmernden Hautoberfläche ab, ein künstlerischer Effekt, der in seiner Virtuosität in krassem Gegensatz steht zu der summarischen Faltenwiedergabe an dem bescheidenen Gewandstück, das auf der Büste klebt und der geradezu stümperhaften Anbringung des "Sockels", von dem sie sich erhebt.

Bei dem Kopf sind Brauen und teilweise Oberlider, Nase und Oberlippe abgeschlagen, Unterlippe und Kinn bestossen, Verletzungen, die in ihrer Art, wie Benndorf feststellte[10], nur absichtlich herbeigeführt worden sein können. Dies ist wichtig festzuhalten, da der Verdacht auf willkürliche Beschädigung auch bei drei weiteren Exemplaren dieses Typus auftreten wird.

1) D.Philios, Eph.Arch.1886,257 ff,pl.10.
2) Hesperia 29,1960,382 ff,pl.85 c,d.
3) a.a.O.383.
4) Philios a.a.O.; ders.,AM 20,1895,256 ff; O.Benndorf,AD I 21; ders., Anz.Akad.Wiss.Wien,phil.-hist.Kl.1887,Nr.25; A.Furtwängler, AA 4, 1889,47,57,147; ders.,Meisterwerke der griechischen Plastik,1893,566; W.Klein, Praxiteles,1898,429 ff; ders.,Geschichte der griechischen Kunst II,1905,379; H.Stuart Jones, The Sculptures of the Museo Capitolino,1912,221; G.Lippold, Kopien und Umbildungen griechischer Statuen,1923,116; ders.,Sarapis und Bryaxis,in: Festschrift P.Arndt, 1925,125; E.Pfuhl, JdI 41,1926,41,Anm.1; G.E.Rizzo, Prassitele,1932, 103; Ch.Picard, Manuel d'Archéologie grecque (IVe siecle), 1954,386 ff; M.Bieber, The Sculpture of the Hellenistic Age,1961,179; W.-H. Schuchhardt, Die Kunst der Griechen, 1940,326 f; S.Karouzou, Archäologisches Nationalmuseum Athen, Antike Skulpturen,1969,172 f; Zögernd verhält sich G.M.A.Richter, Handbuch der griechischen Kunst,1966,167 und dies.,Sculpture and Sculptors of the Greeks, 1970,139,203.
5) Lippold, Hdb.241; ders.,RE XXII 2,1805 s.v.Praxiteles.
6) Gegen die Originalität des Kopfes sprach sich als erster H.Heydemann, 13.Hallisches Winckelmannsprogramm,1888, loff, aus. Vgl. weiters O.Kern, AM 16,1891,28; J.Six, JdI 24,1909,16; C. Blümel, Griechische Bildhauerarbeit,1927,40,45 f,48; L.Curtis, Die klassische Kunst Griechenlands, 1938,385 f; G.E.Mylonas, Eleusis and the Eleusinian Mysteries,1962,199; H.v.Steuben in W.Helbig, Führer durch die öffentlichen Sammulungen klassischer Altertumer in Rom II, 1966,93 f,Nr.1240.
7) Harrison a.a.O.(Anm.2). Auch sie erklärt die eleusinische Büste für eine römische Kopie. Ihr folgen M.Bieber, Alexander the Great in Greek and Roman Art,1964,26; T.Hölscher,Ideal und Wirklichkeit in den Bildnissen Alexanders des Grossen,1971,9; E.Berger,AntK 14, 1971,140,Anm.8; T.L.Shear Jr.,Hesperia 40,1971,273 f.
8) Photos: DAI Athen Hege 1000 (Abb.1), Dr.E.Pochmarski, Graz (Abb.2,3). Gute Abb.zuletzt bei J.Charbonneaux, R.Martin, F.Villard, Das hellenistische Griechenland, 203,Abb.212.- Den Kopf und seine Repliken in Griechenland konnte ich anlässlich eines Stipendiums des Österreichischen Archäologischen Institutes studieren.
9) Philios a.a.O.(Anm.1)

Bemerkenswert an dem Kopf ist sein Ausdruck, der sich dem Betrachter nur schwer erschliesst: Voll blühender, jugendlicher Schönheit, das Antlitz von der umhüllenden Masse der Haare beschattet, ist er von einer gewissen Schwermut erfüllt, sein mildes Wesen bleibt merkwürdig undurchdringlich und bei aller pittoresken Anmut strahlt er eine bukolische Frische aus. So erscheint sein Ausdruck von seltsamer Ambiguität.

Man vertrat vereinzelt die Meinung, dass das Werk ursprünglich als Büste geschaffen war[11], jedoch schon Benndorf hatte richtig erkannt, dass es Teil einer Statue ist[12]. Die Haltung dieser Statue war gänzlich anders, als die frontale Ausrichtung der Büste es uns jetzt weismachen will: Halsgrube und Brustbein sind etwas nach rechts verschoben, was auf eine Drehung der rechten Schulter nach vorn schliessen lässt. Das rechte Schlüsselbein liegt höher als das linke, durch die Kopfdrehung ist der linke Nackenmuskel höher emporgeführt. Die rechte Gesichtshälfte ist grösser und das Haar an der linken Wange weiter ausladend gebildet, sodass der Kopf von der linken Wange weiter ausladend gebildet, sodass der Kopf von halblinks betrachtet werden muss, um die richtigen Proportionen zu erhalten. Im Originalzustand wird die Büste einer Sitzfigur angehört haben, wofür ihr in sich gekehrter Gesichtsausdruck spricht.

Sicher ist es auf eine Beschädigung der Statue zurückzuführen, dass sie zu einer Büste umgearbeitet wurde[13]. Auf eine nachträgliche Überarbeitung weist auch die Tatsache hin, dass der Chiton an einer Stelle niedriger liegt als die nackte Haut: So ist am äusseren Ende des linken Schlüsselbeines eine seichte Delle zu erkennen, die von Chitonfalten überdeckt ist. Spuren von nachträglicher Bearbeitung finden sich weiters am Chitonrand unterhalb des rechten Schlüsselbeines. Die Stümperhaftigkeit in der Ausführung des Chitons und des "Sockels" im Vergleich zur Qualität der übrigen Arbeit wird durch die Feststellung einer späteren Überarbeitung überhaupt erst verständlich. Aber auch ein anderes Problem, das der Kopf bisher aufgab, kann auf diese Weise gelöst werden. Die Frage, ob die Büste nun eine griechische Originalarbeit aus der Zeit um 320 v.Chr. oder eine römische Kopie sei, konnte auch mit Hilfe technischer Untersuchungen nicht eindeutig geklärt werden[14]. Die atmende Frische des Ausdrucks plädierte für die eine Antwort, die tiefen Bohrgänge im Haar, die mit der Bohrtechnik des 4.Jhs.v.Chr. unvereinbar schienen, für die andere. Eine eingehende Betrachtung des Haares aber bestätigt, was schon zuvor über die Büste gesagt wurde, eine nachträgliche Überarbeitung in römischer Zeit. Dabei wurden die Locken mit dem Bohrer in annähernd wagrechter Richtung förmcher Strähnen gar nicht mehr erkenntlich ist, sondern erst anhand der Kopien "rekonstruiert" werden muss (vgl. Abb. 9). Auch das Nackenhaar ist sekundär abgearbeitet. Die Zerstückelung der Lockensträhnen mit dem Bohrer, die an der rechten Schläfe besonders deutlich ist, wurde vermutlich im 3.Jh.n.Chr. vorgenommen. Eine solche nachträgliche Überarbeitung konnte in letzter Zeit auch an einem anderen berühmten Werk, dessen Originalität wegen diverser Unstimmigkeiten bisweilen in Frage gestellt wurde, nachgewiesen werden, am Hermes des Praxiteles[15]. Antike Reparaturen sind keine Seltenheit und lassen sich für den olympischen Zeus des Phidias sogar literarisch belegen[15a]. Auch an der eleusinischen Herme löst die Feststellung römerzeitlicher Überarbeitung das Problem, das das Vorhandensein jüngerer Stilmerkmale wie die tiefen Bohrkanäle sowie die Divergenz in der Qualität zwischen Kopf und Büste bisher aufgab und räumt ihr einen sicheren Platz in den Jahren gegen 320 v.Chr. ein.

a) Kopf Athen,Nat.-Mus.1839 (Abb.2,5)[16], aus Eleusis.

1883 in der Nähe des Telesterions gefunden. Der Bruch, der in Augenhöhe durch den Kopf geht, ist derzeit mit Gips veschmiert. Es hat den Anschein, als ob der Kopf absichtlich zerschlagen worden wäre. Die einst eingesetzten Augen sind verloren, Nase und Unterlippe samt Kinn abgeschlagen, ebenso wie der rechte Teil des Lockensternes über den Stirnlocken. Der Hochstand der Augen von Nr.181 ist hier gemildert, wodurch der Ausdruck verändert wird: Der Kopf lässt viel von der sinnenden Schwermut, die bei der eleusinischen Büste sosehr beeindruckte, vermissen. Er zeigt im Nacken einen dichten Haarkranz, der bei Nr.181 abgearbeitet wurde. Es ist eine gute, lebendige, sicher noch hellenistische Arbeit[17], die in der Bohrtechnik des Haares an den Bart des Zeus des Eukleides erinnert.

10) AD I 21.
11) Furtwängler,Meisterwerke 566; Klein, Praxiteles,429.
12) AD I 21.
13) Benndorf a.a.O. vermutete, dass das Büstenstück in eine Statue eingekittet war und dass der für die Büste verwendete Marmorblock nur verschieden grosse Schulterstücke hergab.
14) Sh.Adam, The Technique of Greek Sculpture,1966,36.
15) W.-H.Schuchhardt, Geschichte der griechischen Kunst,1971,382.
15a) Paus.IV 31,6) J.Frel,AAA V/1,1972,73 ff.
16) Photos:Abb.2 DAI Athen,Neg.1188 (zeigt den Kopf vor der Restaurierung), Abb.5 Dr.E.Pochmarski.- Philios,Eph.Arch.1890,129, Anm.1; O.Kern,AM 16,1891,27 f,Taf.II; J.Svoronos,Eph.Arch.1911, 39,pl.3,3; Lippold, Kopien und Umbildungen griechischer Statuen 116 f; Richter,Sculpture and Sculptors of the Greeks 139,Abb.550; Harrison a.a.O.(Anm.2) 382,Anm. 57 a,Nr.2; Karouzou, Archäologisches Nationalmuseum 173.
17) Karouzou a.a.O.173; Richter, Sculpture and Sculptors of the Greeks,139, hält den Kopf für eine römische Kopie.

b) Kopf Athen,Nat.-Mus.2650, aus dem Gebiet des Militärspitals südlich der Akropolis (Abb.3,6)[18].

Da die Haare nicht von Bohrgängen zerschnitten sind, lassen sich die bei Nr.181 zerstückelten Lockenbahnen in ihrer Anlage besser ablesen, so etwa der Verlauf der langen Locke, die hinter dem rechten Ohr in den Nacken fällt (vgl.Abb.6). Die Tränenkarunkeln sind angegeben, die Unterlider weiter hinabgezogen, wodurch die Augen grösser wirken als bei Nr.181 und der Gesichtsausdruck verändert wird. Die Stirn ist so stark gebuckelt, dass eine tiefe Querfalte entsteht. Die Kopie dürfte in augusteischer Zeit entstanden sein. Der stumpfen, trockenen Arbeit fehlt jegliches Verständnis für das Original.

c) Kopf Athen, Akropolis-Museum 2394[19] Aus Athen, genauer Fundort nicht bekannt. Unpubliziert.

Fragment. Höhe vom Kinn bis zur obersten Locke 0,26 m. Höhe des Gesichtes 0,21 m. Die linke Gesichtshälfte ist abgeschlagen (willkürlich?), das Haar ist auf der rechten Seite bis zum Reifen erhalten, der Hinterkopf fehlt und war gesondert angesetzt, wie ein Bohrloch zeigt. Die Nase ist abgeschlagen, der Mund zur Gänze erhalten, die Lippen jedoch bestossen. Das Kinn ist auf der linken Seite mehr verletzt als auf der rechten. An dem erhaltenen rechten Auge ist die plastisch angegebene Pupille bestossen, ebenso wie die Braue, der Wulst darunter und das Oberlid teilweise abgeschlagen sind. Der Augenwinkel ist mit dem Bohrer eingetieft, die Tränenkarunkel plastisch abgesetzt. Kleine Absplitterungen sind an der rechten Wange festzustellen. Das Haar ist nicht mit dem Bohrer unterhöhlt, die Haarmasse wirkt kompakt und stumpf. Das erhaltene Auge ist gross und liegt nicht so hoch im Gesicht wie bei der eleusinischen Büste, wodurch die Wange verkürzt wird.

d) Kopf Athen, Akropolis-Museum 7285[20]. Aus Athen, genauer Fundort nicht bekannt. Unpubliziert.

Höhe 0,33 m. Das Gesicht ist zur Gänze abgeschlagen, was auf eine absichtliche Zerstörung schliessen lässt, da die in die Stirn fallende Lockenzange noch vollständig erhalten ist. Der Hals ist schräg von links unten nach rechts oben abgebrochen und vorne bestossen. Die Locken sind an den Seiten mit dem Bohrer abgeteilt und unterhöhlt, am Hinterkopf kaum ausgearbeitet, wo sie

vom Längsscheitel aus flach nach rechts und links gestrichen sind. Die Arbeit scheint wesentlich besser gewesen zu sein als Nr.2394.

e) Büste Patras, Archäologisches Museum 12[21]. Unpubliziert.

An der Büste ist wie bei der aus Eleusis der Chiton angegeben. Auf ihrer Unterseite ist ein Zapfen mit Dübellöchern angebracht, reste von Metalldübeln haben sich erhalten. Auffallend ist, dass ofenbar die Büste samt Chiton in eine Statue eingelassen war und die Fuge nicht, wie zu erwarten, entlang des Chitonrades verlief[22]. Chitonfalten sind nur auf der Vorderseite angegeben, die Rückseite der Büste ist nicht ausgearbeitet, sodass ein Steg zwischen Nackenhaar und Chitonrand stehengeblieben ist. Nase, Mund und Kinn sind abgeschlagen. In den Augen sind die Tränenkarunkel angegeben. Der Charakter des Originals ist gut erfasst. Die Kopie ist wohl in späthadrianischantoninische Zeit zu datieren.

f) Büste Agora Athen S 2089 (Abb. 7)[23].

Aus thasischem (?) Marmor, Höhe = 0,615 m, gefunden in einer spätrömischen Befestigungsanlage[24]. Die Büste, die besterhaltene von allen, ist unvollständig geblieben. 7 Messpunkte (2 an den Locken über der Stirn, einer am Kinn, je zwei seitlich am Haar, vgl.Abb. 7a), ein Marmorsteg zwischen Nackenhaar und Rücken sowie Marmorklumpen dort, wo der Bohrer eingesetzt werden sollte, zwischen Gesicht und Haarmasse und unter der Nase, sind stehengeblieben. Auch der unverhältnismässig breite Nasenrücken ist auf den unvollendeten Zustand der Kopie zurückzuführen. Der Streifen rund um die Büste harrte wohl eher seiner Ausarbeitung in einen Chiton, wie ihn die Büsten Athen und Patras zeigen, als dass er eine schützende Oberfläche war, die bei der Fertigstellung abgemeisselt werden sollte[24]. Die Büste erhebt sich über einem Sockel mit Akanthusornament, dessen seitliche Blätter ebenfalls nicht ausgearbeitet sind. Die Augen blicken freier als auf der eleusinischen Büste und sind grösser. Am entscheidendsten aber wird die Physiognomie durch den breiten Nasenrücken verändert. Die Kopie ist an den Anfang des 3.Jh.n.Chr. zu datieren[25].

g) Kopf Rom, Kapitolin.Museum,Inv.-Nr.44 (Abb. 8)[26].

Lunenser Marmor,H = 0,615 m, die Herme ist antik,

---

18) Photos: Dr. E. Pochmarski. Svoronos, Eph. Arch. 1911,39, pl. 3,4; Karouzou a.a.O.173; Harrison a.a.O.383,Anm.57 a,Nr.5.
19) Pfuhl,JdI 41,1926,41,Anm.1; Harrison a.a.O.383,Anm.57 a, Nr.3.
20) Pfuhl a.a.O.; Harrison a.a.O.Nr.4.
21) Harrison a.a.O. Nr.7.
22) Dasselbe Problem stellte sich Heydemann a.a.O. (Anm.6)11 für die eleusinische Büste, da er annahm, ihre sonderbare Zurichtung sei für die Einlassung in eine Statue gedacht, was er als Beweis gegen die Originalität des Werkes nimmt.
23) Photos:Agora Excavations,Neg.Nr.81-696,81-699. Zu allen Einzel-

heiten der Büste vgl.Harrison a.a.O.(Anm.2)382-389,pl.85 c,d; Bieber, a.a.O. (Anm.7)fig.9,10; Adam a.a.O(Anm.14) pl. 18c; H.Jucker, *Das Bildnis im Blätterkelch,* 1961,190, Anm.3; The Athenian Agora, A Guide, 1962,194 f.
24) Harrison a.a.O.385.
25) Die Annahme, die Kopie sei durch den Herulereinfall des Jahres 257 n.Chr. an ihrer Vollendung gehindert worden (The Athenian Agora, A Guide, 194 f) ergibt einen zu späten Zeitansatz für die Arbeit.
26) Photo: Anderson; EA 424; Helbig a.a.O. (Anm.6) II,Nr.1240; Stuart Jones a.a.O.(Anm.4) 221,pl.54,Nr.1; Harrison a.a.O. 383,Nr.9.

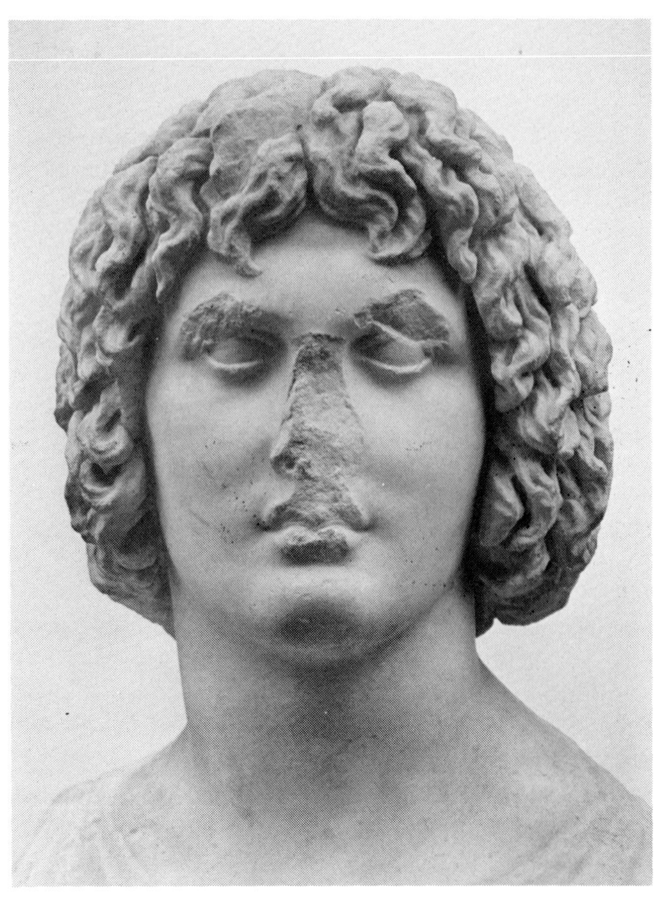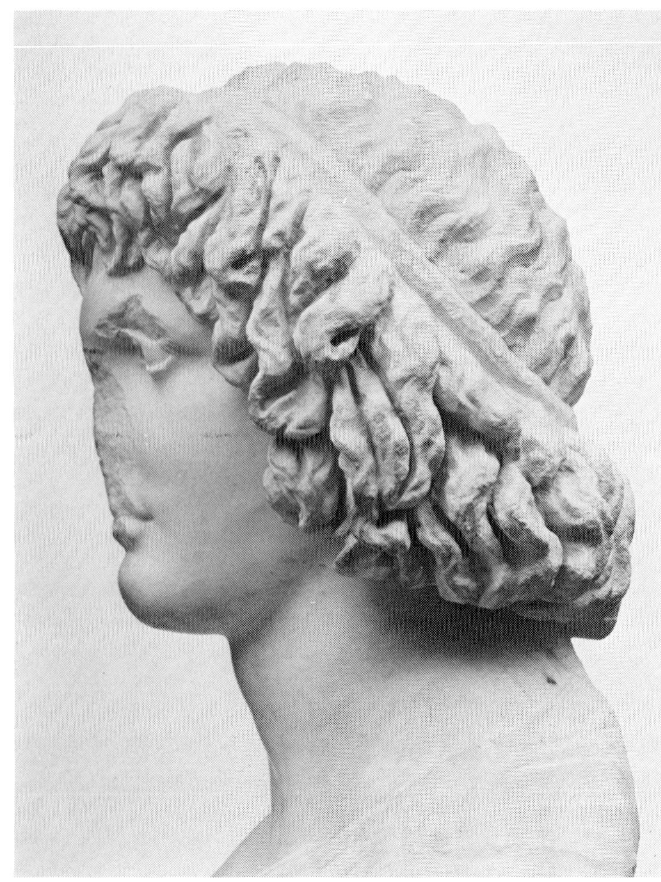

1a-d Eubouleus. Athen 181

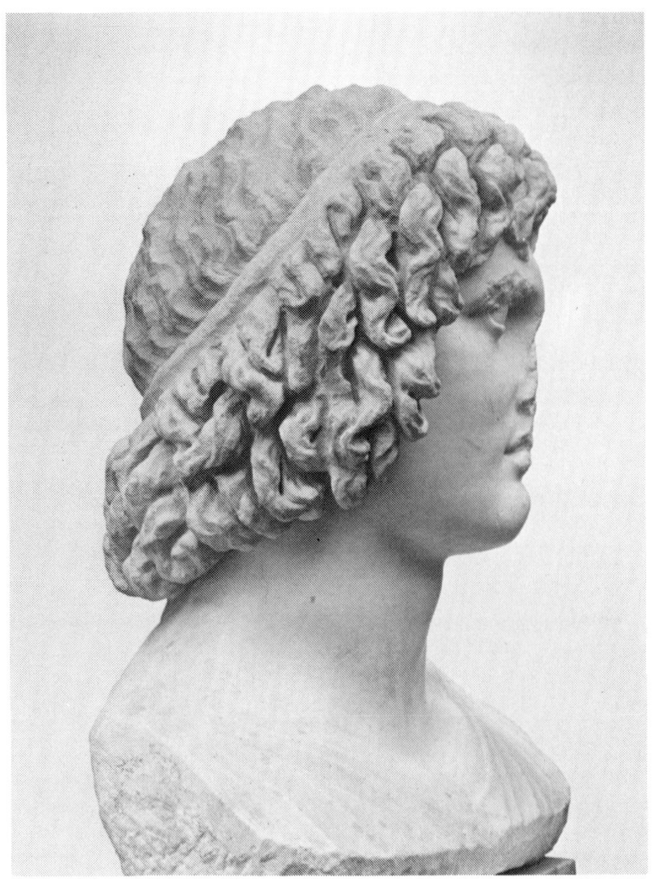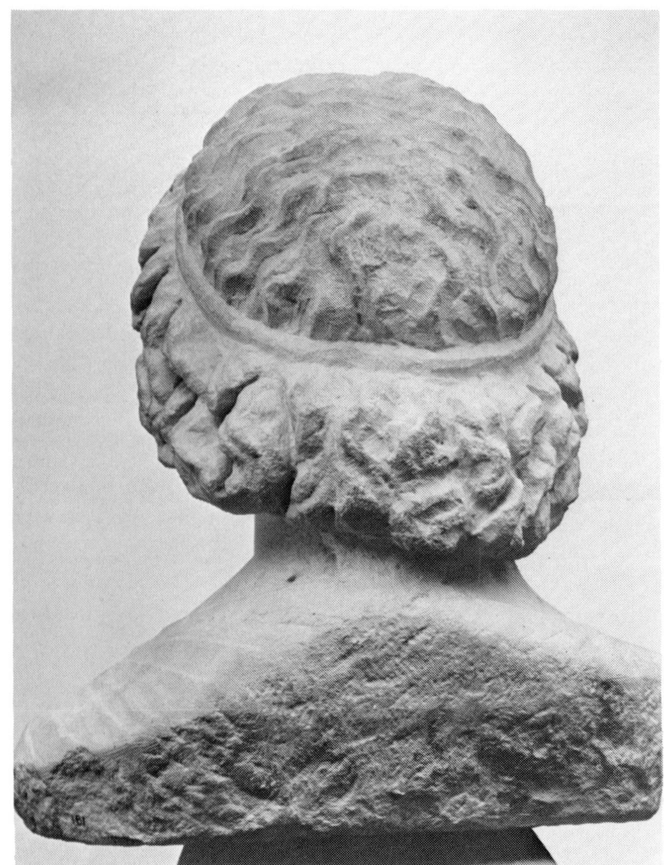

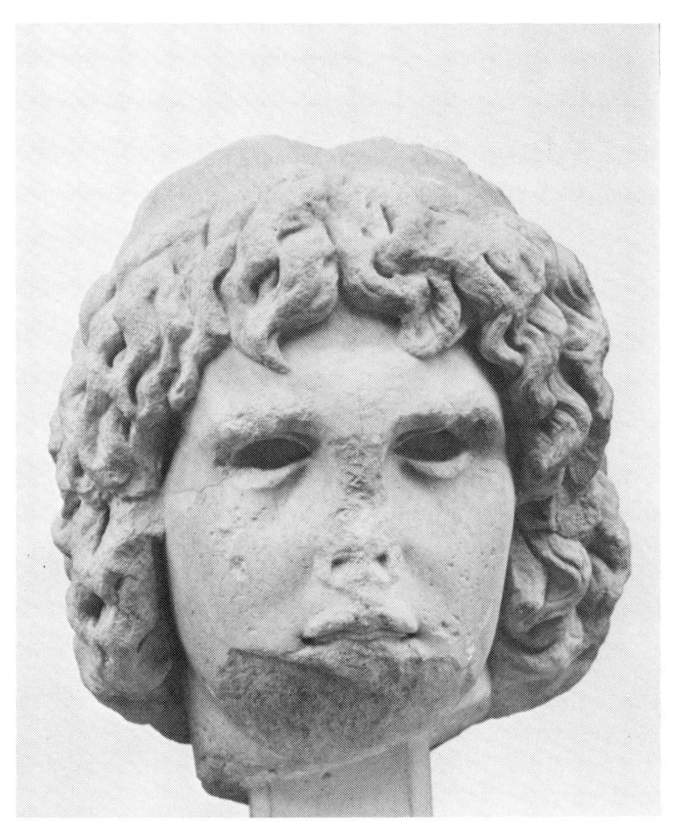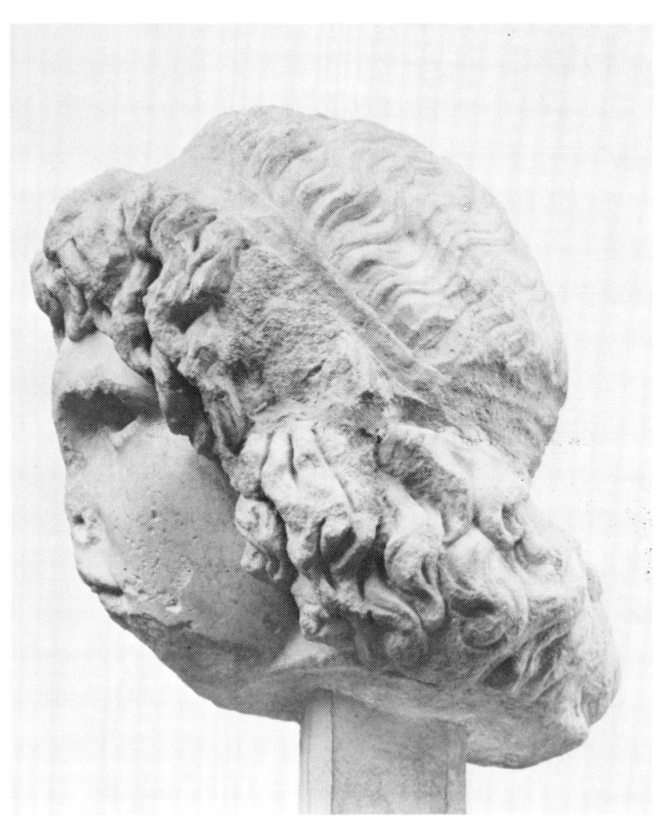

2a-d Eubouleus. Athen 1839

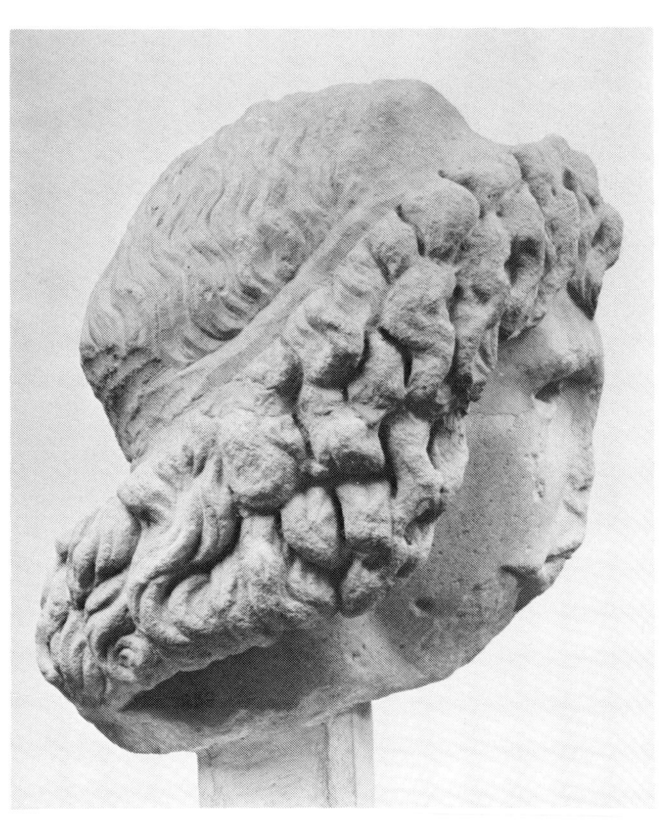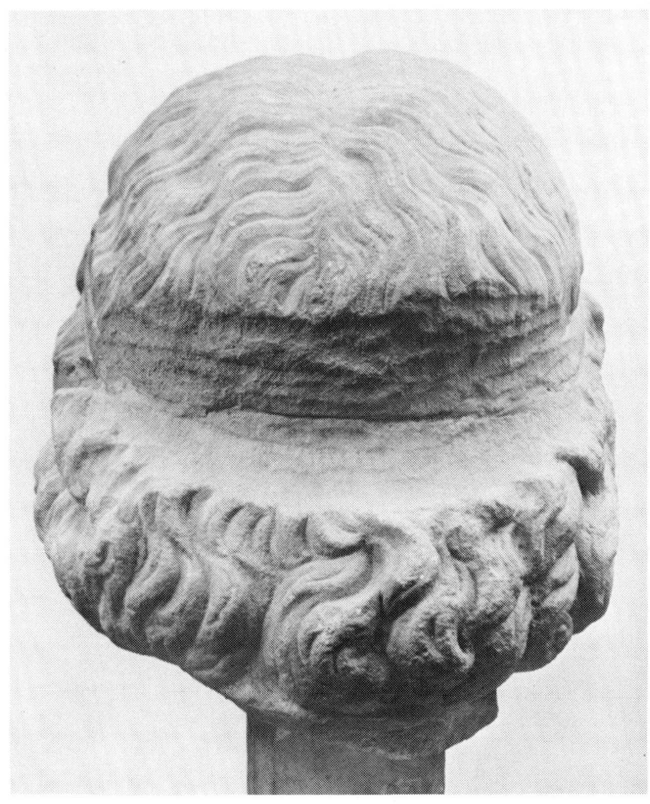

aber nicht zugehörig, die untere Hälfte der Nase ergänzt. Vor der Auffindung der Büste von der Athener Agora war diese die wichtigste weil nahezu vollständigste Kopie. Sie besitzt allerdings nichts Weiches, Gedämpftes wie das Original, sondern ist hart und spröd in den Konturen. Auch gelang es dem Kopisten nicht, die duftige Fülle des Haares wiederzugeben. Der Kopf ist unrichtig in die Büste eingesetzt, da die Neigung fehlt. 2.Jh.n.Chr.?

h) Kopf Mantua, Palazzo Ducale (Abb. 9)[27].

Der sogenannte Vergil. Italischer Marmor, Höhe des Kopfes 0,29 m, des Gesichtes 0,21 m. Hals und Herme sind in Gips ergänzt. Der Kopf ist leicht nach links geneigt, Pupille und Iris sind angegeben. Der untere Teil der Wangen ist in Marmor ergänzt, das linke Unterlid in Gips. Der gesamte untere Teil der Locken, der seitlich unter dem Reifen herabhängt, ist ebenfalls in Gips ergänzt und viel zu lang. Die Haarbehandlung ist locker. Die Kopie dürfte aus dem Ende des 2.Jh.n. Chr. stammen. Das Stück ist modern poliert, die Augen sind retuschiert[28].

Ihr Meister.

Seit eine geistreiche Theorie die im Ploutonion von Eleusis gefundene Büste Athen NM 181 mit einer kopflosen Herme in Rom mit der Aufschrift Εὐβουλεὺς Πραξιτέλους[29] in Verbindung gebracht hatte[30], wobei auch die an derselben Stelle zutage getretene Weihinschrift an Eubouleus mitbestimmend gewesen sein dürfte, wurden immer wieder Stimmen laut, die sich dieser Hypothese anschlossen: Nach Benndorf waren es zunächst Furtwängler[31], Heydemann[32] und Svoronos[33], die die Büste dem Praxiteles zuwiesen. Furtwängler sah in ihr ein Werk aus der mittleren Schaffenszeit des Meisters, während sie Benndorf, dem später Rizzo[34] und Picard[35] folgten, in die Zeit nach dem Hermes datierte. Lippold hielt den Kopf für eine Werkstattwiederholung des praxitelischen Iakchos aus den Jahren um 320 v.Chr.[36]. Philios, der Ausgräber der Büste, erkannte in ihr wohl

praxitelische Züge, die jedoch in jener Zeit Allgemeingut waren und nicht unbedingt für die Hand des Meisters selbst sprechen, eher aber Ähnlichkeit mit den skopasischen Köpfen aus Tegea[37]. Praxitelischen Einfluss glaubten auch Schuchhardt[38] und Richter[39] in ihr feststellen zu können. Andere Wege ging Klein, der das Werk dem vatikanischen Ganymed und dem Steinhauser'schen Kopf an die Seite stellte und es dem Leochares zuwies[40], Six hingegen hielt es für eine Schöpfung des wenig greifbaren Euphranor[41].

Den unmittelbaren Zusammenhang des Kopfes mit den besten der Sarapis-Nachbildungen erkannte als erster L.Curtius und teilte ihn damit dem oeuvre des Bryaxis zu[42]. Aber auch in neuerer Zeit meldeten sich Stimmen zu Wort, die die nahe Verwandtschaft der beiden Werke unterstreichen: J.Charbonneaux sieht Übereinstimmungen in Stirn- und Haarbildung, ohne jedoch den Namen Bryaxis als Künstler der eleusinischen Büste direkt auszusprechen[43]. In einer Grazer Dissertation hat F.F.Schwarz nachdrücklich für eine Zuweisung des Kopfes an Bryaxis wegen der stilistischen Nähe zum Zeus von Otricoli plädiert, der ebenfalls dem Bryaxis zuzuteilen ist[44].

Nunmehr wäre zu prüfen, welche dieser Hypothesen die stichhältigste ist oder ob der Meister dieses faszinierenden Werkes anonym bleiben muss.

Gewiss weist der Kopf in der duftigen, malerisch-unbestimmten Bearbeitung des Haares, das sich auch stofflich von der seidig schimmernden Oberfläche der Haut abzusetzen scheint, Ähnlichkeiten mit dem Hermes in Olympia auf. Da alle Züge des verschlossenen Jünglings, sein Fundort und die mitgefundene Weihinschrift an Eubouleus auf eine eleusinische Unterweltsgottheit schliessen liessen, kam der Hermenschaft in Rom, der einen Eubouleus des Praxiteles nennt, als glänzender "Beweis" für eine Zuschreibung hinzu. Aber abgesehen davon, dass wir nicht wissen, wie der Kopf auf der Herme nun wirklich aussah, so kann ein direkter Zusammenhang der eleusinischen Büste mit Praxiteles nicht beste-

27) Photos:Giovetti,Mantua; EA 17; A.Levi, Sculture Greche e Romane del Palazzo Ducale di Mantova,1931,Nr.34,Taf.32; Harrison a.a.O.Nr.8.

28) Der Kopf im Louvre, den Harrison a.a.O. als 10. Exemplar dieses Typus anführt (Photo:Giraudon 2060), ist keine Replik, sondern eine der zahlreichen Umbildungen, wie sie sich in der Folgezeit häufig finden (vgl.auch Deltion 23,1968 B1,63 ff,Taf.33 b).

29) E.Löwy,Inschriften griechischer Bildhauer,1885,Nr.504; Helbig a.a.O(Anm.6) I,1963,59,Nr.75.

30) Benndorf,AD I 21; ders.,Anz.Adad.Wiss.Wien,phil.-hist.Kl.1887, Nr.25.

31) Meisterwerke 566; ders.,AA 4,1889,47,57,147.

32) a.a.O.(Anm.6) 5.

33) Eph.Arch.1911,39-52.

34) Prassitele 103 ff,108.

35) Manuel (Anm.4) 386 ff.

36) Hdb.241; RE XXII,2 1805 s.v.Praxiteles.

37) Eph.Arch.1886,266; AM 20,1895,256,261,264.

38) Die Kunst der Griechen,1940,327.

39) Handbuch der griechischen Kunst 167.

40) Geschichte der griechischen Kunst II,379;Praxiteles 429 ff.

41) JdI 24,1909,14 ff. Für ihn steht es damit dem Skopas näher als dem Praxiteles.

42) Die klassische Kunst Griechenlands 385 f.

43) MonPiot 52,2,1962,23; vgl.auch Charbonneaux-Villard-Martin, Das hellenistische Griechenland 201.

44) Bryaxis. Eine Studie zur Persönlichkeitsforschung im 4.Jh.v.Chr., Diss.Graz 1962,83 f. Die Zuweisung des Zeus von Otricoli darf nach W. Amelung, Ausonia 3,1908,115 und RA (IV série),1903,II,177-204 als gesichert gelten, vgl. Schwarz a.a.O.

hen. Das dumpfe Brüten des schwerlockigen, breitgesichtigen Jünglings (Abb. 10) hat nichts mit der Verträumtheit praxitelischer Gestalten gemeinsam, auch nicht mit der Versonnenheit eines seiner derberen Burschen, des ausruhenden Satyrs, wie öfter behauptet wurde[45]. Es entspringt einer völlig anders gearteten Geistigkeit, der nicht Offenes und Heiteres eigen ist. Die Kompaktheit und Breite des eigenwilligen Kopfes hat Philios veranlasst, ihn in die Nähe des Skopas zu rücken[46]. Diese Äusserlichkeit kann jedoch nicht darüber hinwegtäuschen, dass von der extrovertierten Leidenschaftlichkeit skopasischer Köpfe an unserem Jüngling nichts zu verspüren ist. Auch sind hier stilistische Bedenken, vor allem in der Augenbildung, anzumelden. Kleins Zuschreibung an Leochares[47] bleibt sehr vage. Die Ähnlichkeit mit dem Ganymed geht über Allgemeinheiten wie den Kopfumriss im Profil, die wohl in der Zeit begründet liegen, nicht hinaus, und vom geistigen Feuer des Steinhäuser'schen Kopfes etwa scheint der dahindämmernde Jüngling völlig unberührt. Die Hypothese von Six, die Büste dem Euphranor zuzuweisen[48], darf als reine Vermutung gewertet werden, da unsere Kenntnis über diesen Künstler viel zu gering ist, als dass wir ihm mit einiger Sicherheit Werke zuteilen könnten.

Bleibt die Bryaxis-Theorie. Seit der Auffindung einer hellenistischen Nachbildung des Sarapis[49] kann ihm sein Platz im 4.Jh.v.Chr. wohl nicht mehr streitig gemacht werden, womit der eigentliche Grund gegen eine sichere Zuweisung an Bryaxis[50] wegfällt. Mit dem Sarapis (Abb.11)[51] aber verbindet den schwermütigen Jüngling nicht nur seine Geistigkeit, der gedämpfte, verschlossene Ausdruck, der ihm gleich nach seiner Auffindung die Benennung auf eine Unterweltsgottheit eingebracht hat, sondern auch eine ganze Reihe von stilistischen Zügen: Wie dem Beherrscher der Unter-

welt fällt auch ihm das Haar schwer und beschattend in die Stirn, die unter einer Querfalte stark gebuckelt ist und sich zu den Schläfen hin verbreitert. Hier wie dort fliesst die Masse der langen Haare an den Seiten ungeordnet tief in die Wangen und verdeckt die Ohren völlig. Dass einzelne Lockenmotive an den Schläfen nahezu dieselbe Anordnung zeigen, stellte schon Curtius fest[52]. Auch die Haarteilung durch einen Längsscheitel am Hinterkopf ist bei beiden analog gebildet[53]. Die kleinen Augen, die seltsam abwesend blicken, scheinen beim Sarapis nach innen, beim sogenannten Eubouleus in weite Ferne gerichtet. Als weiteres gemeinsames Merkmal darf noch die Bekleidung mit einem Chiton sowie die Ähnlichkeit in dessen Anordnung über der Büste erwähnt werden. Die grösste Verwandtschaft aber besteht in dem über den Stirnlocken angebrachten Lockenstern, einer Besonderheit, die geradezu den Charakter einer Signatur[54] trägt. Diesen Lockenwirbel zeigt auch der thronende Asklepios auf einem Votivrelief aus Epidauros im Athener Nationalmuseum, dessen Urbild Charbonneaux wegen der Ähnlichkeit in Haaranordnung und Gesichtsbau mit dem Sarapis ebenfalls dem Bryaxis zuweist[55]. Von dem karischen Bildhauer ist uns ein Asklepios in Megara überliefert[56]. Es ist gut möglich, dass Bryaxis zur Zeit seines Megara-Auftrages auch die Statue für Eleusis schuf, während die Athener Basis[57] in seinen ersten Aufenthalt in Griechenland, in seine Lehrjahre, fällt[58]. Nach Griechenland zurückgekehrt war er bereits ein anerkannter Meister, der am Mausoleum von Halikarnassos[59] und vielleicht auch in Tegea[60] mitgearbeitet hatte und dem bedeutende Aufträge anvertraut wurden.

Die Zuweisung der eleusinischen Büste an Bryaxis ergibt sich nur auf Grund stilistischer Merkmale. Vielmehr spricht alles, was der Kopf an Undurchdringlichem, für griechisches Empfinden wohl nahezu fremd-

45) Furtwängler, Meisterwerke 560; Ähnlichkeit in der Haarbildung: Rizzo, Prassitele 107. Wegen seines runden, lockenumrahmten Gesichtstypus geht Curtius a.a.O.424 soweit, den ausruhenden Satyr dem Bryaxis zuzuweisen.
46) Vgl.Anm.37.
47) Vgl.Anm.40.
48) Vgl.Anm.41.
49) Charbonneaux,MonPiot 52,2,1962,19,Abb.2; C.Rolley,BCH 92, 1968,191, J.Marcadé,Au Musée de Délos,1969,427 f,pl.LVIII. Die Statuette stammt aus dem Sarapeion von Delos und ist durch ihre Inschrift in die Jahre vor 166 v.Chr. datiert.
50) A.Adriani, Alla ricerca di Briasside,1948; L.Castiglione,Bull.du Musée nat.hongrois des Beaux-Arts 12,1958,17-39;Th.Kraus,JdI 75, 1960,96 f; Jucker,Genava N.S.8,1960,113-121.
51) Basaltbüste in Rom, Villa Albani. Helbig a.a.O.(Anm.6) IV,1972, 330,Nr.3353. Photo Alinari Nr.27661.
52) Die klassische Kunst Griechenlands 424.
53) Für den sog.Eubouleus vgl. Abb.7 (Büste von der Athener Agora), für den Sarapis Rolley a.a.O.(Anm.49) 188,Abb.2.

54) Charbonneaux a.a.O.(Anm.49)25.
55) Inv.-Nr.1425; Charbonneaux a.a.O.24 f, Abb.10,11; vgl.auch Charbonneaux-Martin-Villard, Das hellenistische Griechenland 201 f, Abb.211.
56) Paus.I 40,6. Ob sich die Notiz bei Plin.nat.hist.34,73 (Bryaxis Aesculapium...fecit) auf dieselbe Statue bezieht,ist nicht zu sagen. Es wurde der Versuch unternommen, ihm neben dem Asklepios-Kopf aus Melos im British Museum (Charbonneaux-Martin-Villard a.a.O. 200,Abb.209) auch die Asklepios-Statue Mounychia in Athen,Nat.-Mus.Nr.258 (K.Papaioannou, Griechische Kunst,1972,Abb.151) zuzuweisen: vgl.Lippold,Hdb.259; Charbonneaux-Villard-Martin a.a.O. 201.
57) N.Pharaklas, Deltion 24 I,1969,59-65,246.
58) vgl.Schwarz a.a.O.(Anm.44) 77 ff.
59) Vitruv.VII.praefat.12; Plin.nat.hist.36,30.
60) Vgl.J.H.Jongkees, JHS 68,1948,38, wonach Bryaxis zunächst in Athen arbeitete, als Karer sodann zur Mitarbeit am Mausoleum nach Halikarnassos berufen wurde und schliesslich Skopas nach Tegea begleitete. Zum Lehrer-Schüler-Verhältnis von Skopas und Bryaxis

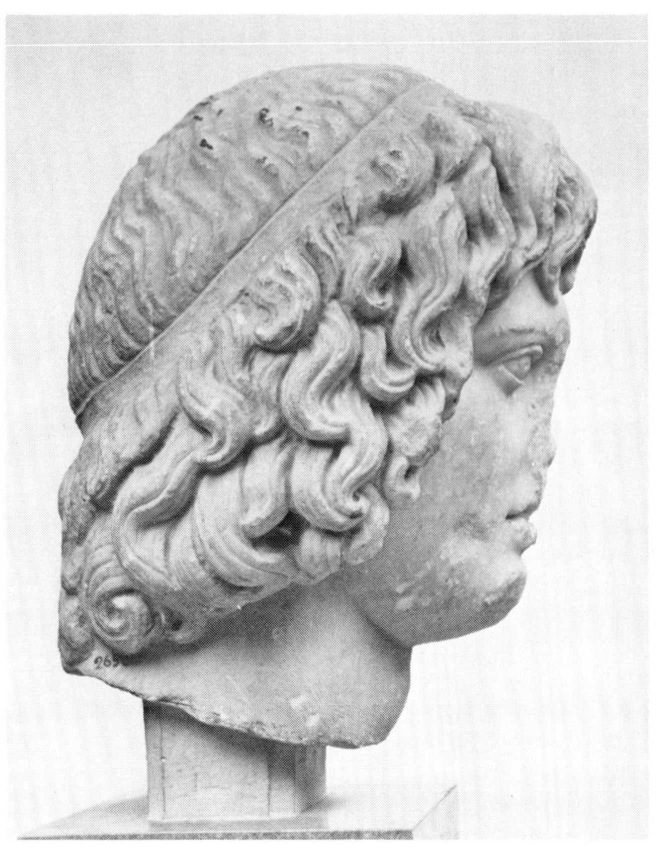 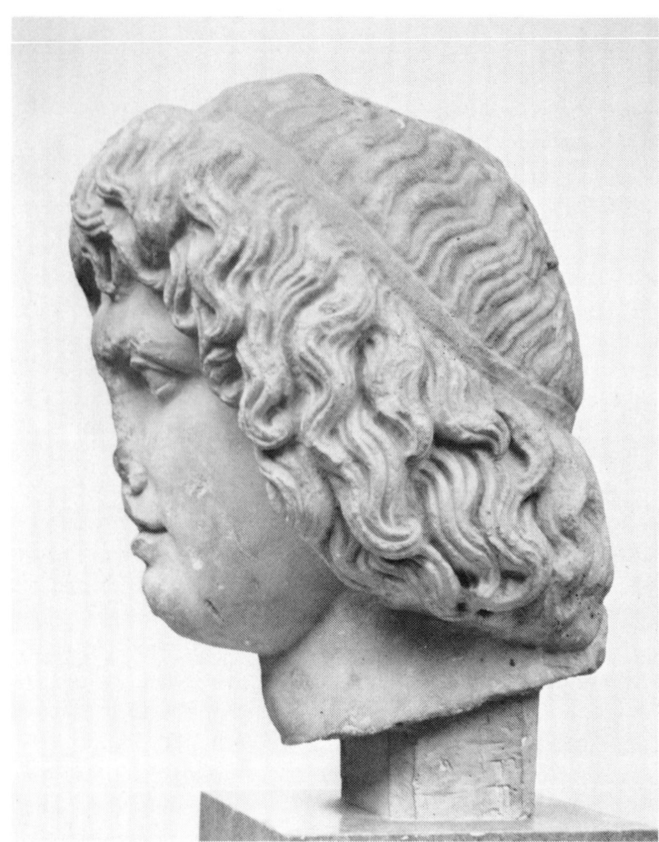

3a-d Eubouleus. Athen 2650

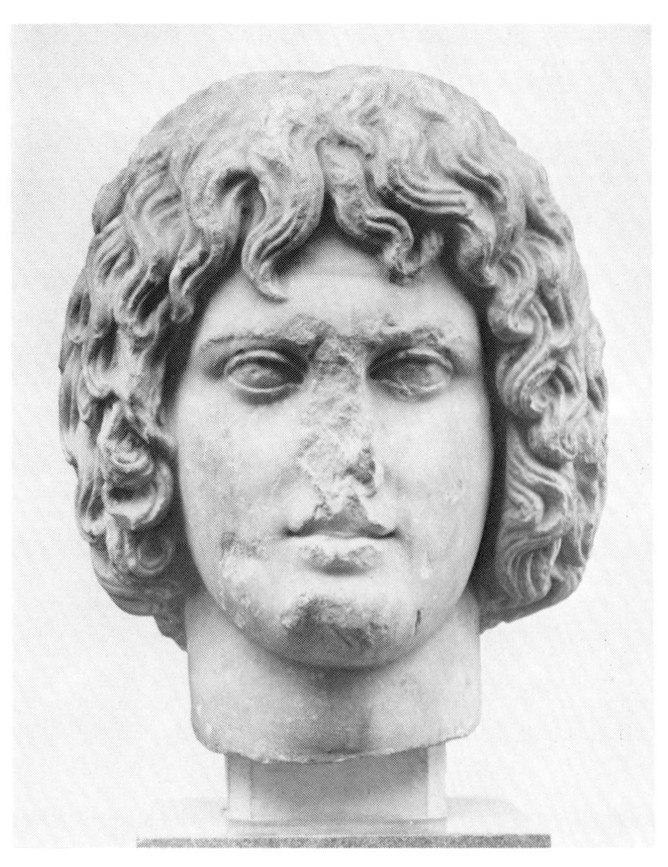 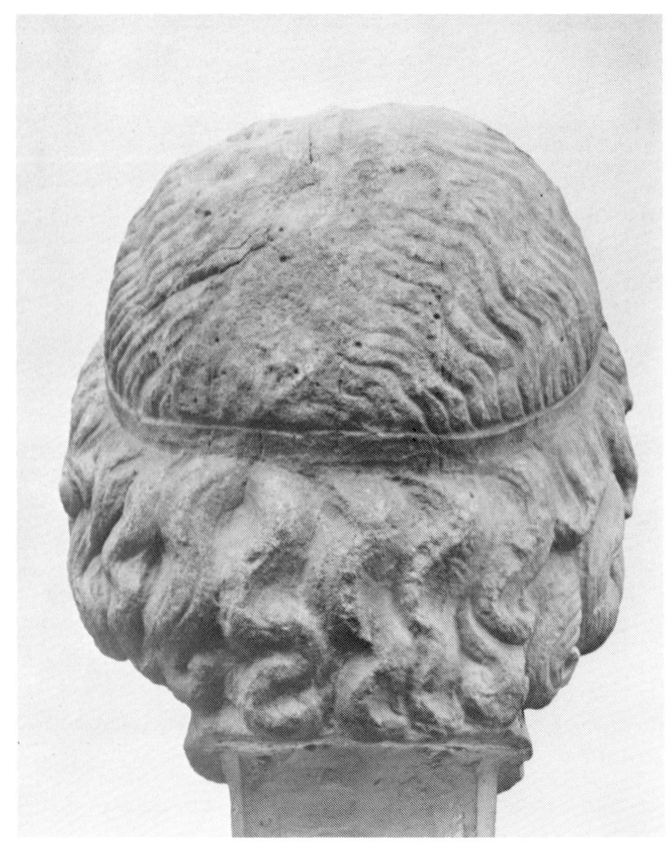

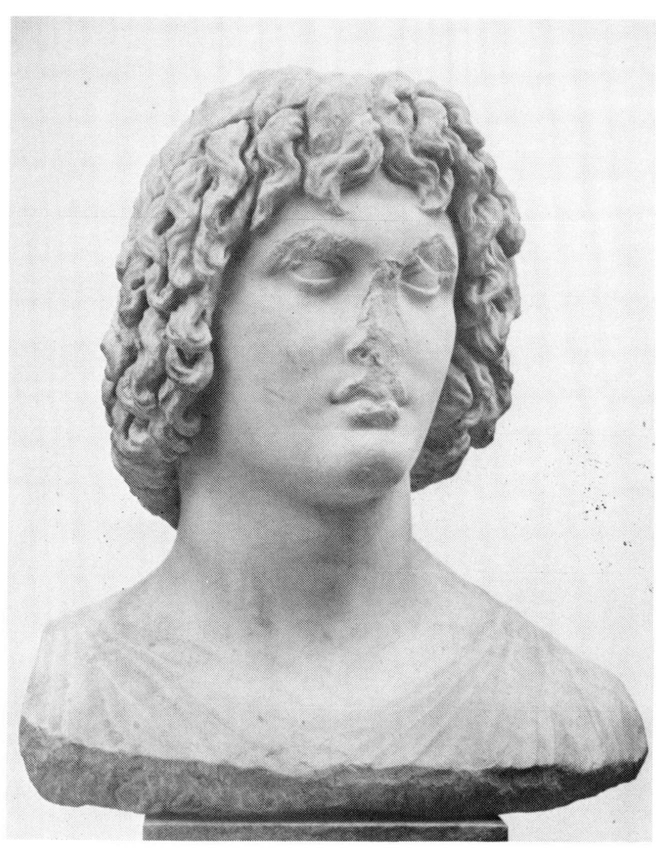

4 Eubouleus. Athen 181
5 Eubouleus. Athen 1839

6 Eubouleus. Athen 2650

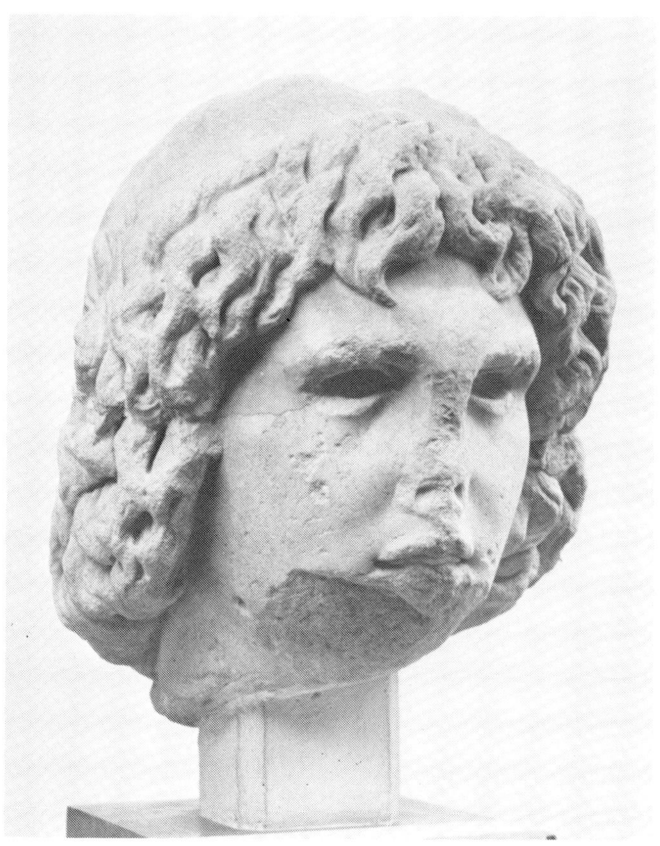

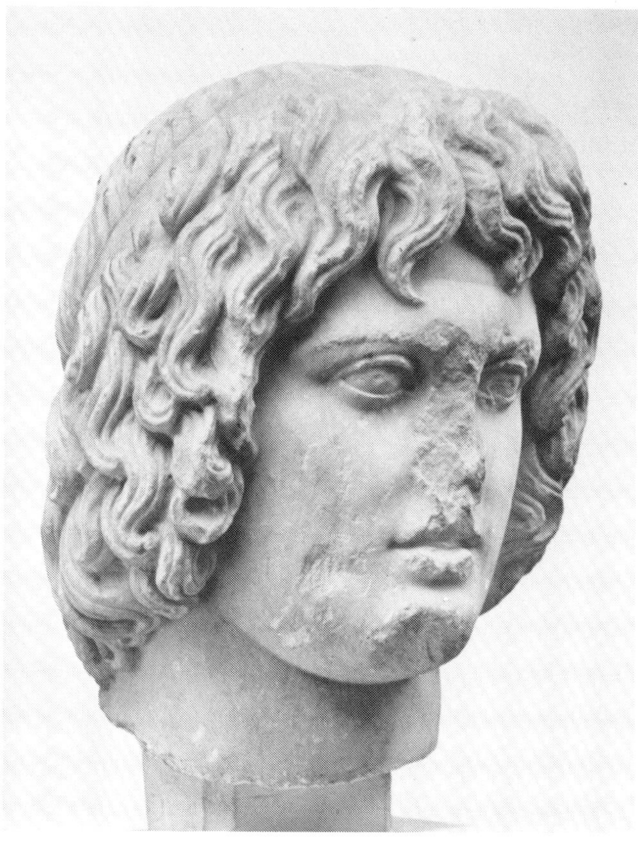

artig Anmutendem und bei aller Jugendlichkeit Gewaltigem an sich hat, für den Geist des Meisters des Sarapis und des Zeus von Otricoli.

Auch die so oft ausgesprochene Zuweisung des Werkes an Praxiteles sowie die Festellung, dass eine gewisse Verwandtschaft mit Skopas besteht, wird so verständlich: Bryaxis hatte Gelegenheit gehabt, die attische Kunst in Athen zu studieren, war bei seiner Arbeit am Mausoleum mit attischen Meistern zusammengetroffen und hatte sich während seiner Tätigkeit in Knidos[61] wieder mit praxitelischer Kunst konfrontiert gesehen, sodass eine Beeinflussung durch den grossen Athener unvermeidlich war, die sich allerdings nur auf äusserliche Merkmale beschränkte. Die Charis und das versonnene Träumen der θεοὶ ῥεῖα ζόντες des Praxiteles bleiben dem erdverbundeneren Bryaxis fremd. Anders steht es mit Skopas. Mit dem Parier verband ihn eine geistige Verwandtschaft, die am besten in den Friesplatten des Mausoleums zum Ausdruck kommt[62], in der Kompaktheit der kraftvoll bewegten Figuren, die ein ähnlich geartetes Temperament der beiden Künstler erahnen lassen. Die Formensprache des Nichtgriechen Bryaxis allerdings erscheint prunkvoller und pompöser als die des Skopas, seine Auffassung vom Kampf realistischer als die des Griechen. So lässt sich die Büste von Eleusis als das Werk eines Meisters verstehen, der zwar vom attischen Stil beeinflusst dennoch seine frèmdländische Eigenart bewahrte, die ihn befähigte, ein Kunstwerk von so ungewöhnlicher, schwer deutbarer Ausdruckskraft zu schaffen.

Deutung.

In der Erstpublikation eleusinischen Büste fühlte sich Philios von ihr an Antinous erinnert[63], ohne dass er nähere Gründe für den ihm porträtartig scheinenden Charakter des Kopfes anzugeben vermochte. Als nächste Parallele stellte er ihm den sogenannten Inopus im Louvre[64] und den Alexanderkopf aus Alexandria im British Museum[65] an die Seite, sprach sich jedoch nicht für eine Benennung auf Alexander den Grossen aus. Vielmehr dachte er an Demetrios Poliorketes, der von den dankbaren Athenern in Gestalt eines Heroen, vielleicht des Triptolemos, nach Eleusis geweiht worden wäre[66]. Die Porträttheorie wurde vor einigen Jahren von E.Harrison nach der Auffindung der Agora-Replik wieder aufgegriffen und entschieden vertreten: In der eleusinischen Büste und den übrigen Köpfen dieses Typus' sei der junge Alexander dargestellt, wahrscheinlich ein Werk des Leochares[67]. Haben wir uns im vorigen Abschnitt schon gegen die Zuweisung an Leochares ausgesprochen, wird nun auch die Identifizierung mit Alexander abzulehnen sein. Zugegeben sei, dass in der Agora-Büste die Physiognomie, wohl durch den unvollendeten Zustand der Nase, mehr ins Porträthafte verändert erscheint, jedoch wird dieser Eindruck von keiner der anderen Repliken bestätigt[68]. Es würde in diesem Zusammenhang zu weit führen, die Problematik des Alexanderporträts im einzelnen zu behandeln, doch muss festgestellt werden, dass diesem Typus gerade das fehlt, was allen Alexanderbildnissen, so verschieden sie auch sein mögen, eigen ist: die grossen Augen, das Aufwärts-und Herausblicken[69]. Auch das Zwillingspaar der Stirnlocken ist nicht in der für Alexander typischen Form gebildet, wonach die linke Locke ein wenig tiefer als die über dem rechten Auge befindliche ansetzt[70], sondern gerade umgekehrt.

Die Agora-Büste ist ein "Bildnis im Blätterkelch". Bis jetzt ist uns jedoch aus vorrömischer Zeit kein einziges Bildnis eines Griechen "im Blätterkelch" überliefert. Unter den Göttern sind nur Sarapis und Antinous, der in Gestalt vieler Gottheiten verehrt wurde, als rundplastische Blätterkelchbüsten auf uns gekommen[71]. Es ist jedoch nichts davon bekannt, dass Alexander in späteren Zeit wie Antinous wegen seines frühen Todes als Heros mit chthonischen Zügen aufgefasst worden wäre[72]. Ausserdem hatte er, soweit wir wissen, keine Beziehung zu Eleusis, die das Auftauchen zweier Köpfe

---

vgl. auch C.Robert, RE III 919 s.v.Bryaxis; Schwarz a.a.O.77.

61) Plin.nat.hist.36,22.

62) Vgl.etwa die Platten British Museum 1013,1014,1015 (abgeb.-neuerdings bei B.Ashmole, Architect and Sculptor in Classical Greece, 1972,Abb.206-208; in Abb.211 ist das 1964 in Bodrum gefundene Bruchstück angefügt) und 1009,1019,1022 (P.Wolters-J.Sieveking, JdI 24,Beil. 2). Zur verschiedenen Aufteilung der Platten an die Künstler vgl. auch Ashmole, JHS 71,1951,17 f, pl.13; Lippold, Hdb.255 ff,Taf.92; B.Schlörb, Timotheos,1965,72 f,Taf.19,20.-Die divergierende Auffassung des Heroismus im Amazonenfries sollte gelegentlich untersucht werden.

63) Eph.Arch.1886,264; ders.,AM 20,1895,263 ff.

64) Encycl.photogr.de l'art:Le musée du Louvre,III,1938,194 f.

65) Richter,The Sculpture and the Sculptors of the Greeks,fig.797. Bezeichnenderweise wurde auch er auf einen chthonischen Gott gedeutet,ja seine Abhängigkeit vom Sarapistypus betont: vgl.K.Gebauer, AM 63/64,1938/39,86.

66) AM 20,1895,265.

67) Vgl.Anm.2.

68) Vgl.Karouzou, Archäologisches Nationalmuseum,172.

69) Vgl.Richter, The Sculpture and the Sculptors of the Greeks 203.

70) Th.Schreiber, Studien über das Bildnis Alexanders des Grossen, 1903,56 ff. Für neue Bildnisse Alexanders und Literaturzusammenfassung vgl. E.Berger, AntK 14,1971,139-44; L.T.Shear, Hesperia 40, 1971,273 f.

71) Jucker, Das Bildnis im Blätterkelch 189. Die Athena-Büste in Eleusis und die Büste im Thermenmuseum in Rom sind Ausnahmen, die die Regel bestätigen (Abb.145-147).

72) Vgl.Mylonas, Eleusis and the Eleusinian Mysteries 199.

dieses Typus' dort erklären würde (A,a). Es wäre aber
gut möglich, dass sowohl der Kopf im Athener Nationalmuseum (b), der im Gebiet des Militärspitals südlich
der Akropolis gefunden wurde, als auch die beiden
Repliken im Akropolismuseum (c,d) aus dem am Süd-
abhang der Akropolis gelegenen Demeter-Heiligtum
stammen[73]. Die Büste von der Athener Agora (f), die
in der spätrömischen Befestigungsanlage geborgen
wurde, könnte leicht aus dem Eleusinion gekommen
sein, das bei dem Herulereinfall im Jahre 267 n.Chr.
zerstört und dann zum Teil von der Befestigungsmauer
überdeckt wurde, wobei Spolien aus den von den
Herulern verwüsteten Bauten Verwendung fanden[74].
Auch ein Tempel der Demeter und Kore und einer des
Triptolemos befand sich in nächster Umgebung des
Eleusinions, wie Pausanias zu berichten weiss[75].

Die Feststellung absichtlicher Verstümmelung an
vier der Köpfe (A,a,c,d) lässt auf religiösen Fanatismus
schliessen, der an den Stätten heidnischer Mysterien
besonders erbittert wütete[76]. Wer aber ist dieser schwer-
mütige Jüngling, der in römischer Zeit offenbar noch so
viel Ansehen genoss? Nach seiner ganzen Aufmachung
und dem Fundort von zumindest zwei (A,a), wahrscheinlich aber auch allen auderen in Athen befindlichen
Exemplaren (b,c,d,f) im Bereiche eines Demeter-Heilig-
tums doch gewiss eine eleusinische Gottheit.

Durch die Zuweisung des Werkes an Bryaxis ist die
These, die es mit dem Eubouleus des Praxiteles identifiziert, hinfällig geworden. Es wäre nun zu klären, ob
die Benennung auf Eubouleus auch ohne Zusammenhang mit Praxiteles beibehalten werden könnte, oder ob
diese Stimmen im Recht sind, die erklärten, für ein so
bedeutendes weil oft kopiertes Werk käme eine Deutung
auf einen zweitrangigen Dämon wie Eubouleus nicht
in Frage, der nur im engsten eleusinischen Kreis eine
Rolle spielte[77]. Dass Eubouleus, der Schweinehirt,
Bruder des Triptolemos, der beim Raub der Kore durch
Hades samt seinen Ferkeln vom Erdspalt verschlungen
wurde[78], noch im 1.Jh.v.Chr. als selbständige Gottheit
Verehrung genoss, erweist das Relief des Lakrateides[79].
Und in der römischen Hermeninschrift sprechen Künst-
lername und Auffindungsort für die Bedeutung und

73) J.Travlos,Bildlexikon zur Topographie des antiken Athen,1971,
Abb.5.
74) Travlos a.a.O.161,199.
75) I 14,1-14. Der Demeter-Kore-Tempel wurde mit dem Südost-
Tempel auf der Agora identifiziert, vgl.Travlos a.a.O.199. Die Lage des
Triptolemos-Tempels ist noch ungewiss.
76) M.P.Nilsson, Geschichte der griechischen Religion II,1961,351.
77) Kern,AM 16,1891,19 ff (besonders 28); v.Steuben a.a.O.(Anm.6).
78) Nilsson a.a.O.I,1967,119,402,463 f,663.
79) Philios,EphArch.1886,25,pl.3,2; Mylonas a.a.O. 197f, fig. 71;
Nilsson a.a.O.I,470,Anm.6,Taf.40.

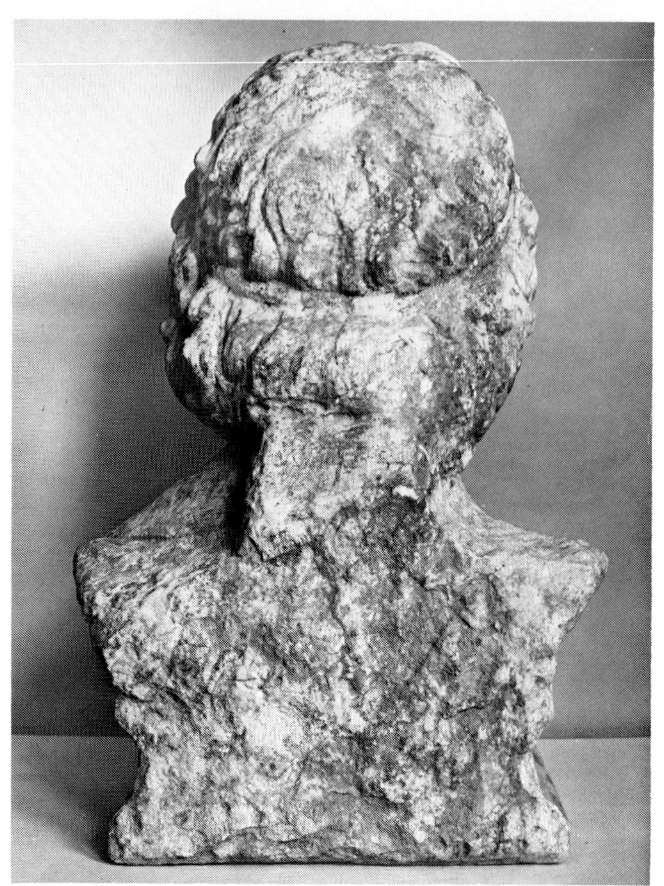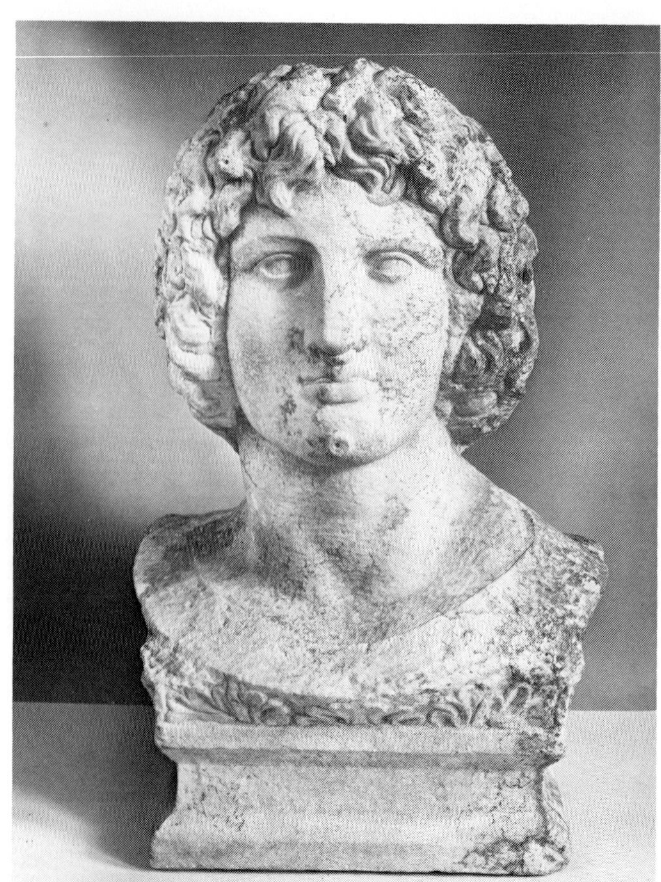

7a-b   Büste des Eubouleus. Athen, Agora
8   Eubouleus. Rom, Kapitolinisches Museum

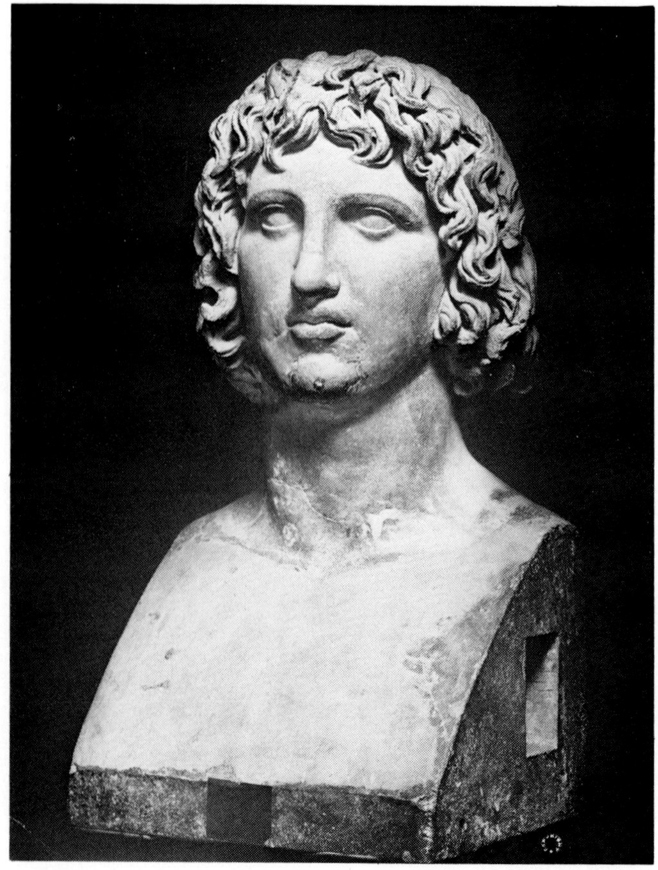

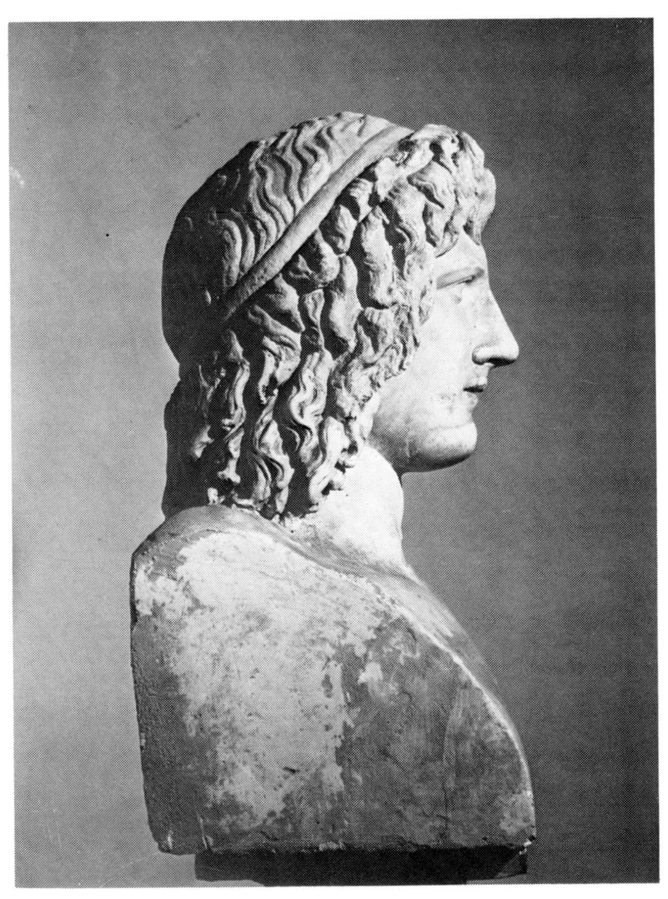

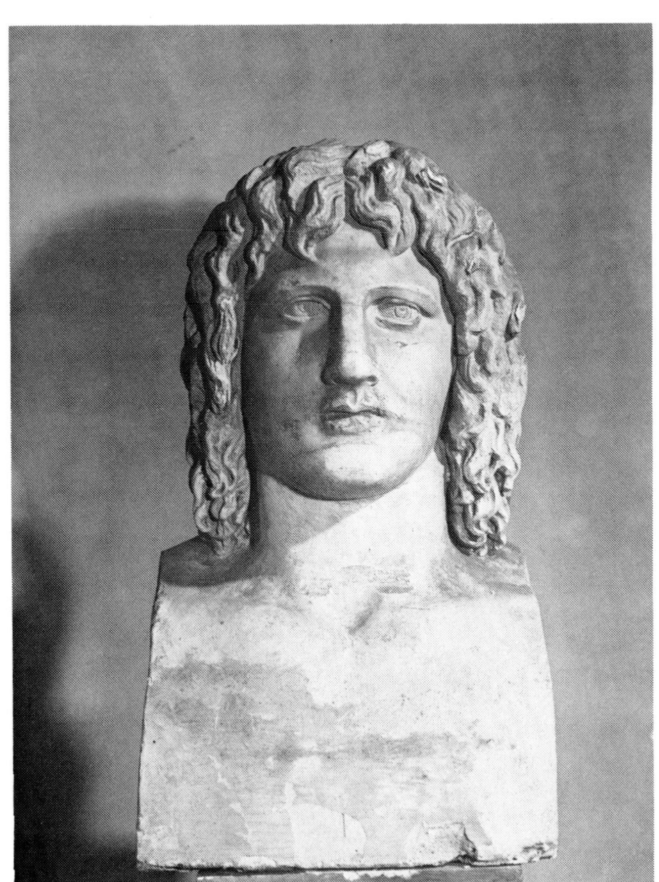

9a-b Eubouleus. Mantua
10   Eubouleus. Athen 181

11   Sarapis. Rom, Villa Albani

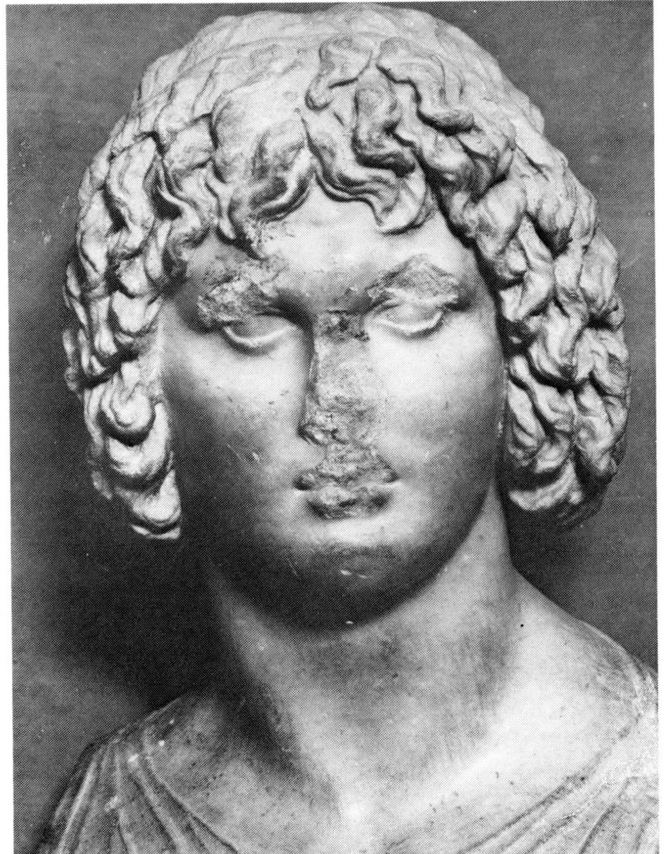

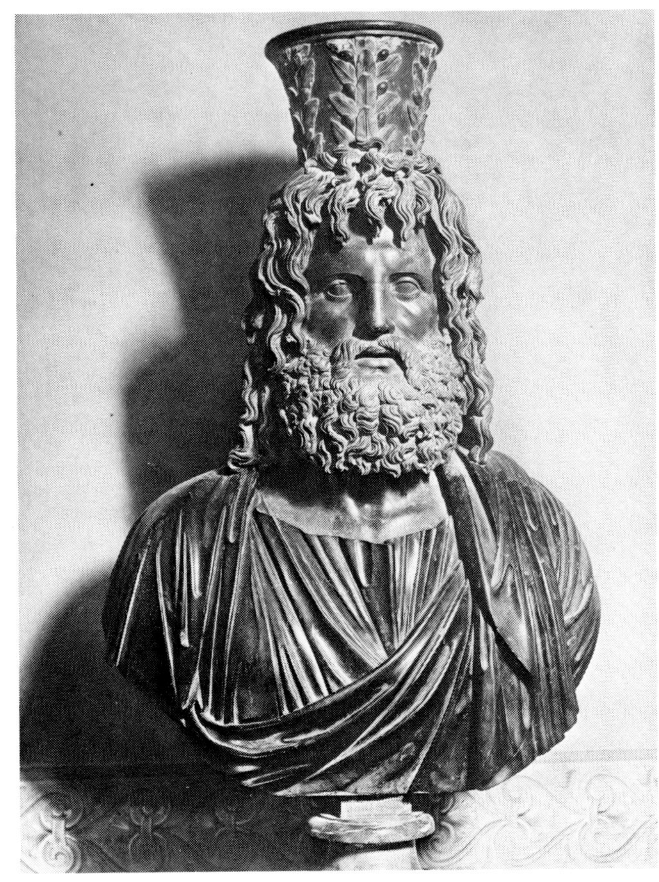

Verbreitung der Gestalt. Wir müssen also annehmen, dass Eubouleus sehr wohl eine Figur war, an der sich die künstlerische Phantasie entzünden konnte, und die auch weitab von Eleusis bekannt war, wenn auch die Existenz einer Kopie in Rom eher auf den berühmten Namen Praxiteles zurückzuführen sein wird als auf kultische Gründe. Gewisse bukolische Züge, die der eleusinischen Büste, dem "étonnant campagnard"[80] anhaften, weisen tatsächlich in den Kreis des königlichen Schweinehirten.

Von manchen, die sich mit der Eubouleus-Benennung nicht zufrieden gaben, jedoch am Zusammenhang des Werkes mit Praxiteles festhielten, wurde der Jüngling als Iakchos gedeutet[81], den Praxiteles mit Demeter und Kóre zu einer Gruppe vereinigt darstellte[82]. Dieser Versuch fand in der Fachwelt wenig Widerhall, kein Wunder, lässt sich doch der stille, sinnende Jungling schwerlich mit dem nächtlich schwärmenden Fackelträger identifizieren, den schon Sophokles mit Dionysos gleichsetzte[83]. Zudem erscheint er zu isoliert, zu sehr in sich versunken, als dass er Teil einer Gruppe gewesen sein könnte. Der Iakchos der praxitelischen Gruppe stand fackeltragend zur Rechten der Demeter[84], den eleusinischen Jüngling jedoch haben wir uns sicher sitzend und als selbständige Statue vorzustellen.

Da seine Zugehörigkeit zum eleusinischen Kreis gesichert schien, war es kein grosser Schritt zu einer weiteren Benennung: Es sei Triptolemos in ihm dargestellt, der eleusinische Königssohn, der den Menschen Demeters Ährengeschenk überbrachte und sie den Ackerbau lehrte[85]. Dass er als selbständige Gottheit auch ausserhalb von Eleusis verehrt wurde, steht fest, da er mehrere Tempel besass[86]. Ein im Museum von Eleusis befindliches Votivrelief zeigt ihn in demselben langlockigen Kopftypus[87], was bereits Philios auffiel[88]. Der Einwand von Curtius, in dem Jüngling könne nicht Triptolemos dargestellt sein, weil dieser stets mit nacktem Oberkörper wiedergegeben werde[89], wird durch den Ausweis zahlreicher Vasenbilder des 5.Jhs.v.Chr. widerlegt, die den Königssohn voll bekleidet auf seinem Flügelwagen zeigen[90]. Eine Vorliebe für volle Bekleidung seiner Statuen nach orientalischer Sitte dürfen wir bei dem Karer Bryaxis ja wohl voraussetzen. So spricht alles dafür, in dem Jüngling Triptolemos zu erkennen, den wir uns auf dem Flügelwagen thronend[91] vorzustellen haben. Das Aufleuchten des Gesichtes aus dem Schatten der Haare, das als chthonischer Zug gedeutet wurde, steht ihm als eleusinischer Fruchtbarkeitgottheit wohl an, ebenso sein milder, bukolischer Charakter. Die Vielzahl der auf uns gekommenen Köpfe passt zu der Bedeutung, die Triptolemos innerhalb der Mysterien einnam: Er bildete mit Demeter und Kore die Heilige Familie[92].

Die gewisse Individualität, die unserem Triptolemos—etwa in dem starken Hals[93]—anhaftet, darf jedoch nicht überbewertet werden und dazu verleiten, in ihm ein Bildnis Alexander des Grossen sehen zu wollen. "Das leise Individuelle der Züge findet man seit der Spätklassik immer häufiger auch bei göttlichen Wesen", so formuliert Schefold diese Erscheinung[94]. Vielleicht fühlte sich auch Bryaxis etwas durch die Züge Alexanders des Grossen inspiriert, als er die Statue des Triptolemos schuf. Eine Gleichung Triptolemos=Alexander lag durchaus nahe, da bereits Nearchos[95] und Onesikritos[96] auch den makedonischen Herrscher als Kulturbringer priesen, als der Triptolemos im besonderen verehrt wurde[97].

Damit sind jedoch nicht alle Fragen, die sich um die Büste von Eleusis und ihre Repliken ranken, beantwortet. Die grosse Wirkung, die sie auf die Folgezeit ausübte und ihr Weiterleben bis in frühchristliche Kunst soll an anderer Stelle behandelt werden.

Gerda Schwarz
Universität Graz

80) Picard a.a.O.(Anm.4) 386.
81) Svoronos,Eph.Arch.1911,39-52; Lippold,Hdb.241; ders.,RE XXII 2,1805 s.v.Praxiteles.
82) Paus. I,2,4, vgl.Lippold RE XXII 2,1789 f. Die Statuen befanden sich im Demetertempel in Athen.
83) Ant.1150 ff., vgl.Nilsson a.a.O.I,318,599f,664.
84) Vgl.Lippold, RE XXII 2,1789 f.
85) Kern,AM 16,1891,26; Klein,Geschichte der griechischen Kunst II,379.
86) Nach Epiktet.I 4,30 hatte er in der ganzen Welt Tempel und Altäre. Tempel in Eleusis:Paus.I 38,6; in Athen:Paus.I 14,1.
87) Lippold, Hdb.237, Anm.7,Taf.85,4; Charbonneaux-Martin-Villard, Das klassische Griechenland 214,Abb.246.
88) AM 20,1895,255 ff (256,261).
89) Die klassische Kunst Griechenlands 423.
90) Recueil Ch.Dugas,1960,123 ff; H.Metzger, Recherches sur l'ima-

gerie athénienne,1965,7-32; G.Schwarz,ÖJh 50,1973 (im Druck).
91) Auch auf dem Relief in Eleusis ist Triptolemos auf einem mit Schlangen und Flügeln ausgestatteten Thron dargestellt,vgl.auch Rizzo, Prassitele 103.
92) E.Simon, Opfernde Götter,1953,69.
93) Vgl.auch den breiten,"naturalistisch" gebildeten Hals der etwa gleichzeitig enstandenen Demeter von Knidos: B.Ashmole,JHS 71/ 1951,13 ff.,pl.1-5.
94) P.Auberson u.K.Schefold, Führer durch Eretria,1972,172. Vgl. auch Lippold,Hdb.268:«So ist auch später zwischen Idealporträts und Götterbildern, die Züge des Alexanderbildnisses benutzen, oft schwer zu unterscheiden."
95) Arr.Ind.40,6; Strabo XI 524; vgl.W.Hoffmann, Das literarische Porträt Alexanders des Grossen im griechischen und römischen Altertum,1907,10.
96) Strabo XI 517.
97) Nilsson, Geschichte der griechischen Religion I,665.

Four "Fayum Portraits" in the Getty Museum

Among some one hundred thirty painted mummy portraits from Roman Egypt now in North American collections there are large and important groups in three major museums: the Metropolitan Museum of Art, New York; the Museum of Fine Arts, Boston; the Royal Ontario Museum, Toronto. Each of these groups was gathered primarily in the half-century which followed the first major finds of "Fayum portraits"—by Graf at Er-Rubayat, by Petrie at Hawara—at a time, in short, when such pieces were widely marketed and readily available. But mummy portraits were not discovered in quantity at any site after about 1912[1] and since the 1930's—when the remainder of Graf's collection was auctioned following his death—quality examples of this art form have been only infrequently available. Considering this state of affairs it is all the more remarkable that the J. Paul Getty Museum has succeeded during the past few years in acquiring four mummy paintings which rank in aesthetic merit with the very finest examples of this genre.

1. Portrait of a man (Fig. 1).
Inv. 71.AI.72; acquired by the museum in 1971.
Encaustic on wood.
H: 47.5 cm.; W: 24.1 cm.; Thickness: *ca.* 0.4 cm.
References: *Apollo* XCI (n.s. no. 96: February, 1970) xxxv, ill. (col.); R. Symes, *Ancient Art* (sale catalogue: London, 1971) no. 25, col. pl.; D.L. Thompson, "A Patchwork 'Fayum' in Toledo," *AJA* 77 (1973) 439 n. 4; C.C. Vermeule and N. Neuerburg, *Catalogue of the Ancient Art in the J. Paul Getty Museum: The Larger Statuary, Wall Paintings and Mosaics* (Malibu, 1973) 41 no. 91, fig. 91.
Provenience: Hawara.
Date: A.D. 100-125.

The first "Fayum portrait" to have been acquired has already appeared in preliminary publication but merits further consideration. Its preservation is good; the thin panel shows the warping which normally results from the forced conformity to the physical shape of the mummy, while four cracks along grain lines of the wood (one of which extends the panel's entire length) do not seriously detract from the portrait's integrity. The panel was roughly cut away at the top before being inserted into the mummy.

The painted surface is very much intact and shows no signs of either repainting or restoration. There is some minor encrustation (sand or dirt) evident in the hair while fragments of the cartonnage remain in the areas over and beyond the subject's left ear. Strokes of the paint reveal the two methods of application which are typical of "Fayum portraits": the brush was used for broad areas of color—*i.e.,* background and garment—while the *cestrum* (a metal instrument similar to a modern paint knife) was used for greater detail and desiredly thicker paint within the face, neck, and hair.

The colors on the whole seem rather dark although a brighter aspect will certainly appear when the portrait eventually is cleaned. The background is gray, while the garment is white with shades of gray and a maroon *clavus*. The remainder of the palette is based on the subject's dark complexion: his skin is dark brown, with brick-red highlights; the eyes are brown, the brows a light chocolate tone. The lips are deep ruby-red; flesh tones appear as highlighting on the ridge of the nose and within the eyes.

As noted by Vermeule and Neuerburg, the portrait is fairly plain in that it contains no symbols of rank or profession. The aquiline nose, dark skin, and long, narrow eyes of the subject suggest a racial mixture. Intermarriage of the native Egyptians with their Greek and then Roman masters, and blood additions of whatever elements from African and Near Eastern neighbors produced the racially complicated types seen in many "Fayum portraits."

Although the artist of this portrait cannot now be identified with certainty in other pieces[2] it is clear that he worked at Hawara (or at Arsinoë, for which Hawara seems to have served as a cemetery). The subject's sharp turn from his right, the manner in which the cloak is draped over the left shoulder and is yet partially visible behind the right, the width and position of the *clavus*—all find precise parallel in a large number of portraits of documented Hawaran origin, including examples in Brooklyn and Baltimore.[3] And while it is by no means a definite index of provenience, the particular cut of the top of the panel—nearly rounded—also suggests Hawara.

Although the moustache first became an accepted element of fashion under Hadrian, the short cut of the

---

1) The last year of Gayet's excavations at Antinoopolis; Petrie's second campaign at Hawara was completed in 1911. For the most complete discussion of the history of recovery of "Fayum portraits" see K. Parlasca, *Mumienporträts und verwandte Denkmäler* (Wiesbaden, 1966, hereafter *Mumienporträts*) Chap. I, 18ff.
2) A portrait in Brighton (Art Gallery and Museum, inv. R137; K. Parlasca, *Repertorio d'arte dell'Egitto greco-romano*, Ser. B, Vol. I [Palermo, 1969, hereafter *Repertorio* B:I] 79 no. 192 [although the data appear there incorrectly under no. 193], pl. 47 fig. 2 [listed incorrectly in the text as pl. 47 fig. 3]) which was excavated by Petrie at Hawara is very probably by the same hand although its poor condition forbids absolute certainty.
3) Brooklyn Museum, inv. 11.600B (*ibid.* 35 no. 34, pl. 9 fig. 2) and Walters Art Gallery, inv. 32.3 (*ibid.* 40 no. 52, pl. 13 fig. 4) respectively; *cf.* the portrait in Brighton (*supra* n. 2) which is perhaps the closest parallel.

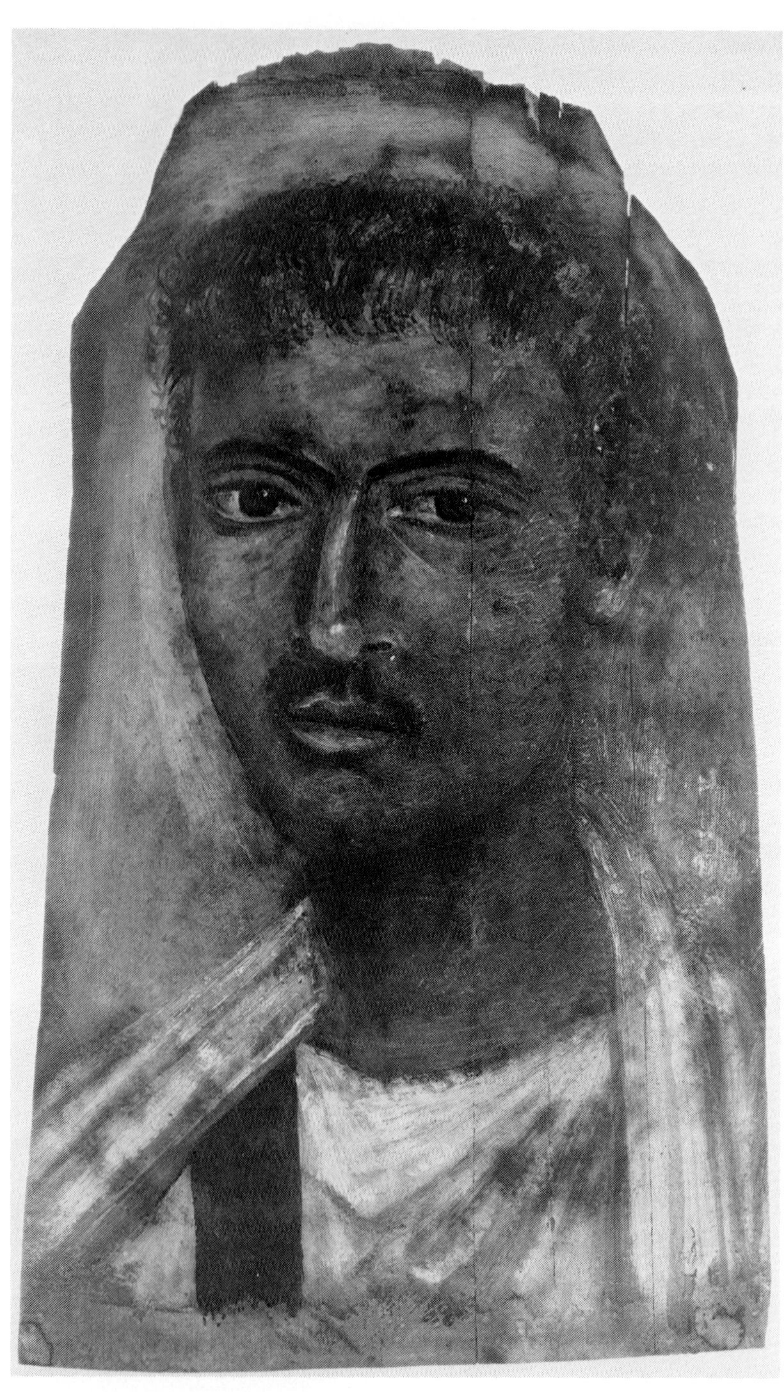

1   Malibu, J. Paul Getty Museum,
inv. 71.AI.72. Phot. Museum

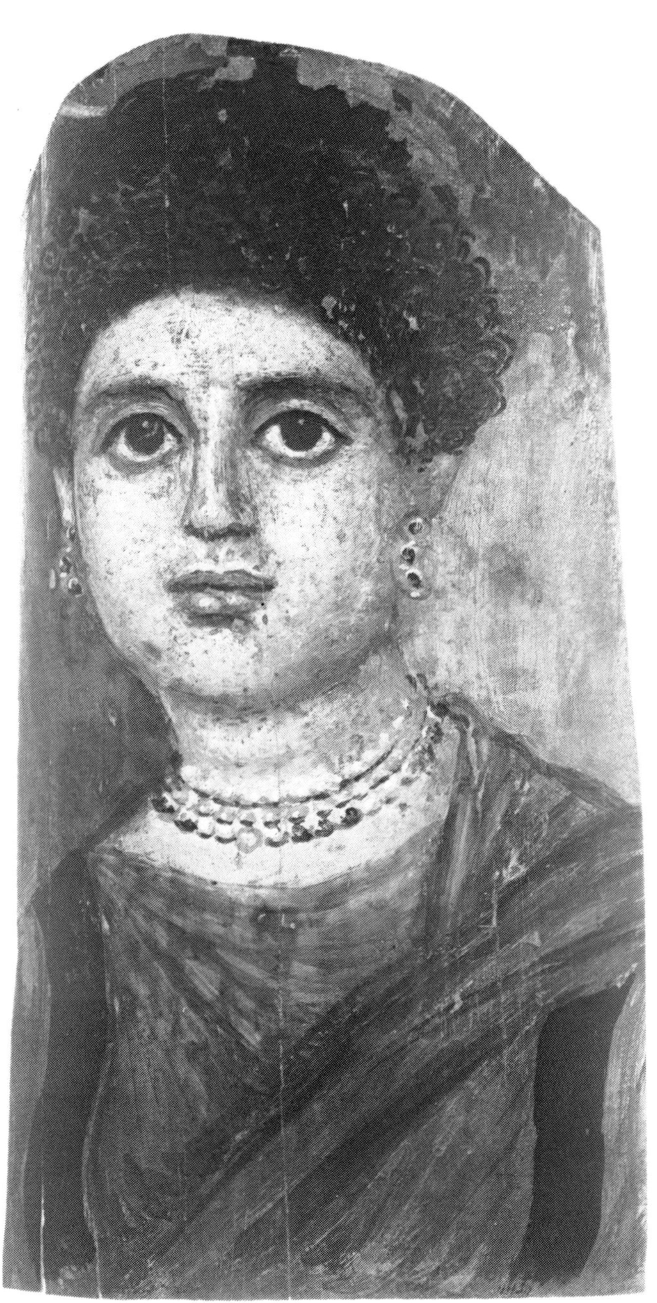

2   Malibu, J. Paul Getty Museum,
inv. 73.AI.91. Phot. Museum

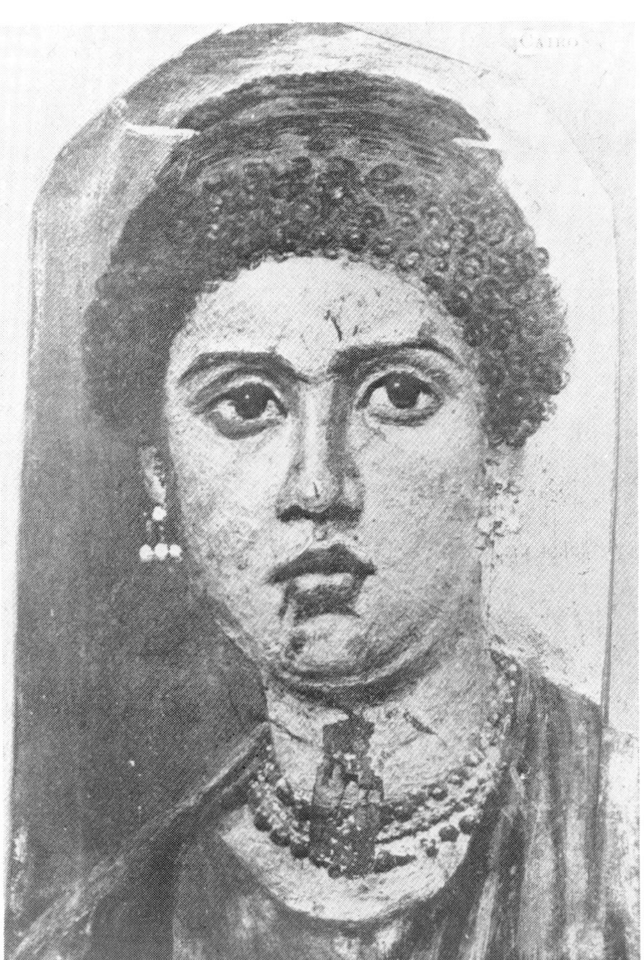

3   Cairo, Egyptian Museum, inv. C.G. 33237

subject's hair suggests the styles made popular by Trajan. This, combined with the intensity of portrayal, suggests a date early in the first quarter of the second century A.D.[4]

2. Portrait of a Flavian matron (Fig. 2).
Inv. 73.AI.91; acquired by the museum in 1973.
Encaustic on wood.
H: 40 cm.; W: 20 cm.; Thickness: *ca.* 0.2 cm.
Unpublished.
Provenience: Hawara.
Date: *Ca.* A.D. 100.

The female portrait acquired in 1973 is certainly the most colorful of the Getty pieces. The panel itself is again in very fine condition: the wood is extremely thin and extensive warping has occurred, but only four partial cracks are present. Some flaking of the paint is evident—in the upper right portion of the panel—and that some repainting had been effected prior to its acquisition can been seen especially around the brows and on the shaded side of the subject's neck; the surface is otherwise clean and intact.

The overall aspect of the portrait is very bright, enhanced by its artist's lively sense of color. The flesh and salmon tones of the subject's face stand out sharply against the dark gray background and against the rich red and black of the garments and *clavi* respectively. Highlight and shadow are achieved within the face in tones of maroon and beige, within the garments in gray and black. Earrings and a triple-tiered necklace are painted in white and green (to suggest pearls and the favored emeralds or semi-precious stones) with gold-leaf or gilt paint to represent the settings.

The rounded shape of the panel at the top initially hints at an Hawaran origin, which is confirmed by comparison with examples of documented provenience. Specifically, the painter of this portrait can be identified in at least two other examples—a poorly preserved portrait of a male child and one better preserved showing a young woman (Fig. 3; name: "Demos"; age at death: 24 years)—both excavated at Hawara by Petrie and now in Cairo.[5] The Getty portrait is the finest of the three examples and we might therefore call this artist the Malibu Painter. This precise pose and hairstyle, moreover—as well as an overall "family resemblance"— appear on at least a dozen or so other portraits of similar origin but different artistic hand, suggesting a circle to which the Malibu Painter belonged. The hairstyles of all the female subjects are extremely similar, late Flavian

in style; this school of portraitists must have worked at Hawara (or at Arsinoë) late in the first and early in the second century A.D.

That this and the preceding example both come from Hawara raises an interesting point. Though most of the extant "Fayum portraits" of documented provenience originate at Er-Rubayat, those to have appeared for sale recently have in many cases been from Hawara. Theodor Graf was a clever businessman and it seems he exploited rather fully and in a relatively short time the necropolis of Er-Rubayat. He, his agents, and his workmen cleaned the site of portraits quickly and efficiently (albeit with no regard for matters archaeological) and most Er-Rubayat portraits originate in the Graf collection. Petrie, however, was driven by scientific rather than by profit motives and therefore excavated Hawara with some deliberation; in addition, his work there was interrupted by excavational commitments at several other sites. During Petrie's absences—as he himself reports (and as Parlasca confirms[6])—a very large number of portraits slipped away from Hawara in the hands of others, and we might therefore say that those examples documented in Petrie's reports represent only a small percentage of the extant portraits which originate at Hawara. It is therefore no surprise to find "new" (previously unknown) Hawaran portraits in some abundance.

3. Portrait of a bearded man (Fig. 4).
Inv. 73.AI.94; acquired by the museum in 1973.
Encaustic on (cedar) wood.
H: 43 cm.; W: 22.5 cm.; Thickness: *ca.* 0.3 cm.
Reference: *Apollo* XCIII (n.s. no. 112: June, 1971) 149, ill.
Provenience: Probably Er-Rubayat.
Date: A.D. 150-175.

Also acquired during 1973 was this Semitic-looking gentleman. The wood, which appears to be cedar, is partially warped but unusually sound; none of the six longitudinal cracks extends the entire length of the panel. Large fragments of the cartonnage (both white and blue linen) remain in the lower portion of the panel as well as on its reverse. Fairly extensive flaking of the paint in the neck area appears to have resulted when the portrait was originally removed from its mummy. The hair has been somewhat retouched; no other restoration is evident.

The color scheme is simple and straightforward but very striking. The subject's complexion is somewhat pale and chalky, rendered in combinations of beige,

---

4) Two examples of comparable style and date are in the Egyptian Museum, Cairo: inv. J.E. 42790 (*ibid.* 67 no. 147, pl. 35 fig. 2) and inv. C.G. 33219 (*ibid.* 71 no. 164, pl. 39 fig. 3).
5) Egyptian Museum, inv. C.G. 33240 (*ibid.* 47 no. 78, pl. 19 fig. 1) and inv. C.G. 33237 (*ibid.* 47 no. 79, pl. 19 fig. 2) respectively. Parlasca reports (here as earlier: *Mumienporträts* 79 n. 120) that the two portraits originate in the same grave; he quite plausibly suggests that they represent mother and child.
6) *Mumienporträts* 32ff.

flesh tones, and white; the background also is white. In sharp contrast, the lips are rich ruby-red with salmon highlights, while the hair, beard, and eyes are black, occasionally enriched with beige and light brown. No garment is visible; it appears likely that none was originally painted.

The extreme simplicity of the portrayal contains only hints of the artist's identity, but it is likely that he also painted a well known female portrait from Er-Rubayat in West Berlin.[7] The subject's luxuriant hair and beard are characteristic of Antonine court fashion; a date in the mid-second century is most likely.[8]

4. Portrait of a bearded man (Fig. 5).
Inv. 74.AI.11; acquired by the museum in 1974.
Encaustic on wood.
H: 37 cm.; W: 21 cm.
Reference: *Apollo* XCVIII (n.s. no. 142: December, 1973) 95, ill. (col.); *Recent Acquisitions: Ancient Art* (exhibition catalogue; Malibu, 1974) no. 26, ill.
Provenience: Er-Rubayat.
Date: A.D. 175-225.

This most recently acquired portrait is certainly the most vivid portrayal, as well as the best preserved of the group. The painted surface and the panel as a whole are in excellent condition; two hairline cracks, some discoloration from the mummification materials, and a small cartonnage fragment which clings at the top do not in any significant way detract from the portrait's superb state. The panel was broken roughly but only slightly at the top corners before being inserted into the mummy.

The subject is again racially striking: his sharp and piercing almond-shaped eyes, almost negroid lips, wiry curled hair, and dark skin all suggest an extremely mixed heritage. The background is neutral grayish-white, while browns dominate the ruddy complexion. The subject's lips are deep brown-red while his eyes are a curious olive-brown, delicately outlined in black. The garment is the usual white, with an extremely narrow *clavus* painted in raspberry-red. The artist's mastery of the encaustic medium is evidenced by the vigor and care accorded the face; the thick black curls of the hair also reveal especially skillful use of the *cestrum*.

The narrow *clavus* is a feature which commonly appears on portraits from the Graf collection; this initially suggests an Er-Rubayat origin for our example.

Precisely identical garment schemes, and the same shading at the neckline appear on at least two other portraits: that of a young man recently offered by a London dealer (Fig. 6)[9] and one of a bearded male, heavily restored, in Montreal (Fig. 7). When we add a list of anatomical similarities (lips, nose, eye shading and lashes, the moustache and beard patterns of the two bearded subjects) it becomes evident that the three portraits are the work of the same hand.[10] He might be called the Montreal Painter even though the Getty portrait is the finest and most careful of the three. Since the Montreal portrait is documented to originate in the Graf collection it is clear that the Montreal Painter worked at Er-Rubayat (or at Philadelphia); while the beard and hairstyle of the subject recall Antonine court fashion, the style of painting could also allow for an early Severan date.

David L. Thompson
University of Georgia

---

7) Staatliche Museen, Ant. inv. 31161/7; *Repertorio* B:I, 90f. no. 240, pl. 59 fig. 1. This attribution should, however, be taken with caution since—as Frel has observed ("Deux portraits de momie à Prague," *ArOr* 20 [1952] 315, pl. 32 figs. 2-3)—the portrait has been somewhat repainted.
8) *Cf.* for example the superb male portrait of Antonine date in Buffalo (Albright-Knox Art Gallery, inv. 38.2; G.M.A. Hanfmann, *Roman*

Art [Greenwich, Conn., n.d.=1964] pl. XLVII).
9) Sale notice: *Apollo* XCVIII (n.s. no. 141: November, 1973) 125, ill. (col.).
10) A portrait in Toronto (Royal Ontario Museum, inv. 946.54.2; W.H. Peck, *Mummy Portraits from Roman Egypt* [exhibition catalogue: Detroit, 1967] 27 no. 18, fig. 18) has many similar characteristics, but its style and later date suggest a follower of the Montreal Painter.

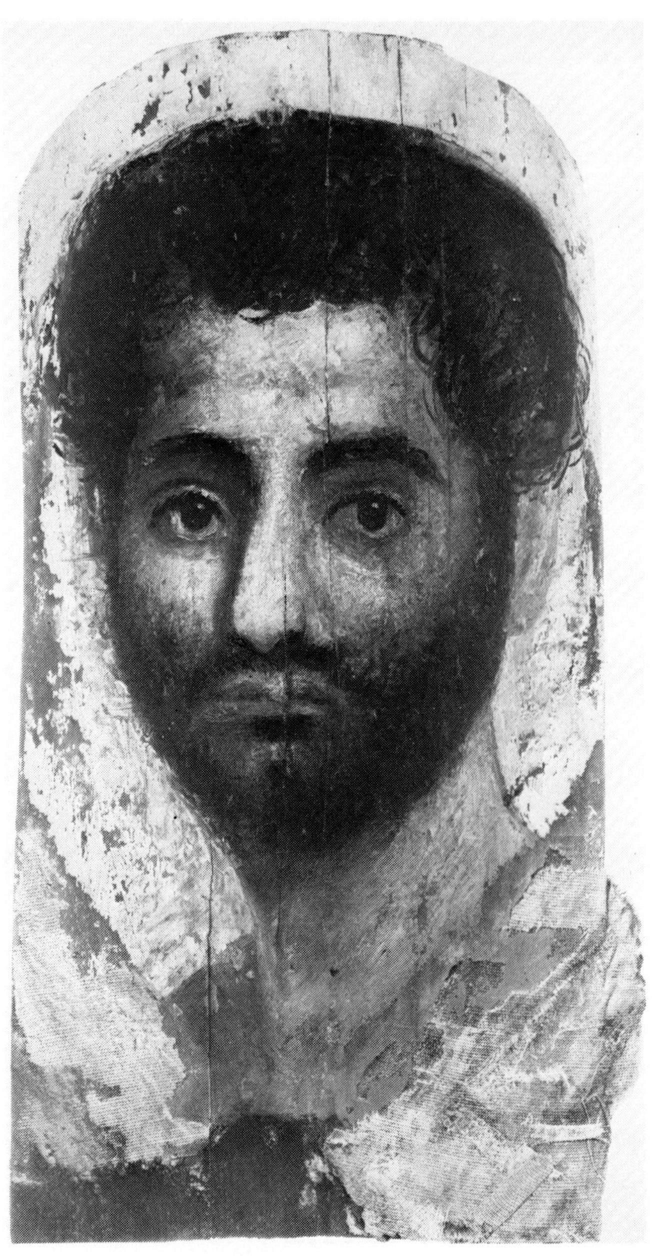

4   Malibu, J. Paul Getty Museum,
     inv. 73.AI.94. Phot. Museum

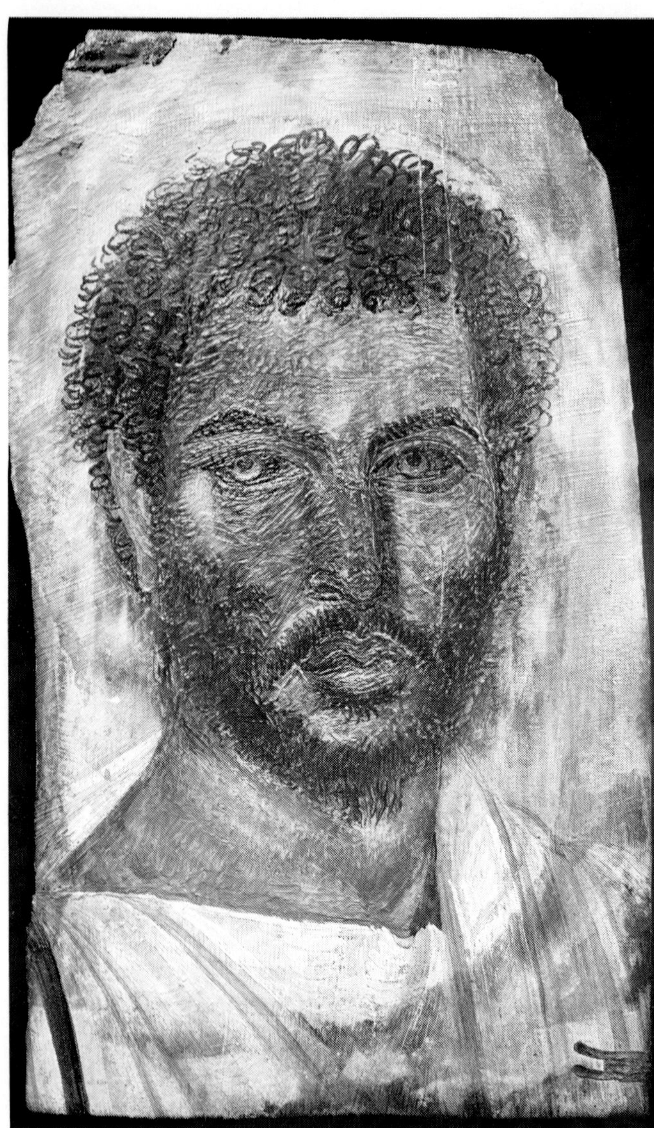

5   Malibu, J. Paul Getty Museum,
     inv. 74.AI.11. Phot. Museum

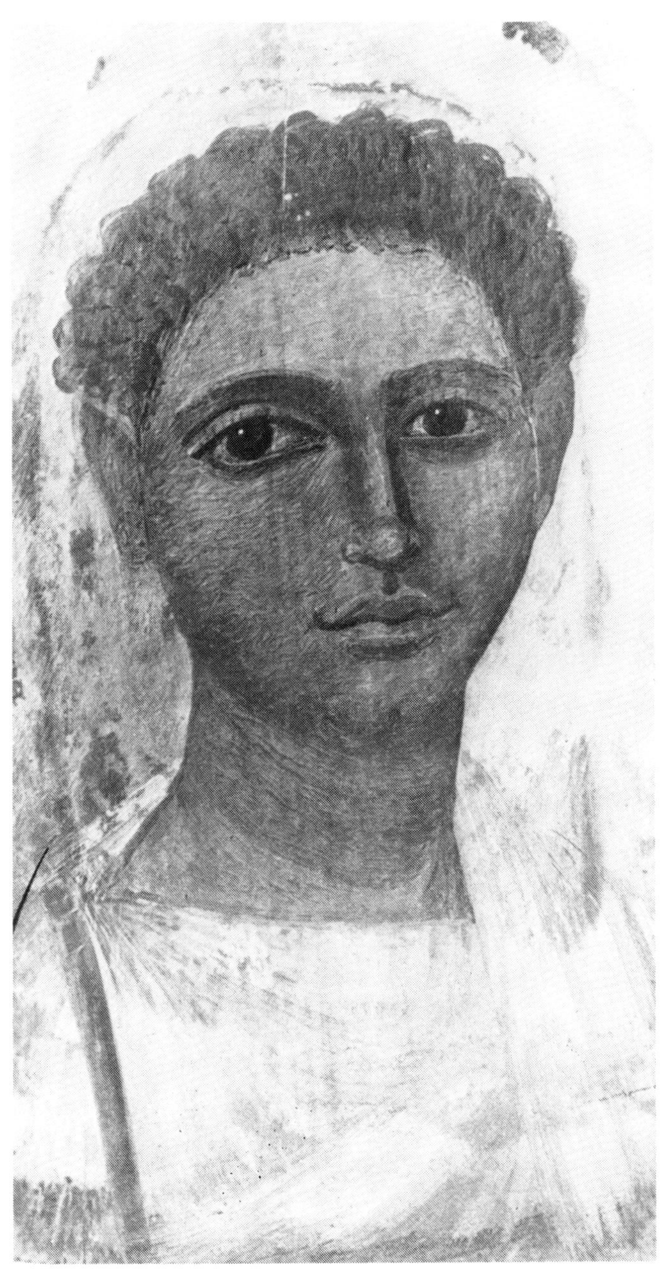

6   London market, 1973

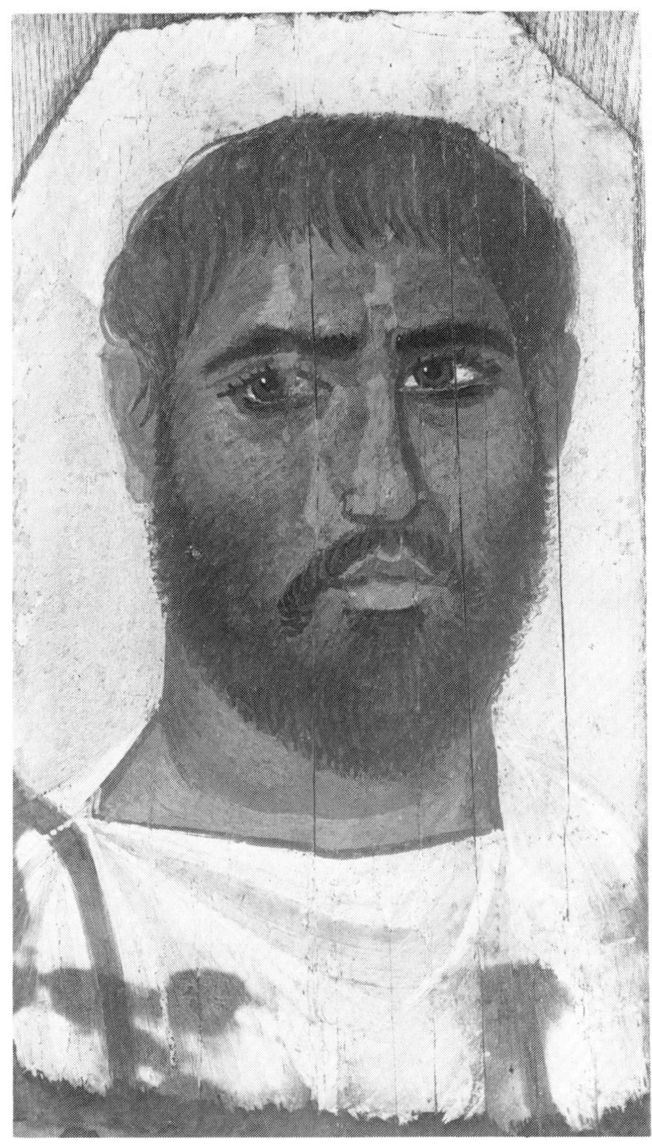

7   Montreal, Museum of Fine Arts, inv. 62.B.3.
The F. Cleveland Morgan Collection,
1962. Phot. Museum

APPENDIX:
"Fayum portraits" in North American collections

The following are listed by inventory number; only true mummy portraits are included. Six examples of doubtful authenticity have been omitted, while private collectors are grouped anonymously at the end.

Ann Arbor: Kelsey Museum of Ancient and Mediaeval Archaeology, University of Michigan (4): 26574, 26801, 26802, 26803.

Baltimore: Walters Art Gallery (6): 32.3, 32.4, 32.5, 32.6, 32.7, T.L. 149.50 (loan from Goucher College = 1895.1).

Berkeley: Robert H. Lowie Museum of Anthropology, University of California (12); 5-2327, 6-21374, 6-21375, 6-21376, 6-21377, 6-21378, 6-21378A, 6-21379, 6-21380, 6-21381, 6-21382, 6-21383.

Bloomington: Indiana University Art Museum (1): E-1958-26.

Boston: Museum of Fine Arts (9): 93.1450, 93.1451, 02.825, 11.2891, 11.2892, 50.650, 54.993, 59.340, L104.1972 (loan from private collector).

Brooklyn: Brooklyn Museum (4): 11.600B, 40.386, 41.848, 54.197.

Buffalo: Albright-Knox Art Gallery (1): 38.2.

Cambridge: Fogg Art Museum, Harvard University (5): 1923.59, 1923.60, 1924.80, 1939.111, 1946.44.

Charleston (South Carolina): Charleston Museum (1): 32.98.46.

Chicago: Art Institute of Chicago (2): 22.4798, 22.4799.

Chicago: Oriental Institute Museum, University of Chicago (2): 2053, 9137.

Cleveland: Cleveland Museum of Art (3): 71.135, 71.136, 71.137.

Detroit: Detroit Institute of Arts (1): 25.2.

Kansas City (Missouri): William Rockhill Nelson Gallery and Atkins Museum of Fine Arts (1): 37-40.

Malibu: J. Paul Getty Museum (5): 71.AI.72, 73.AI.91, 73.AI.94, 74.AI.11, 74.AI.20.

Milwaukee: Milwaukee Public Museum (1): A24428-6700.

Montreal: Montreal Museum of Fine Arts (2): 45.Dv.20, 62.B.3.

New Haven: Yale University Art Gallery (2): 1939.263, 1939.264.

New York: Metropolitan Museum of Art (14): 08.202.8, 09.181.1, 09.181.2, 09.181.3, 09.181.4, 09.181.5, 09.181.6, 09.181.7, 09.181.8, 11.139, 18.9.2, 26.5, 44.2.2, 44.7.

Northampton (Mass.): Smith College Museum of Art (1): 32:9-1.

Omaha: Joslyn Art Museum (1): 1944.167.

Ottawa: National Gallery of Canada (1): 570.

Philadelphia: Philadelphia Museum of Art (1): 63-181-263.

Philadelphia: University Museum, University of Pennsylvania (3): E16212, E16213, E16214 (+frame E16215).

Princeton: Art Museum, Princeton University (1): 37-356.

Providence: Museum of Art, Rhode Island School of Design (3): 17.060, 39.025, 39.026.

Richmond: Virginia Museum of Fine Arts (1): 55-4.

Saint Louis: Saint Louis Art Museum (2): 63.59, 128.51.

Santa Barbara: Santa Barbara Museum of Art (2): 59.18, 59.19.

Seattle: Seattle Art Museum (3): 56.Cs32.1, 46.Cs32.3, 50.Cs32.5.

Stanford: Art Gallery and Museum, Stanford University (2): 22225, 22226.

Toledo: Toledo Museum of Art (2): 06.172, 71.130.

Toronto: Royal Ontario Museum (12): 918.20.1, 918.20.2, 918.20.3, 918.20.4, 946.54.1, 946.54.2, 946.54.3, 946.54.4, 946.54.5, 946.54.6, 946.54.7, 952.50.

Washington: Dumbarton Oaks Collection, Harvard University (1): 37.32.

Washington: Smithsonian Institution (1): 230149.

Worcester: Worcester Art Museum (3): 1924.111, 1935.140, 1935.141.

Private collections: 14 examples.

Columellam ... Aut Mensam ... Aut Labellum
Archaeological Remarks on Cicero's De Legibus II 66

In the year of the archon Demogenes, Demetrios of Phaleron gave laws to the Athenians, 'Αϑήνησι νόμους ἔϑηκεν in the wording of the Marmor Parium.[1] Some of these *nomoi* are mentioned by Cicero in *De Legibus* II 66: Sed ait rursus idem Demetrius increbruisse eam funerum sepulchrorumque magnificentiam, quae nunc fere Romae est; quam consuetudinem lege minuit ipse; fuit enim hic vir, ut scitis, non solum eruditissimus, sed etiam civis e re publica maxime tuendaeque civitatis peritissimus. Is igitur sumptum minuit, non solum poena, sed etiam tempore; ante lucem enim iussit efferri. Sepulchris autem novis finivit modum; nam super terrae tumulum noluit quicquam statui nisi columellam tribus cubitis ne altiorem aut mensam aut labellum et huic procurationi certum magistratum praefecerat.[2]

The crucial passage, *nam super terrae tumulum noluit quicquam nisi columellam tribus cubitis ne altiorem aut mensam aut labellum,* has been taken without question by editors and translators to mean that Demetrios permitted three monuments: "...nothing should be built above the mound of earth except a small column no more than three cubits in height, or else a table or small basin."[3] Conze's illustration, published in 1922,[4] presents the archaeologist's acceptance of this interpretation of three monuments: the columella, the mensa and the birdbath-like labellum.

The first decisive step toward equating Cicero's account with the archaeological evidence was made by Brueckner in 1891.[5] Following the identification of the columnar-shaped grave monuments with Cicero's columellae, he pointed out: "Nahe verwandt der Form dieser Säulchen sind ein paar Monumente, welche nach unten sich verbreitern ... Bestimmte technische Indizien,

darunter je ein grosses viereckiges Einsatzloch auf ihrer oberen Fläche sprechen dafür, dass es einstmals Stützen für weite Schalen gewesen sind, so dass das vollständige Grabmal die Form eines antiken Weihwasserbeckens, eines περιρραντήριον, hatte. Unteritalische Vasen bieten Parallelen für die Verwendung solcher Becken als Grabmäler in der Zeit um 300."[6]

These sentences have become the foundation for what we may call the "Labellum Theory."

Eight years later Brueckner's interpretation was further stabilized by Wolters' second article on the pottery found in the dromos of the Menidi tholos.[7] Arguing from the combination of finds—small terracotta shields, horsemen figurines, and the relatively large quantity of conical-shaped foot fragments of "bauchiger Kessel auf hohem Fuss,"[8] and the "Ort selbst,"[9] Wolters explained the dromos as the location of a hero-cult practiced from the 8th to the early 5th century. The most frequent and most obvious vessel, often equipped with pouring spout (Gussschnauze), the bellied cauldron on a high foot,[10] he identified[11] as louteria.[12] The presence of these louteria he connected convincingly with bath rituals performed in the cult of the dead. Then he summarizes: "Die Darbringung des Bades an die Toten ist ... bezeugt, und die Gefässe in Menidi haben damit ihre Erklärung erhalten, um uns sogleich ihrerseits einen weiteren Aufschluss zu geben. Das aus Cicero (De legibus II, 66) bekannte Gesetz des Demetrius von Phaleron beschränkte die erlaubten Grabdenkmäler auf drei Formen, columella, mensa, labellum. Was wir darunter zu verstehen haben hat Brückner, leider bisher nur ganz kurz, überzeugend dargelegt (Arch. Anz. 1892 S. 23): es sind die bekannten Säulen, die länglichen basenartigen Aufsätze und schalenartigen Gefässe auf hohem

---

The text of this article is an only slightly edited version of a paper read at the General Meeting of the Archaeological Institute of America in San Francisco, December 1969. Some of the material used (see notes 50, 56) is still unpublished. The columellae and labella of the Kerameikos were studied by the author in 1962-63, with the generous assistance of the Deutsches Archäologisches Institut, Athen, for which I am greatly indebted to the Second Director of the German Institute, Professor Dr. Franz Willemsen.

1) For text cf. Felix Jacoby, *Das Marmor Parium,* Berlin, 1904, p. 22.13 (especially line 114 +2 = 116). For date, cf. Jacoby's comment, *ibid.,* p. 198 and Munro's review in *Cl. Rev.,* XIX, p. 269; and *F. Gr. Hist.,* II b, No. 239, p. 700 *sub* D. Zeittafeln line 11 and note 15.

2) Whether Cicero's source is actually Demetrios' περὶ τῆς 'Αϑήνησι νομοϑεσίας, as Conze (*Die Attischen Grabreliefs,* IV 1922, p. 5, with reference to Diogenes Laertius, *Vit. Philosoph.,* V, 9) assumes, may remain undiscussed here, along with the debated question of when, precisely, the decree was issued.

3) Cicero, *De Re Publica, De Legibus,* C. W. Keyes, 1970 (Loeb), pp. 453, 455; cf. also C. D. Yonge, *The Treatises of M. T. Cicero,* London and New York, 1892, p. 459, "...save a little column, three cubits high, or a tombstone (sic! for mensa), or tablet (for labellum?)."

4) A. Conze, *Die Attischen Grabreliefs,* IV, 1922, p. 9. For a recent discussion of the meaning of columella, mensa, labellum, see D. C. Kurz and J. Boardman, *Greek Burial Customs,* Ithaca, 1971, pp. 166-169.

5) Report to the German Archaeological Society, Berlin, December 1891; published as "Die Entwicklung der Bestattung in Attika," *AA,* 1892, pp. 19-24.

6) *Ibid.,* p. 23. There is no doubt that some of the South Italian vases actually show perirrhanteria in sepulchral contexts. Whether, however, it is legitimate to claim them as "parallels," thus implying a) that these vase representations actually depict contemporary burial rites and burial monuments, and more importantly b), that if a) is correct for South Italy these representations prove the existence of identical practices and monuments in Attica, seems questionable. Cf. Eva Brann, *Hesperia,* XXX, 1961, p. 315 ad F22, H 18-19.

7) P. Wolters, *JdI,* XIV, 1899, pp. 103 ff.

8) *Ibid.,* p. 125.

9) *Ibid.,* p. 127.

10) *Ibid.,* pp. 128f.

11) *Ibid.,* p. 132.

12) Cf. *JdI,* 1899, p. 108 fig. 10; p. 126 fig. 29; also Hedwig Kenner, *ÖJh.* XXIX, 1935, p. 134, fig. 55.

Fuss. Dass Demetrius diese, von seiner Zeit an für lange ausschliesslichen Formen z.T. erst geschaffen habe,[13] kann ich nicht glauben; höchstens die den bestimmten Zweck in so nüchterner Weise anstrebende Säule könnte man für eine solche Erfindung halten; die mensa ist es zweifellos nicht, und das charakteristische und schwerlich bedeutungslose labellum lässt sich doch auch nicht leicht so erklären. Aber es fehlten bisher die Monumente, welche den Ursprung erkennen liessen. Dies hat uns jetzt das Grab von Menidi geschenkt: wenn wir dort das Wasserbecken auf hohem Fuss als typisches Gerät des Totenkultes verwendet und beim Grab aufgestellt sehen, dürfen wir ähnliche Sitte auch sonst in Attika voraussetzen und aus ihr die Denkmalform herleiten, welche Demetrius neben jenen beiden anderen noch weiter bestehen liess."[14]

Wolters' main argument for his interpretation of the shallow, or bellied, Menidi bowls as louteria rests on the spouts, surviving on some examples, assumed for others,[15] being indeed characteristic for the vessel. "Er (i.e. the spout) ist aber an einer flachen oder auch bauchigen Schüssel so auffallend, dass wir von ihm aus schliessen müssen. Niemand wird ein Gefäss zum Eingiessen, eine Kanne, so gestalten. Diese Schusseln waren vielmehr offenbar bestimmt, eine Flüssigkeit aufzunehmen, die nach dem Gebrauch als wertlos fortgegossen wurde, mit einem Wort, es sind Waschbecken... λουτήρια..."[16] This leads him to his next conclusion, that the large number of louteria found in the dromos rules out the idea "(dass sie) nur als Weihgeschenke ohne besondere Beziehung aufgestellt worden seien, vielmehr ist es ohne weiteres klar, dass es hier üblich war, den Heroen als Opfergabe ein Bad darzubringen."[17]

The literary sources as used by Wolters[18] seem to concur with this idea. He quotes, among others, Sophocles' *Elektra*,[19] Aischylos' *Choephoroi*,[20] Zenobios' definition of chthonia loutra,[21] all of which attest that loutra were carried out to the graves. And finally, Athenaeus' description[22] which, I think, could be considered rather a testimony against the use of the louteria than in their

favor: "But there is a special use of the word *aponimma* in Athens, where it is applied to the ritual in honour of the dead, or to the purification of the unclean, as (Kleidemos) says in the work entitled *The Expositor*. For after some preliminary remarks on offerings to the dead, he writes: 'Dig a trench on the west side of the grave. Then standing beside the trench face the west, and pour over it the water, reciting these words: "Water to you for whom it is meet and lawful." After that pour scented oil.'"[23]

Conze's introductory chapter[24] on the columellae, mensae, and labella summarizes and accepts the Brueckner-Wolters identification. His passage on the labella, however, betrays that Conze is only too aware of the shakiness of Wolters' conclusions with regard to the post-Demetrian labella. Not a single one of the monuments which he entered as labella represents an intact sepulchral specimen of the assumed birdbath type: they are without exception stands of washbasins re-used as columellae.

Hedwig Kenner's article, *Das Luterion im Kult,*[25] added a new link to this chain. In interpreting the representation of a bowl with two tripartite handles and spout which appears on an Attic red-figure spout fragment in the Vienna University collection,[26] she relies heavily on Wolters' louterion theory. Miss Kenner's argument runs as follows: Wolters has proved the custom of the "Totenbad,"[27] closely related to which are the bath rituals dedicated to heroes (Menidi) and deities (Delphi).[28] The Viennese spout belongs to a louterion of precisely the same shape as the representation shown upon it.[29] According to Kenner it is to be dated between 350 and 318,[30] and to be considered a late offspring of the Menidi bowls. To close the gap between the latest of the Menidi bowls and the Vienna Hapax[31] she turns to the sanctuaries.[32] There she finds not only the counterparts of the Geometric and post-Geometric grave louteria, but also their stone successors, the variety of "basin-on-a-pedestal." The same kind of washbasin, she points out, served different purposes, since found in private

---

13) As it appeared to Brueckner, see *op. cit.,* p. 24, "...wie es scheint...."
14) Wolters, *JdI,* 1899, p. 134.
15) To support this assumption Wolters refers to his figs. 10, p. 108, and 29, p. 126; cf. also p. 129 note 25.
16) Wolters, *op. cit.,* p. 132.
17) *Ibid.* p. 133.
18) Wolters, *op. cit.,* pp. 133 f.
17) *Ibid.* p. 133.
18) Wolters, *op. cit.,* pp. 133 f.
19) Line 84: πατρὸς χέοντες λουτρά; line 434: λουτρὰ προσφέρειν πατρί.
20) Wolters quotes line 130: χέουσα τάσδε χέρνιβας φϑιτοῖς; however *Aeschyli Tragoediae,* editio altera, Gilbert Murray ed., Oxford, 1964, line 129: κἀγω χέουσα τάσδε χέρνιβας νεκροῖς.
21) Zenobios, VI.45, Göttinger Parömiographen I S. 174; Wolters,

op. cit., p. 134 with note 54.
22) Athenaeus, *Deipnosophistae,* IX, 409-410.
23) Athenaeus, IV, G. B. Gulick, London, 1930 (Loeb), p. 357. I have used the Loeb translation for the corresponding Greek passage quoted in Wolters' text, p. 134, substituting here Wolters' Kleidemos for the Loeb Anticleides (cf. Gulick, p. 356 note 2 and p. 357 note c).
24) Conze, *op. cit.*
25) *ÖJh.,* XXIX, 1935, pp. 109-154.
26) *Ibid.,* p. 110, fig. 49.
27) *Ibid.,* p. 132.
28) *Ibid.,* pp. 132, 135 f.
29) Cf. Kenner's drawing, *op. cit.,* p. 109 and fig. 49, p. 110.
30) *Ibid.,* p. 154.
31) *Ibid.,* p. 142.
32) *Ibid.,* p. 135.

houses, public places, sanctuaries,[33] and in cemeteries.[34]

Finally Johannes Kirchner, at the First International Congress for Epigraphy in Amsterdam, September 1938, read a short paper on the sumptuary decree of Demetrios of Phaleron.[35] "Was man unter dem bei Cicero an dritter Stelle erwähnten labellum zu verstehen hat, *ist nicht ganz sicher* (italics mine). Wie die Darlegungen von Brueckner und Wolters es wahrscheinlich gemacht haben, haben wir als labella Säulchen mit schalenförmiger Ausweitung zu einem breiten Fuss anzusehen (Abb. 10).[36] Obenauf befindet sich bei den Labellen meist ein Einsatzloch, bestimmt einen Aufsatz zu tragen."[37]

By that time the confusion over Cicero's *labellum* seems to have been complete. Plate II of IG II[2] shows on the left a columella adapted from the unfluted foot of a washbasin.[38] A better choice would have been to show a columella made from a fluted foot (e.g. Conze, 1754, 1755), which occurs more frequently than the illustrated type. The caption here should read "columella e parte inferiore labelli adaptata," rather than "labellum (pars inferior)"—for where and when, until now, have the fragments of a single basin belonging to a louterion been found in an Athenian necropolis:[39] Twelve specimens answering the description "columella e labello adaptata" are still kept in the Kerameikos.[40] *Nine* of these are published in IG II[2]; only *two* correctly described as "colu-

mella e labello adaptata,"[41] *two* referred to as "labellum,"[42] and *five* as "columella."[43] The remaining *three* examples are unpublished.[44]

Back to Cicero: Nam super terrae tumulum noluit quicquam statui nisi columellam tribus cubitis ne altiorem aut mensam aut labellum.

The word *columella* describes very well the columnar-shaped grave monuments that do exist. More than 4,000 of them were found in Athens, very few of them outside Attica.[45] Brueckner's identification therefore seems to hold, particularly since none of the grave columns can be dated earlier than the very end of the 4th century.

The word *mensa,* as generally applied by archaeologists and epigraphers, conceals rather than describes a variety of shapes. We have to distinguish three types:

1) the "house type";[46]
2) a mensa used as a base for another monument, a loutrophoros as in the monument of the Messenians, or a stele;[47]
3) and, finally, the simple box-shaped mensa either decorated with moldings or unadorned.[48]

Are these really the monuments indicated by Cicero's word mensa? No one has ever seriously questioned that assumption.[49] But does the Kerameikos material stand the test?

---

33) To perirrhanteria in private houses, public places and sanctuaries add: D. A. Amyx, *Hesperia,* XXVII, 1958, pp. 221-228; E. Brann, *Hesperia,* XXX, 1961, pp. 314-316; B. B. Shefton, *Hesperia,* XXXI, 1962, pp. 331-334; B. Sparkes and L. Talcott, *Athenian Agora,* XII, Princeton, 1972, pp. 218-221; H. A. Thompson and R. E. Wycherley, *Athenian Agora,* XIV, Princeton, p. 79 note 229, pp. 118-119.

34) Cf. Kenner, *op. cit.,* pp. 142-146. It should be noted that she does not refer to a *single* louterion with even vestiges of a bowl preserved found *in* an Attic cemetery and of post-Demetrian date.

35) "Das Gesetz des Demetrios von Phaleron zur Einschrankung des Gräberluxus," *Die Antike,* XV, 1939, pp. 93-97.

36) Abb. 10 = IG II 3559; the same illustration: Conze, pl. CCCLXXVII, no. 1752 and IG II[2], pl. II, 11084.

37) *Ibid.,* p. 95.

38) See note 37 above.

39) Cf. Kenner, *op. cit.,* pp. 142 f.: "Eine Reihe von Beckenuntersätzen...tragen Namensinschriften, sind also sicher Reste von Grabzeichen, d.h. Grabluterien (Conze S. 11, Nr. 1750-1753). ...wohl alle ...3. Jahrhundert v. Chr." I find it extremely difficult to agree with this statement. A permanently attached basin on a foot no higher than "0.38-0.57 m." would have concealed any inscription, in a position so close under the bowl as e.g. Conze, No. 1752, to any viewer standing on the same level. Can Kenner's argument be correct? If so, then we may safely assume that the louteria cited must have belonged in the large 4th century grave precincts along the "Gräberstrasse" (= Weststrasse, cf. *AA,* 1965, cols. 333-334, Abb. 31), standing just within high retaining walls—in other words, well above eye level for a passerby in the street. Even then, however, the legibility of their inscriptions would have been doubly reduced, for *most of the day* by the deep shadow of the basin and *always* by distance.

I much prefer to believe that Kenner's "sicher(e) Reste von Grabzeichen, d.h. Grabluterien" also were inscribed only at the time of reuse, i.e., after they had ceased to be louteria due to the destruction of their basins. The only difference between them and those listed by Kenner on p. 143 (generally accepted as re-used louteria/labella stands): they have not even been reworked!

40) See, in note 59 below, Nos. 1, 2, 3, 6; 5, 7, 8, 11, 15, 16, 17; 4.

41) Nos. 5, 7.

42) Nos. 11, 15.

43) Nos. 1, 2, 6, 8, 16.

44) Nos. 3, 4, 17.

45) This rough count is based mainly on the columellae listed in IG II[2]. Considering the large number of columellae visible almost everywhere in the walls and at street corners of Athens' Plaka, most of them still awaiting rescue and publication, the figure "more than 4000" is a rather conservative understatement. Outside of Attica I know genuine columellae of the common Attic type only at Eretria, and there but a small number. The variations kept in the courtyard of the Museum of Boeotian Thebes, though possibly remote relatives of the Attic columns, can hardly be added here (e.g. A. Wilhelm, *Beiträge zur griechischen Inschriftenkunde.* Vienna, 1909, p. 74, fig. 36, from Thespiai).

46) E.g. Conze, *op. cit.,* p. 13, No. 1768 (illustr.).

47) E.g. A Brueckner, *Der Friedhof am Eridanos.* 1909, fig. 64 (Messenians); Conze, *op. cit.,* pl. CCCLXXVIII, No. 1769.

48) Conze, *op. cit.,* p. 13, mensa of Hegesias Hegesiou ex Oiou (IG II[2] 6994). Cf. also *Kerameikos,* VI. 1, Taf. 3, the best illustration of the stemma of mensa types 1) and 3).

49) Save for Conze's (*op. cit.*) extremely cautiously phrased assessment of the material, and its recent echo in Kurz and Boardman, *op. cit.,* p. 168.

Of the 32 mensae listed in the Kerameikos inventory,[50] 27 are dated, mainly by lettering and in a few instances by prosopographical evidence,[51] to the 4th century B.C., covering the span from approximately 360 to 320.[52] One of these was re-used in the 2nd century B.C.[53] One, the controversial Melis trapeza, seems to have been inscribed in Augustan times; its molding and shape, however, suggest for the mensa proper a date in the 4th century again.[54] Only one out of 32 mensae seems to qualify as a genuine (?) 1st century B.C. representative: Ker. Fol. 57, No. 3 = IG II² 10281, Ker. Inv. I.352, KER Phot. 5888. Thus we are left with only three mensae which give us the result of our analysis. The type of grave monument commonly called mensae is represented between ca. 300 and 200 B.C. by only three instances:

1) Ker. Fol. 57, No. 35 = IG II² 6540 = Ker. Inv. I.378, KER Phot. 15 (left), 5945.5946 (inscr.), properly described in IG II² as "marmor quadratum (mensa videlicet)", dated ante med. s. III a. Does the columella IG II² 13006 = Ker. Inv. C 1/7, post fin. s. IV a., belong?
2) Ker. Fol. 57, No. 11 = IG II² 6084 = Ker. Inv. I.358, KER Phot. 5900.5901 (inscr.), fin. s. III a.—The jointly inscribed names of the couple occur separately on the two columellae IG II² 6080 (Mus. Nat. EM 11699) and

---

50) The handwritten inventory, labelled "Grabtische (Fol. 57)," is kept in the apotheke of the Kerameikos excavations. Actually this inventory lists 43 running numbers. Of these, however, 11 entries have unfortunately to be disregarded, since: 3 (Nos. 5, 16, 32) remain blank; 6 are either safely (Nos. 9, 18, 27, 38) or most likely (Nos. 42, 43) without inscriptions and unpublished; 1 (No. 1 = Ker. Inv. I. 350, KER Phot. 5884, inscr.) unpublished; and 1 (No. 39) not inventoried since not found in April 1960, apparently unpublished.
51) IG II² 6831 = Ker. Inv. I.357. Kleandros from Oia, line 2, is attested as diaitetes in 325/4 BC in IG II² 1926, 89; IG II² 6747 = Ker. Inv. I.373. Cf. IG II² 6738 and 6732; IG II² 6953 = Ker. Inv. I.382; Cf. *PA* 8177 = IG II² 1524, 187 (II 758B, col. II, 13), tab. curat. Brauronii c.a. 334 a; IG II²5728 = Ker. Inv. I.383. Philagros Phalereus, in line 2 = *PA* 14215 = IG II² 1622, 549 (II 803d, 118) νεωρίων ἐπιμελητής a. 348/7.
52) IG II² 8678 = Ker. Inv. I.354; IG II² 5242 = Ker. Inv. I.359; IG II² 9062 = Ker. Inv. I.371 (?date); IG II² 6738 = Ker. Inv. I.374 (?date); IG II² 7429/30 = Ker. Inv. I.375; IG II² 11831 = Ker. Inv. I.376; IG II² 5918 = Ker. Inv. I.377 (?date); IG II² 11089 = Ker. Inv. I.366; IG II² 6953 = Ker. Inv. I.382; IG II² 5678 (II 1872) = Ker. Inv. I.351; IG II² 5678 (II 1873.1874) = Ker. Inv. I.355; IG II² 7100 = Ker. Inv. I.356; IG II² 5645 = Ker. Inv. I.365 (re-used 2nd c. BC); IG II² 9347 = Ker. Inv. I.367; IG II² 9347 = Ker. Inv. I.368; IG II² 9347 = Ker. Inv. I.369; IG II² 8505 = Ker. Inv. I.372; IG II² 5728 = Ker. Inv. I.383; IG II² 5676 = Ker. Inv. I.353; IG II² 5677 = Ker. Inv. I.360; IG II² 7400 = Ker. Inv. I.361; IG II² 6602 = Ker. Inv. I.362; IG II² 6226 = Ker. Inv. I.364; IG II² 6747 = Ker. Inv. I.373; IG II² 5725 = Ker. Inv. I.379; IG II² 5756 = Ker. Inv. I.380; IG II² 6831 = Ker. Inv. I.357.
53) IG II² 5645 = Ker. Inv. I.365.
54) IG II² 9768 (III 2753) = Ker. Inv. I.363, KER Phot. 5911.5912 (inscr.) = Conze, No. 1766 and pl. CCCLXXVIII. Brueckner, *FaE,* p. 81: "Die Formen des Grabtisches schliessen sich in der zierlichen Profilierung an die des vierten Jahrhunderts an; die Inschriften... (sc.

6083 = Ker. Inv. A 2/8; cf. Brueckner, *FaE,* p. 64.
3) Ker. Fol. 57, No. 25 = IG II² 7148 = Ker. Inv. I.370,
KER Phot. 5926.5927 (inscr.), fin. s. III a. with columella
IG II² 12723 = Ker. Inv. C 1/79. For father see columella
IG II² 8024 = Ker. Inv. C 2/29; cf. Brueckner, *FaE,*
p. 119.

On the other hand, of the three pre-Demetrian types
of mensa at least one, type 2, served as a basis. This
type shares its function with the flat slabs which supported columellae from the third century on.[55] Could
we not call this poorest type of basis, that supporting a
columella, mensa as well?

Let us turn now to the so-called labella (louteria) of
the Kerameikos.[56] Twelve of them are safely "columellae
e labellis adaptatae," re-using the fluted variety. In
several of these the tenon-hole, once in the top of the
labellum stand to hold the bowl, now appears on the
bottom of the columella (Nos. 5, 7, 8, 11, 15, 16, 17 in
note 56). These are safely recognizable as upside-down,
re-used, originally fluted washbasin (= louterion) stands.
No. 4 differs from the previous group only by location
of the tenon-hole which is now visible on top of the

IG II² 9768 and 9767) sind nicht viel jünger zu datieren. Aus der glei-
chen Zeit, rund dem dritten Jahrhundert..." Kirchner, init. s. I p.
(Augustan). Rhusopulos, *Eph. Arch.,* 1862, 299, no. 351, Hadrianic.
55) E.g., 1) post med. s. III a.: IG II² 7598 and addendum, p. 882 =
Ker. Inv. A 3/1. *AA,* 1932, cols. 189-190, Abb. 2, Beil. 1; Riemann,
Kerameikos, II, pp. 44 ff., No. 42 (P 659), Taf. 14; Peek, *Kerameikos,*
III, pp. 44 ff, 38a, Taf. 15, 1.2.
2) s. II a.: IG II² 7271 = Ker. Inv. A 3/4. *Kerameikos,* III, p. 48, 38d.
(Do columella and basis actually belong together?)
3) s. II/1 a.: IG II² 6741 = Ker. Inv. E 2/7. *AA,* 1942, cols 233 ff.
4) s. I a./ s. I p.: IG II² 6545 = Ker. Inv. B 3/26. Brueckner, *FaE,* pp.
49 f., No. 25; Conze, No. 1777.
5) init. s. II p.: IG II² 5484 = Ker. Inv. B 1/51-53. Brueckner, *FaE,*
pp. 50 f., No. 35 = Conze, No. 1749 and Nachtrag, p. 125.
56) Total number: 17 +1. (1) IG II² 5260 = Ker. Inv. C 3/13; (2) IG II²
5354 = Ker. Inv. C 1/40; (3) Unpublished. Ker. Inv. 112; (4) Unpublished. Ker. Inv. B 1/6; (5) IG II² 6623 = Conze 1755 (cf. also IG II²
6625). Ker. Inv. F 1/22; (6) IG II² 6887 = Ker. Inv. C 1/70; (7) IG II²
8845 = Ker. Inv. F 1/1; (8) IG II² 9229 = Ker. Inv. C 3/7; (9) IG II²
9249 = Ker. Inv. A 2/3; (10) IG II² 10299 = Conze 1750. Ker. Inv. B
1/27; (11) IG II² 11314a = Ker. Inv. C 2/8; (12) IG II² 11817 = Conze
1751 (belongs to mensa IG II² 6226). Now lost; (13) Unpublished. Ker.
Inv. K-N/II, 144; (14) IG II² 12457 = Ker. Inv. C 3/5; (15) IG II² 12548
= Conze 1761. Ker. Inv. C 2/9; (16) IG II² 12611 = Ker. Inv. C 3/3; (17)
Unpublished. Ker. Inv. C 3/12; (18) IG II² 5646: questionable. Ker.
Inv. B 1/55. This list includes, besides a), 11 re-used once-fluted washbasin stands (Nos. 1-7, 11, 15-17); b) 3 safely re-used washbasin stands,
however without traces of fluting (Nos. 8, 13, 14); c) 1 now lost "labellum," cf. IG II² 11817 (II 3841), "olim prope mensam Calliphanis
Thoricii, n. 6226, periisse videtur," here No. 12; d) 2 columnar-shaped
specimens, at least one of them (No. 9) worked from an abandoned
washbasin stand without the customary torus but with "dowel-shaped"
top section, the second (No. 10) identical in shape; e) 1 example whose
shape resembles suspiciously that of the trumpet-shaped washbasin
stands, which was actually worked from an abandoned section of a
small column shaft (?). Here No. 18.

columella, betraying that the washbasin foot was re-used in its original orientation.[57] Four other examples, Nos. 1, 2, 3, 6, show the same traces of partially removed flutes as the preceding specimens, but lack tenon-holes. Without a tenon-hole it is impossible to determine whether the labellum stand was re-used upside down or in its original position.

Three other examples, Nos. 13, 14, 18, have the general shape of the louterion stand, however no traces of fluting and none of the other characteristics indicating the re-use of actually finished basin stands, e.g. tenon-holes or moldings. Most likely these columellae were worked out of washbasin stands abandoned at an early state of the cutting process, later on re-used with slight modifications only. All of these are fashioned with the neck-ring (torus) typical of the columella.

Closely related to these are three further examples, Nos. 9, 10, 12, the tops of their shafts showing a reduced diameter, slightly resembling a tenon[58]. One of them is to be dated around 315 B.C.[59] The second,[60] still *in situ super terrae tumulum,* cannot be later than the middle of the third century.[61] The third of this group, No. 9, the marker of Σωτήριχος Μάγνης, is dated in IG II² 9249 ca. s. II a. Only these three stones could be suspected of having carried Aufsätze (bowls?), no traces of which have been recorded, to my knowledge, in Koumanoudes' or Brueckner's excavation diaries. Nor have there been any finds of this nature during more recent excavations. The large diameter and the height of their tenon-like projections should warn us against taking them for actual tenons.[62]

To summarize: Only the following types of grave monument found in the Kerameikos have safely been made in the years following 317/6 B.C.:

A number of unpretentious cippi which can be disregarded in this context; and

Columellae, the lower ends of their shafts appearing in three varieties:

1) unworked, to be dug into the ground—the unworked part comprising at least one third, more often almost one half of the entire length of the monument;

2) bottom flat-cut or tenon-shaped, to be inserted into a base;

3) footing trumpet-shaped since made from a labellum. In these instances the wide foot or top of the original stand, whichever was better preserved, served as basis.

There is no third type of monument to be added.

Two points about the accepted interpretation of Cicero's passage strike me as peculiar: (1) Only the columella is restricted in height; (2) Only one of the three grave monuments mentioned by Cicero has yet been found—the columella. Furthermore, the earliest specimens of this category have one characteristic in common, that is, a wide footing provided *either* by a base (mensa) *or* by the flaring end of a re-used washbasin stand (labellum).

I would therefore suggest a reinterpretation of the crucial Cicero passage: Nothing should be built above the mound of earth except a small column no more than three cubits in height, either (supported by) a mensa or (re-using) a labellum.[63]

Jochen R. A. Twele
University of Denver

---

57) It remains uncertain whether this unsightly hole was for the purpose of re-use filled or intentionally left open to receive the tenon of some unknown object for which there is no evidence.

58) Brueckner, *FaE,* p. 63: "...mit oben abgesetztem Rande...."

59) IG II² 11817 = Conze, No. 1751, missing since 1907. See No. 12, note 56 above, under c). The date, paullo post a. 317/6, in IG II² is based on Brueckner's argument, *FaE,* pp. 63 f.

60) See No. 10, note 56 above, under d).

61) Cf. IG II² 10299, based on Brueckner, *op. cit.,* pp. 33 f. For illustration see *ibid.,* p. 31, fig. 14 and Conze, *op. cit.,* pl. CCCLXXXVI, No. 1750.

62) No. 9, IG II² 9249: Tenon height 0.0415; tenon diam. 0.214; shaft diam. 0.234; No. 10, IG II² 10299: Tenon height 0.078; tenon diam.

0.20; shaft diam. 0.26; No. 12, IG II² 11817: Tenon height (?); tenon diam. 0.21; shaft diam. (?) Cf. Brueckner, *FaE,* p. 63 f., sub f = Conze, No. 1751.

63) That the puritanical observance of this law—which was apparently strictly obeyed for at least decades—did not remain in effect *ad infinitum* has been masterfully proven by Johannes Kirchner's article "Attische Grabstelen des dritten und zweiten Jahrhunderts v. Chr.," *Arch. Eph.,* 1937, pp. 338-340.

NOTE: In 1969, wondering about the reaction of a philologist to the interpretation suggested here, I asked for the always generous advice of Professor George Duckworth of Princeton University. After careful deliberation, he gave the theory his blessing. His agreement encouraged me; if, however, the idea may not pass review, the error is entirely mine.

The Westmacott Jupiter: An Enthroned Zeus of Late Antique Aspect

Introduction

The J. Paul Getty Museum is rich in masterpieces of Greek and Roman sculpture, works like the Lansdowne Herakles, the Mazarin Venus, or the Crouching Aphrodite from Sir Francis Cook's and Lord Anson's collections which were as famous in their homes in the British Isles or western Europe as they are now at Malibu. Catalogues, guides, standard histories of Classical art, and specialized articles have featured these statues and reliefs. Under the direction of Burton Fredericksen and his colleagues, the Getty Museum has also acquired a number of Greek and Roman sculptures of prime interest to students of ancient civilization rather than chiefly to critics and admirers of ancient beauty. One of these statues is discussed in these pages. Like many other marbles in the Getty Museum, the Westmacott Jupiter has the virtue of having once belonged to a distinguished Briton, a leading exponent of official sculpture in marble in the New-Classic style, and of having acquired an important pedigree in the days of Queen Victoria, if not at an even earlier date.

The Westmacott Jupiter has gone virtually unnoticed for its contribution to Greek imperial art, and on this count alone the statue merits consideration at this time. I should like to dedicate this short study to Professor Bernard Ashmole, from whom I learned much about Greek sculpture in the United Kingdom a quarter of a century ago, and with whom in recent years I have discussed many of the marbles in the J. Paul Getty Museum both in person and by correspondence. As a connoisseur, his eye has few rivals; as a teacher, he yields to no one in kindness and understanding.

The Statue

One of the ugliest, in classical terms, and, seemingly, least interesting small statues in the J. Paul Getty Museum may have been a cult-image of considerable ethnic and political significance, and may prove to be both important and rewarding in identifying the latest, pre-Christian stages of pagan antiquity in the Roman Empire (Figs. 1a,b and 2a,b,c,d). The statue came most immediately from Laguna Beach. Long before acquisition by Mr. Getty, the ensemble had been mentioned and recorded as part of the small collection of the British Neo-Classic sculptor Sir Richard Westmacott (1775 to 1856) in London. In his survey of the classical and related antiquities in the British Isles, Adolph Michaelis wrote,

in 1882, "At the residence of WESTMACOTT, the sculptor, Count Clarac, in the year 1833, found a number of marbles with regard to the actual whereabouts of which I have no information to give. Clarac had published the following statues or statuettes, apparently for the most part rather seriously restored." Michaelis listed number one as, "Statuette of Serapis, restored as Zeus"[1] (Fig. 3).

The right arm and hand with a thunderbolt and the left with a scepter-staff are now missing. They may have been restorations, as Michaelis has suggested, but this question should have little effect on the iconography of the statue as a whole. Such parallels as do exist might suggest a phiale or patera as a better attribute for the extended right hand.

The arrangement of the chiton under the himation and the rows of four curls over the brow (Fig. 4a,b,c,d) are characteristics of Sarapis rather than Zeus, but the fact that the himation is pulled up over the back of the head and that there are two eagles, or the remains of same, as supports for the arms of the throne would confirm that this is a representation of Zeus derived from the Graeco-Roman statues of Sarapis in the Hellenistic tradition. This particular version, by its sculptural detail, certainly dates no earlier than the Severan period of the Roman Empire. A clue to dating the statue in the third century A.D., perhaps as late as the beginning of the last quarter of the century, seems to be provided by the eagle on the surviving armrest, the style of the drapery, and the cutting of the feet on a statue or very high relief of Zeus, evidently from an Asiatic sarcophagus, published as in the Museum at Konya (Iconium).[2] This handsome fragment, a superlative demonstration of classicism's survival and modification in the later Hellenistic to imperial worlds, might also confirm an atelier in western Asia Minor as ultimate origin for the "Westmacott Jupiter."

Related Statues

The Hadrianic or early Antonine enthroned Zeus from Salamis on Cyprus offers a good comparison in more traditional, Greek imperial terms (Fig. 5). While earlier in date by about a century, this Zeus from the major city of later Roman Cyprus is a sculpture of equal quality, with greater fluidity of body and confident simplicity of drapery, as befits excellent carving based ultimately on an older prototype. The upper torso is bare, not covered by a chiton, in the tradition of the Jupiter Capitolinus and, ultimately, of the Pheidian Zeus.[3] The small statue

1) A. Michaelis, *Ancient Marbles in Great Britain,* Cambridge 1882, p. 486; S. Reinach, *Répertoire de la statuaire grecque et romaine,* I (*Clarac de poche*) Paris 1906, p. 193, no. 1 (Clarac, III, 410A, 669B). Miss Mary Comstock, Professor Jiri Frel, Mr. and Mrs. Kyriakos Nicolaou, and Miss Marion True have helped me in preparing this article.
2) G. Ferrari, *Il Commercio dei sarcofagi asiatici,* Rome 1966, p. 115,

pl. 27, fig. 3.
3) V. Karageorghis, C. Vermeule, *Sculptures from Salamis,* I, Nicosia 1964, pp. 31f., no. 25, pl. XXIX; volume III, forthcoming, will document the rediscovery (mentioned and illustrated in the excavation reports of 1969) and rejoining of the eagle's head. J. Frel reminds me that the seated "Capitoline" Jupiter with the Macon treasure indicates

"

from the Gymnasium at Salamis also provides an excellent illustration of the relationship between this figure and the widely-diffused, early Hellenistic images of Sarapis, to be discussed presently, for a seated Sarapis of similar date, in bluish-gray Cypriote marble with Parian extremities, was also found in the Gymnasium and bath complex at Cypriote Salamis. The so-called "Infernal Jupiter" in the British Museum presents another comparable, in many respects more timely statue and also serves as an iconographic middle ground between the Capitoline Jupiter and the Hellenistic Sarapis. The "Infernal Jupiter" has the three-headed dog Cerberus and the traditional eagle either side of the footrest, but otherwise the statue agrees in all other respects with the "Westmacott Jupiter" as a probable representation of Zeus in his non-Egyptian aspects as Hades.[4] It seems possible but not likely that a small figure of Cerberus occupied the broken area of the plinth near the right foot of the Westmacott statue.

A full description of the Jupiter or Zeus in the British Museum and comments on this statue are based on A.H. Smith's catalogue of the classical sculpture in that collection. The "Chthonian or Infernal Zeus", both arms restored, was purchased by Charles Towneley in Rome in 1773 and appears frequently in later Neo-Classic literature.[5] "He is seated on a throne with a footstool. He has long flowing hair, bound with a taenia; *a chiton with short sleeves, a large mantle* (italics mine), and sandals. The figure is restored as holding a thunderbolt and sceptre. On the right of the throne is an eagle, and on the left Cerberus. The combination of these symbols indicates that in this statue the Olympian and Chthonian divinities are united in one type. Such mixed types were common in late Roman art. 2nd cent. A.D. (?)." This statue thus not only bespeaks a fusion of the traditional images of Zeus with those of Sarapis, as conceived at the outset of the Hellenistic age, but also follows the main details of the "Westmacott Jupiter" insofar as they can be divined from Clarac's plate or the work, in both instances, of the restorer.

The same processes of modification from several prototypes, seen in the London and Malibu statues, also characterized other cult-statues in the late Hellenistic and Roman imperial periods. These processes can be adduced in the development of small marble figures of Tyche-Fortuna, based on older images of the enthroned Hera or of Demeter and circulated in varying forms from east to west and vice versa in the Roman Empire. The relationship with major models of the fifth and fourth centuries B.C. soon became lost or at least blurred, and the attributes of these Roman imperial images could be interchanged, or the positions of the arms altered, to create new variations on old stereotypes.[6] Routine though this may seem to the modern eye accustomed to viewing Greek sculpture in the light of Pheidias (his Zeus at Olympia) or Polykleitos (the Hera at. Argos), this predictable elaboration of old stereotypes was a standard aesthetic practice in the creation of new devotional sculptures in the four hundred years from 75 B.C. to 325 of the Christian era. The Westmacott-Getty Zeus represents a creative phase in ancient sculpture which can only be explained against the background of a multi-national Graeco-Roman world in which traditions other than those of Athens of Sikyon in the Golden Age shaped the imagery of public temples and private chapels.

The Style of the Westmacott Jupiter

If the "Westmacott Jupiter" seems distorted or ill-formed in terms of traditional concepts of the Pheidian Zeus or its early Hellenistic successors, the marble now at Malibu has its chronological parallel and stylistic counterpart in a monumental bronze statuette in the Museum of Fine Arts, Boston (Fig. 6). This Zeus, once seated on a chair, a throne, or even a geographic symbol, held a scepter-staff in the raised right hand and extends a four-sided pyramid with a ball on each corner in the left.[7] This is a well-documented Greek imperial symbol for Mount Argaeus in Cappadocia, appearing on Antonine to Severan coins of Caesarea. It must, therefore, be concluded that this bronze came from Cappadocia and reproduces a famous late Hellenistic or imperial cult-image in a temple near Caesarea. Its curly head set slightly askew, the elongated upper body, the small lower limbs, and the flat, zig-zag folds of drapery are

---

the presence of such statuary in Roman cult groups, with a number of gods and goddesses: H. B. Walters, *Catalogue of the Silver Plate (Greek, Etruscan and Roman) in the British Museum,* London 1921, pp. 10f., no. 35, pl. VI.

4) S. Reinach, *op. cit.,* p. 184, no. 6.

5) A. H. Smith, *Catalogue of Sculpture in the Department of Greek and Roman Antiquities,* III, London, British Museum, 1904, p. 6, no. 1531. "Restorations: both arms with attributes, head of eagle, part of plinth, and of throne." For varying types of Hades and Zeus, see S. Reinach, *op. cit.,* IV, Paris 1913, pp. 10-11. Compare, also, the bronze in the British Museum, with Zeus-Hades-Sarapis seated, radiate crown and modius on the head, an eagle at the left side, once balanced by a

Cerberus. All this made the perfect, supreme, all-purpose divinity: A. B. Cook, *Zeus, A Study in Ancient Religion,* I, Cambridge 1914, pp. 188-189, fig. 137. Cf. also a Hellenistic terracotta relief in Munich, reproducing a statue of Hades-Sarapis: R. Lullies, *Eine Sammlung griechischer Kleinkunst* (Munich, 1955), no. 208.

6) See the references under L. Budde, R. Nicholls, *A Catalogue of the Greek and Roman Sculpture in the Fitzwilliam Museum Cambridge,* Cambridge 1964, pp. 64-65, no. 101, pl. 34. The Sarapis and Cerberus from Salamis is also in Cambridge: Budde, Nicholls, *op. cit.,* pp. 31-32, no. 56, pl. 18.

7) Museum of Fine Arts, Accession no. 1972.920; from a private collection in Germany. H.: 0.205m.

characteristics, in their own way, of the enthroned Zeus "Sarapis" in the Getty Museum. It seems reasonable to conclude from these shared stylistic features that this is how the Father of the Gods in cult form came to be represented in the first half of the third century A.D., in a period when, to modern critics examining them in retrospect, many of the principles of Late Antique sculpture become recognizable.

Cult-Images of Zeus or Sarapis

The Father of the Gods is inevitably portrayed half-draped or in the heroic nude. Representation with a chiton covering the chest does relate to the image of Sarapis-Hades-Osiris created for the temple in Alexandria by Bryaxis the Younger around 300 B.C., but other manifestations of the major Greek divinity were fully clothed in variations on the chiton or tunic and himation or cloak. There is ample evidence that the Hellenistic and Graeco-Roman worlds saw the creation of cult images in which Zeus was fully clad as befitting the ancient Near Eastern divinities and despots with which he came to be identified or which sought assimilation in his image. Unusual forms of Zeus were expected in the classical world in Syria or Mesopotamia, in Egypt or the desert to the west where Ammon reigned, but western Asia Minor, Greece, Italy, Gaul, and Spain demanded, or could tolerate, only minor variations in the traditional iconography of Zeus-Jupiter. It was out of this atmosphere that Zeus came to be clad in garments resembling those of Sarapis in later classical times.

The Westmacott Jupiter and
Zeus- Hadad- Jupiter- Ba'al-shamin

There can be little coincidence in the fact that the high relief, half-figure "bust" of Zeus-Hadad from Khirbet Tannur, southeast of Jerusalem and north of Petra in Arabia, is a virtual replica of the Westmacott-Getty figure.[8] There is, to be sure, little to connect the Julio-Claudian through Antonine sculptures of Arabia with the Severan to mid-third century period of the Roman Empire, save one important historical consideration. The Emperor Philippus I, known as the Arab (A.D. 244 to 249), *came* from this part of the Hellenistic and Roman worlds. It is therefore very plausible that the decade before the middle of the century might have been the time when the Westmacott Jupiter was carved and set up, presumably in Italy, perhaps as a reminder that the Zeus of Syria or Arabia had his place in the most conservative fashion, in the homeland of Jupiter Capitolinus. Such a statue would have had great appeal in a com-

8) N. Glueck, *Deities and Dolphins, The Story of the Nabataeans,* New York 1965, pp. 330, 470, pl. 154.

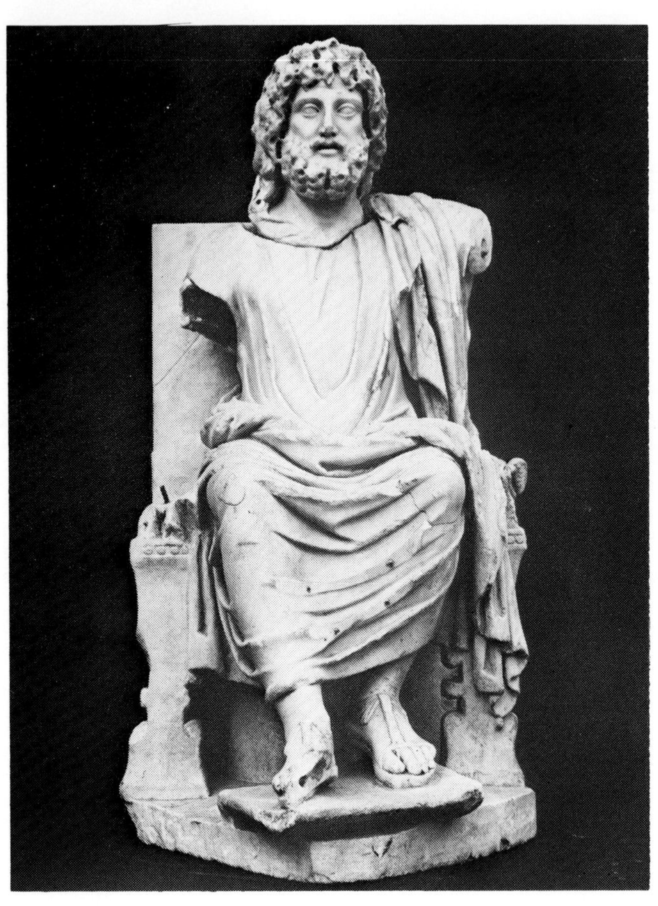 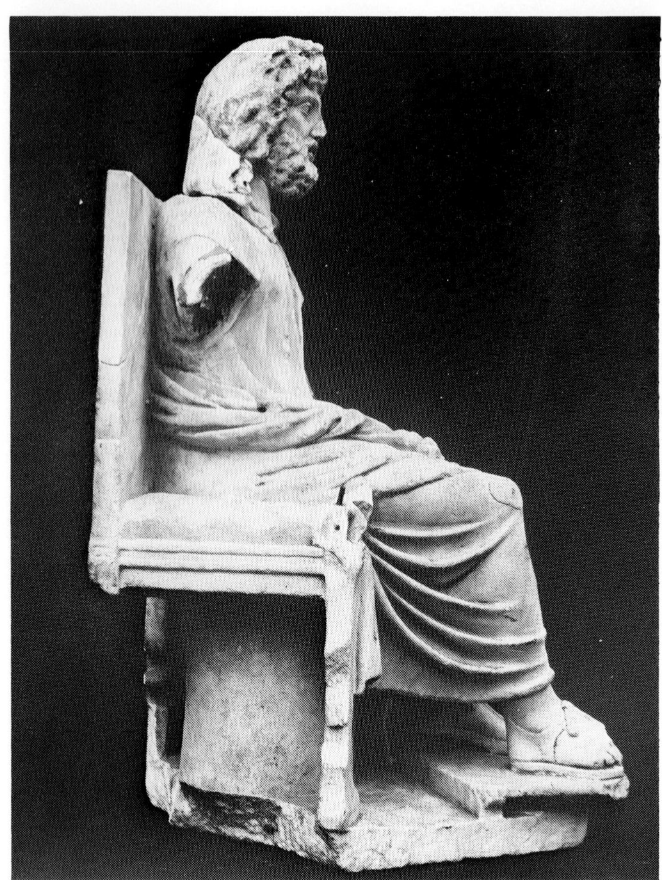

1a,b   The Westamacott Jupiter. J. Paul Getty Museum
70.AA.124. With restorations

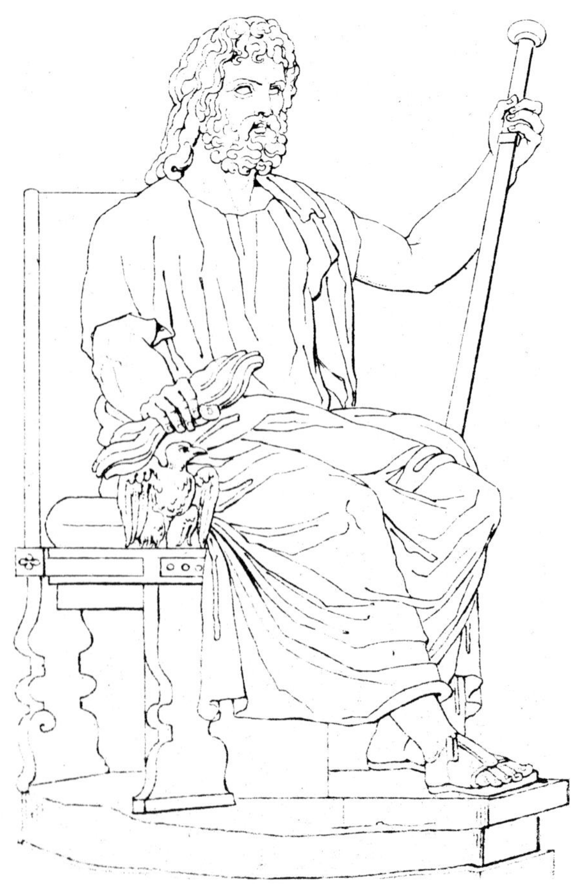

3   The statue as published by the Comte de Clarac

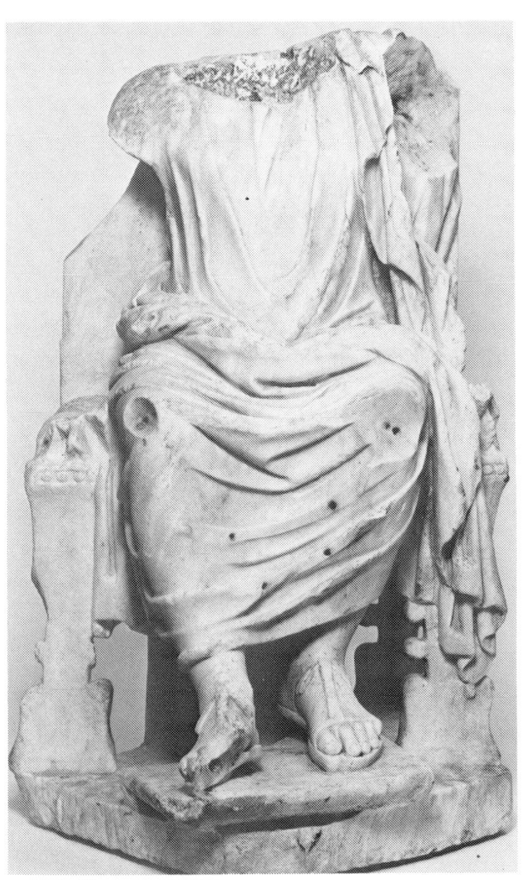

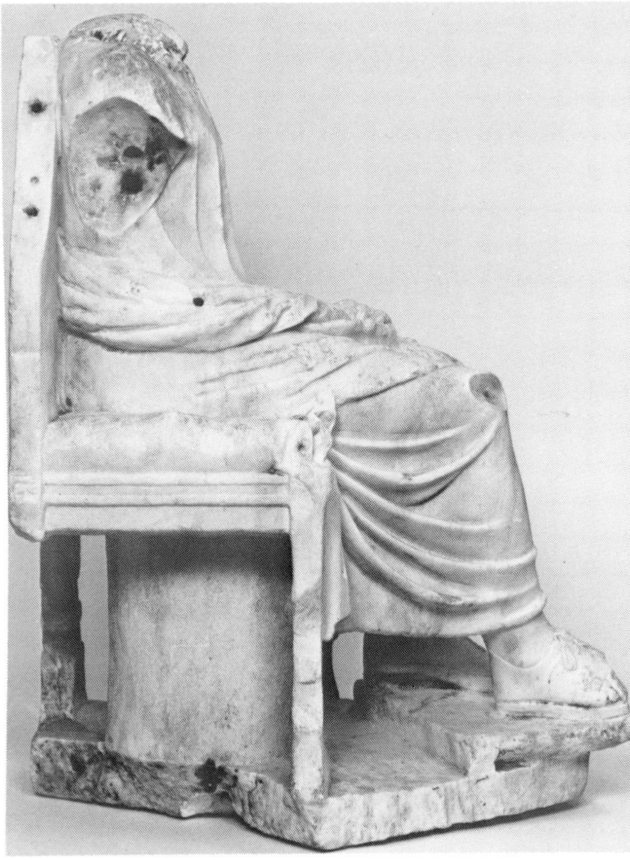

2a,b,c,d   The Westamacott Jupiter, without restorations. J. Paul Getty Museum, 70.AA.124

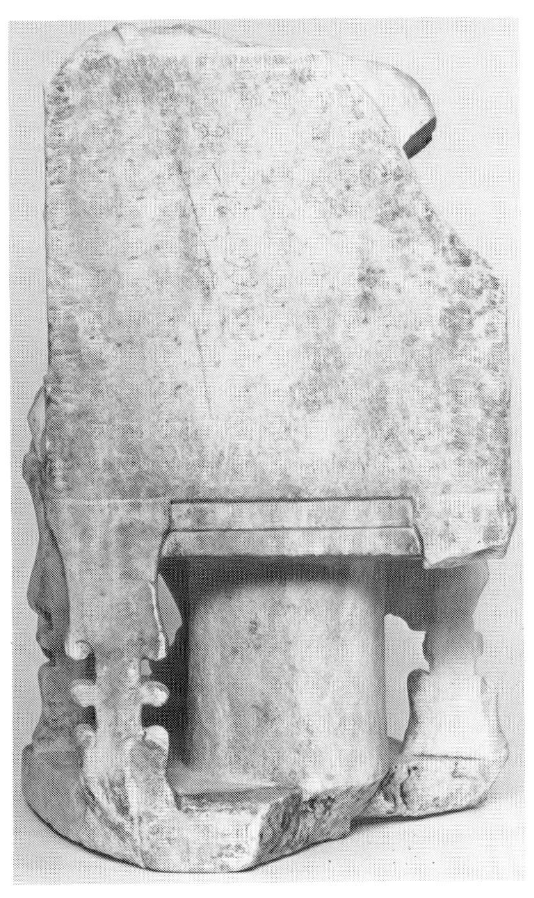

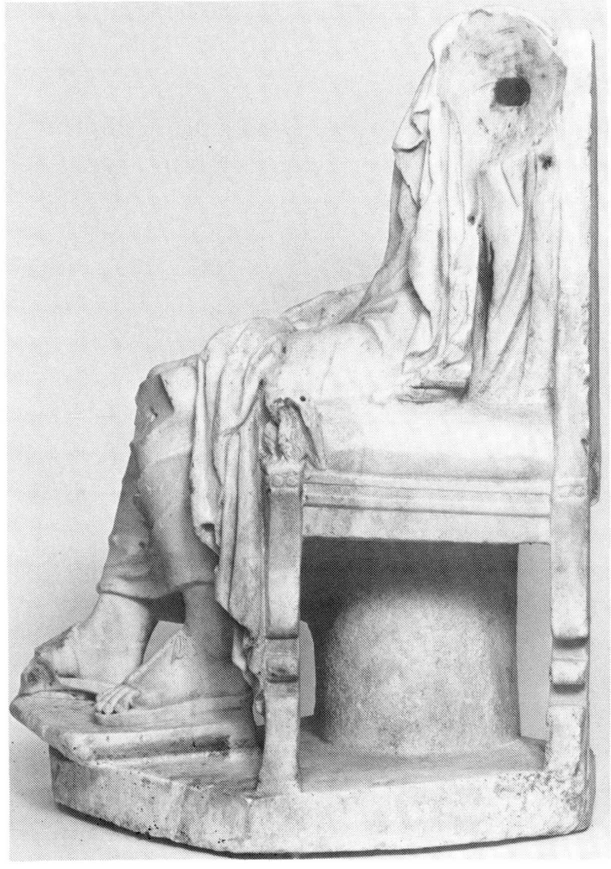

munity of Syrians or Arabians settled in Rome, in the Alban Hills, or a port such as Ostia. Since a number of Roman Emperors in the thirty years from A.D. 255 to 285 had intimate connections with the East, there is every additional reason beyond sculptural parallels in Asia Minor (the Zeus at Konya), to date the Westmacott Jupiter in these decades. Other monuments, statuary, reliefs, mosaics, and minor arts, testify to the prosperity of the Oriental communities in Italy during these years.

Zeus and the Roman Emperors

A further reason for presentation of an imperial Zeus in conservative garb may lie in the relationship of this figure with later representations of the Roman emperor as an enthroned magistrate. As the Emperors became more clad in ceremonial and more connected with the obscure parts of the Empire and their customs or costume, a trend toward conservative, Eastern divinities became noticeable, a reaction to the nudity and doubtless the mental liberties of Greece's Golden Age. This form of Zeus carries over into the iconography of Christ in apse mosaics of the churches in Rome of the fourth through the seventh centuries A.D., both in presentations of the enthroned God the Father and similar representations of God the Son.[9] That the Hellenistic world of about 200 B.C. was prepared for the visual juxtaposition of a half-draped Zeus and a fully-clad, enthroned figure is apparent in the famous "Apotheosis of Homer" relief signed by Archelaos, son of Apollonios of Priene, where Zeus reclines comfortably with his eagle above while Homer sits enthroned and erect, looking exactly like a Hades or Sarapis, in the lowest register below. The transition from the humanistic Zeus to the Jovian Homer, and vice versa, is an easy one to make in statuary, in Graeco-Roman cult images, given the statuesque quality of such figures in reliefs of this nature.[10]

Another reason for a shift from the half-draped to the fully-clad Zeus in the Roman imperial period stems from the fact that a clothed Zeus was popular in Archaistic decorative art, in various reliefs created in general imitation of Archaic statues and carvings in relief. Three-sided candelabra, set up in shrines and villas throughout Italy, were particularly cherished vehicles of this art, as the example in Copenhagen reputed to have been found in Campania.[11] This form of visual revival of the past

<hr>

9) See A. B. Cook, *op. cit.,* I, pp. 49-51, figs. 23 and 24.

10) Cook, *Zeus,* I, pp. 129-132, pl. XIII, fig. 98.

11) F. Poulsen, *Catalogue of Ancient Sculpture in the Ny Carlsberg Glyptotek,* Copenhagen 1951, p. 210, no. 282, Billedtavler pl. XX: here the standing Zeus holds a scepter and an eagle. This type of Zeus, updated, was very popular in Phrygia and Lycia in Greek imperial times. A terracotta votive lamp of about A.D. 50 shows this Zeus enthroned in a temple, his eagle at his feet; Athena and Hera are visible

doubtless also conditioned the Latin West to the intro-
duction of a Zeus in the full garb of the ancient East.
A small bronze statuette in the Walters Art Gallery,
Baltimore, presents a modern, Graeco-Roman version of
just such a Zeus, standing, carrying a patera in the right
hand and an eagle on the left wrist. Although the costume is the classical chiton and himation, it is unusual
enough in this context to give the figure as a whole,
clearly Zeus or Jupiter from the attribute, an appearance
to be equated with the noble past and the philosophic
East rather than with the immortal humanism of the
major divinities. Dorothy Hill noted, rightly, in cata-
loguing this statuette, "The complete drapery is unusual
and may be due to provincial origin. The date is
Roman."[12]

Conclusion

The Westmacott Jupiter is not merely a curiosity of the
later Roman imperial age. This statue represents an
importation into the Latin West, as a cult-image, of a
Zeus which flourished and had developed in Asia Minor,
Syria, Arabia, and Egypt, in the last area in relation to
the traditional Sarapis of Bryaxis. The aim was to present
an alternative to the Jupiter Capitolinus, a conservative
variation which would have been palatable to the large
communities from the Hellenistic East settled in the
commercial centers of the Latin West. The fact that
Emperors such as Elagabalus (A.D. 218 to 222) and
Philip the Arab came from these regions certainly stimulated an official interest in images such as this.

Ptolemaic Egypt gave to Cyprus a curious, folk-art
image of Zeus (Ammon), enthroned and fully draped, in
which can be seen echoes of a major statue of the fifth
century B.C. (Fig. 7).[13] The dumpy little god has ram's
horns and holds a cornucopia in one hand, a phiale in
the other. He wears his himation as a cloak around his
shoulders and over the long chiton at his knees. Two
rams flank the high-backed throne, serving almost as if
they had been elaborately carved armrests on the archi-
typal cult-image. It is a long road from this little Cypriote

within the columns either side; *Gods and Men in the Allard Pierson
Museum,* Amsterdam, 1971, p. 13 (reference kindness of Prof. J. Frel).
12) D. K. Hill, *Catalogue of Classical Bronze Sculpture in the Walters
Art Gallery,* Baltimore 1949, p. 10, no. 16, pl. 6. The classicizing, late
Republican or early imperial, section of the base or comparable architectural panel in the J. Paul Getty Museum, from Rome, features a
cult-image of the general type discussed in these pages (a Dionysos like
that of Alkamenes in Athens?) being carried in procession in a cart:
see *The J. Paul Getty Collection,* The Minneapolis Institute of Arts,
June 29-September 3, 1972, no. 4.
13) Compare V. Karageorghis, *Bulletin de correspondance hellénique*
87, 1963, pp. 338-339, no. 5, fig. 20 and references. These statuettes
are found in clay (terracotta) as well as limestone. They are occasionally
equated with the Syrian god Baal Hamman.

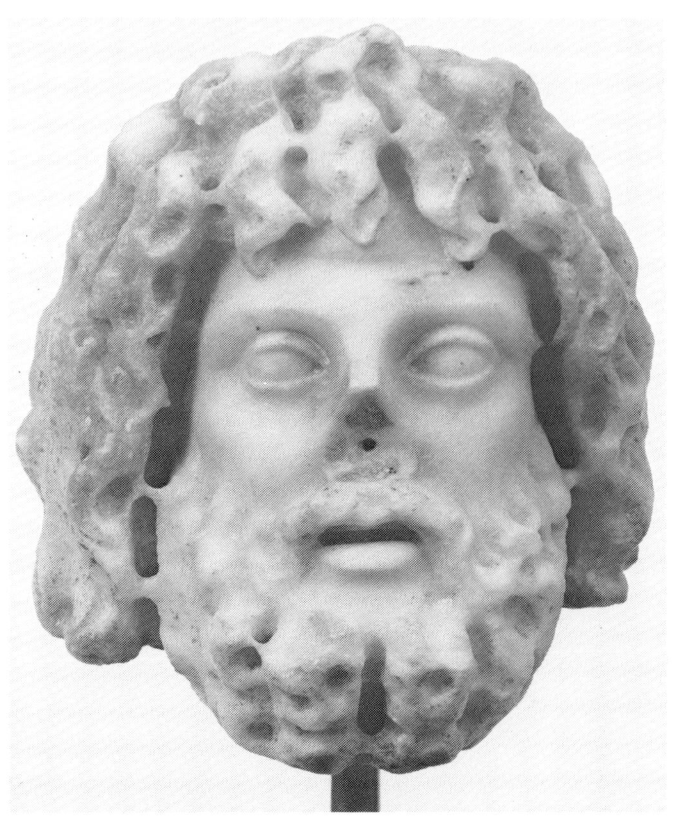
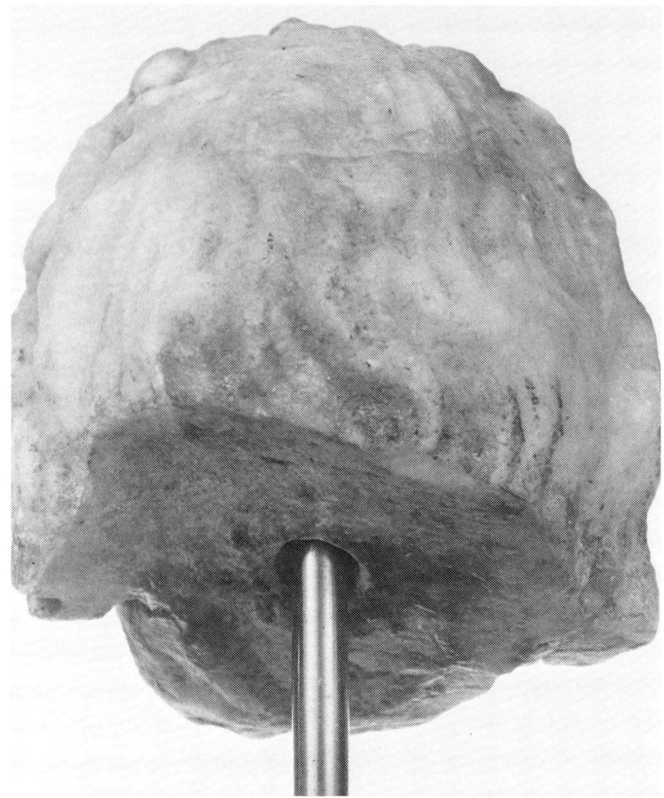

4a,b,c,d   Head formerly on the Westmacott Jupiter

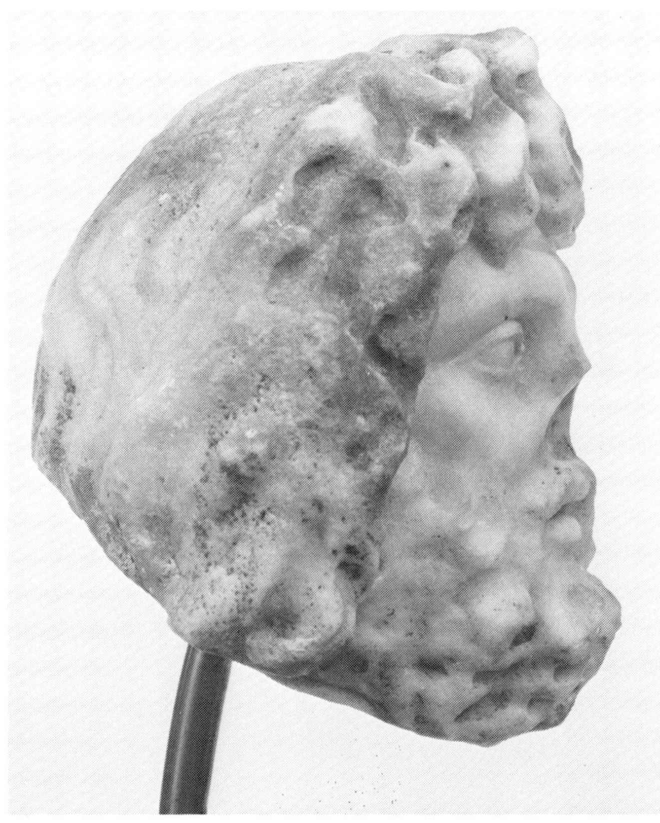
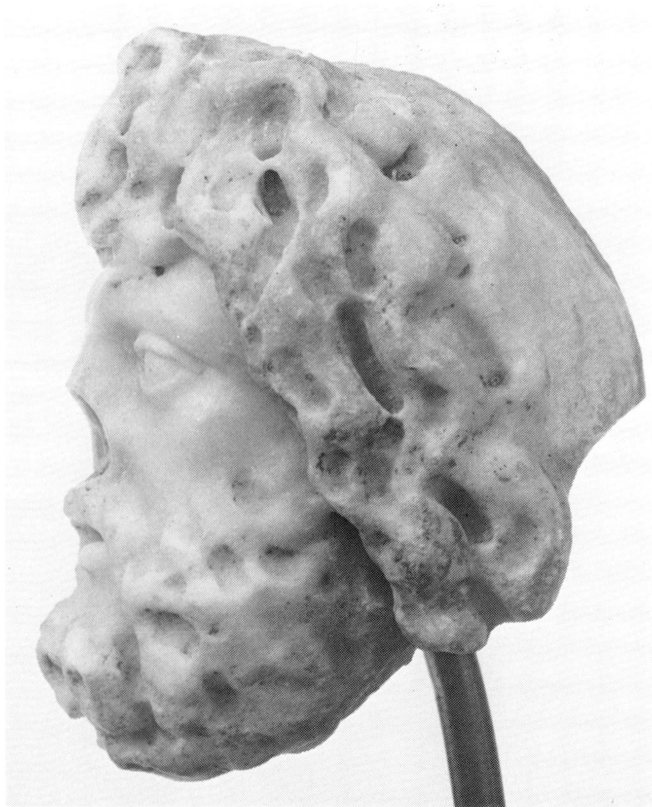

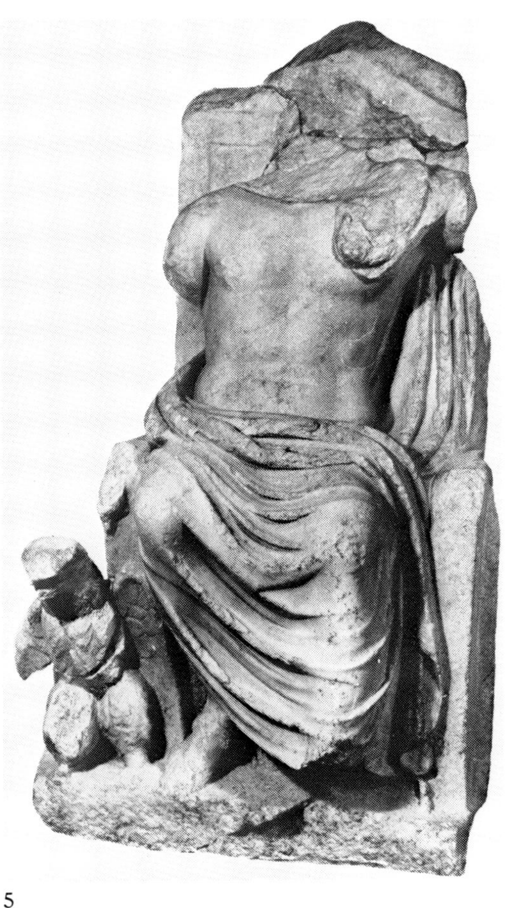

5

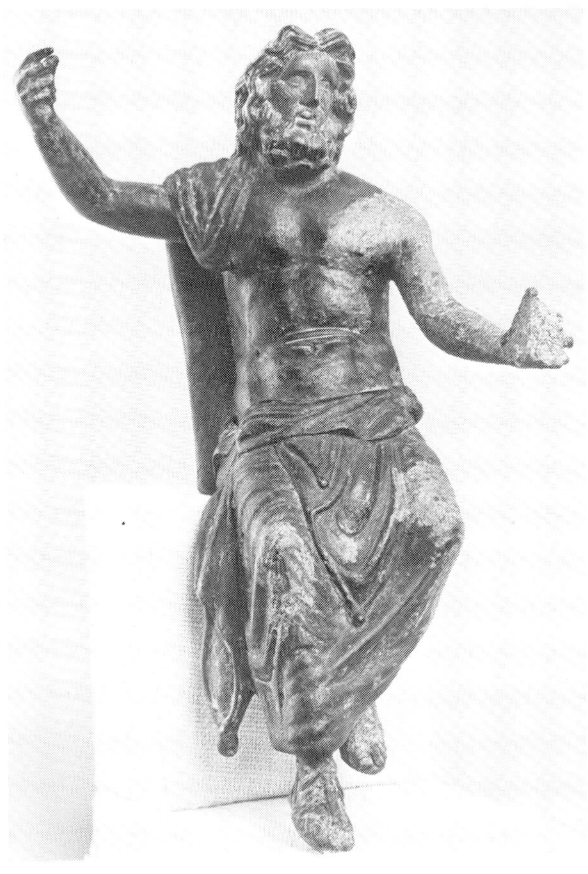

6

5   Zeus from Salamis on Cyprus. Nicosia, Cyprus Museum. Photo courtesy of the Department of Antiquities, Republic of Cyprus

6   Bronze Zeus after a statue in Cappadocia. Boston, Museum of Fine Arts, Edwin E. Jack Fund

7   Limestone Zeus Ammon, enthroned between two rams. Nicosia, Cyprus Museum. Photo courtesy of Dr. Vassos Karageorghis

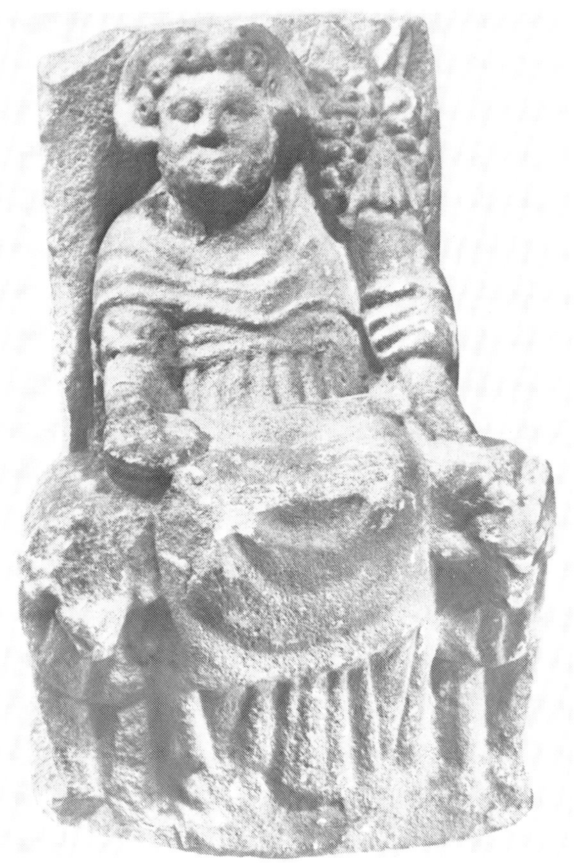

7

Zeus Ammon to the immediate world of the Westmacott Jupiter, but common notions of an eastern Hellenistic or Greek imperial Zeus produced parallels of costume and iconography (rams and eagles) for both statues. Set alongside the little Cypriote Zeus Ammon, the Westmacott Jupiter emerges as the largest, one of the grandest, of a series of East Greek cult-images, most of which were circulated in or near the lands of their origin. The Westmacott Jupiter, therefore, is doubly important, not only for its own iconography but also because it brought the draped, enthroned Zeus into the old heart of the Roman Empire in the West.

Cornelius Vermeule
Boston Museum of Fine Arts

Addendum

In the summer of 1974 the Westmacott Zeus was submitted to conservation treatment in the Conservation Department of the J. Paul Getty Museum. The restorations, most of them mentioned in C.C. Vermeule's paper, were removed, as well as the numerous iron pins. As a result, it was concluded that the head does not belong to the body. There is, of course, no material join, but the marble is different and the proportions are not consistent with the body. However the head may have belonged to a comparable piece, or to a similar small statue of a seated Sarapis, as suggested by the three locks of hair hanging over the forehead. The scholarly contribution made by C.C. Vermeule's article is not affected by these material facts.

David Rinne
Jiří Frel

The contents of this article will not be new to Professor Ashmole. He kindly read and criticised an earlier draft, and it is hoped that he will find this version to his liking. The paper has its origins in a lecture I once gave on Mantegna's classical prototypes to Dr. Françoise Henry's History of European Painting Seminar in University College, Dublin. It appeared to me then, as it does now, that Andrea Mantegna saw fragments of the *Ara Pacis Augustae* during his stay in Rome between 1488 and 1490, or at least knew drawings or engravings of them, for certain details of the *Triumph of Caesar* recall the *Ara Pacis* too closely for the resemblance to be coincidental. There is, however, one major obstacle to be removed before any comparison can be made between the two works, namely, the widely held belief that substantial remains of the *Ara Pacis* first came to light only in 1568. Three quotations will suffice to show what are generally held to have been the circumstances of its re-appearance in modern times:

'Le prime notizie scritte se riferiscono alla estrazione di vari pezzi, che si scopersero nei cavi fatti per i lavori del 1568 dai Peretti, nipoti de Sisto V, allora proprietari del palazzo in Campo Marzio.'[1]

'In 1568, when the foundations were laid for the Palazzo Peretti (now Fiano) in the Via in Lucina, some marble slabs with reliefs on both sides were discovered.'[2]

'Als man gegen 1568 del Palazzo Peretti erbaute, würden neun Blöcke der Umfassungswand entdeckt und für die Familie Medici erworben.'[3]

The documents referred to in the first quotation (from Moretti) are four letters from Cardinal Ricci de Montepulciano (who regularly collected works of art for the Medici collections) written between 11th February and 16th June 1569 to the Grand Duke of Tuscany, describing how 'XV o XVIII pezzi di marmi' bearing 'figure di trionfi' on one side and 'festoni' on the other, had been found 'sotterrati' at Rome.[4] Nothing, in fact, was said about the findspot, merely that people said that they were from a triumphal arch built by Domitian.[5] Since

the nearby *Arco di Portogallo,* which spanned the Corso until 1662, was popularly thought in the fifteenth century to have been an arch of Domitian,[6] it seems likely that the reliefs had been found on the site of the *Ara Pacis.*

But wherever the reliefs were found, it was not the construction of the Palazzo Peretti which brought about their discovery. The existing *palazzo* only passed into the hands of the Peretti family in 1585 when Cardinal Alessandro Peretti became the titular of the neighbouring church of S. Lorenzo in Lucina.[7] The owner of the site in 1568 was Cardinal Fulvio Corneo to whom it had been granted by Pius V in February 1566.[8]

The story of the site begins, so far as we are concerned, in 1084 when soldiers of Robert Guiscard are reported to have almost reduced to nothing the quarter where S. Lorenzo in Lucina is situated.[9] The original Palazzo di S. Lorenzo in Lucina was begun at some time between 1281 and 1287, by Cardinal Hugh of Evesham and was remodelled by a succession of title cardinals from 1427 onwards. An inscription, now lost, but recorded by Martinelli, recorded how Cardinal Jean de Rochetaille (created cardinal 1426, died 1437) found the church and its neighbouring *palazzo* in a dilapidated condition and restored them, rebuilding the *palazzo* from the foundations. The relevant part of the inscription reads as follows:

. . . preamble]   AD VRBEM

```
15  ROMVLEAM VENIT RVPE DE SCISSA IOANNES
    CARDINE APOSTOLICO DOMINO DECORATVS AB IPSO
    HVIVS ET ECCLESIAE TITVLO REMANENTE PRIORI
    ROTHOMAGI ECCLESIAE MERITO COGNOMINE PATRI.
    ISTE DOMVM QVASI COLLAPSAM ET PROSTRATA
       RVINAE
20  FVNDAMENTA VIDENS NAM VT PRISCA RECENSVIT
       AETAS
    VNVS CARDINEO ANTISTES PRACLARVS HONORE
    ANGLICVS HAEC OLIM FVNDASSE PALATIA FERTVR
    VLTRO OPVS AGGREDITVR TEMPLVMQ. DOMVMQ.
       CADENTEM
    CVNCTA NOVANS REPARAT PARTIMQ. PALATIA TEMPLI
25  FVNDITVS INSTAVRAT SVBLATAQ. IVRA REDEMIT
    CVI DECVS ET MERITAE MANENT PER SECVLA
       LAVDES.10
```

A draft of this paper was kindly read by Professor Ashmole, Professor C.M. Robertson and Professor J.M.C. Toynbee. It has benefited from their comments, but any remaining mistakes are my own. My thanks are also due to my colleague Mr. Christopher Lloyd for his advice on Mantegna.

1) G. Moretti, *Ara Pacis Augustae* (Rome, 1948) 13.

2) E. Nash, *Pictorial Dictionary of Ancient Rome* (London, 1961) 63.

3) E. Simon, *Ara Pacis Augustae* (Tübingen, 1967) 7.

4) The relevant extracts are quoted by E. Petersen, "L'Ara Pacis Augustae," *Römische Mitteilungen* IX (1894) 224-225.

5) "Dicono d'un Arco Trionfale, che fece Domitiano," Petersen, *loc. cit.*

6) R. Krautheimer, *Corpus basilicorum christianorum Romae* II (Vatican City, 1959) 165. See too Albertini, quoted in n. 11 below.

7) A. Reumont, "Il Palazzo Fiano di Roma," *Archivo della Società romana di storia patria* VII (1884) 549-554; R. Lanciani, "Miscellanea topografica," *Bullettino Communale* (1891) 18-19; T. Magnuson, *Studies in Roman Quattrocento Architecture* (Stockholm, 1958) 227; Krautheimer, *op. cit.* 163. G. Berton and J. P. Migne, *Dictionnaire des cardinaux* (Paris, 1857) 1360, are incorrect in saying that Peretti was appointed to the title of S. Lorenzo in Damaso.

8) The deed is quoted in full by Lanciani, *Storia degli scavi di Roma* IV, (Rome, 1912) 27.

9) "Immo ipse cum suis totam regionem illam in qua aecclesiae sancti Silvestri et Sancti Laurentii in Lucina site sunt penitus destruxit et fere ad nichilum redegit." L. Duchesne, *Le Liber Pontificalis* II (Paris, 1886) 290. Cf. Krautheimer, *op. cit.* 161.

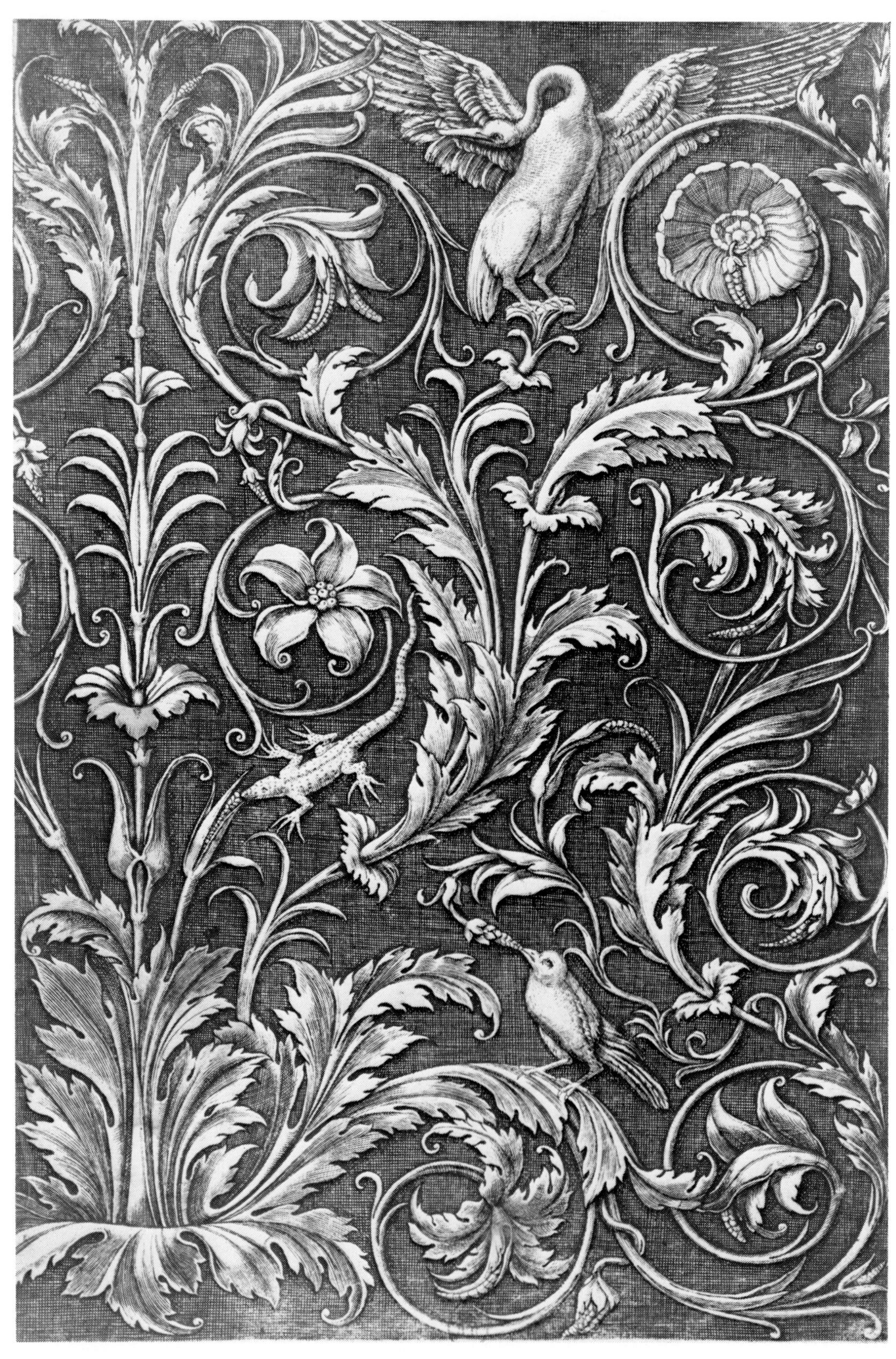

1   Engraving of *Ara Pacis* dado slab,
attributed to Agostino Veneziano.
Photo Bibl. Nat. Paris

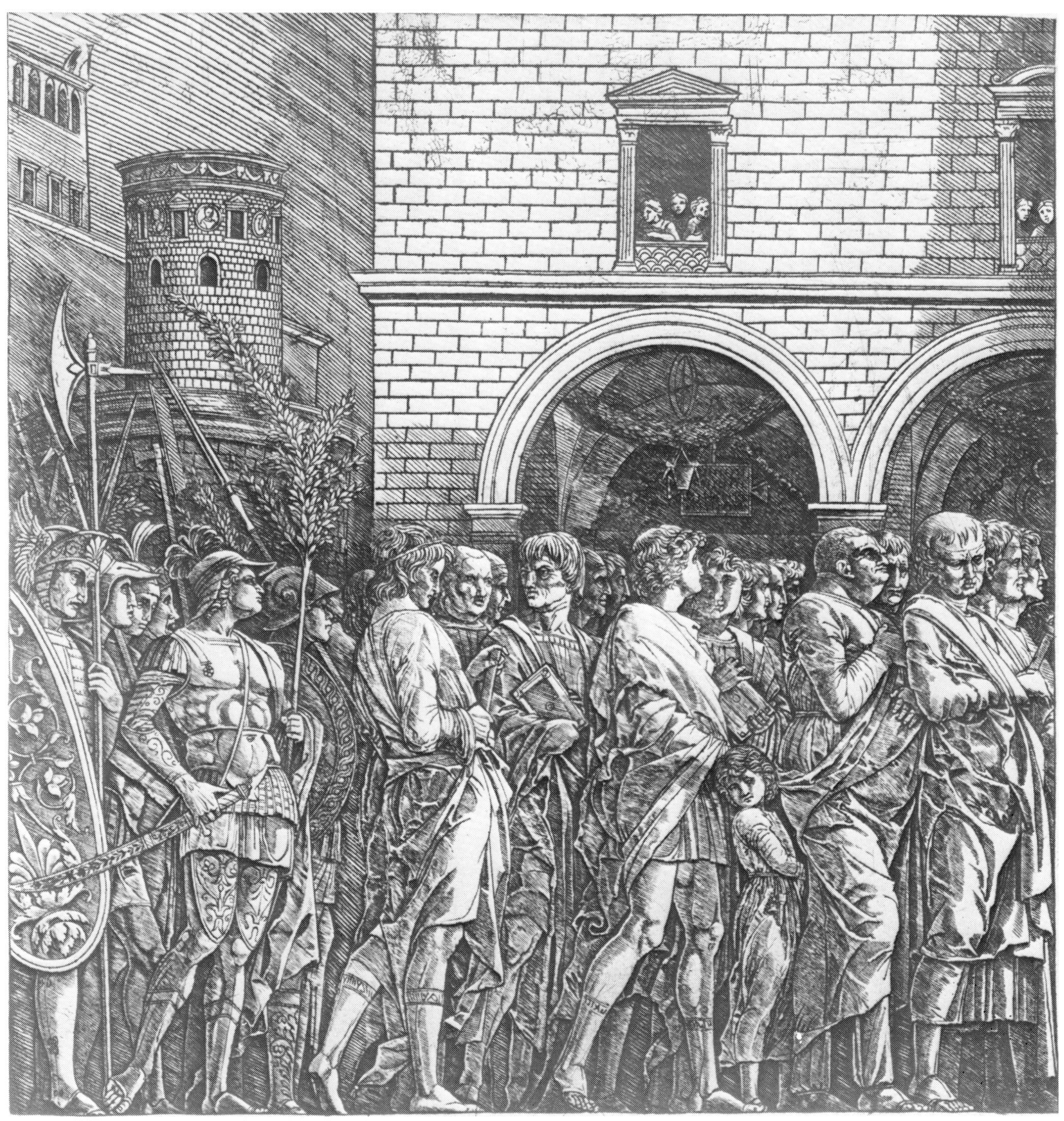

2 Mantegna, *Triumph of Caesar:*
'Senators,' engraving British Museum

Work continued from 1439 under Cardinal Jean le Jeune de Contay, bishop of St. Jean de Maurienne (Cardinal Morinense), reckoned to be the richest ecclesiastic of his day. The *palazzo* was still unfinished at his death in 1457, but had already won the admiration of Flavio Biondo.[11] Cardinal Filippo Calandrini, who succeeded to the title, carried on the work, but even when he died in 1476 the *palazzo* was still incomplete. Cardinals Giovanni Battista Ciba (1476-1484), afterwards Innocent VIII, and Jorge Costa of Lisbon (1503-1508), added their contributions, and the building was completed in about 1510 by Cardinal Fazio Santorio.[12]

In view of so many centuries of activity on the site of the *Ara Pacis* it would have been remarkable if some of its sculptured decoration had *not* come to light before 1568, and there is in fact quite definite evidence for at least one slab having been known before then. There are two engravings in the Département des Dessins in the Louvre which depict one of the dado slabs of the *Ara Pacis* decorated with acanthus scrolls surmounted by a swan displayed. One version is unsigned, but the other bears the initials AV and has been attributed to Agostino Veneziano (Fig. 1). Although the precise dates of the birth and death of Agostino are unknown, it can be established that he was born around 1490 and that his last dated engraving is 1536. His engraving of the *Ara Pacis* fragment was most probably made before this date, or at least not very long afterwards. As E. Michon has already observed, it points to fragments of the *Ara Pacis*

10) Martinelli, *Roma ex ethnica sacra* (Rome, 1638) 138; reproduced in V. Forcella, *Inscrizioni delle chiese e d'altri edificii di Roma* V, (Rome, 1874) 120, no. 345. Cf. Krautheimer, *op. cit.* 162.

11) Flavius Blondus, *Roma instaurata* [c. 1447] (Verona, 1481) Book II, xiv-xv: "*Arcus domitiani triumphalis.* Nec dubitamus quin triumphalis ex marmore arcus ille qui nunc pene integer cernitur triphali dictus: ecclesias inter sanctorum Sylvestri et laurentii in lucina viam amplexus flamminiam Domitiani fuerit honori positus: in quo ipsum cernere est qualis a Suetonio describitur Statura procerum sed tuuc [sic] sedentem dormientemque et minervam quam supersticiose colebat somniantem exedere sacrario: negantemque se ultra eum tueri posse exarmata esset a Jove ut consequens etiam sit magnos fornices et amplissima fundamenta super quibus aedificatum est nobile pallatium quod Joannes ex Galliis Picardus cardinalis morinensis nunc habitat. Domitiani operum partem esse id pallatium ad annum salutis trecentesimum supra millesimum a cardinale anglico in praedictis Domitiani operum ruinis aedificatum Johannes cardinalis Rothomagensis anno nunc vigesimo supradictus tanto ampliavit ornavitque impendio ut nullam praeter pontificale palatium sancti petri domum urbs roma nunc habeat pulchriorem".

12) F. Albertini, *Opusculum de mirabilibus novae et veteris urbis Romae* (Rome, 1510) liber iii, de domus Cardinalium: "Domus sancti Laurentii in lucina apud arcum domitiani a pluribus card. ampliata. s.a. Ioanne morine[n]si, et a Philippo Calandrino summo penitentiario: postremo vero a Io. bap. Cibo et a Giorgio ulisbone[n]si patria portugall: cardinalibus, cui quide[m] Fatius car. sanctae sabinae nonnulla pro co[m]modidate addidit pro ut eius insignia indicant."

having been found well before 1568.[13]

And now we come to Mantegna. The movement on the extant scenes of the *Triumph of Caesar* in the Royal Collection in Hampton Court is all from right to left, but there is an engraving which is generally supposed to have been based on the original designs—the 'Senators' in the British Museum (Fig. 2)[14]—in which the movement is from left to right. It is, of course, possible that the change in direction is attributable to the fact that we are dealing with an engraving, a medium in which a mirror-image of an original is easy enough to achieve. But if we take the 'Senators' at face value, they recall the Senators on the North frieze of the *Ara Pacis* (Fig. 3),[15] who are not only moving from left to right as well, but also bear a remarkable similarity in detail to Mantegna's 'Senators'. It would be going too far to suggest that correspondences can be demonstrated man for man, but given the way in which Mantegna departs from known classical proto-types,[16] the resemblance is very close indeed. Mantegna's serried ranks are deeper, it is true, but the togate senator on the far right, for example, with his arm resting in the *balteus* of his toga and the senator in the centre holding a box and looking back over his shoulder have their immediately recognisable counterparts on the *Ara Pacis*. Children also occur on the North frieze (Fig. 4),[17] standing close to their parents, though they do not turn towards the spectator—only those of the South frieze do. But before we look at the South frieze, there is a general point to be made concerning both friezes that is relevant to the argument. Both friezes are remarkable for the lack of what has been called 'atmospheric space' above the figures' heads. They are carved in the manner of reliefs of the fifth century B.C. and thus differ from most Roman reliefs of the Julio-Claudian and Flavian periods, and especially to reliefs of the Arch of Titus, which supplied the formal model for the *Triumph of Caesar*. Although there is a large building behind and above Mantegna's senators, there is nevertheless a feeling that

13) E. Michon, "Les bas-reliefs historiques romains du Museé du Louvre," *Monuments Piot* XVII (1909) 180-4, fig. 5. Cf. E. Simon, *op. cit.*, 7. The pieces of the Ara Pacis mentioned by Lanciani as having been seen by Aldrovandi before 1550 in fact belonged to another monument: *Storia degli scavi di Roma, loc. cit.,* and *The Ruins and Excavations of Ancient Rome* (London, 1897) 468.

14) Tietz-Conrat, *op. cit.,* fig. 55.

15) Moretti, *op. cit.,* pl. 11, centre; J.M.C. Toynbee, "The Ara Pacis reconsidered and historical art in Roman Italy," *Proceedings of the British Academy* XXXIX (1953) pl. 20; Simon, *op. cit.* pl. 16, bottom.

16) I. Blum, *Andrea Mantegna und die Antike* (Strasbourg, 1936) *passim,* but cf. A. Braham's comments in "A reappraisal of 'The Intro-duction of the Cult of Cybele at Rome' by Mantegna," *Burlington Magazine* cxv (1973) 462, n. 20.

17) Moretti, *op. cit.,* pl. 11, left; Toynbee, *op. cit.* pl. 22; Simon, *op. cit.* pl. 16, top.

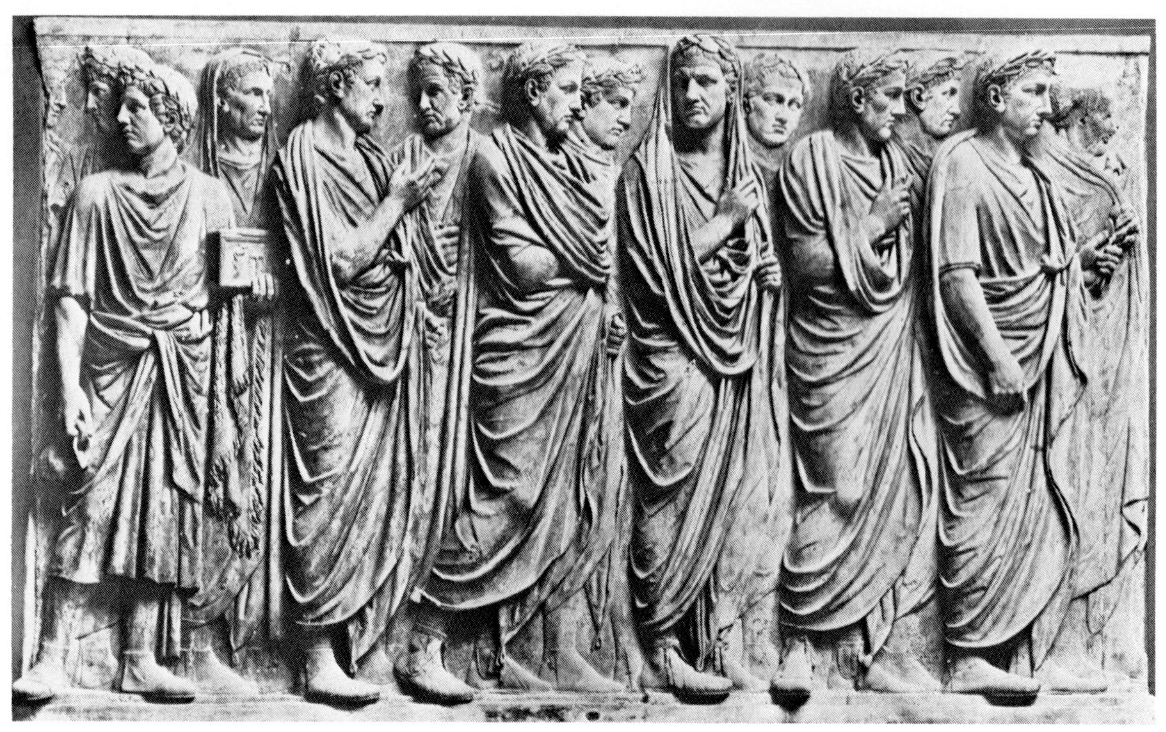

3-4   North frieze of *Ara Pacis*

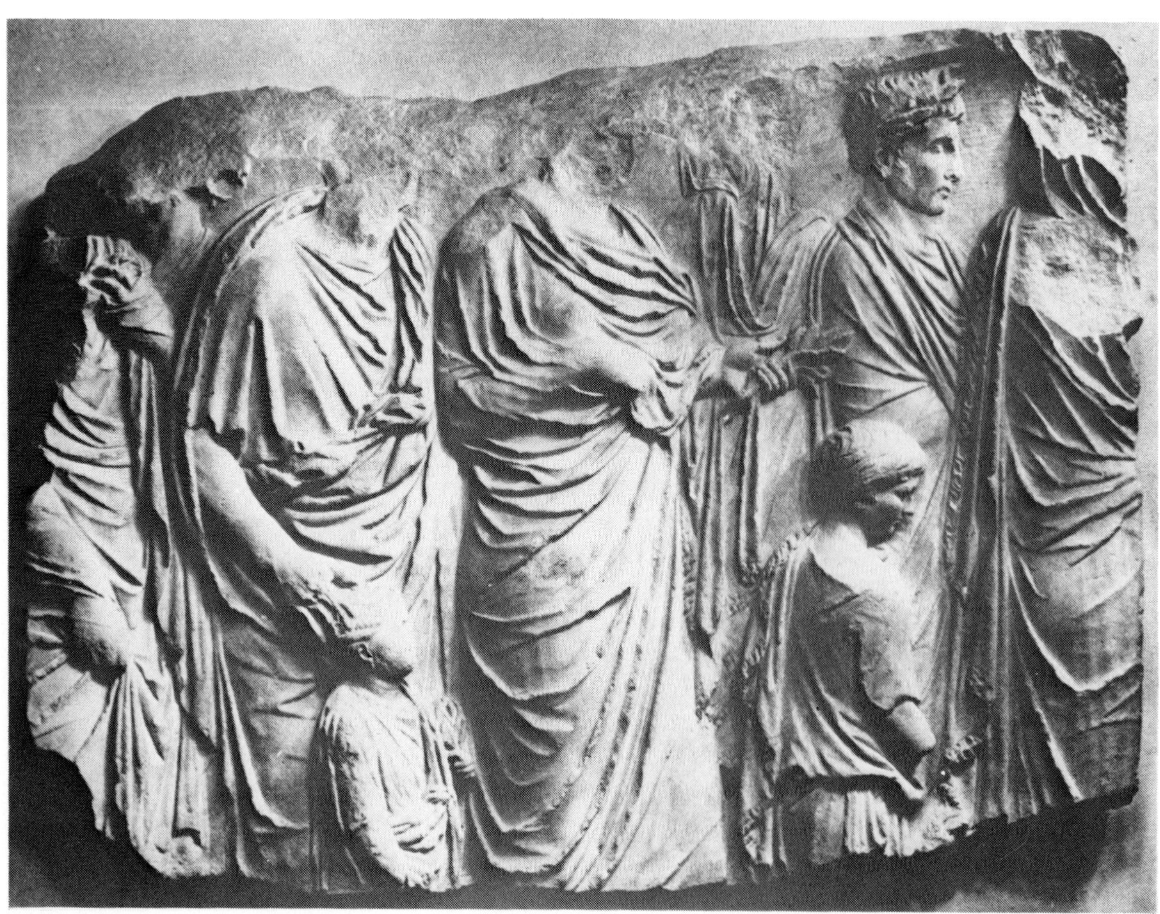

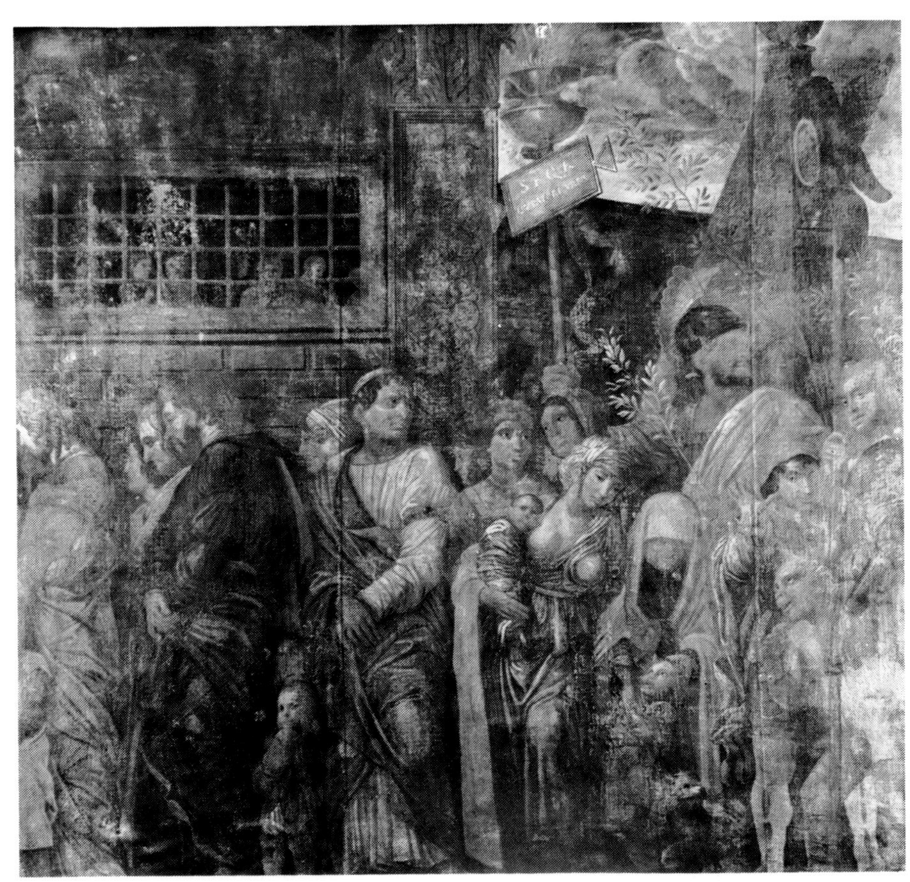

5   Mantegna's Triumph of Caesar:
     'Captives,' painting, Hampton
     Court Palace

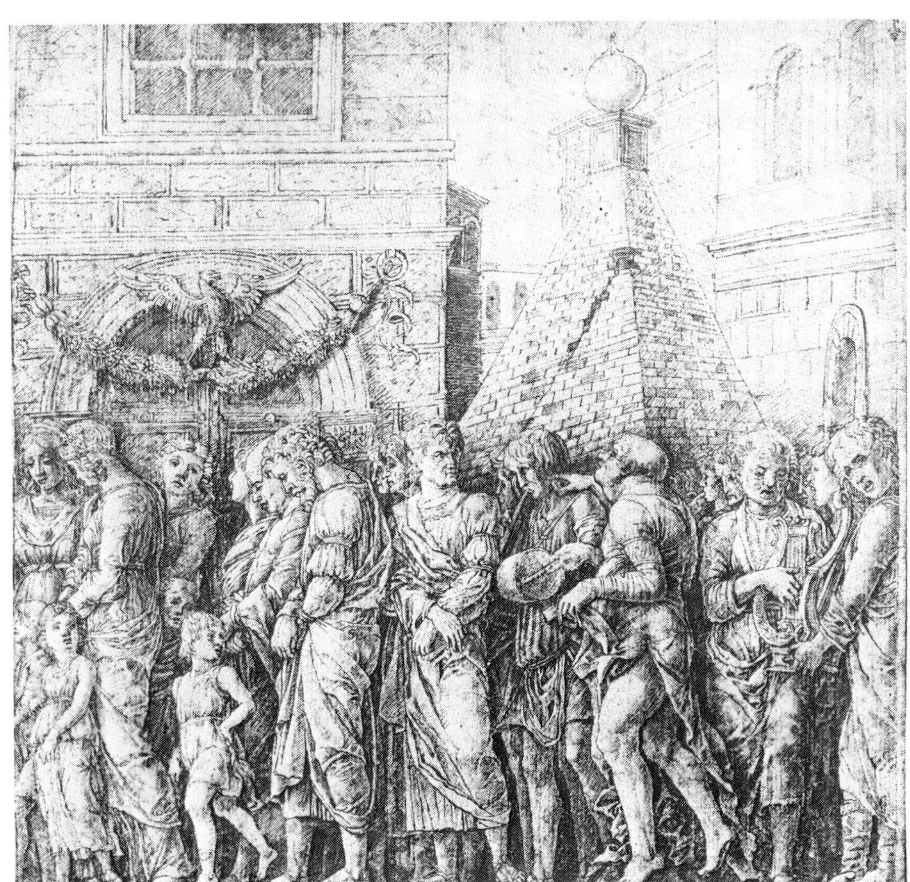

6   Mantegna's 'Captives,' drawing, Musée
     Condé, Chantilly. Photo. Giraudon

this part of the picture stops at the capitals from which the arches of the portico spring (in contrast with the left part of the picture, where atmospheric space is created by the spears and halberds of the soldiery), and this feature probably owes its inspiration to a classical prototype which possessed the same characteristic.

There are two versions of the 'Captives', one the painting in Hampton Court (Fig. 5)[18] and the other a drawing—a copy of an early design—in the Musée Condé, Chantilly (Fig. 6).[19] The captives themselves, in the bottom left-hand quarters of their respective pictures, are similar though not identical. In other respects, however, the pictures differ considerably from one another, with the exception of the *Meta Romuli* which occurs in the right background of both. Notice first the natural break between the last male captive on the left, and the women, children and grotesques on the right of the painting, and the musicians on the right of the drawing. There are also soldiers holding standards on the right hand side of the painting, one helmeted and the other bareheaded. The buildings behind the captives differ too: on the painting we see a couple of courses of drafted masonry and a grille above, and to the right a delicately carved pilaster. On the drawing, on the other hand, we have a doorway adorned with an eagle displayed standing on a swag, a pair of stringing courses and another, smaller grille.

These two pictures are full of references to classical monuments, some more obvious than others. The *Meta Romuli,* already mentioned, survived until 1500,[20] but judging by the drawing, was already in a dilapidated condition when Mantegna saw it. The eagle on the swag is based on the one now in the porch of SS. Apostoli, found in Trajan's Forum and placed in its present position by Julius II before his election to the papacy in 1503.[21] Professor Ashmole points out to me that the helmeted soldier in the painting and the frontal lyre player on the drawing were probably inspired by two of the figures on the slab of the so-called Altar of Domitius Ahenobarbus now in the Louvre (Figs. 7 and 8).[22] These reliefs were first recorded in 1683, in the Palazzo Santo Croce,[23] but their presence in the Mantegna corpus indicates that they were known much earlier. But the principal source

18) Tietz-Conrat, *op. cit.,* pl. 114.
19) *Ibid.* fig. 57.
20) Nash, *op. cit.* i, 59; cf. Blum *op. cit.,* 84.
21) F. Wickhoff, *Roman Art* (London, 1900) pl. 9; E. Strong, *Roman Sculpture* (London, 1907) pl. 69; *ead. La scultura romana* (Florence, 1923) 206, fig. 121.
22) See e.g. H. Kähler, *Seethiasos und Census; die Reliefs aus dem Palazzo Santo Croce in Rom* (Berlin, 1966) pls. 5 and 9.
23) R. Fabretti, *De Columna Traiani Syntagma* (Rome, 1653) 155; cf. Kähler, *op. cit.,* 7-8.

of inspiration for the 'Captives' was, as Ilse Blum pointed out, panel 91 of Trajan's Column (Fig. 9).[24] Despite its height and relative inaccessibility, the details of the monument were well known in the Renaissance.[25] The figures on the Column which Mantegna used as models were not in fact captives, but spectators at a sacrifice. Nevertheless, the overall composition is much the same: the men to the left of the relief with the children on the left-hand side of both the painting and the drawing, and the young woman with a babe in arms to the right of the centre of the painting and the elderly woman bending down to attend to a child bear a generic similarity to two of the figures on the Trajanic relief.

What follows is very much in the realm of speculation, although it does follow on from a remark made almost in passing by W. Weisbach to the effect that the 'Captives' give the impression that Mantegna used as prototypes Roman reliefs 'von der Art der Ara Pacis'.[26] We have already noted that the 'Senators' bear a more than coincidental resemblance to the *Ara Pacis,* and were in all probability taken from it; a case, though perhaps not so strong, can be made for some aspects of the 'Captives' being similarly dependant. Once again there is a lack of any real atmospheric space above the figures on the left. The grille on the painting and the swag on the drawing can be regarded as little more than interchangeable filling ornaments. Take away the filling ornament and we are left with figures disposed in the same way as those on the *Ara Pacis.* Furthermore, it seems likely that the figure of a woman who only appears on the drawing is directly derived from that part of the South frieze of the *Ara Pacis* where we find Antonia Minor and Drusus (following Professor Toynbee's identification) taking part in Augustus' procession (Fig. 10.)[27] The woman in question appears on the engraving below the eagle's right foot, towards the back. The visible part of her body is seen from the side, but her head is turned outwards towards the spectator. The woman immediately behind Drusus on the *Ara Pacis* looks out towards us in just the same way. About the only difference is that the captive woman is not wearing a wreath, but then we should not expect her to do so. Another suggestive piece of evidence

24) C. Cichorius, *Die Reliefs der Trajansäule,* Tafelband II (Berlin/ Leipzig, 1900) pl. 66 (whence fig. 9); K. Lehmann-Hartleben, *Die Trajansäule* (Berlin/Leipzig, 1926) pl. 42; F. B. Florescu, *Die Trajansäule, Grundfragen und Tafeln* (Bucarest/Bonn, 1969) pl. 78.
25) Cf., for example, the activities (cited by Blum, *op. cit.* 75) of Jacopo Ripanda da Bologna: "...que Trajani Columnae picturas omnes ordine delineavit, magna omnium admiratione, magnoque periculo circum machinis scandendo."
26) W. Weisbach, *Trionfi* (Berlin, 1919) 45.
27) Moretti, *op. cit.,* 13, fig. 2, pl. 0 and pl. 12, right; Toynbee *op. cit.,* pl. 18; Simon, *op. cit.,* pl. 15.

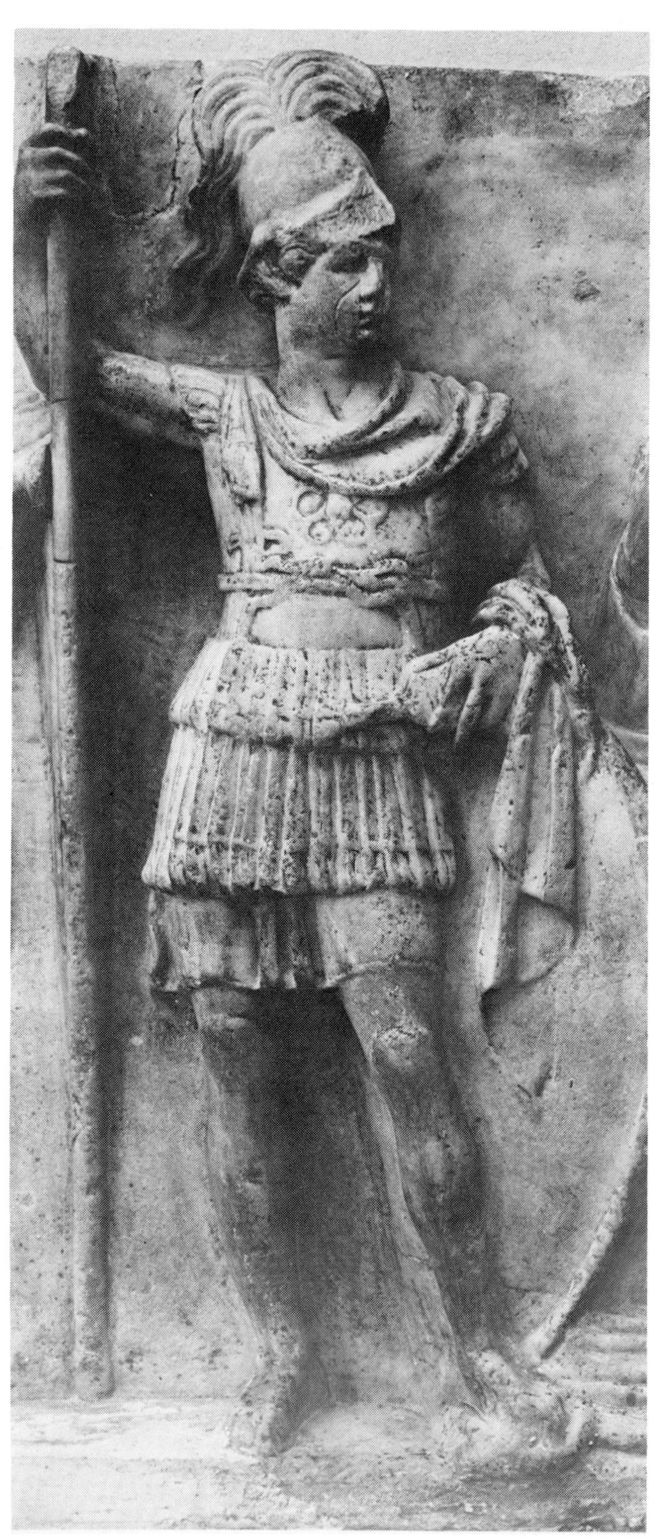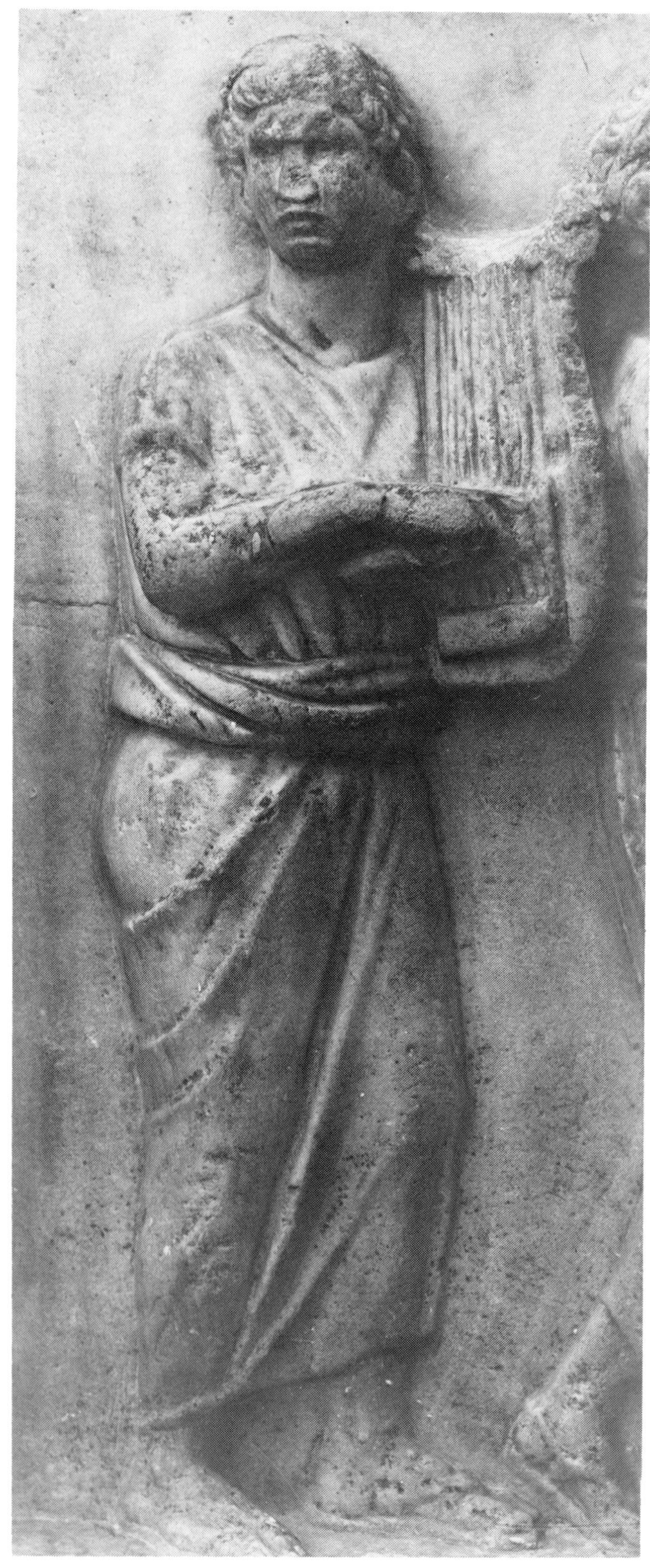

7-8 Details from the so-called Altar of Domitius
Ahenobarbus. Louvre, Paris. Photo.
Bildarchiv Marburg, 180465 and 163039

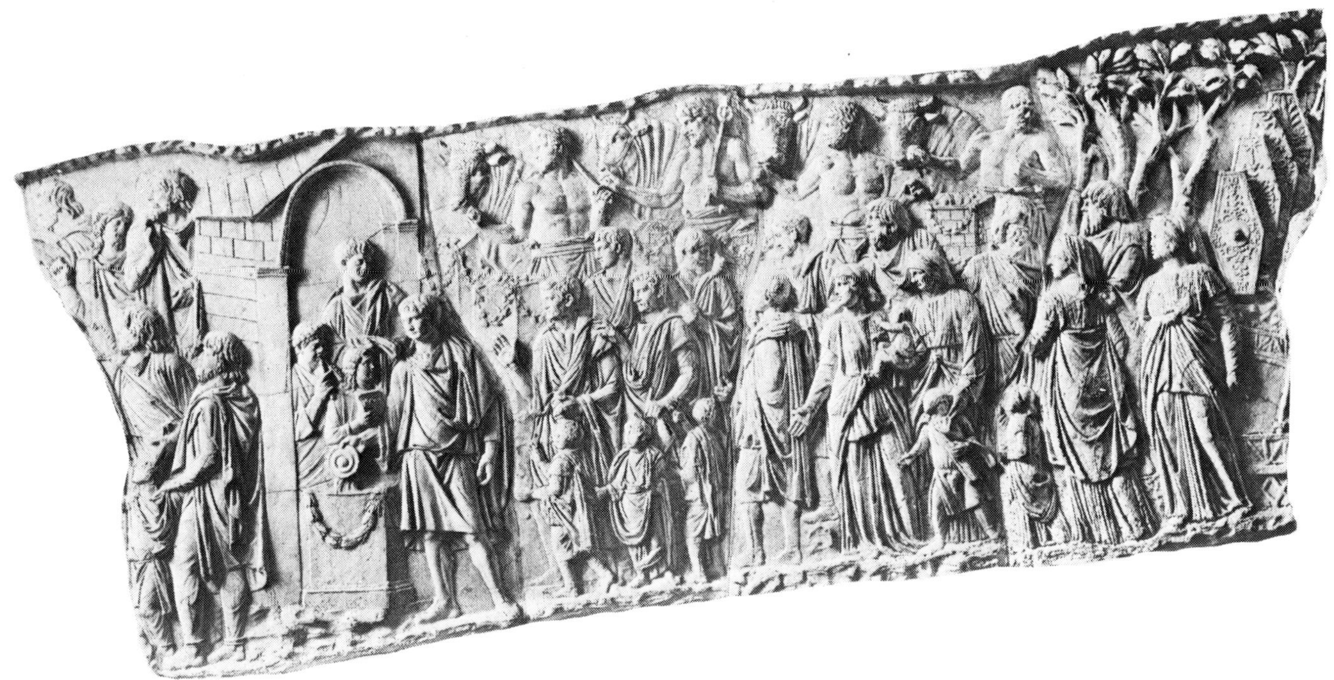

<table>
<tr><td>9   Panel 91 of Trajan's Column</td><td>10   Part of the South frieze of the Ara Pacis</td></tr>
</table>

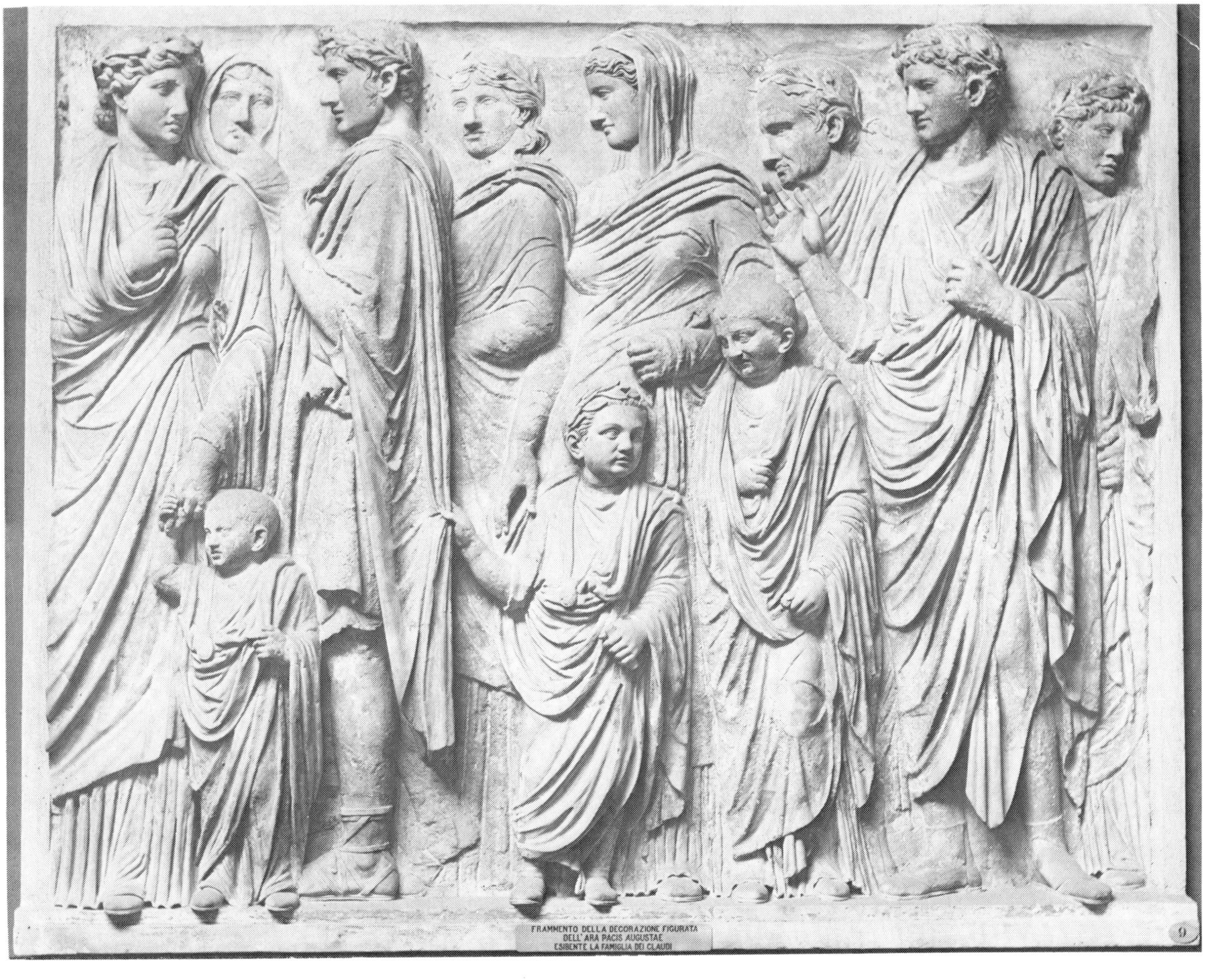

is the pilaster in the centre of the painting, which, though badly preserved, is very similar, with its delicate symmetrical acanthus scrolls, to the corner pilasters of the *Ara Pacis*.[28]

There were, of course, ancient copies or adaptations of details of the *Ara Pacis*. The *Tellus* group is echoed on a relief from Carthage,[29] and the *Sacrifice of Aeneas* panel clearly inspired the reverse of a bronze medallion struck for Marcus Aurelius as Caesar.[30] But these were self-contained compositions, and while it is possible that Mantegna saw copies in some medium of the particular sections of the *Ara Pacis* that we have discussed, but which have not survived, it is difficult to see why anyone should have wanted to copy an extract from a long procession. If the features we have observed are not fortuitous, the simplest explanation for them is surely that parts of both the North and South friezes of the *Ara Pacis* had come to light in the fifteenth century and had been copied, before they were lost and subsequently re-found in 1568. The fact that the *palazzo* had recently come into new ownership can hardly have been unconnected with their rediscovery.

Michael Vickers
Ashmolean Museum, Oxford

28) E.g. Moretti, *op. cit.* 29, fig. 17, 43, fig. 31, pls. I-IV; Toynbee, *op. cit.* pls. 6-7, 26, 32; Simon, *op. cit.* pls. 1, 3, 6, 18.
29) E. Simon *op. cit.,* pl. 32; J.M.C. Toynbee, *op. cit.,* 81 n. 9 (further references), pl. 14.
30) F. Gnecchi, *I medaglioni romani,* II, (Milan, 1912) pl. 66, no. 6.

Four Boeotian Ape Figurines from the J. Paul Getty Museum [1]

The antiquities collection of the J. Paul Getty Museum includes four small terracotta figurines representing animals, usually recognized as monkeys or apes,[2] in a squatting position. This type of primitive figurine, depicting the animal with its forepaws resting on the hindpaws and decorated with simple stripes, is well-known and is generally thought to have been manufactured in Boeotia. Of the twenty-six examples which have been published or are otherwise known of, only thirteen have been found in a certified context, either at Rhitsona[3] or at Tanagra,[4] and only at Rhitsona can dates be determined with any assurance.

Despite their primitive appearance, which has led some scholars to date them in the Mycenaean or early Geometric Periods,[5] figurines of this type have been uncovered in graves of the early and middle sixth century at Rhitsona, and this context provides a good *terminus ante quem* for their manufacture. As far as can be determined, no squatting ape figurines of this sort were produced after 550 B.C. The *terminus post quem* is, however, far more difficult to establish, and the figurines themselves provide few chronological clues. Equally difficult to determine is the precise significance of the ape figures, and it is hoped that this study will result in answers, however tentative, to these problems.

The following is a description of the four figurines in the Getty Museum.[6]

1. 71.AD.133: fig. 1. H. 0.09 m. Fine pink-tan clay and slip, lustrous red/black paint. Head convex, ears protrude horizontally; one ear chipped; pointed snout. Applied circles for eyes and breasts at top of arms. Forepaws pinched onto hindpaws, claws indicated by three incised strokes. Broad tail pinched out for support. Baby held on lap within mother's arms; in same position as mother, less carefully made. Legs and back attached to mother with extra blobs of clay shoved in at sides. Applied circles for eyes. Fairly regularly spaced narrow stripes, horizontal across body and head, arms and legs; vertical stripes on top of head and short vertical strokes on middle of back.

2. 71.AD.377: fig. 2. H. 0.088 m. Tan clay, lustrous brown/black paint, worn. Head rounded, no indication of ears. Small pointed snout; eyes gouged out with sharp instrument; short incised line for mouth. Forepaws rest on short hindlegs; broad tail pinched out for support. Horizontal stripes of irregular width and spacing across face, chest, arms, and back; oblique stripes across belly.

3. 71.AD.378: fig. 3a,b,c. H. 0.07 m. Fine orange-tan clay, lustrous red/black paint, worn. Crudely executed. Small head; ears pinched out horizontally, small pointed snout. Body leans back, rests on broad pinched-out tail. Forepaws make wide curve outward from chest creating small "shelf" at chest level. Plain horizontal bands of fairly regular width on head, belly, and arms, oblique stripes on back.

4. 71.AD.379: fig. 4a,b,c. H. 0.085 m. Fine yellow-tan micaceous clay, lustrous red paint, worn in back. Crudely made. Small head, large pointed ears; snout long and tapers downward. Large tail pinched out for support. Many narrow horizontal stripes across arms; vertical stripes down hind legs and back, coming over head and ending on face just above snout.

These four figurines, while differing widely in details and quality of execution, are quite remarkable in their consistency, both in position and in mode of decoration. They are rarely well-made, although No. 1 does have more details and refinements than the other three. Nos. 3 and 4 were made with extreme carelessness and apparent

The following abbreviations will be used for books commonly referred to in the text:

BM Cat - R. A. Higgins, *Catalogue of the Terracottas in the Department of Greek and Roman Antiquities, British Museum. I. Greek: 730-330 B.C.* (Oxford, 1954).

Breitenstein - N. Breitenstein, *Catalogue of Terracottas: Cypriote, Greek, Etrusco-Italic, and Roman. Danish National Museum, Department of Oriental and Classical Antiquities* (Copenhagen, 1941).

Chesterman - J. Chesterman, *Classical Terracotta Figures* (London, 1974).

CVA - *Corpus Vasorum Antiquorum.*

Deltion - Ἀρχαιολογικὸν Δελτίον

Grace - F. R. Grace, *Archaic Sculpture in Boeotia* (Cambridge, Mass., 1939).

Higgins - R. A. Higgins, *Greek Terracottas* (London, 1967).

Louvre Cat - S. Mollard-Besques, *Catalogue raisonné des figurines et reliefs en terre-cuite grecs, étrusques, et romains. I. Epoques préhellénique, géométrique, archaïque, et classique* (Paris, 1954).

McDermott - W. C. McDermott, *The Ape in Antiquity* (=*Johns Hopkins Studies in Archaeology,* 27; Baltimore, 1938).

Paul - E. Paul, "Die böotischen Brettidole," *Wissenschaftliche Zeitschrift der Karl-Marx-Universität Leipzig. 8 Jahrgang. 1958-59. Gesellschafts - und Sprachwissenschaftliche Reihe. Heft I.* pp. 165-206.

Roes - A. Roes, *De Oorsprong der Geometrische Kunst* (Haarlem, 1931).

Ure, *Rhitsona* - P. N. Ure, *Aryballoi and Figurines from Rhitsona in Boeotia* (Cambridge, 1934).

Ure, *VI and V Cent.Pott.* - P. N. Ure, *Sixth and Fifth Century Pottery from Rhitsona in Boeotia* (Oxford, 1927).

Winter, *Typen I* - F. Winter, *Die Typen der figürlichen terrakotten. Die Antiken Terrakotten,* ed. Kekulé von Stradonitz, Vol. III, Pt. I (Berlin, 1901).

1) I wish to express my gratitude to Dr. Jiři Frel for his generosity in allowing me to work with these figurines.

2) McDermott pp. 162 ff., Nos. 2-18, No. 64.

3) Ure, *Rhitsona* pp. 66 and 86.

4) McDermott pp. 162 ff., Nos. 2-3, 5, 6, 8-14; *Deltion* III (1888) p. 217 Nos. 68 and 70 (possibly No. 69, but this has been omitted).

5) *CVA* Baltimore 1 (USA 4) p. 28.

6) All four of the Getty figurines were purchased from an art dealer in New York, and there is no good information on their provenance.

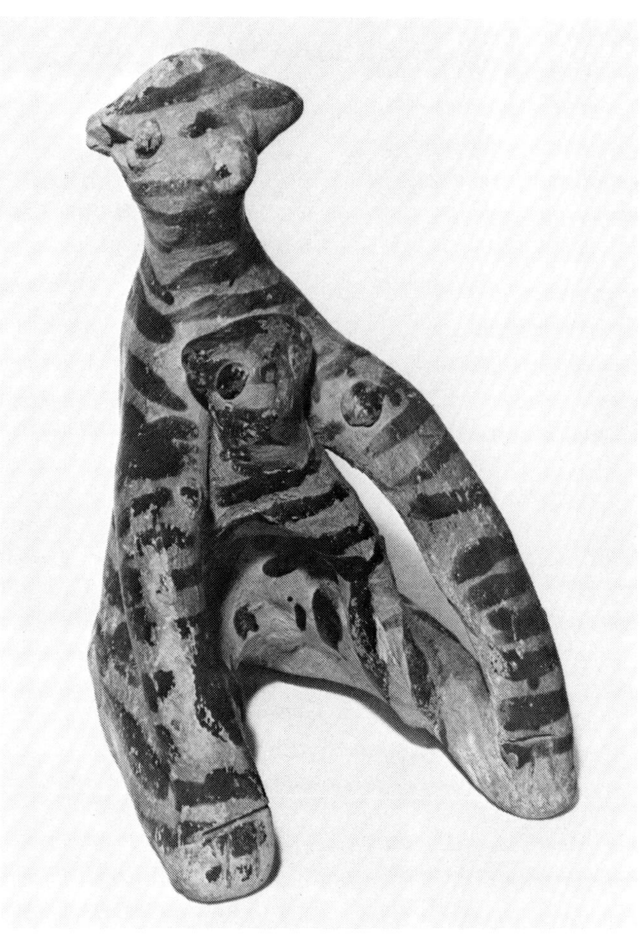

1   J. Paul Getty Museum 71.AD.133

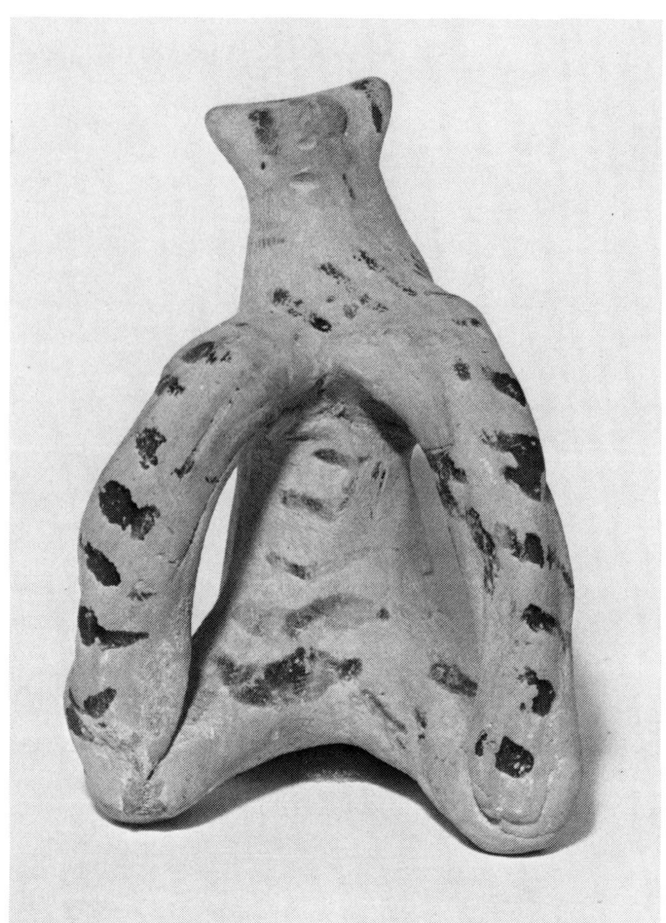

3a,b,c   J. Paul Getty Museum 71.AD.378

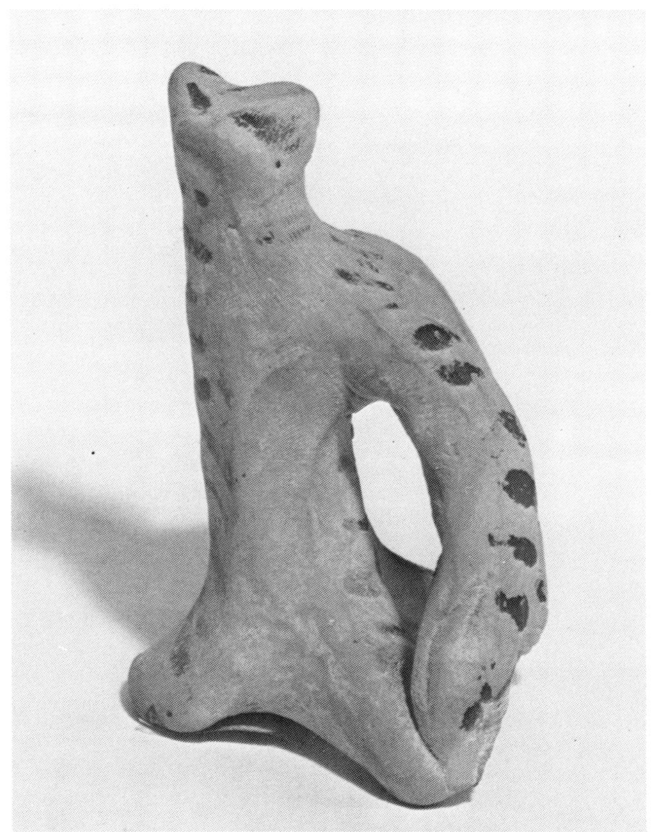

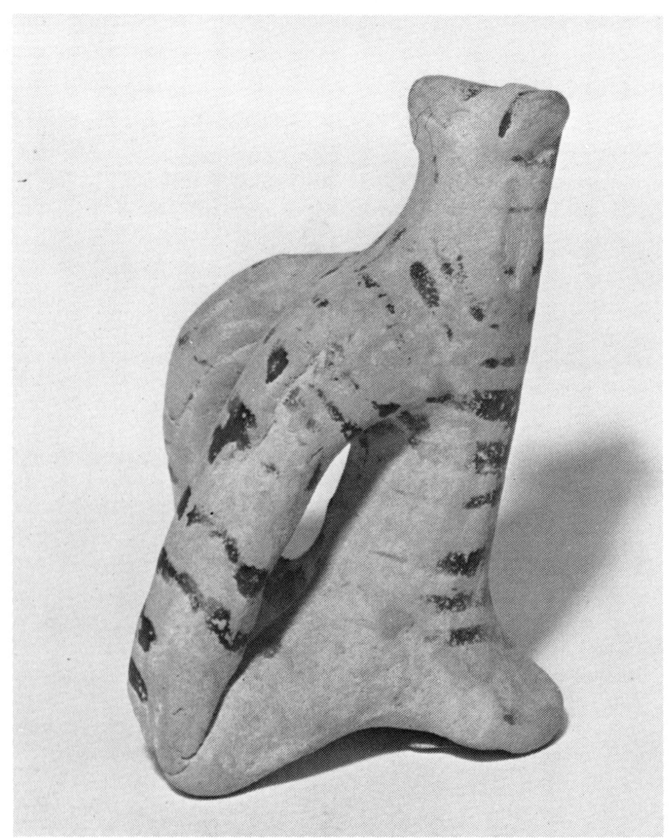

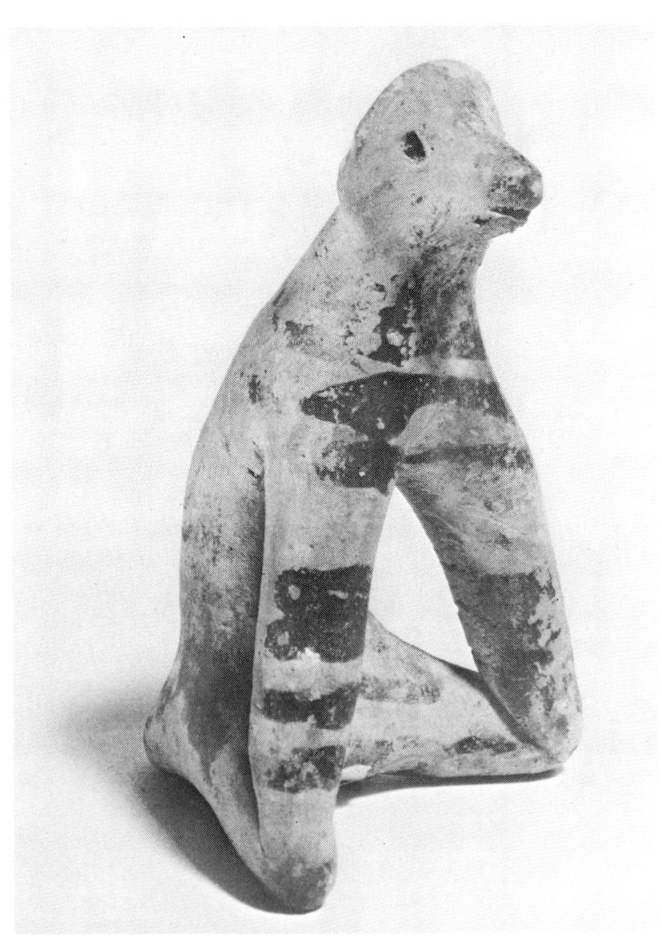

2   J. Paul Getty Museum 71.AD.377

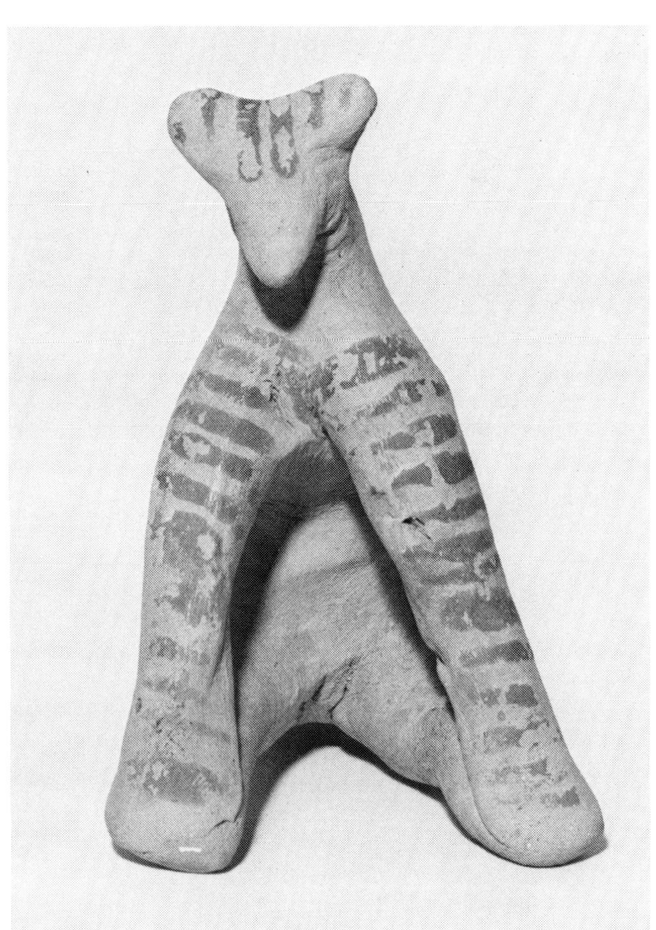

4a,b,c   J. Paul Getty Museum 71.AD.379

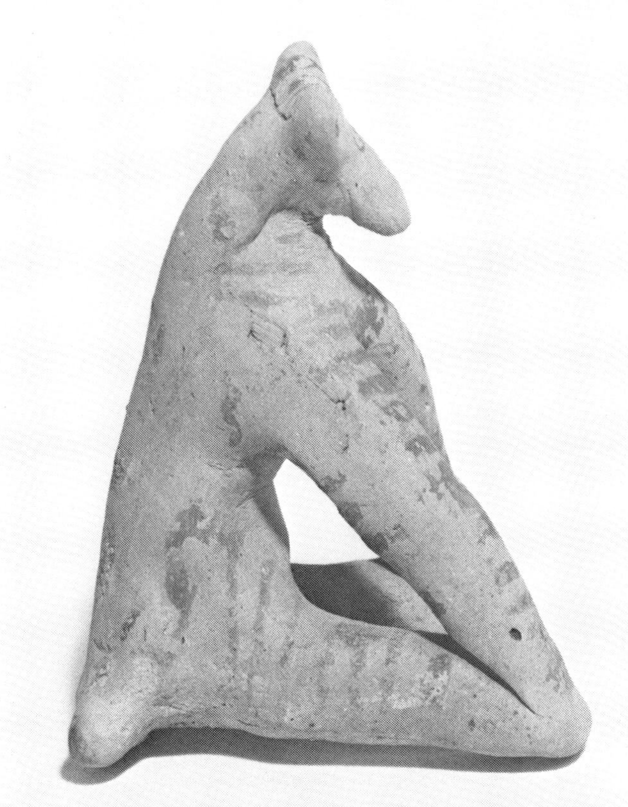

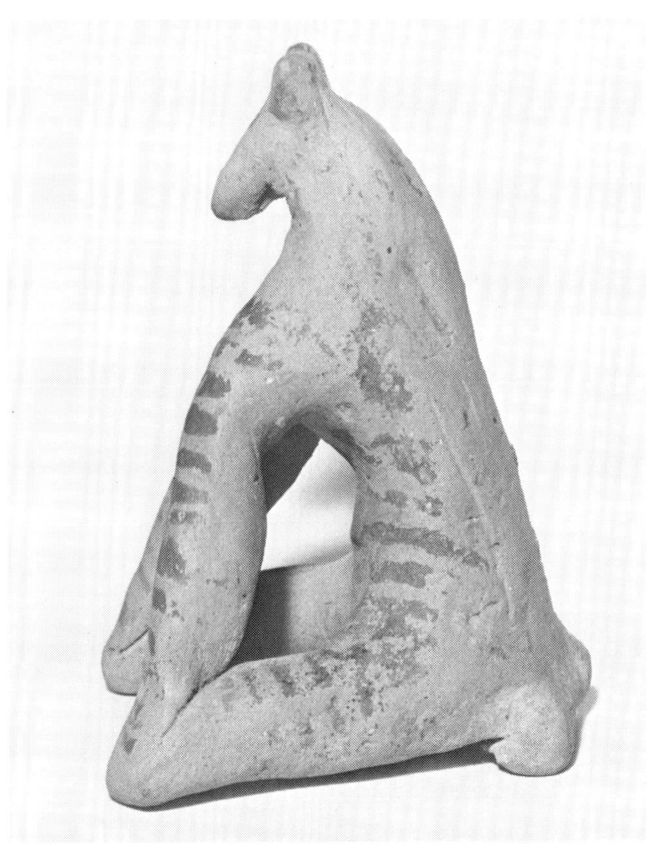

haste, since their makers did not bother to smooth off their fingerprints from the surface or even, in the case of No. 4, knead the clay enough to remove all the air bubbles. Despite these differences in quality, the four seem to have been made in the same way, and they appear to comprise part of the potter's craft rather than that of the terracotta manufacturer's. Basically these figurines were made in the simplest way using cylinders of clay; one large cylinder made up the body, and smaller ones formed the arms and legs. The various details were pinched out (snout, ears), incised, or added (facial features). In technique the apes resemble most of all the handles on large Boeotian Geometric amphorae, which are of similar shape and are also decorated with stripes.[7] This is far removed from the mould-made technique already in use at this time in other parts of Greece. In addition to the technique and the squatting position, other unifying elements among the figurines are the size and the decoration. The size, which ranges from 0.07-0.09 m. in height, places these terracottas well within the category of minor arts. The use of simple striped decoration is common to all, although again there is a wide variation in the quality and details of execution. No. 1 has been more carefully handled in its decoration than the others, as in everything else, and it does contain a slight variation, unknown elsewhere,[8] of short vertical strokes amid the horizontal ones covering the back of the figure.

Similar to the four Getty figurines are possibly as many as twenty-six other terracottas which are published or otherwise known. The following list of known examples does not purport to be complete; probably more such figures exist, many in the hands of dealers or private collectors, but it does include all the examples which are published or mentioned in publications.

From certified excavations: 5. Rhitsona 99.53. Ure, *Rhitsona* pp. 66, 86; pl. XVII; McDermott p. 163. Thebes Museum. 6. Rhitsona 101b.36. Ure, *Rhitsona* pp. 66,86; pl. XVII; McDermott p. 163. Thebes Museum. 7. Rhitsona 101b.37. Ure, *Rhitsona* pp. 66,86. Like No. 6, but not pictured. 8. Rhitsona 126.126. Ure, *Rhitsona* p. 66; pl. XVII; Ure, *VI and V Cent.Pott.* p. 96; McDermott p. 163; Roes p. 122, fig. 129. Thebes Museum. 9. Seven examples from Tanagra, now in the Skimitari Museum. No photographs. McDermott p. 163 Nos. 8-14; Winter *Typen I* p. 222, id; possibly mentioned in *Deltion* III (1888) pp. 35 and p. 217 Nos. 68-70. 10. Athens, National Museum 11 E. From Tanagra. McDermott p. 162, pl. I,2; Winter, *Typen I* p. 222, 1b. 11. Athens, National Museum 1047. From Tanagra. McDermott p. 162, pl. I,3; Winter, *Typen I* p. 222, 1b.

Not from certified contexts: 12. Athens, National Museum 3904. McDermott, p. 162, pl. I,1. 13. British Museum 774. From Lake Copais. *BM Cat* p. 207, pl. 102; Higgins p. 46, pl. 19, D. 14. Danish Museum 155. Breitenstein p. 17, pl. 16. 15. Louvre CA 2229. From Attica. *Louvre Cat* No. B10, p. 4, pl. III. 16. Chesterman 104. From Boeotia. Chesterman p. 35, No. 24 and p. 94. 17. Baltimore, Robinson Collection. From near Mycenae. *CVA* Baltimore 1 (USA 4) p. 28, pl. XII No. 14 (*USA* pl. 145). 18. Louvre CA 531. From Tegea. *Louvre Cat.* No. B155, p. 26, pl. XIX; Roes p. 122, fig. 129; Winter, *Typen I* p. 222, 2. 19. Parke Bernet Galleries, *Antiquities Catalogue,* Nov. 5, 1971, No. 207, p. 24. 20. Cincinnati, Private Collection.

Others mentioned in publications but not pictured: 21. Ashmolean Museum 1893.109. From Thebes. *BM Cat* p. 207 n. 2. 22. Possession of Art Dealer, 1887. From Boeotia. McDermott p. 163 No. 7; Winter, *Typen I* p. 222, Ic 23. Collection of Dr. Otto Rubensohn. McDermott p. 163 No. 15. 24. Collection of Wilson College, Chambersburg, Pa.

Although few of these figurines come from certified contexts, the majority of them are said to have been found in Boeotia, and their manufacture is generally thought to have been limited to that area. Only three are known to have been found outside Boeotia; No. 15 is said to be from Attica, No. 17 from near Mycenae, and No. 18 is from Tegea. Nos. 15 and 17 are so close to those from Boeotia that it seems best to consider them as imports into Attica or the Argolid, although only a scientific analysis of their clay could prove this. No. 18 has a variation in that it carries its young on its shoulder rather than on its lap. While ape figurines carrying their young in this way are not unknown,[9] this is the only example in the category of squatting apes. This may be a local variation on the Boeotian type of ape figurine, but the figure is otherwise so similar to its Boeotian counterparts in position, decoration, and execution that it seems more likely to be another import from Central Greece. All the present evidence supports the prevailing theory that this type of figurine does have a strict geographical limit, although examples may have been imitated in or exported to other areas in small quantity.

---

7) N. Coldstream, *Greek Geometric Pottery* (London, 1968) pl. 45,c. It has been suggested of the similar figure in Baltimore that it was made as an ornament for the lid of a Geometric pot, much as figures of horses decorate many Attic lids of that period. See *CVA* Baltimore 1 (USA 4) p. 28. This does not seem to have been the case with the Getty figurines, which show no signs of having been attached to pottery, but the observation about the technique is well-taken.
8) This may not be unique, but it is impossible to determine from photographs which give only a front or oblique view of the figure.
9) Winter, *Typen I,* p. 222, 5. See also n. 23.

The problem of defining the development and the chronological limits for the figurines is more complex and the answer less easy to find. There is a remarkable unity of style among the figures and it is difficult to break them down into different types. A study of the published examples does show, however, that there are three distinguishable groups of ape figurines.

Type I: Nos. 5, 14, 18. This type is characterized by rather squat proportions in general, and by heads which are larger in proportion to the bodies. Much attention has been given to the facial markings; in all cases mouths and eyes are indicated, usually by incisions (5, 18) or by applied circles (14). There is no consistency in style of decoration; the photograph of No. 5 gives no indication of any decoration, although the description in the text indicates the use of paint on the figure. No. 14 has fairly thick and even stripes, and those of No. 18 are more irregular. Nos. 5 and 18 have claws indicated by incisions.

Type II: Nos. 2, 11, 16, 19. Possibly these figures represent a different type or species of ape. The chief characteristic is an absence of ears, which gives these figures an appearance quite different from the usual *cynocephalus* baboon. Otherwise the group is similar to the others; the faces have pointed snouts, mouths indicated by incisions, and gouged-out eyes. The stripes are thick and irregular; No. 19 seems to have a thick vertical stripe down half of its belly, which is unique.

Type III: Four subgroups comprise this type. a) Nos. 1, 12, 13, 17, 20. These are similar in proportions: rather large heads with big ears and a tall neck. The eyes are generally attached circles, although No. 12's are gouged out. Nos. 1, 17, and 20 have their young seated on their laps; Nos. 1 and 17 have applied circles for breasts at the tops of their arms, while No. 13 has breasts but no baby. Otherwise, sexual attributes are not indicated on any of the figurines. The figures in this group have regular densely-spaced stripes and are more carefully made. Nos. 13 and 17 are so similar that they could have been made by the same hand. b) Nos. 3, 6, 10, 15. The figurines in this subgroup are similar to those in a), but are not so carefully made. The heads are smaller in proportion to the bodies. The stripes are regular and densely-spaced; Nos. 10 and 15 have vertical instead of the more usual horizontal stripes on the belly. c) No. 8. This figurine is similar to a) in general appearance and decoration, but the proportions are quite different: it is more elongated, and the head is smaller and thrown back. Possibly it does not represent an ape at all, but it must be classed with the others because of the basic similarity. d) No. 4. This figure is similar to those in subgroup a), but it is less well-made and has a head of an unusual shape. Like No. 8, it may not even be meant as an ape. It is unusual in having vertical rather than the more common horizontal stripes on its back.

There seems to be little chronological significance to these different types, but a slight development can be seen from an observation of the three dateable Rhitsona figures. A comparison of Nos. 5 and 6, of early sixth century date, with No. 8, of the mid-sixth century, indicates a development in proportions from squatness to more elongation and a diminution in head size in proportion to the size of the body. In decoration, too, there seems to be a development; on the earlier examples the stripes are irregular and on the later one they are dense and more regular. There is apparently a change, noted by Paul in other Boeotian figurines,[10] toward a more abstracted, less "realistic" form, which makes No. 8 look less like an ape than the others. On this basis Types I and II would seem to be earlier than Type III, although none of the figures seems to be earlier than Nos. 5 and 6 nor more developed than No. 8.

With regard to the chronology of the Boeotian ape figurines, the majority of the published examples seem to fall within the first half of the sixth century, and none were produced after 550. Their primitive appearance suggested to some archaeologists that they go back well into the Geometric Period, although there is no concrete evidence to support such a theory and some to deny it. To a certain extent the problems of dating these figures must be considered as part of the more general problem centered around the whole group of so-called Primitive Boeotian figurines, a group which also includes the protopappades, "Bird-faced figurines," and the series of horses with or without riders. Like the apes, these other primitive figurines have been found in secure context only at Rhitsona, where the picture is the same: nearly all the examples have been found in graves of the first half of the sixth century.

P. N. Ure, the excavator of Rhitsona, believed that the primitive figurines started considerably earlier and that the same potters who produced the latest of the large Boeotian Geometric vases also made the horse figures and the protopappades.[11] Grace, in his definitive study of archaic Boeotian sculpture, decided that while the primitive figurines could be placed back into the seventh century, the close unity of style, particularly among the Bird-faced figurines, suggests that they were produced over a short space of time.[12] E. Paul, on the other hand, believed that these primitive figurines all belong to the

---

10) Paul p. 186.
11) Ure, *Rhitsona* p. 54.

12) Grace pp. 22 and 24.

sixth century and cannot be dated earlier;[13] the same seems to be true of the ape figurines. While they may have a primitive appearance, they are clearly not Geometric; they are too carelessly executed, even for Boeotia. A comparison with the handles on late Geometric Boeotian amphorae, which are similar both in technique and style, shows that even these handles have been made with more care and more attention to a uniform decoration than the terracottas.[14] More figures from certified contexts are needed to clarify the chronological development, but they are not Geometric; their great uniformity and the apparent lack of a well-defined evolution indicates that they were produced over a short span of time, no more than 50 years.

The question of the function and significance of the figurines still remains to be answered. The term "ape" has been used throughout this discussion, even though not all of the figurines are clearly recognizable as simians. The published examples have also been identified as bears[15] or dogs,[16] but most of them do seem to represent the *cynocephalus* or dog-faced (hamadryas) baboon,[17] with the possible exception of those in Type II. Nevertheless, the figurines are so primitive and so little attention has been paid to zoological detail that it is not always possible to determine the animal represented. The position of the figures is more natural for an ape than for any other animal, even though the striped decoration, probably meant to indicate hair, looks as though it belongs more on a hedgehog. In fact, many of the figurines resemble nothing so much as "teddy bears," a fact which, I believe, has some bearing on their function.

Context is of little use in helping determine the function of the terracottas. Both at Rhitsona and Tanagra they appear in graves, although there is no consistency in the types of graves in which they have been found.[18] The fact that the terracottas were buried as part of the grave goods might suggest that they were intended to serve a funerary purpose, whether religious or apotropaic, but such an assertion must be made cautiously. No habitation sites of the Archaic period have been systematically explored in Boeotia, and the small terracottas might just as well have formed part of the ordinary domestic accoutrements placed with the dead. Thus the figurines cannot definitely be said to have a connection with the dead, although the possibility cannot be entirely dismissed.

In general it appears that the ape did not have a strong religious significance for the Greeks.[19] McDermott suggests that the ape may have had some connection with the Cabiric worship at Thebes and possibly even an association with the cult of Orpheus, but although the small terracotta apes may have had some slight religious connotation, in reality they were probably meant to amuse.[20] The ape is basically a comical figure because of its similarities to man. Its appearance in Greek literature, which begins in the sixth century, is almost always as a figure of fun whose imitation of man often brings it to grief.[21] Much is made of its grotesque appearance. Surely the Boeotian figurines were produced in keeping with this humorous aspect of the ape; they should thus be viewed as toys or amusing knickknacks. This interpretation is in keeping with the careless rendering of the figures; although they are recognizable as apes, they bear the same resemblance to the real animal as a teddy-bear does to a live bear.

Finally, mention must be made of a terracotta figure of a man, roughly contemporary with the ape figurines and said to be from Boeotia or Attica, who sits in the same squatting position as the apes.[22] The position is highly uncomfortable, if not impossible, for a human, and the figure must have been made in imitation of the ape figurines. If the apes were considered humorous imitations of man, then this is one step further — the grotesque imitation of a monkey by a man.[23]

Leslie E. Preston
California State University, San Diego

---

13) Paul p. 167.
14) Coldstream, *op. cit.*
15) Ure, *Rhitsona* pp. 66,86; Breitenstein p. 17.
16) *CVA* Baltimore 1 (USA 4) p. 28.
17) McDermott pp. 102 ff.
18) No. 5 accompanied a child burial in a shaft grave; Nos. 6, 7, and 8 were found in pithos burials one of which was large enough to accomodate an adult although none had any trace of bones. The earth was very damp, which probably accounts for the disintegration of the bones. Ure, *Rhitsona* pp. 10-11; *VI and V Cent.Pott.* p. 4.
19) Not as much as for the Egyptians, who associated the animal with Thoth; for the Mesopotamians it served an apotropaic function. See McDermott pp. 156-7.
20) McDermott pp. 126, 156.
21) McDermott p. 27, pp. 110 ff. It appears in Archilochus, Simonides, and Aesop.
22) *Kunstwerke der Antike.* Münzen und Medaillen A.G., Basel. Auktion 51 (14-15 March, 1975) No. 184.
23) Since the writing of this paper, I have learned of the existence of three more apes. Two are in the Kanellopoulos Museum, Athens: one of normal size and shape, surface eroded, still traces of stripes, the eyes and breasts in the form of rounded buttons; the other about ⅔ normal size, modelled in a block, with the arms down the sides and not detached from the body. A third, from Mycenae but probably not Mycenaean, has a ruff on the neck, with shoulders pierced for suspension: McDermott p. 162 No. 1, Schliemann, *Mykenae* p. 82 fig. 115, Roes p. 132 fig. 144. The identification of these animals as apes is confirmed by a new sample on the market, where the baby rides on the mother; realistically shaped head. *Greek and Roman Terracottas III* (1975), 30.